THE WELSH
Selected readings in the social sciences

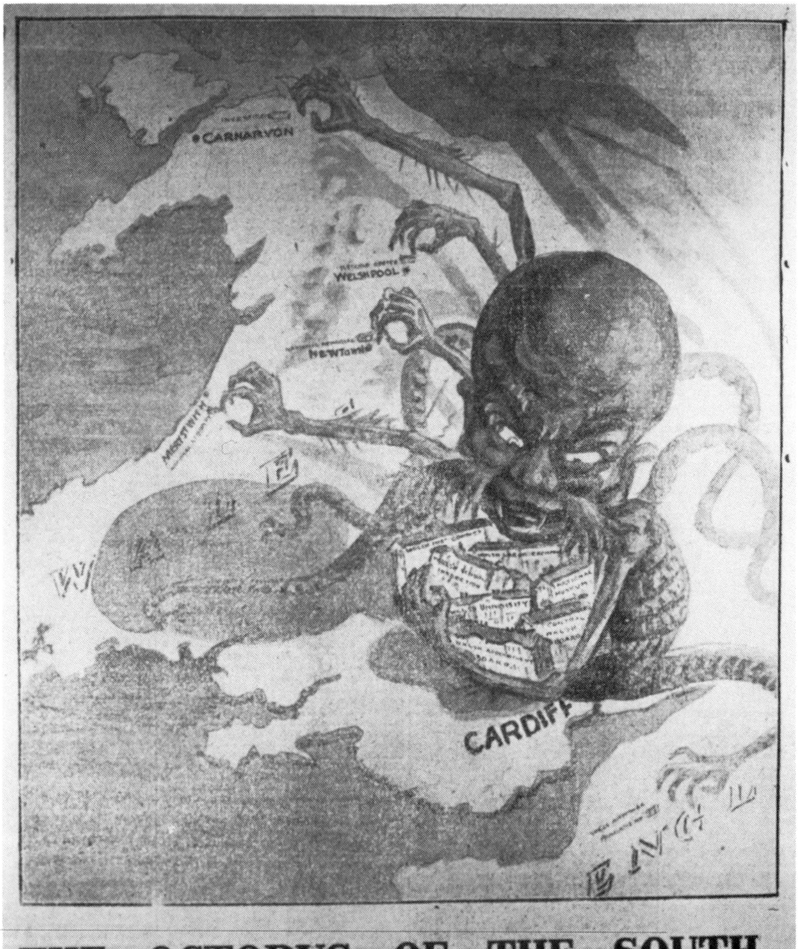

A northern comment on the process of nation building

This cartoon, entitled 'The octopus of the south' was published on p. 5 of the *Montgomeryshire Express & Radnor Times* on June 17, 1913. Many important Welsh institutions are shown as already secure in the bosom of the south east. Cardiff, not designated formally as Capital of Wales until 1955, is preceived as extending covetous tentacles towards the remaining national institutions elsewhere including the Investiture ceremony for the Prince of Wales (Caernarfon), a proposed Record Office for Wales (Welshpool), the National Memorial (Newtown) and the National Library (Aberystwyth). The Referendum on devolution of government to Wales raised similar objections in 1979.

THE WELSH AND THEIR COUNTRY
Selected readings in the social sciences

edited by
Ian Hume and W. T. R. Pryce

GOMER PRESS
1986

First impression — February 1986

ISBN 0 86383 245 8

Gomer Press
Published in association with the
Open University

Printed in Wales
at Gomer Press, Llandysul, Dyfed

I FYFYRWYR
Y BRIFYSGOL AGORED
A GWBLHAODD
D423: Cymru—astudiaeth o hunaniaeth diwylliannol a chenedlaethol
yn 1982/83

FOR THE STUDENTS OF
THE OPEN UNIVERSITY
WHO COMPLETED
D423: Wales—A study of cultural and national identity in 1982/3

Joyce Andrews, Y Barri
Gerald Camm, Ynysowen: Merthyr Vale
Eiluned Davies, Oxted, Surrey
Sylvia Davies, Grimsby
Elsie Grattidge, Penarth
Megan Hall, Porthcawl
Kenneth Harris, Llanfair Caereinion
George Hart-Jones, Aberdaugleddau: Milford Haven
Mansel Jones, Caerdydd: Cardiff
Stanley Jones, Aberystwyth
Ray Kensett, Caerdydd: Cardiff
Margaret Laming, Caergybi: Holyhead
Robert Lewis, Dolgellau
Shandy Mathias, Eastbourne
Christine Mendlson, Portsmouth
Peter Rowland, Leamington Spa
Graham Williams, Ystradgynlais

AC I
FYFYRWYR
NEWYDD

AND
FOR NEW
STUDENTS

Contents

		Page
Figures		viii
PREFACE: Emrys Jones		x
INTRODUCTION: I. Hume and W. T. R. Pryce		xiii

Section 1..SPATIAL IDENTITY

Chapter 1	Language Areas and Language Change in Wales: 1961-1981 Harold Carter and John Aitchison	1
Chapter 2	Wales as a Culture Region: Patterns of Change 1750-1971 W. T. R. Pryce	26
Chapter 3	The Geography of Wales as a Background to its History E. G. Bowen	64

Section 2............................THE TRADITIONAL SOCIETY

Chapter 4	Community Studies in Wales: An Overview Trefor M. Owen	91
Chapter 5	The *Gwerin* of Wales: Myth and Reality Prys Morgan. Translated by the author.	134
Chapter 6	The Sociology of Wales: Issues and Prospects 1979 and 1985 Graham Day	153
Chapter 7	Recent Trends in the Sociology of Wales Glyn Williams	176

Section 3...IDEOLOGIES

Chapter 8	Culture and Politics in Wales T. Nairn	195
Chapter 9	Towards a Theory of Ethnic Change Michael Hechter	217

Chapter 10 The Shadow of the Swastika? 234
R. Tudur Jones. Translated by Eirian E. Edwards and B. P. Jones.

Chapter 11 What is *Adfer*? 244
Emyr Llywelyn. Translated by Ann Davies.

Chapter 12 Language Planning and Minority Group Rights 253
Colin H. Williams

Section 4............THE CONTEXT OF POLITICAL IDENTITY

Chapter 13 Wales: A Separate Administrative Unit 273
D. Foulkes, J. B. Jones and R. A. Wilford

Chapter 14 Organisations, Political Movements and their Backgrounds 292
Ian Hume

Chapter 15 Mass Media and Society in the 1980s 324
Ian Hume

Index 348

Figures

page

Frontispiece. A northern comment on the process of nation building.

1. Absolute numbers of Welsh speakers (aged 3 years and over) in communities, 1981. 5
2. Proportions of the population (aged 3 years and over) able to speak Welsh, 1981. 8
3. Literacy levels amongst Welsh speakers, 1981. 10
4. Percentage of the population able to speak Welsh 1901-81. 12
5. Percentage change in the numbers able to speak Welsh, 1961-71 and 1971-81. 14
6. Percentage rates of change amongst Welsh speakers within communities, 1961-71 and 1971-81. 15
7. Increases in the actual numbers of Welsh speakers within communities, 1971-81. 18
8. Language areas, 1981. 20
9. Language areas 1981: minimum variance cluster analysis. 22
10. Language areas 1961-71 and 1971-81; change statistics. 22
11. Welsh monoglots, bilinguals and patterns of change in relation to population movements, 1901-71. 28
12. Inter-censal changes in the population (aged 3 years and over) able to speak Welsh, 1901-71. 30
13. Principal language zones in the mid-eighteenth century. 39
14. Long-term changes at specific locations c.1750-1900 and the principal language zones in 1900. 48
15. The territorial shrinkage of *Cymru Gymraeg*, c.1750-1971. 57

16. The distribution of Welsh speakers, 1901 and 1971. 59
17. Wales: Norman manors in the fourteenth century. 73
18. The Welsh Heartland: combined relief, rainfall and natural vegetation characters. 79
19. Distribution of Puritan churches, c.1715 (after the list of Dr. John Evans) 81
20. Modern mass communications in Wales. 86
21. Over and under representation of Welsh speakers and the population born outside Wales, Gwynedd 1981. 186
22. Newspapers of Wales: contents analysis. 343
23. Categories of news coverage in daily papers and in *Y Cymro*. 344
24. Welsh newspaper circulations. 344
25. News broadcasting in Wales: early evening television news services, 1981/82 and 1984/85.345
26. Early evening television news services of BBC Midlands' Region. 346
27. News broadcasting in Wales: early morning news bulletin, 1985. 346
28. HTV Wales: hours of service in English. 347

Preface

Since World War II nation states in the western world have been consolidated into greater, and fewer, power blocs. Paradoxically, these developments, together with the growing disregard of national boundaries by the great multinational companies, have been paralleled by an increasing awareness of identity by small cultural groups which, to all intents and purposes, had already been subsumed within the organisation of stronger neighbours. It may well be that self awareness and a recognition of cultural individuality are automatic acts of preservation within dominant universal cultures and their frequently deadening uniformity. In Wales, certainly, a gentle 'nationalism' which was in danger of becoming no more than a sentimental folk memory has become a live issue, culturally, economically and politically.

It would be too simple to think of this merely as the expression of a continuous traditional feeling which has waxed and waned for well over a millennium. Nor are these changes in ideas and organisation products of neatly defined periods, temporally self-contained and explicable only in terms of contemporary issues beyond Wales. History is a tapestry woven on the warp of continuity and the weft of change. Both find their place in this volume: the first perhaps more familiar, the second more challenging. Neither is accepted at face value, and differences in interpretation and in belief enliven the issues and should make for intellectual stimulation. Both refer to the same homeland, and here, perhaps, lies the most intriguing of all problems: how does one interpret or understand a dynamic social situation within a static territory? It is very difficult to bound culture, impossible to locate ideology. But national identity is a unique combination of how we live and where we live. The chapters in this book go a long way towards providing a basis for a better understanding of the diverse and complex issues underlying this apparently simple statement. The editors have done Wales a signal service in collating material for a reasoned and fruitful discussion of the problem.

Emrys Jones
Emeritus Professor of Geography
The London School of Economics
December 1, 1985

Introduction

The title of this volume derives from our desire to present the territories of Wales as both spatial and non-spatial in nature. Naturally there is a country, a spatial entity, called Wales, and within this there is a variety of distinctive culture regions. From their geographical location in these latter, Welsh people—whether knowingly or unconsciously—enjoy ties of identification with locality. In turn, the character of these locations, however various or divergent in nature, contributes to a larger identity which is national in character. But, in addition, there are also those Welsh worlds which cannot be bounded by space that are defined by factors of emotion, attachment, and imagination. Whatever the ties of locality and aspects of identity that can be associated with territorial space, these ties must be seen in the context of those changing but ever-present ideas—whether social, cultural or political in nature—which continually operate to enhance and develop contemporary Welsh life. These Welsh worlds thus are ones defined by the subjective; yet these are no less real because of this characteristic. Ideas can and do become material forces which, in the end, can change objective reality. Ideas of Welshness, therefore, do not only depend upon a simple attachment to a country as defined by territorial boundaries: they develop in association with inspiration and influence from within and from outside Wales—whether from Welsh communities elsewhere or from other 'national' cultures existing within 'host' nation states other than the United Kingdom of Great Britain. The *patterns* of these spatial and non-spatial factors influencing Welsh cultural and national identity, and the *processes* whereby they are formed and transformed are of crucial importance in understanding Wales as it appears to be in the later decades of the twentieth century.

What sort of book, therefore, does *The Welsh and their country* turn out to be? First and foremost we have tried to produce a new contribution dealing with the Wales of our times—the Wales of the 1980s rather than, say, the 1880s. Moreover, to complement existing studies, this is a collection of key papers written primarily within the paradigms of the social sciences. Here, you will notice, we use the term in the plural for although our colleagues share a good range of analytical approaches, there are no all-embracing approaches which individual disciplines—geography, sociology, political anthropology—share fully and completely. Rather, as readers of this volume will find, there exists a considerable diversity of methods and points of focus.

Inevitably, though, in setting out to explore the inner, essential qualities of modern Wales, of necessity we must address ourselves to that central question of what contribution should we draw from colleagues cultivating the same fields but with different tools, namely specialists on the history of Wales. As the poet, R. S. Thomas, points out in *Welsh landscape*, 'You cannot live in the present, at least not in Wales'.[1]

In this book the reader will find frequent references to events in Welsh history and many of our contributors draw on the published work of Welsh historians. Indeed, Dr. Prys Morgan, the author of Chapter 5, is himself a distinguished professional historian. It would be quite unthinkable that anyone could ever set out to explore the nature of the Welsh, their society and cultural identity without resort to events in the past; and the contextual interpretations placed on these events and movements by Welsh historians. Therefore, in this volume 'history' is drawn on insofar as it helps to explain the present, but these explanations are primarily within the conceptual frameworks used by social scientists the world over. As a general principle we have eschewed the narrative approaches of traditional history whereby explanations of contemporary life are reached only after past events have been dealt with layer by layer as in the peeling of an onion. We offer this volume, then, not as a replacement but as a complement to recent scholarly writings, on twentieth-century Wales by traditional historians.

ORIGINS AND SCOPE OF THE BOOK

Of course, collaborative work such as this book owes much to its origins. In 1982 and 1983 the editors wrote, presented and taught an advanced honours-level undergraduate course in the Open University entitled, *D423: Wales—a study of cultural and national identity*. This was designed to be completed by extended studies of selected works dealing with the geographical, social and political nature of the country in the early 1980s. The course was proposed and sponsored by the University's Faculty Board of Social Sciences. In itself this very fact is significant for it determined the specific ways in which the topics of enquiry were selected and interpreted within the syllabus of study. The course attracted much interest, both within and outside the University; and an enthusiastic group of part-time students, living at many different locations throughout England and Wales, was enrolled. In the planning stages it became clear that although several existing books could have been adopted as set texts, none managed to deal adequately with a representative range of the topics which awaited exploration. Some of the essential reading had been published in Welsh and therefore was beyond the reach of students without a reading knowledge of that language. Others, despite their publication in English, were accessible only with considerably difficulty. These had been printed in specialist journals and some students found that the public library service was unable or unwilling to obtain copies for them.

It soon became apparent that the publication of a collection of key papers on contemporary Wales would go some way to meeting the steadily growing demands of a readership outside of as well as within our own University. Once the Gomer Press had accepted our proposals, we realised that this venture would provide the various authors with opportunities to correct, modify and update their original statements. Thus, whilst Chapters 3, 10 and

11 were first published in the Welsh language, all, except Chapter 3, appear in this book in an undated English translation for the first time. Chapters 2, 4, 6, 7 and 12 were published in the English language as research papers in specialist journals but here they appear as revised versions. Chapter 1 (dealing with language), Chapter 14 (political organisations) and Chapter 15 (the role of the mass media) are concerned with topics which, in the context of this book, of necessity need to reflect ongoing changes right up to the date of publication. Therefore, these particular contributions have been specially written for this volume.

As the contents list shows, the fifteen chapters have been grouped into four sections or themes. In Section 1 we start with the idea that primarily Wales is itself a territorial expression and that language and the long-standing interaction with England gives the country a certain distinctiveness. Section 2 contains contributions which set out to explore aspects of what some scholars formerly regarded archetypically as traditional Welsh societies. This section also includes two important reviews of the various ways in which approaches to the sociology of Wales have changed in recent times. Section 3 is concerned primarily with the intellectual templates for structuring various analytical approaches, including those relating to questions of planning and the maintenance of the Welsh language and the culture it represents in the 1980s. Finally, Section 4 rounds off the substantive themes by looking closely at organisations and administrative structures and the ways in which these have grown up or been adapted to reflect the distinctive identity of Wales in political terms.

Pattern and Process

Another manner of interpreting this rich medley of themes is to accept them as statements concerning pattern or process. Wales is and, in the foreseeable future, will remain an integral part of the British nation state. Like Brittany and other indigenous 'cultural nations' it continues to radiate a most distinctive and separate identity. Yet, at the same time there are many similarities with the other countries of Britain. By *pattern* we are referring to what exists in reality—political boundaries, the very fact that the Welsh language contines to be used in everyday life alongside English, and the institutions and public bodies established specifically to meet Welsh needs. Once identified, we can recognise all these differences for what they are. In part, the distinctiveness of Wales in the 1980s lies in having a different arrangement of that which is found elsewhere in Britain as, for example, in the sphere of public education or the local government system. In other words, in Wales the 'British pattern' has been re-jigged and modified for specific Welsh purposes. But at the same time, and in substantial measure, Wales still retains its own indigenous 'patterns' as, for example, in the continued existence of the Welsh language and regional differences in the distributions of its speakers. It is clear that linguistic considerations constitute a key pattern, exerting much influence on many other aspects of Welsh life—more so in the past, perhaps, than at present; more effectively, perhaps, in some domains of Welsh life than in others.

Conversely, by *process* we are referring to underlying currents of change: how patterns, structures, attitudes and perceptions are modified and the impact of these changes on other aspects of life. Whilst some patterns and their attendant processes are inherently spatial phenomena and give rise to regional differences, other key processes do not relate primarily to territorial and regional considerations. Thus, for example, social and administrative structures provide contexts for change. Here the processes which operate may turn out to be formal (as, for example, in the re-organisation of local government) or, as in the roles played by pressure groups or through the exercise of influence and/or patronage, they are of an informal nature, operating outside or beyond statutory provisions.

The identification of relevant patterns begins in this book in the chapters of Section 1 where we are particularly concerned with linguistic data and territorial affiliations. Pattern recognition in relation to the distinctive national and cultural character of modern Wales also occurs elsewhere, particularly in Section 3 where both Nairn (Chapter 8) and Hechter (Chapter 9) set out to offer explanatory frameworks of relationships over time between Wales and England. Again, in Section 4 where formal administrative structures and institutions are reviewed, we are still concerned with the identification of distinctive patterns. Although in all these chapters there is much discussion of processes in relation to observed and changing patterns, it is to the contributions included in Section 2 (The traditional society) and 3 (Ideologies) that the reader has to turn to be made fully aware of the processes which are thought to have been significant in the retention of Welshness in our own time.

Review of Contents

In Chapter 1 Professor Carter and Dr. Aitchison take great care to point out the statistical advantages and shortcomings of census data for studies of linguistic distributions in the Wales of the 1980s. They emphasise, in particular, the need to consider *absolute* (or actual) numbers as well as the use of the percentage (a *relative* measure) which has had long traditional usage. Some administrators and some formulators of public policy have tended to base all their recommendations on percentages and thus have ignored the simple fact that actual numbers of Welsh speakers may be greater in what appears, in relative terms, to be the anglicized south and northeast. From their analysis of the 1981 census figures it is clear that in terms of actual numbers, today the main areas for Welsh are predominantly industrial and urban! This, they point out, is in contrast to the traditional public conception which tends to associate the Welsh language with the remoter and more upland regions of rural Wales. They go on to point out that whilst still remaining areas with low densities of Welsh speakers, some of the greatest increases amongst the young in the decade 1971-81 were found not in the Welsh heartland areas but within the anglicized communities of south-east and north-east Wales. These results demand close and careful study. Clearly this opening chapter is, in many respects, a bench-mark study which provides an authoritative survey as to the territorial and numerical significance of the Welsh language which, even today, for many remains a meaningful badge of their nationality.

The themes of linguistic and territorial identity are continued by Dr. Pryce in Chapter 2. This sets out to explore the idea that Wales can be thought of in terms of a distinctive culture area—a large territory where regional components have been changed significantly since the pre-industrial circumstances of the later-eighteenth century. Following the Devolution Referendum of 1979 and the rejection of the Labour Party's proposals for an elected Welsh Assembly, *Barn*, the influential current affairs journal, singled out the original version of this paper for detailed comment, arguing that the findings of the research showed a depressing situation for the survival of 'our nation, our language and culture'.[2] Yet, the significance of the research on which Chapter 2 is based is that the culture region model lifts the discussion above immediate partisan interests; it raises the 'Welsh question' beyond the somewhat pedestrian contexts in which it is often treated in the popular media and facilitates international comparisons. And, as later chapters show, the culture region model identifies the contexts in which present-day concerns can be intelligently discussed.

Chapter 3 by the late Professor E. G. Bowen rounds off the treatment of spatial identity by providing a number of wide historical perspectives. Since its first broadcast as the Annual Radio Lecture of BBC Wales in 1964, Bowen's interpretation of the geography of Wales as the backcloth to its history has continued to attract much interest. Early Welsh Life was developed by individuals, Bowen points out, in the relative loneliness of their scattered rural settlements.

> It was in the isolation of these farms that so much emphasis was placed on the non-material culture, music, poetry, philosophy and religion to say nothing of their interest in later times in eisteddfodau, singing festivals, and the religious revivals of the eighteenth and nineteenth centuries.

And, he continues, linked with these intellectual pursuits was the development of rural crafts. The ordinary people, he points out,

> . . . were possibly very poor in their material resources but indeed very rich in the things of the mind and the spirit. The most important element in their culture was their language and the usage closest to hand was the spoken word . . . It is no wonder, therefore, that the word *iaith* (language) was used in the Middle Ages to denote 'nation'.

Bowen then moves on to identify 'centrifugal' and 'centripetal' forces which throughout the ages have shaped the cultural life of Wales. These, which include the profound influences of intense industrialisation after c.1780, have given rise, he contends, to two territorial provinces: 'Inner Wales' in the north and west; 'Outer Wales' in the east and south. Inner Wales has always been strong in its indigenous character—so strong, indeed, that invariably, incoming ideas and movements were Cymricized and modified so that they became integral to the national culture. Conversely, in Outer Wales local and regional characteristics were themselves changed as a result of contact with England.

Whilst welcoming these ideas some scholars displayed initial reservations, especially the older generation of Welsh historians. Professor Glanmor Williams, for example, appreciated the 'clear, incisive, widely-ranging' nature of Bowen's basic tenets which were, 'stimulating to the point of being venturesome', but felt that a longer in-depth study was needed. This, he argued, could then offer a 'finer-toothed analysis' to 'take greater account of social conditions, the product of historical change as well as geographical features . . .'. In general, Williams felt that the distinction between Inner and Outer Wales was, perhaps, 'too broadgauged and unsophisticated to be more than preliminarily useful'. Nevertheless, although now dated and, in some respects overtaken by more recent studies, as Professor Williams himself was careful to emphasise, Bowen's ideas still remain stimulating because they offer new perspectives on old themes.[3]

Section 2 of this book changes the focus from geographical to much more overtly sociological considerations. In Chapter 4 Trefor M. Owen looks back over the achievements of the now, world-famous studies of Welsh rural communities which commenced with Alwyn D. Rees's book, *Life in a Welsh countryside: a social study of Llanfihangel-yng-Ngwynfa* (Cardiff: University of Wales Press), first published in 1950. Despite recent criticisms, quite rightly Owen still finds value in these case studies. Despite their empiricism they still provide much information as to former cultural and social characteristics, insights not accessible by more 'objective' techniques. The strength of Chapter 4 lies, however, in the ways in which Owen contrasts the methods and the specific topics selected by the various researchers—in particular, the differences of approach between 'insiders' and 'outsiders': that is, between those writing from within or from outside the ambits of Welsh cultural life; the differences of emphasis, insight and the nuances that can be detected between native researcher or newly arrived scholar. In contrast, Chapter 5 explores a range of intriguing ideas which, even today, are still deeply rooted in the Welsh language. In dealing with the changing concept of *y werin* (ordinary people) Dr. Prys Morgan makes available a whole cluster of images and evaluations which it is essential for all observers of the Welsh scene, whether or not they speak the Welsh language, to understand and appreciate if they are to gain access to some of the innermost recesses of national identity in Wales.

Whilst Chapters 4 and 5 deal with aspects of the traditional society, Chapter 6 (by Graham Day) and Chapter 7 (by Dr. Glyn Williams) offer wide-ranging reviews of the main talking points that have occupied sociologists—particularly members of the Sociology of Wales Research Group—throughout the 1970s and in the early 1980s. Day argues that 'underdevelopment' constitutes a serious problem in modern Wales. This he states, is characterised by its one-sidedness and the fact that executive decisions are taken outside Wales. Moreover, as he points out, until recently earlier researchers had failed to acknowledge this fact. In his assessment the community studies reported in Chapter 4 give rise to numerous methodological problems in sociological terms because they tend to depict rural Wales as a series of warm, intimate, 'radical' communities. The researchers, by the very way in which their findings were presented, effected a 'closure' on certain topics, so preventing a fuller discussion of wider issues, especially class considerations. A stronger theoretical framework is needed, he argues: questions of cultural identity, language usage and changes, ethnicity and nationalism are more fruitfully pursued in the proper 'structural contexts' in which they arise. Day's post-script, written specially for this volume, takes a cool look at what has actually been achieved since the publication of his original paper in 1979. He concludes that, whilst there have been encouraging signs of numerous changes of approach, the sociology of Wales still continues to be written with an inherent bias towards economic rather than sociological or political considerations.

Much the same ground is covered by Dr. Glyn Williams in Chapter 7. Here, however, the main differences are ones of emphasis rather than topic or context. Like Day, Williams is critical of the ultimate value of the community-study approach on methodological grounds and he goes on to review, in particular, the significance of the ideas of Professor Michael Hechter (see Chapter 9) that Wales is an 'internal colony' within the British nation state, in the past exploited by and, in consequence, now dependent on England. In his vision of Wales in the 1980s Williams identifies the continuance of economic inequalities. He recognises that lack of access to certain opportunities is one of several consequences that stem from the 'colonial' nature of the country and, in particular, from the 'cultural division of labour' within dominantly Welsh speaking areas such as Gwynedd. This, he argues, has been brought about by processes of re-structuring and the results work against the maintenance of Welsh cultural identity. It is clear that Chapter 7 raises a number of crucial matters which need further research and evaluation. Taken together, the contributions in Chapters 6 and 7 neatly chart a whole series of change-processes that are now operational throughout much of the Welsh heartland areas identified in earlier chapters.

The role of ideologies and ideas in patterning social and political action is a key feature of Section 3; also prominent are analytic frameworks offered by contemporary social scientists—frameworks which offer differing interpretations of this complex reality. Tom Nairn's vivid comparison of Wales and Scotland (Chapter 8) located both countries not only within the context of the British Isles, but also within a larger process, that of the decline of the British imperial state.[4]

Using the idea of uneven development as developed by Marxist scholars, he sees the differing responses of Wales and Scotland to this process as products both of indigenous and external factors. Locating both of these differing territories in 'Europe's new wave of national movements' requires a theory which is capable of combining a wide variety of economic, political, cultural and historical evidence without robbing it of its unique features. This is where a comparison with the ideas of Professor Michael Hechter (Chapter 9) is particularly instructive, for Nairn specifically criticizes him on this point—he 'lumps too many different things together'. Whatever our view on this, Hechter's contribution to the study of contemporary Wales is of considerable importance—for just as Nairn does, he locates Wales within a wider framework of international comparisons. Just as capitalist development created colonies throughout the world so, believes

Hechter, it also did within its own original territories. Thus, Britain developed 'internal colonies' in its 'Celtic fringe'. Once again the mode of analysis depends upon the notion of uneven development, but this time it is much more closely related to Weberian concepts of status, rather than to Marxist ideas of class. Therefore, it is interesting that Hechter's work should have become a model for many scholars who normally would have been preoccupied with the class paradigm. Because of their relevance to the new alignments and vigour of politics within the national regions of Britain at that time, both Nairn and Hechter considerably influenced academic and political debate in the 1970s. This re-assertion of key concepts relating to national and cultural identity was wide-ranging; however, the least well-documented of all new developments was the emergence of the idea, and of the movement, *Adfer*.[5] Only very rarely have Emyr Llewelyn's writings and speeches been referred to in the English language media. Highly rhetorical in style, these form an ideological underlay to a significant development (or re-development) in contemporary realms of political ideas and action. It is therefore important for this volume to include the newly-commissioned translation 'What is *Adfer*?' (Chapter 11); equally important is the need to include one of the major criticisms of the ideology of the *Adfer* movement by Principal R. Tudur Jones, translated here as Chapter 10.

Today, 'the rights of the individual' seem to be a general preoccupation of liberal-democratic theory and related practice, including planning. But where sizeable areas and communities with specific Welsh characteristics still exist, should these latter be given the status of key factors in social and economic planning? The concentration on the idea of the *individual* in the community has been apparent. Is it now time to re-assert the idea of the *community*? In particular, Chapter 12 by Dr. Colin Williams addresses itself to the validity and desirability of using areal or regional linguistic characteritics as a distinct factor in planning. The idea of planning for communities, long since accepted in other spheres of activity, has been relatively neglected in relation to language in Wales and we hope that this chapter may help to re-invigorate and inform debate.

Finally, Section 4 examines the existing structures and the processes at work in the field of politics. Chapter 13 (Foulkes, Jones and Wilford) concentrates on the description of formal structures; Chapter 14 by Ian Hume also emphasizes the role of informal and non-party structures and their relationship to other social and cultural processes. In Chapter 15 Hume looks further at aspects of these processes as illustrated by the state of the Welsh mass-media. Its conclusion, that the diversity of Welsh social and cultural life is relatively poorly served by the mass-media—particularly those in the English language—sets out to add a further dimension to our understanding of ideological influences on contemporary Welsh political life.

Acknowledgements

This book could not have been completed without the enthusiastic help of a substantial number of people. We are indebted to the fourteen contributing authors for allowing us to use their work and the substantial revisions and updating that some of them completed to earlier published versions of their papers. Dr. Prys Morgan, Eirian E. Edwards and B. P. Jones, and Ann Davies translated Chapters 5, 10 and 11 respectively. We acknowledge the informed and sympathetic ways in which they have rendered into good English, works originally published in the Welsh language.

We have received much advice and guidance from Emeritus Professor Emrys Jones of the London School of Economics who has acted as external assessor to this volume. Several other colleagues have offered stimulating critical insights, particularly Dr. Cyril Parry of the University College of North Wales at Bangor. The views and ideas expressed in the book are however the responsibility of the original authors and, where indicated, the editors.

A central role has been played, also, by Jacquie Griffin, secretary to the Faculty of Social Sciences at the Open University in Wales, Cardiff, who prepared much of the material in readiness for the printer.

Finally, we thank the Gomer Press for undertaking the publication of this book, especially John Lewis and Cathryn Gwynn who have assisted us in numerous practical ways. Before joining the National Museum of Wales Dr. I. D. Elis-Gruffydd was a key member of staff at the Gomer Press; we acknowledge his quiet efficiency and friendly encouragement when this book was in the initial stages of development.

We hope that you, our readers, will derive as much pleasure from this volume as we ourselves have had in its compilation.

Ian Hume The Open University in Wales,
W. T. R. Pryce Cardiff.

References

1 R. S. Thomas, *Selected poems, 1946-1968*. London: Hart-Davis, MacGibbon, 1973, 9.

2 'Cymru a'i phobl', *Barn*, Rhif 195, Ebrill 1979, 590.

3 G. Williams, 'Geography and Welsh history', *Welsh History Review*, 2 (1965), 275-8.

4 In his book (1977), *The break-up of Britain: crisis and neo-nationalism*, London, New Left Books, Nairn fully describes what he sees as this process of decline, of break-up. The work reprinted here occurs as a chapter in that volume.

5 *Adfer* is the Welsh verb-noun meaning 'to return' or 'to restore' and hence 'restoration'.

Contributors

John Aitchison, BA, MA, PhD
Senior Lecturer in Geography, University College of Wales, Aberystwyth.

The late E. G. Bowen, BA, MA, DLitt, LLD, DUniv, DipEd, FSA, FRGS,
Emeritus Professor of Geography, University of Wales.

Harold Carter, BA, MA, DLitt,
Gregynog Professor of Human Geography, University College of Wales, Aberystwyth.

Graham Day, BA, MPhil,
Lecturer in Sociology, University College of Wales, Aberystwyth.

D. Foulkes, BA, LLM, Barrister,
Professor of Law, University of Wales Institute of Science and Technology, Cardiff.

Michael Hechter, BA, PhD,
Professor of Sociology, University of Arizona, Tucsan, Arizona.

Ian Hume, BA, MScEcon, AIB,
Staff Tutor in Government and Politics, The Open University in Wales, Cardiff.

J. B. Jones, BA, MA,
Lecturer in Politics, University College, Cardiff.

R. Tudur Jones, BA, DD, DPhil,
Rev. Principal of the Bala-Bangor College, Bangor.

Emyr Llewelyn

Prys Morgan, MA, DPhil,
Senior Lecturer in History, University College, Swansea.

T. Nairn, MA,
Author and journalist

Trefor M. Owen, BA, MA, FSA,
Curator, Welsh Folk Museum, St. Fagans, Cardiff.

W. T. R. Pryce, BSc, MSc, PhD, Dip Ed,
Staff Tutor in Geography, The Open University in Wales, Cardiff.

R. A. Wilford, BSc, MSc, PhD,
Lecturer in Politics, The Queen's University of Belfast.

Colin H. Williams, BScEcon, PhD,
Principal Lecturer and Course Tutor in Geography, North Staffordshire Polytechnic.

Glyn Williams, BSc, MA, PhD,
Lecturer in Sociology, University College of North Wales, Bangor.

SECTION 1
SPATIAL IDENTITY

Chapter One

Language Areas and Language Change in Wales: 1961-1981

Harold Carter and John Aitchison

The character and vitality of a culture is to a large extent language-dependent. Language helps to preserve traditions, shapes modes of perception, and profoundly influences patterns of social intercourse and behaviour. As Mandelbaum (1949,162) has stated, it is an illusion to imagine 'that language is merely an incidental means of solving problems of communication or reflection. No two languages are ever sufficiently similar to be considered as representing the same social reality. The worlds in which different societies live are distinct worlds, not merely the same world with different labels attached'. According to this view a culture gains identity and significance from its associated language. For a minority culture in particular, the absolute and relative strength of its language serves as a diagnostic and tangible indicator of that culture's general well-being and long-term viability. Whilst other indicators might be cited, comprehensive data on such features are seldom available. For instance, statistics on religious affiliation—a significant variable in the Welsh cultural equation—are not recorded in the British national censuses (apart from the census of 1851) and reliable data on such matters can be difficult to accumulate (Williams, 1982). It is for this reason, and because of its intrinsic importance, that academic and political analysts of cultural change frequently focus on trends in the ability to speak, read and write a language.

The central aims of this study are to map and examine the spatial distribution of Welsh speakers, as enumerated in the 1981 census; to comment on broad patterns of change, especially between 1961 and 1981; and finally to identify language areas by reference to a composite set of criteria. Before broaching these substantive issues, however, it is necessary to detail the nature of the data sets to be analysed and to draw attention to problems of interpretation and inference that arise in treating aggregate census information.

The Interpretation and Mapping of Aggregate Language Statistics

The section of the 1981 census relating to the Welsh language is based on a series of questions which seek to identify whether the respondent is able to speak Welsh, and if so, whether or not he/she can read or write it. The first of these would appear to be straightforward since it is based on a seemingly simple statement of fact. In reality, however, the question on the census form—'Do you speak Welsh?'—is open to widely differing interpretations. The quality or fluency of the Welsh spoken, for instance, is not specified. When dealing with aggregate statistics (as in this study) it has to be assumed that such variations in interpretation will be similar in all areas and, therefore, can be ignored in assessing regional patterns. A further complicating issue concerns the treatment of those respondents who indicate that they are monoglot Welsh. Two completely different factors make this a difficult matter to resolve. It is evident that a number of those returned as monoglot Welsh will be young children over the age of three—the age at which the language enumeration begins—and who have not yet learned to speak English. In sharp contrast are those who, for political or cultural reasons, will deny that they are able to speak English. Given the complexities of these issues the incidence of monoglot Welsh speakers will not be considered in this particular study (but see Aitchison and Carter, 1985).

Since 1971 the census has collated data on abilities to read and write Welsh. Spatial variations in 'literacy' levels are worthy of special consideration since they serve as a further and important indicator of the strength and well-being of the language. In the 1981 census only 72.1 per cent of those able to speak Welsh claimed a facility to read and write the language. In assessing regional differences in literacy levels, together with changes in the numbers of Welsh speakers, three closely related 'structural' issues need to be taken into account. Firstly, in a colonial situation—and it is not unusual to treat Wales as an internal colony (see Chapters 6, 7, and 9 in this book)—the vernacular remains as a means of oral communication, but in an increasingly bureaucratic and urban world the colonizing language (English) dominates in formal, official and written transactions. Secondly, the ability to read and write Welsh is age specific. The older element of the population was educated at a time when English was the exclusive medium in schools and Welsh expressly forbidden. Welsh was spoken at home but not formally learned at school. Literacy was achieved in English only. This is supported by the fact that in 1981 only 66.2 per cent of those over 55 could read and write Welsh, compared with 81.7 per cent in the 10 to 24 age group. Since it has a differential spatial impact, it should also be added that the overall literacy percentage in an area will be reduced by the number of very young Welsh speakers who at the time of the census had not yet learned to read or write Welsh. Finally, it has to be recognized that it is possible to interpret the relatively low levels of literacy recorded as a symptom of language decline. Where the Welsh cultural tradition as whole is becoming increasingly attenuated, where doubts are felt as to the 'value' of the language in commercial terms, and where a variety of other social and economic goals and aspirations are deemed to be more important than a facility in Welsh, then it could be argued that whilst the spoken language might well be acquired on the hearth, for many there will not be sufficient motivation to extend this to a facility in the reading and writing of the language.

These and many other factors can be cited to explain spatial differences in the numbers able to speak Welsh and in degrees of literacy, but the precise impact of each, particularly when the analysis is set at an aggregate level, is difficult to ascertain. They interact and, operating at different scales, their separate influences cannot be readily isolated and measured. Accordingly, in considering selected language distributions this study is descriptive in tone; explanations of particular spatial patterns are proffered but these are not formally tested.

The analysis itself is based on data for the communities of Wales (since 1974 the Welsh equivalent of parishes in England) and draws information from the 1961, 1971 and 1981 censuses. To overcome the problem of boundary changes a number of communities have had to be amalgamated. Only by so doing is it possible to measure absolute and relative changes in the numbers of Welsh speakers from one census to another. This process of amalgamation resulted in the delimitation of 993 community areas out of the original 1,005 communities included in the 1981 census. The latter are maintained in the mapping of 1981 statistics, the former have been used for plotting patterns of change between 1961 and 1981. A further complication that needs to be noted is that whilst in 1961 and 1971 the enumerated population related to persons present at midnight on the day of the census, in 1981 it referred specifically to the 'usually resident population'. Fortunately, for purposes of comparison, language data for 1981 (i.e. numbers able to speak Welsh and to read and write Welsh) are available for both of these bases, although without a breakdown according to age.

Welsh Language Distributions 1981

(i) Absolute numbers of Welsh speakers

In Wales at the 1981 census 503,549 out of the total 'usually resident' population of 2,645,114 claimed an ability to speak Welsh. Figure 1 records absolute numbers of Welsh speakers at the community level. The distribution highlights two main areas of concentration. The first, and by far the largest, covers the urban and old industrial heartland of south Wales. Communities with

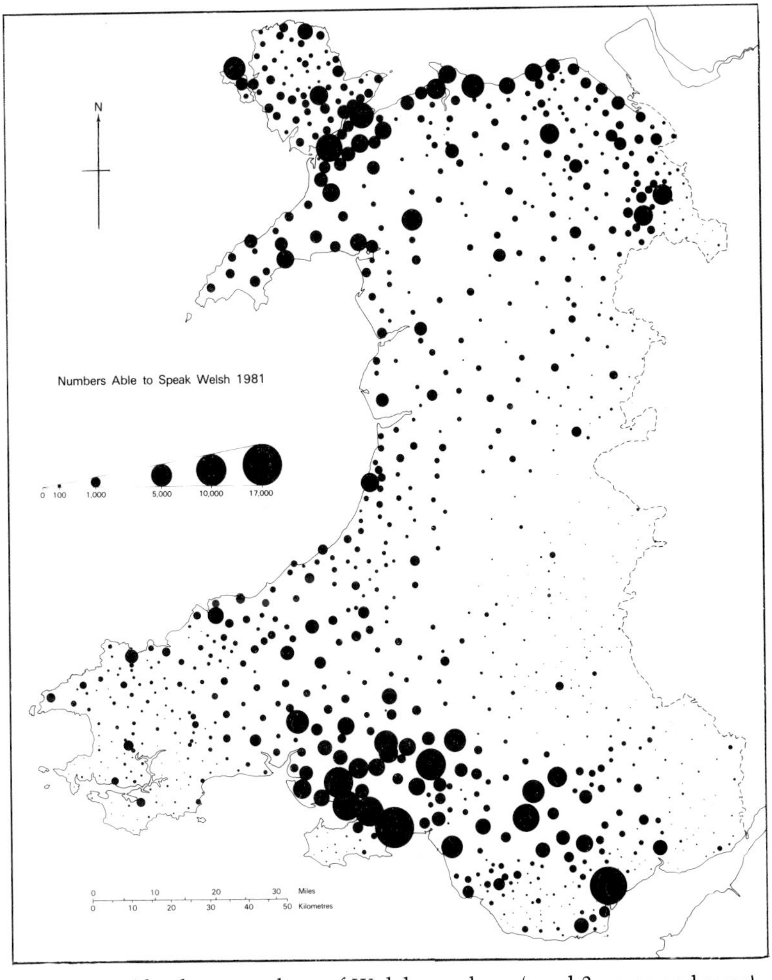

Figure 1. Absolute numbers of Welsh speakers (aged 3 years and over) in communities, 1981.

the highest numbers of Welsh speakers include Swansea (16,427), Cardiff (13,877), and Llanelli Urban and Rural (17,472). Significant numbers are also recorded in the heads of the valleys settlements of Mid Glamorgan, such as Aberdare (4,948) and Merthyr Tudful (4,183), and in the 'hearts of the valleys' (e.g. Rhondda—7,377). The main core area, however, is the western part of the coalfield in south-east Dyfed and West Glamorgan. Of the total population of Welsh speakers a notable 23.8 per cent are to be found in the districts of Llanelli and Dinefwr. Around the margins of this extensive zone of concentration, along the coastal and borderland fringes of south Wales and in the upland interior of central Wales, absolute numbers of Welsh speakers are clearly much smaller.

The second zone with a high population of Welsh speakers extends in an arcuate band along the coast of north Wales, from Caernarfon in the west to Flint in the east. It then continues southwards and inland to include the urban and rural communities of Wrexham and Rhiwabon (Ruabon). Here, the largest totals are recorded by Caernarfon (7,761), Bangor (6,225), Conwy (3,281), Llandudno (3,280), Colwyn Bay (5,582), Wrexham (4,176) and Rhosllanerchrugog (3,907).

Away from these two main areas locally high values are associated with a string of coastal settlements in west Wales; for example, Holyhead (5,380), Pwllheli (3,182) and Aberystwyth (3,655). Market towns set within productive agricultural lowlands also have relatively large populations of Welsh speakers. Examples include Carmarthen (5,652) in the Vale of Tywi, and Denbigh (4,023) in the Vale of Clwyd.

The spatial pattern displayed in Figure 1 demonstrates that, in terms of absolute numbers, the main Welsh-speaking areas are predominantly industrial and urban in character. This is in contrast to the traditional public conception which tends to associate the language with the remoter and more uplands regions of rural Wales. One possible explanation for this is that in the past analysts have tended to lay more emphasis on the *relative* dominance of Welsh speakers, and have mapped proportions rather than raw totals. Which of these measures is the more appropriate is open to debate. The two are evidently inter-related but many would argue that a culture survives, and is seen to be regionally identifiable, only where it is dominant. From this point of view it is the relative rather than the absolute importance of the language that is critical. Cardiff, for example, may have a large number of Welsh speakers but it is not predominantly a Welsh-speaking area. Conversely, there may be a much smaller number of Welsh speakers in places such as Pwllheli but often they constitute a high proportion of the total population and have a major formative influence on the social life of the community and the Welshness of the milieu. The significance of this distinction between the absolute and relative strength of the language has been elaborated upon by Aitchison and Carter (1985).

(ii) Welsh speakers: proportionate dominance

Figure 2 categorizes the communities of Wales according to the proportion of the total population over three years of age that is able to speak Welsh. The distribution highlights five main areas where proportions generally exceed 70 and, in places, even 80 per cent. The first is the central and south-western parts of Ynys Môn (Isle of Anglesey). The highest percentage of Welsh speakers within this compact region is returned by the community of Llangwyllog with a figure of 96 per cent. Only around the port of Holyhead and along the east coast of the island—a notable retirement area—do values fall below 70. The districts of Dwyfor and Arfon constitute a second major core, separated physically from Ynys Môn by Afon Menai (the Menai Straits) and almost wholly severed from the Welsh-speaking mountain heartland of Wales by a band of strongly-anglicized communities. This band follows the valley of the Conwy and then sweeps around the southern fringes of the Snowdonia Massif to include such centres as Capel Curig and Beddgelert. This linguistic fracture within what is conventionally called 'Welsh Wales' is perhaps unexpected, but it is, of course, a consequence of the long-developed tourist industry with all its social and economic ramifications. In this second core area the highest proportion is recorded by the community of Llanaelhaearn in Dwyfor (90.9 per cent).

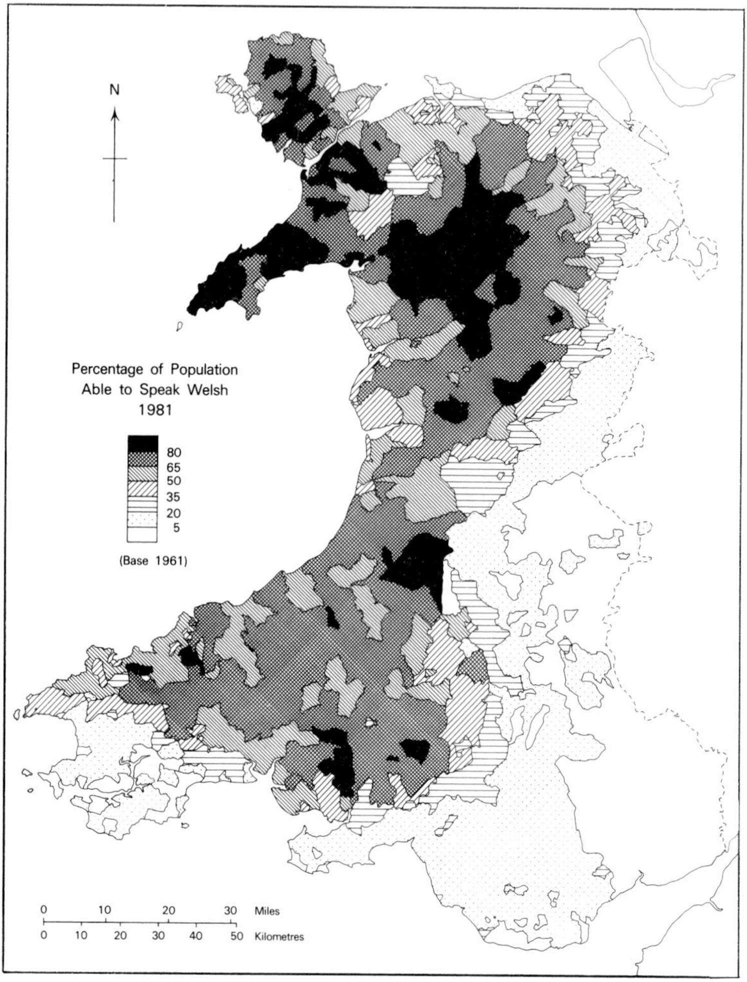

Figure 2. Proportions of the population (aged 3 years and over) able to speak Welsh, 1981.

The third region with distinctively high porportions of Welsh speakers covers much of Meirionydd, and extends northwards to Mynydd Hiraethog and southwards to the River Dyfi. More remote than the four other zones of concentration, this large core area constitutes a major bastion for the language. In many communities the proportion of Welsh speakers exceeds 85, with Llanuwchllyn recording a figure of 93.2 per cent. This said, however, percentages are seen to fall sharply towards the west coast. Here, the development of tourism is known to have had a strong anglicizing influence. The Dyfi marks the divide between the Meirionydd heartland and the fourth area of concentration which lies to the south. Broadly following the Cambrian Mountains of upland Dyfed, this zone is made up of a number of fragmented clusters of communities. More clearly delineated is the fifth and final core region which includes communities in south-east Dyfed and neighbouring parts of West Glamorgan. This area, like others in south Wales, has high numbers of Welsh speakers (Fig. 1). The distinguishing feature of this particular zone however, which is focused on the Gwendraeth and Amman valleys, is the proportion of the population that is able to speak Welsh. Here, unlike other areas, percentages generally exceed 70 per cent—the highest figure being returned by the community of Quarter Bach (86.7 per cent).

It is evident from Figure 2 that, away from the five main areas of concentration identified above, the proportions of Welsh speakers at community level decline sharply, with gradients being at their steepest in south and central Wales. Having established this overall pattern of regional variation it is appropriate to continue with a consideration of literacy levels.

(iii) Proportions of Welsh speakers unable to read and write Welsh

In 1981 almost 28 per cent of Welsh speakers were *unable* to read and write the language. Figure 3 is of interest in this regard for it shows that literacy rates are at their highest in the four Welsh-speaking core areas of the north and west. In the core region of south-east Dyfed and West Glamorgan, and especially in neighbouring regions to the east, the picture is much less impressive. In many communities the percentage of speakers unable to read

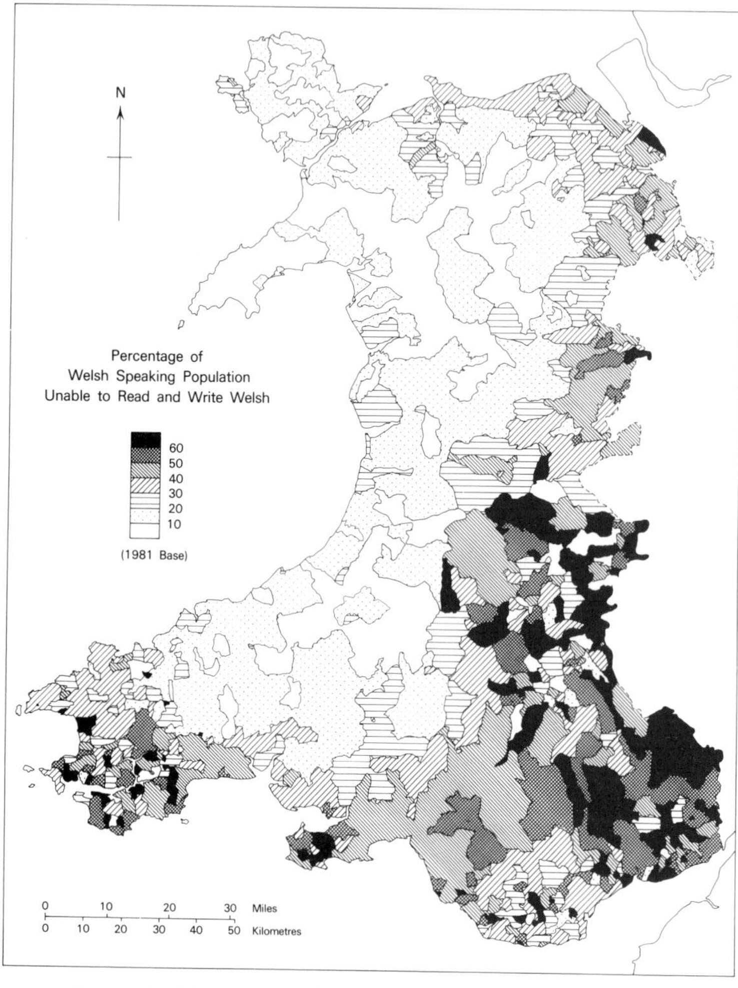

Figure 3: Literacy levels amongst Welsh speakers, 1981.

and write Welsh frequently ranges between 30 and 40. It has been suggested earlier that the low levels of literacy recorded in these heavily industrialized environments reflect the colonizing dominance of English as the language of more formal, commercial and bureaucratic communication. This may be so, but the fact that the proportion of Welsh speakers over 65 years of age is greater here than anywhere else in Wales is also of some relevance. In many parts of the region well over 30 per cent of the Welsh-speaking population fall into this age category. As far as the future of the language is concerned the situation is clearly disturbing, and all the more so because it applies to an area with the greatest absolute concentration of Welsh speakers (Fig. 1). This said, however, it is notable that in certain parts of Wales—the hinterland of Cardiff and the Wrexham-Mold region, for instance—literacy rates are generally higher than might be expected, given the low proportion of Welsh speakers. As will be seen, the numbers of Welsh speakers in these areas are increasing; a growth which manifests itself in a high demand for Welsh medium schools. Aitchison and Carter (1985) argue that developments in these areas reflect a changing attitude to the language on the part of young urban professionals—at least in as far as the education of their children is concerned. The precise significance of these localized developments, and the motivations that underpin them (personal, social, economic, political and cultural), cannot be analysed in detail here, but they are of import when it comes to considering the patterns of change in the numbers of Welsh speakers over the past twenty years.

Language Change 1961-1981

The process of language change can be quantified using various absolute and relative measures. From statistics relating to successive censuses, reference can be made either to absolute differences in the numbers able to speak Welsh, to differences in the percentage of Welsh speakers within individual communities or to percentage rates of change.

Figure 4 records changes in the proportionate dominance of Welsh speakers in each of the former counties of Wales between 1901 and 1981. The figures graphically capture the widespread and persistent decline in the relative strength of the language. Differences in the percentage of Welsh speakers for the period are seen to be greatest for the

Figure 4

Percetage of the population able to speak Welsh, 1901-81

County (pre-1974)	1901	1911	1921	1931	1951	1961	1971	1981
Anglesey	91.7	88.7	84.9	87.4	79.8	75.5	65.7	61.0
Brecon	45.9	41.5	37.2	37.3	30.3	28.1	22.9	19.3
Caernarfon	89.6	85.6	75.0	79.2	71.7	68.3	62.0	59.7
Cardigan	93.0	89.6	82.1	87.1	79.5	74.8	67.6	63.2
Carmarthen	90.4	84.9	82.4	82.3	77.3	75.1	66.5	60.0
Denbigh	61.9	56.7	48.4	48.5	38.5	34.8	28.1	24.2
Flint	49.1	42.2	32.7	31.7	21.1	19.0	14.7	13.5
Glamorgan	43.5	38.1	31.6	30.5	20.3	17.2	11.8	10.0
Merioneth	93.7	90.3	82.1	86.1	75.4	75.9	73.5	68.2
Monmouth	13.0	9.6	6.4	6.0	3.5	3.4	2.1	2.7
Montgomery	47.5	44.8	42.3	40.7	35.1	32.3	28.1	24.0
Pembroke	34.4	32.4	30.3	30.6	26.9	24.4	20.7	18.1
Radnor	6.2	5.4	6.3	4.7	4.5	4.5	3.7	5.0
WALES	49.9	43.5	37.1	36.8	28.9	26.0	20.8	18.9

counties of Denbighshire and Flintshire. In both cases the difference between percentages in 1901 and 1981 are in excess of -35. A considerable dilution of the language is also evidenced in the counties of Glamorgan, Anglesey and Carmarthenshire. Focussing on percentage differences at community level between 1961 and 1981 Aitchison and Carter (1985) have drawn attention to significant changes within the main Welsh-speaking core areas. Thus, whereas in 1961 (for Wales as a whole) there were 279 communities with over 80 per cent of their population able to speak Welsh, by 1981 there were only 66.

Whilst a consideration of differences in the percentage dominance of Welsh speakers is revealing and of import, it is clearly necessary to take account of associated changes in absolute numbers of Welsh speakers. This can be achieved either by charting crude differences in totals, or by expressing the change in percentage terms. Such measures need to be adopted since it is possible for an area to show a decrease in the relative strength of the language (i.e. a decline in the proportion of people able to speak Welsh) but at the same time for the actual numbers of Welsh speakers to be on the increase.

The reverse situation is also possible, but in practice is less frequently encountered. A comparison of Figure 4 with the percentage change statistics presented in Figure 5 confirms that such conditions apply at the county level. Between 1971 and 1981, for instance, the proprortion of Welsh speakers in the areas covered by the old counties of Anglesey and Flintshire fell, whilst actual numbers of Welsh speakers increased. Similar tendencies can be discerned at community level but will not be considered here. Reference will simply be made to a classification of communities according to rates of change in the numbers of Welsh speakers for the two inter-censal decades 1961-71 and 1971-81 (Fig. 6), and to absolute increases in the numbers of Welsh speakers between 1971 and 1981 (Fig. 7).

Figure 5

Percentage change in the numbers able to speak Welsh
1961-71 and 1971-81

County (pre-1974)	1961-71	1971-81
Anglesey	-0.03	5.98
Brecon	-21.18	-10.30
Caernarfon	-8.49	-2.28
Cardigan	-7.10	-1.79
Carmarthen	-14.15	-10.27
Denbigh	-14.45	-6.99
Flint	-10.22	4.48
Glamorgan	-14.96	-29.79
Merioneth	-10.37	-4.77
Monmouth	-35.85	27.78
Montgomery	-14.80	-3.74
Pembroke	-10.74	-2.98
Radnor	-17.09	58.17
WALES	-17.31	-6.34

(i) Percentage rates of change 1961-1971 and 1971-1981

The categorization presented in Figure 6 summarizes directions of change for the first period (i.e. increase, decrease or stability in numbers between 1961 and 1971) and, for the second period (1971-81), indicates whether or not there has been a change in the pace or direction of change (i.e. an acceleration or deceleration of decrease or increase, a reversal of the direction of change or a pattern of stability). The resulting map yields a rather complex and fragmented spatial picture.

Category 1 (i.e. decrease-acceleration of decrease) identifies a dispersed collection of communities surrounding the main Welsh-speaking core areas identified earlier. Although not forming a continuous band, this cluster of communities can be seen as marking the critical moving frontier of language decline. The frontier follows the line of the Pembroke Landsker, extends through south Dyfed to the Swansea-Neath valleys, and thence continues

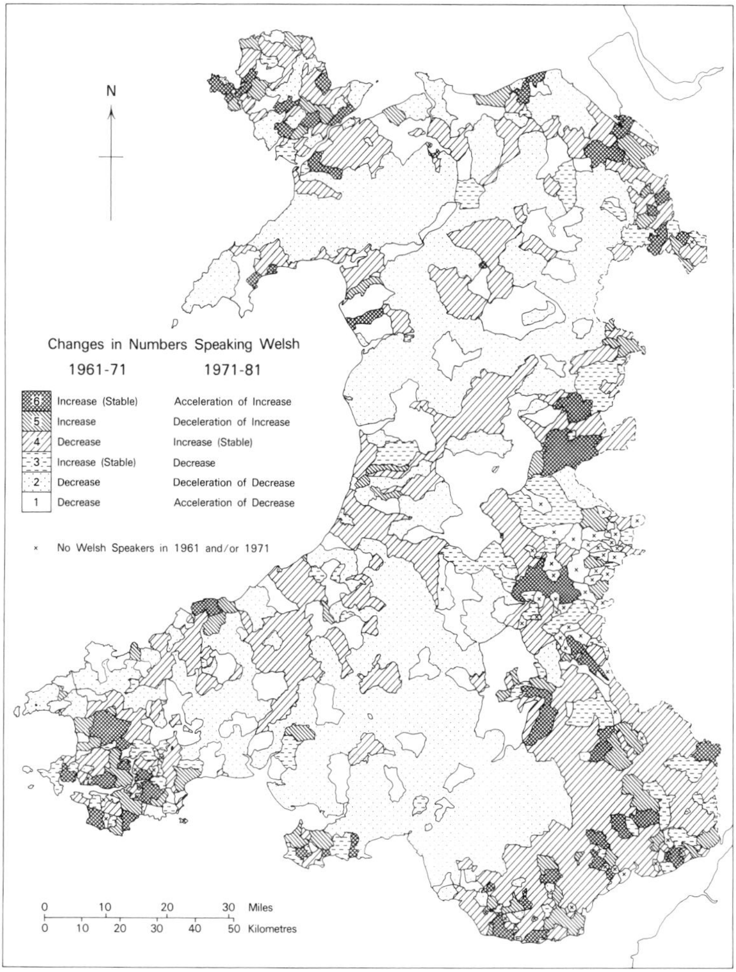

Figure 6. Percentage rates of change amongst Welsh speakers within communities, 1961-71 and 1971-81.

northwards across central Wales to the Vale of Clwyd and coastal regions of north Wales. It will be recalled that the proportion of Welsh speakers in this zone that claimed a facility to read and write the language was also of a relatively low order (Fig. 3). Together the two distributions underline the weakness and vulnerability of the language in the communities of this marginal area. An absolute decline in the numbers likewise characterises the situation in the main core areas of Welsh speakers (category 2), but here, and in much of Mid Glamorgan where there are quite large populations of Welsh speakers (Figure 1), the rate of decrease slackened between 1971 and 1981. Be this as it may, clearly it is disturbing that categories 1 and 2 should apply in the main to both rural and urban regions of 'Welsh Wales'. However, within the heartland some communities did register an increase in the number of Welsh speakers between 1971 and 1981, after a period of decline (category 4). The majority of these are seen to be located in Ceredigion and parts of Ynys Môn, Arfon and Dwyfor. In regard to these areas it has to be recognized that whilst absolute numbers of Welsh speakers have increased, their relative significance within the population at large has, in most instances, decreased. The counter-urbanization or 'rural retreating' phenomenon—the search for alternative 'rural' as opposed to 'urban' life-styles by people from England—together with the impact of tourism (Bowen and Carter, 1975), the development of second homes and in-migration associated with retirement are largely responsible for this problematic state of affairs.

Interestingly, by far the largest number of communities belonging to category 4 are situated in south-east Wales (Fig. 6 again). The most extensive grouping includes communities in the Vale of Glamorgan, southern sections of Mid Glamorgan, Gwent and south-eastern Brecknock. It is notable that these regions also include communities belonging to the two remaining growth categories (categories 5 and 6). Whilst the changes recorded in many of these areas are of import, it has to be emphasised that the absolute numbers of Welsh speakers involved are often relatively small. The rate and direction of change in communities of this type can be dramatically modified by the introduction of one Welsh evening class or one bilingual nursery school. This is also true of the many communities throughout the borderland, in south Pembrokeshire and southern parts of Preseli which also belong to categories 5 and 6. The fickleness and variability of the situation in these regions is further underlined by the frequency of communities where the number of Welsh speakers increased (or remained stable) between 1961 and 1971, but then decreased between 1971 and 1981 (category 3). Perhaps more significant, as far as the survival of the language is concerned, is the rather limited number of communities within the Welsh-speaking core areas that have managed to maintain growth through each of the inter-censal periods. Of those that have, the majority are located on Ynys Môn.

(ii) Absolute increases in numbers of Welsh speakers 1971-1981

In order to highlight absolute magnitudes of growth Figure 7 identifies those communities which showed an increase in the number of Welsh speakers between 1971 and 1981. This distribution confirms many of the changes previously alluded to and, in particular, focusses attention on developments in the Cardiff region and in the area around Mold in north-east Wales. The efforts of *Cymdeithas yr Iaith Gymraeg* since 1960, the effect of the Welsh Language Act of 1967 and the report of the Council for the Welsh Language in 1978 have done much to promote the language in Wales as a whole, but on their own these are not sufficient to explain the strong concentration of growth points in urban parts of the borderland. The factors of relevance here are manifold. They include the rise of a Welsh bureaucracy and a general expansion of the Welsh-oriented mass media (epitomised by the establishment of the Fourth Television Channel in Wales, *Sianel Pedwar Cymru*). In these areas attitudes to Welsh have also changed. Whereas a facility to speak Welsh was once regarded as of little economic advantage, now it has a certain social cachet and is seen to open up wider economic opportunities. Pressure in the educational sphere, particularly from influential, middle class sections of metropolitan society, has likewise resulted in an expanding provision of Welsh-medium and bilingual schools

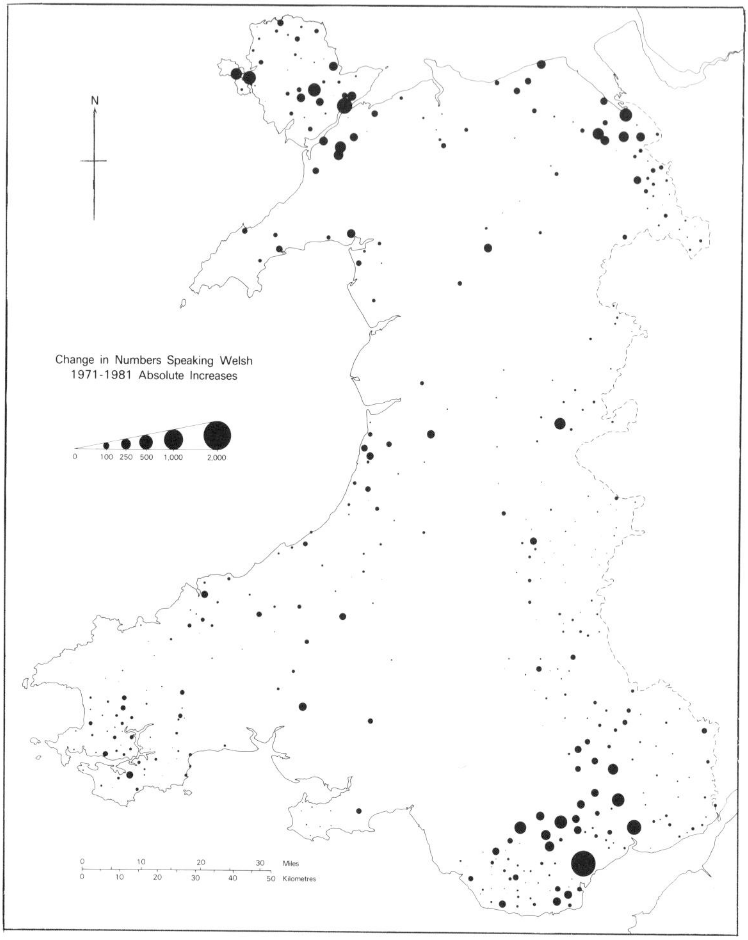

Figure 7. Increase in the acutal numbers of Welsh speakers within communities, 1971-81

(from *ysgol feithrin* to secondary levels) throughout Wales, and most especially in the Cardiff region. The impact of these developments in this latter area, and in north-east Wales, is indirectly captured in maps prepared by Aitchison and Carter (1985) which indicate above average incidences of Welsh speakers under the age of 15 years. It is difficult to assess whether this is a transitory phenomenon of the 1970s or the basis of a new resurgence in the language. Much will depend upon the depth of commitment to the language and on employment prospects in the region. Certainly the language itself shows different characteristics, and the culture based on it, should it continue to develop, will be in considerable contrast to that traditionally associated with rural Wales.

Language Areas: A Multivariate Regionalization

The discussion thus far has concerned itself with an analysis of individual map distributions. By way of conclusion it is appropriate to consider a composite regionalization based not upon single characteristics but upon a multiple set of diagnostic language attributes. To this end the 993 communities have been subjected to a 'minimum variance' cluster analysis. The statistical procedure adopted here has been widely used by geographers and by analysts of census data (Oppenshaw, 1983), and need not be elaborated upon here. Suffice it to say that it is an 'objective' classificatory procedure which allows areas with similar language characteristics to be grouped together.[1] Of particular interest to this study is the location and nature of the areas that belong to each of the groups (clusters) identified. The analysis itself is based on five language attributes derived from the 1981 census:

(i) the percentage of the total population over 3 years of age able to speak Welsh.
(ii) the percentage of the Welsh-speaking population able to read and write Welsh.
(iii) the percentage of the Welsh-speaking population under 15 years of age.
(iv) the percentage of the Welsh-speaking population 65 years of age and over.
(v) the number of Welsh speakers per square kilometre.

---

[1] In carrying out the 'minimum variance' clustering procedure the data were first 'ortho-normalized' (using principal components analysis) to remove the distorting effect that strong inter-correlations between the five attributes would have on the calculation of the various 'distance' and 'variance' measures used in

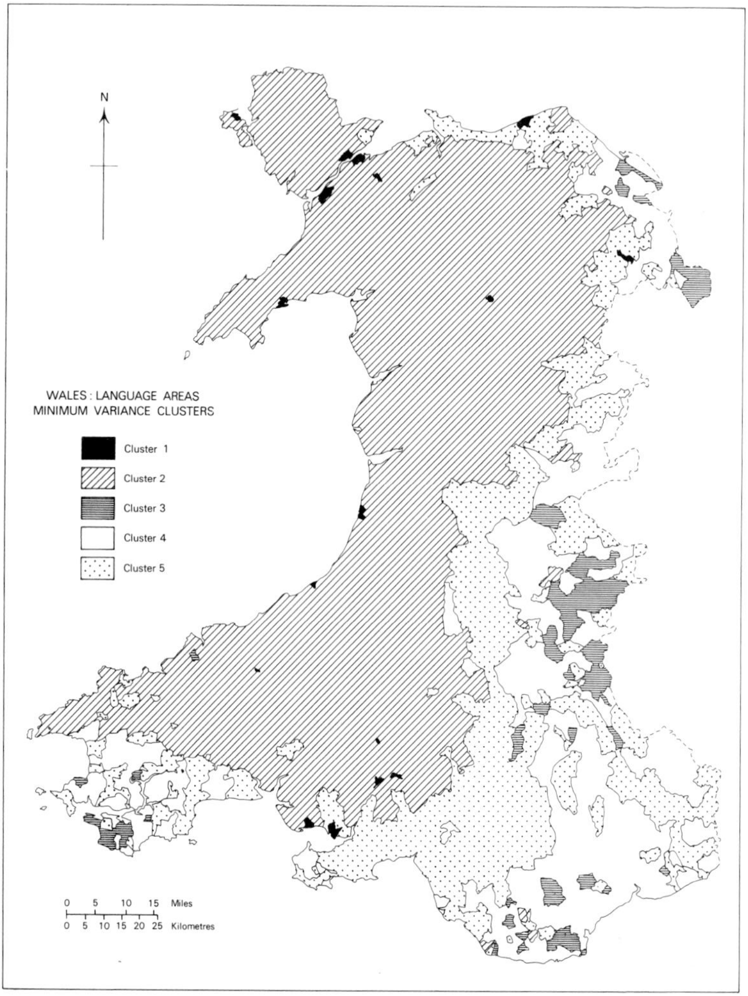

Figure 8. Language areas, 1981

the analysis. It is to be appreciated that by allocating individual areas to a small number of groups (in this case, five) there will inevitably be a loss of local detail. In compensation, however, there is a considerable gain in the resultant level of generalization. Cluster analysis serves a useful purpose in helping to distinguish broad patterns of regional variation using multivariate sets of information. It allows the analyst to develop an integrated classification and regionalization of language areas.

Figure 8 shows the distribution of communities associated with each of the five clusters and Figure 9 lists associated mean statistics for the five attributes. It is apparent that the resulting spatial pattern draws together many of the features either emphasised in the analysis of the various individual language maps (Figs 1-3, 6-7) or raised in discussion. In this sense it can be regarded as a composite or summary picture. Together, the first two clusters clearly delimit the linguistic heartland of Wales. Cluster 1 identifies the main urban areas within or on the margins of the zone. As Figure 9 indicates, the eighteen communities that make up this cluster tend to have slightly lower percentages of Welsh speakers, lower literacy rates and a more aged Welsh-speaking population than those belonging to cluster 2. Inevitably, they also have much greater densities of Welsh speakers, with a mean of 789 persons per km^2. The majority of the communities in cluster 1 are enveloped by communities in cluster 2. This cluster is the largest of the five, and includes 418 essentially rural communities. Here the percentage of Welsh speakers averages 66.8, whilst the mean proportion of the Welsh speaking population able to read and write the language reaches 83.9 per cent. Unlike cluster 1 the proportion of Welsh speakers under 15 years is generally greater than the proportion over 65 years. Although not used in the classification it is pertinent, in considering average language characteristics within these and subsequent clusters, to make brief reference to associated patterns of change. Accordingly, Figure 10 lists total absolute changes in the numbers of Welsh speakers for each of the clusters, as well as mean rates of percentage change at community level. These summary statistics show that within the areas included in both clusters 1 and 2 there was a persistent decline in the number of Welsh speakers. The communities in cluster 2 lost over 28,000 speakers between 1961 and 1971, with a mean rate of change of -12.9 per cent. The pace of absolute and relative change slackened somewhat between 1971 and 1981, but for both clusters it continued in a negative direction.

Figure 9

Language areas, 1981: minimum variance cluster analysis

		Community attribute means				
Clusters	Numbers of Communities	% population Welsh-speaking	% Welsh speakers able to read/write Welsh	% Welsh speakers under 15 years of age	% Welsh speakers aged 65 years and over	Welsh speakers per Km^2
1	18	63.1	73.3	16.5	24.3	789
2	418	66.8	83.9	20.3	18.4	32
3	62	6.5	69.5	56.9	4.4	9
4	263	6.2	43.1	16.1	12.1	11
5	232	15.4	53.4	9.1	32.7	34

Figure 10

Language areas, 1961-71 and 1971-81: change statistics

	Numbers of Welsh speakers			
	Total absolute change		Mean percentage rates of change	
Clusters	1961-71	1971-81	1961-71	1971-81
1	-11,120	-6,603	-5.7	-3.3
2	-28,315	-8,137	-12.9	-4.0
3	893	1,905	41.4	45.0
4	-10,427	8,397	2.7	20.4
5	-64,435	-29,956	-9.3	-0.6

Previous discussion has drawn attention to a critical and problematic fringe zone, skirting the main heartland region, where considerable erosion of the language has taken place. In Figure 8 this fringe zone is largely associated with cluster 5. This cluster does, however, include communities located at some distance from the main Welsh-speaking core areas (e.g. in Gwent), with the result that the average percentage of Welsh speakers reaches only 15.4. A particularly diagnostic feature of the cluster is the very high percentage of Welsh speakers that are of 65 years of age and over. The implications that this might have for the future of the language in the areas concerned have already been noted. From Figure 10 it is evident that the communities within cluster no. 5 lost a massive number of Welsh speakers between 1961 and 1981 (mainly from West and Mid Glamorgan), and were responsible for much of the decline registered for the nation as a whole. This said, it has to be emphasised that on average the proportionate rates of change in these areas were lower than those returned by the communities in rural 'Welsh Wales' (cluster 2). Of the final two clusters the most interesting is undoubtedly cluster no. 3. Although made up of a scattered collection of communities (62 in all), the cluster brings together those areas experiencing a limited but steady growth in the numbers of Welsh speakers. The actual percentage of Welsh speakers may be low (with a mean of only 6.5) but of these a very high proportion are less than 15 years of age. Literacy levels are also well above average (Fig. 9 again). The distinctive developments that have taken place in these areas, and most especially in the immediate hinterland of Cardiff and Mold, have already been examined. The 263 communities that make up cluster no. 4 are largely located along the Welsh borderland, with an outlying group asserting itself in south Pembrokeshire. Although highly anglicized (the mean community figure for the percentage of Welsh speakers being only 6.2), these regions collectively recorded absolute gains in the number of Welsh speakers between 1971 and 1981. This growth is all the more significant given the large losses registered in the previous inter-censal period (Fig. 10). Literacy levels and the age structure of the Welsh-speaking population are not as favourable as those displayed for cluster no. 3, but the signs are at least encouraging. Whether it is possible to talk of a turning of the tide in the borderland areas of south-east and north-east Wales it is much too early to say. For these and other regions of the Wales the next decade will be a testing and revealing time.

Conclusion

Recognising that the state and status of the language is of paramount significance to Welsh culture, this study has endeavoured, through an analysis of selected map distributions, to distinguish broad patterns of regional variation in the incidence of Welsh speakers in 1981. Consideration has also been given to absolute and relative changes in the number of speakers at community level between 1961 and 1981. Although constrained by the aggregate nature of the data, the analysis has attempted to move beyond a simple description of regional differences. The variable spatial impact of major forces of change, both macro and micro, have been identified and their implications assessed. It is clear, however, that the richness and complexity of the patterns warrant, and deserve, more detailed research. Population movements and their impress on demographic structures, transformations of local economies and societies, changing attitudes to the language both at a family level and beyond to higher political echelons, and the pressures and problems associated with the emergence of an increasingly 'transactional', metropolitan society, are just some of the issues that need to be more carefully scrutinized.

References

Aitchison, J.W. and Carter, H. (1985) *The Welsh language 1961-1981: an interpretative atlas*, University of Wales Press, Cardiff.

Bowen, E. G. and Carter, H. (1975) 'Some preliminary observations on the distribution of the Welsh language at the 1971 census', *Geographical Journal*, 140, 43-442.

Mandelbaum, D.G. (ed.) (1949) *Selected writings of Edward Sapir. A study in phonetic symbolism*, Berkeley.

Oppenshaw, S. (1984) *Cluster analysis programs*, Centre for Urban and Regional Development Studies, Department of Town and Country Planning, University of Newcastle upon Tyne.

Williams, C. (1982) Religious affiliation in Wales, in Carter, H. and Griffiths, H. (eds.) *National atlas of Wales*, University of Wales Press, Cardiff. Sheet 3-3.

Chapter Two

Wales as a Culture Region: Patterns of Change 1750-1971[1]

W. T. R. Pryce

Local government in Wales was reorganized in April 1974 when eight new counties were introduced. In consequence, whilst publishing retrospective statistics for these new administrative units, the official census reports did not include the appropriate data which would have permitted the long-term trends described in this chapter to be extended to 1981.

Today, very few informed Welshmen are unaware of the very special role played by the Honourable Society of Cymmrodorion in fostering the distinctive identity of Wales. When this most distinguished Society was established in 1751 Wales was a very different country to what it is in the late 1970s. First and foremost it must be remembered that Welsh society was then essentially of a pre-industrial nature, sustained on a rural subsistence with, here and there, the unmistakable signs of incipient industrialization derived from the working of minerals. In many respects the economy and social structures of 'old' Wales can now be regarded as having been somewhat comparable to those of an underdeveloped country in the 'third world' of our own times.[2] Before the tremendous social and cultural changes which were to be ushered in with industrialization, the small but important chancery towns of Carmarthen, Brecon, Caernarfon and Denbigh operated as the primary regional centres and, therefore, they dominated the urban hierarchy.[3] These were to be reduced considerably in importance during the nineteenth century in favour of newer centres which grew rapidly in population and influence in the northeast and in south Wales.[4] Eventually industrialization and urbanization were to give rise to what can be termed the 'new' Wales and this had emerged by the early 1900s.

The distinctiveness of Wales as a spatial entity and the regional patterns of culture change leading up to present-day circumstances are the themes which are explored in this paper. Outside the long-established Englishries of south Pembrokeshire, Gower, Radnorshire and borderline parishes actually contiguous with England itself, informed estimates suggest that in 'old' Wales the sole language spoken by the overwhelming majority of the people was Welsh.[5] Even as late as the early 1870s E. G. Ravenstein calculated that 71 per cent of the population still retained Welsh and that 22 per cent spoke no other language.[6] A century later the linguistic situation had been reversed: now only 21 per cent of the population were able to speak Welsh and between one and two per cent of the people were returned as Welsh monoglots.[7] Yet irrespective of their fluency or otherwise, questions concerning the survival of the language have become of very considerable significance to Welshmen, especially in the last two decades. Much has been written already on the plight of Welsh but if we are to derive anything approaching a full and balanced understanding of the processes at work it is necessary to examine long-term changes. For reasons of context and perspective first we can begin by looking briefly at prevailing trends since the early 1900s.

The Welsh Language 1901-1971

Principal trends in the decline of Welsh during the twentieth century are displayed in Figure 11.[8] In 1901 50 per cent of the population of the country claimed to be able to speak Welsh and over 15 per cent were returned as Welsh monoglots. But, as at the present time, there existed considerable regional variations. These ranged from the northern (Anglesey, Caernarfon and Merioneth) and western (Cardigan, Carmarthen) counties where over 90 per cent of the population spoke Welsh down to only 6 per cent in Radnor and 13 per cent in Monmouth. In Glamorganshire, where the bulk of the population of Wales was

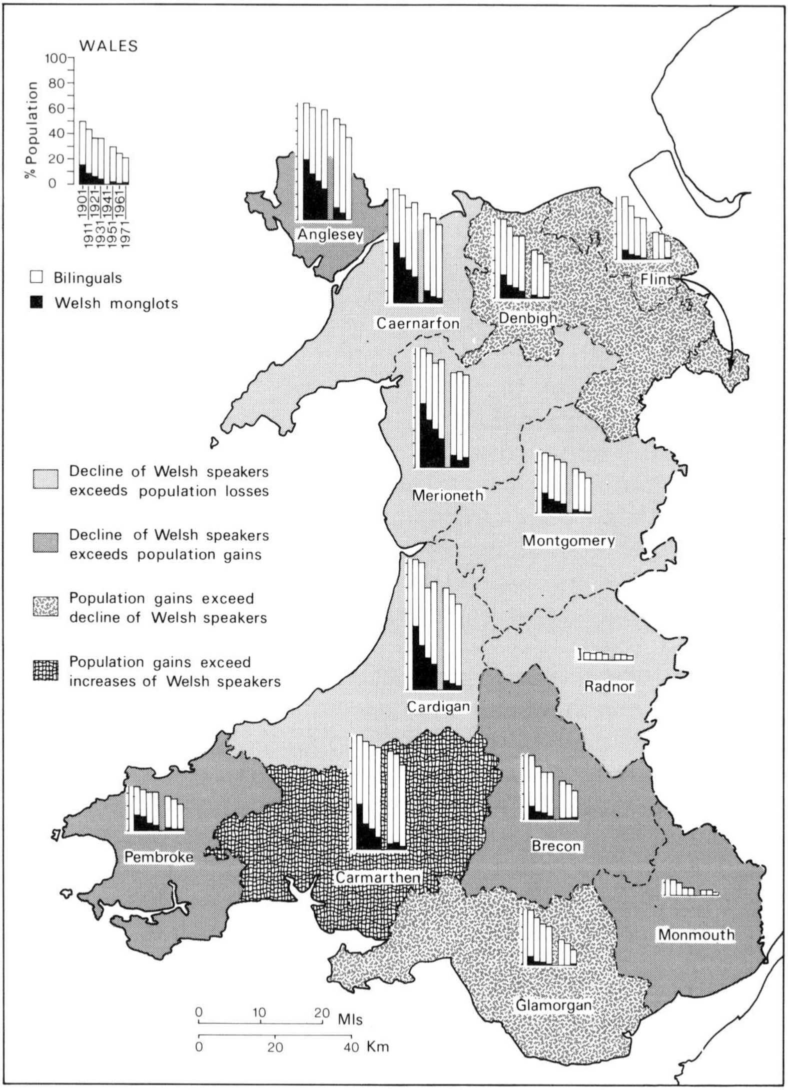

Figure 11: Welsh monoglots, bilinguals and patterns of change in relation to population movements, 1901-1971.

enumerated in 1901, 44 per cent of them spoke Welsh. Everywhere the proportions of Welsh speakers were to fall progressively during the first half of the twentieth century. By 1971 the counties of the north and west recorded over 60 per cent of their populations as Welsh speakers compared with just 4 per cent in Radnor, 2 per cent in Monmouth and 11 per cent in the old county of Glamorgan. Close examination of the graphs in Figure 11 indicates that the proportions of Welsh monoglots in the county populations have declined much more rapidly during this century than the proportions of bilinguals. Indeed, it is the view of some commentators that this very feature is central to an understanding of the processes of language decline. In the aggregate it seems that at first the declining number of bilinguals was offset by the addition of Welshmen who only recently had acquired full fluency in English. Once this source of replenishment was used up then a rapid decline in the numbers of bilinguals set in.[9]

Inter-censal changes in the numbers of Welsh speakers are displayed in Figure 12. From columns 3-8 of this table it can be seen that in the majority of counties (including those in the most heavily industrialized south and north-east) maximum inter-censal declines came 1931-51, that is in the decades spanning the economic recession of the 1930s and the end of World War II. More recently, maximum declines have been recorded in those counties which hitherto had come to be widely regarded as areas where the language could be self-maintaining through 'natural' means.[10] If all these intercensal changes are summed, then the counties can be ranked *inversely* by the accumulated rates of decline. From Figure 12 (columns 1 and 2) it is clear that counties in the south and east have experienced more substantial inter-censal losses during this century than those in the west and north.

It is quite clear that the proportion of Welsh speakers has declined everywhere irrespective of whether the population in each county has been increasing or declining. Relative movements in the decline of Welsh and overall demographic trends are indicated by the shaded areas in

Figure 12

Inter-censal changes in the population (aged 3 years and over) able to speak Welsh, 1901-1971

Percentage decreases are shown in italics with modal changes in bold print.

(1) WALES/ Administrative Counties (ranked according to col. 2)	(2) summation of inter-censal percentage changes, 1901-1971	(3)	(4)	(5)	(6)	(7)	(8)
		inter-censal changes					
		1901-1911	1911-1921	1921-1931	1931-1951	1951-1961	1961-1971
		per cent (+ = increase − = decrease)					
Carmarthen	6.6	+13.0	+ 5.7	+ 3.7	− *9.8*	− *5.0*	− **14.2**
Anglesey	15.7	− *0.3*	− *4.0*	− *1.5*	− **6.3**	− *3.5*	− *0.1*
Cardigan	31.8	− *3.7*	− *7.0*	− *3.7*	− **12.2**	− *5.2*	− *7.1*
Caernarfon	35.2	− *2.4*	− **8.5**	− *2.2*	− *7.4*	− *6.1*	− **8.5**
Pembroke	36.0	− *2.3*	− *4.5*	− *3.6*	− *8.8*	− *6.0*	− **10.7**
Denbigh	39.2	+ 2.9	− *8.5*	+ 2.6	− **14.5**	− *7.3*	− **14.5**
Flint	39.7	− *0.4*	− *10.5*	+ 2.5	− **14.5**	− *6.6*	− *10.2*
WALES	48.7	+ 6.7	− *6.3*	− *2.2*	+ **21.3**	− *8.3*	+ *17.3*
Merioneth	50.9	− *7.6*	− *10.7*	+ 0.7	− **15.7**	− *7.3*	− *10.4*
Radnor	61.2	− *15.6*	+ 21.5	− **30.1**	− *12.0*	− *7.8*	− *17.1*
Brecknock	62.2	+ 0.2	− *6.7*	− *5.0*	− *20.5*	− *9.1*	− **21.2**
Montgomery	69.3	− *7.4*	− *8.9*	− *8.2*	− **18.6**	− *11.3*	− *14.8*
Glamorgan	73.4	+ 16.0	− *6.9*	− *4.6*	− **34.8**	− *13.2*	− *29.9*
Monmouth	108.5	+ 1.9	− *25.4*	− *8.0*	− **43.5**	+ 2.3	− *35.9*

Figure 11.[11] In Caernarfonshire and in the rural counties of central Wales the decline of Welsh was greater in percentage terms than overall decreases in the enumerated population. In the great majority of counties, particularly the industrialized northeast and in the southeast, the relative decline of Welsh was very much greater than the growth in population. Carmarthenshire is the only county where the use of Welsh increased as the population grew.

The post-industrial decades of the twentieth century have seen, therefore, the rapid decline of Welsh in numerical as well as in territorial terms. In every respect the situation in the second half of the twentieth century can be regarded as the end product of processes which gathered momentum during the industrialization of the nineteenth century. Before pursuing these matters further it is necessary to clarify the relationships between language and the national culture. Moreover, since the country of Wales, with all its regional variations, is itself a distinctive territorial expression we need to seek out conceptual frameworks for the exploration of changing regional structures.

Language, Culture and the Idea of the Culture Region

'Culture' is one of those terms which in the end eludes an absolute definition. Yet, for operational reasons we need a definition. From the outset, therefore, in this paper we shall not be using the term just to denote 'high culture' —certain forms of say, music, literature or the visual arts. Here, the term *culture* is applied to the every-day circumstances of people in order to describe value systems, attitudes and other considerations interacting in a distinctive way of life. The working definition first formulated by the American anthropologists Kroeber and Kluckhohn is one which still has considerable merits:

> . . . the essential core of culture consists of traditional (i.e., historically derived and selected) ideas and especially their attached values; culture systems may, on the one hand, be considered as products of action, on the other as conditioning elements of further action.[12]

Drawing on a large number of scholarly works Wilbur Zelinsky has elaborated on these basic ideas. He points out that culture must be envisaged as an assemblage of ideas deriving from learned behaviour. These ideas, he points out, are of a complexity and durability not found in animal societies. Individual cultures can be very distinctive and highly specific to particular nations, ethnic and social groups. Zelinsky emphasizes that cultures survive not through biological transference but rather through 'symbolic means, *substantially but not wholly through language*'. Culture is itself a 'macro-idea' but any culture needs the contributions from individual minds by way of sustenance. Yet, long after individuals have ceased to exist cultural systems will survive. In these respects culture can be regarded as a phenomenon pertaining to social groups rather than individuals. Zelinsky concludes that in its ultimate, most essential sense culture is '. . . an image of the world, of oneself and one's community'.[13]

Since 1927 and the publication of the official report *Welsh in education and life* a remarkable series of educational policy recommendations have enshrined these very same notions in the context of Wales.[14] In *The place of Welsh and English in the schools of Wales* (1953) the Central Advisory Council for Education in Wales set out to define their understanding of what is meant by the word 'culture'. Although the Council was not unanimous on the proper employment of the term they did arrive at the following consensus:

> . . . culture is the manifestation of an attitude of mind which gives to a class or a people its distinctive niche in the history of man . . . culture consists of the acquired or cultivated behaviour and thought of individuals within a community, based on a common tradition and conditioned by a common environment . . .[15]

Because individual cultures manifest themselves in many guises and because the very notion of culture is so all-embracing, there can be no universal or absolute means of its measurement. In these circumstances the adoption of the most salient feature or features of the culture milieu under consideration (such as language or, perhaps, religious affiliation) seems appropriate for purposes of identification and measurement. Of necessity such indicators have to be resorted to in the social sciences as surrogates for situations which, in the ultimate, cannot perhaps ever be fully recorded. Thus, for example, just as a person's full-time employment can be used as the surrogate for social class, in Welsh studies linguistic differences can be selected as appropriate indices of culture differentiation. In their 1953 report the Central Advisory Council for Education fully recognized existing differentials in the use of the Welsh and English languages in Wales. In putting forward the need for genuinely bilingual policies they were careful to emphasize the important role which English has to play in the education of Welshmen. Yet, they argued, fundamentally Welsh is still of the utmost significance:

> . . . the language which has expressed the older and deeper native culture is Welsh, and if it were to disappear a great part of the culture of our nation, as now described, would of necessity die with it.[16]

The incidence of spoken Welsh as a surrogate measure of the distinctive culture that is Wales has been emphasized by generations of scholars. For example, in his pioneering study of cultural changes amongst Welsh emigrants to the U.S.A., Professor Emrys Jones was able to pinpoint stages in the process of culture assimilation and how these changes were to be measured:

> . . . Language is one of the most important elements in the cultural heritage, not only as a means of communication and expression but for its close association with certain institutions . . . the significance of . . . language can easily be underestimated . . . Welsh remains the indispensable medium for expressing Welsh cultural values.[17]

As we have seen, culture must be regarded as a phenomenon pertaining to social groups rather than individuals. Within pluralistic societies several cultures may co-exist as, for example, within the social ecology of great cities. Spatial segregation may have occurred so that individual cultural and ethnic groups sometimes can be identified in terms of location. Much more likely, however, is the situation where cultural distinctiveness is reflected primarily as facets of the social structure. On the other hand, where just one or two cultures are overwhelmingly dominant over considerable areas then their spatial configurations and inter-relationships give rise to distinctive territorial patterns and the idea of the culture area or region.

In what is now regarded as a series of classic contributions to the human geography of north America D. W. Meinig has identified the structural features of the culture region model. Within each culture region three component zonal elements can be recognized. First there is the *core*. This can be regarded as the inner zone of concentration. In it is to be found the greatest density of occupation, intensity of social organization, strength and homogeneity of the prevailing culture. All the principal characteristics of the culture are dominant here. Moving out from the core we next pass into a secondary zone which Meinig termed the *domain*. Here the same culture is dominant but with less intesity and complexity than in the core, Moreover, in contrast to the core, regional peculiarities are more evident. Finally, there is the *sphere*. This is the zone of outer influence and it is often a zone where peripheral acculturation is occurring. Here the over-whelmingly dominant culture of the core is represented only by certain of its elements and its people often reside as minorities amongst those of a different culture or cultures. It is quite important to recognize that these zonal relationships within the culture region cannot be regarded as fixed: over time changes take place due to the extension or regression of the component elements.[18]

The first meaningful application of the basic concept of the culture region to the evolution of Wales had been made, however, some years before the recognition of these zonal structures by D. W. Meinig. It was the late Professor E. G. Bowen who, drawing on the classical tradition of the French regional geographers, characterized the predominantly Welsh-speaking northern and western counties as the essential heartland of *Le Pays de Galles.*[19] With a scholarly resort to principal events in Welsh history, subsequently he postulated the long-standing existence of two basically different culture areas. Rooted in the northern and western parts of the Principality is *Inner Wales*, a culture province which has always drawn on its own resources, fostering and upholding Welsh culture traits to such an extent that innovations from outside were adapted and absorbed into the cultural fabric. Therefore, until recent times and the advent of modern mass communications, Inner Wales has been able to maintain its identity. Conversely, *Outer Wales* is to be found in the southern and eastern parts of the country. Because it was easily penetrated on successive occasions throughout the centuries by external influences, Outer Wales has become less homogeneous in terms of language and culture. This dualism in the cultural geography of Wales, whilst not always so clear-cut in territorial terms, has been manifest throughout the centuries but, as Bowen emphasized, its expression was reinforced and heightened by industrialization in the eighteenth and nineteenth centuries when the more densely-peopled industrial communities themselves grew up in Outer Wales. These ideas were advanced by Bowen as a set of basic propositions needing further exploration and verification.[20]

Data for the Reconstruction of the Welsh Culture Region

Despite the first population census in 1801 it was not until 1891 that the census attempted to enumerate the number of Welsh speakers.[21] It is clear, therefore, that if we are to deal effectively with linguistic distributions in Wales during its transition from a rural peasantry to one of the world's most highly industrialized societies by the end of the nineteenth century, then we have to look to other sources. There are now very considerable grounds for believing that the language or languages as used regularly in Anglican church services closely reflected local circumstances. In 1563 a Parliamentary Act had provided for the translation of the Bible into Welsh. The same measures provided that '... the whole Dyvyne Service should be used and sayd by the Curate and Ministers ... where the Welshe Tongue is commonly used in the said Britishe or Welsh Tongue'. Until litigation leading up to the 'English services in Wales Act' of 1863 this arrangement was interpreted in law as not merely permissive but obligatory.[22] For these statutory reasons and because or rival challenges from non-conformists it is clear that Anglican clergy took special care to retain their congregations by ensuring that the language or mix of languages used in their churches was appropriate to local needs.[23] Thus, we find that from the early eighteenth century bishops asked for specific returns from every curate, vicar and rector throughout Wales as to the use of Welsh and English in their services. In addition, in the Diocese of St. Asaph rural deans made regular inspections of local arrangements before reporting back in writing to their superiors. It is on a very large number of these returns that we can draw to pin-point the changing expressions of Wales as a culture region before the availability of census data.

Visitation enquiries and returns

Much of this information was obtained by including specific questions in the surveys made by bishops prior to their official visitations. The range and quality of the data collected in this way can be illustrated from successive returns relating to one location, the small town of Llanfair Caereinion in the former county of Montgomery. After inspecting local arrangements the rural dean reported back to his bishop in 1749 as follows:

> ... Here is a Charity School for 8 poor Childn.—The publick Service is performed mostly in Welsh: but once a month in

English. For which I can see no Reason, there being I believe not One in ye Parish who does not both speak & understand Welsh better than English & most ye greater Part understand no English at all:

There are & have been for these sevl. years past a good many Methodists in this Parish . . . [24]

Despite the rural dean's protestations it is clear that by the early nineteenth century the linguistic situation was changing and probably for quite inevitable reasons:

Question: Is public service duly performed twice every Lord's Day in your Church, and in what language? And is one or more sermons in Welsh or English preached? On what days besides are prayers read there, and in what language?

Answer: Divine Service is performed in our Church twice every Sunday, two Sundays successively in the Welsh and the third in the English Language: but Evening Service is Read in the English Lanugage all the Year around. There is one Sermon preached every Sunday in the same Language as the Service happens to be. Prayers are read on every Holyday and St. Days and on Wednesdays. and Fridays in Lent always in the English Language. [25]

In general it is in the eighteenth and early nineteenth century returns that we find the bulk of the detailed comments which throw considerable light on local conditions and how the roles for Welsh and English were perceived. Because the original returns seem never to have been preserved the information relating to conditions in St. Asaph Diocese in the mid-nineteenth century (dated *c.* 1844) takes the form of brief notes surviving in a pocket book. Pehaps this had been compiled for ease of consultation by the bishop and his officers during their travels on horseback around the diocese. On this occasion the entry concerning Llanfair Caereinion is brief but for our purposes it does contain all the essential information:

Llanfair Caereinion V[icarage].
Revd. P. G. Moulsdale—Resident.

Services three on Sunday—2 Sermons
12 [underlined for emphasis!] Diss. Places of Worship.
. . .

Pop. 2514
Service W[elsh] & E[nglish] altern.
Rep. Val. £400.[26]

Printed forms with standardized questions had been introduced in the later eighteenth century but by 1900 much more statistical detail was requested from the clergy. Thus, the return for 1902 from Llanfair Caereinion takes the form of a printed table with blank spaces for the respondent to indicate the location and time of every service (weekdays as well as on Sundays), the language of worship and the 'average number' of attendants.[27]

Language Zones Before Industrialization

In order to reconstruct the territorial relationships of Welsh and English at specific dates in the past it is necessary to standardize the visitation returns so that every parish can be identified as falling into one of the six categories shown in the point symbols on Figure 13. The appropriate symbol is then placed on the map at the site of the parish church. Using these as control points, language divides are next interpolated and the three principal language areas or zones—Welsh, bilingual, English—can be identified. Using these techniques, large masses of data, quite specific in time and place, can be drawn on to provide fresh and original approaches to the study of the evolving regional complex.[28]

The territorial dominance of Welsh

Before the early industrialization of northeast Wales and the later growth of metallurgical and mining industries in the south, on the evidence of the visitation returns Wales was overwhelmingly a Welsh-speaking country (Fig. 13). From the vast majority of churches no other observation was received beyond the fact that Welsh was the sole language used in public worship. These conditions, however, did not prevail everywhere for towards

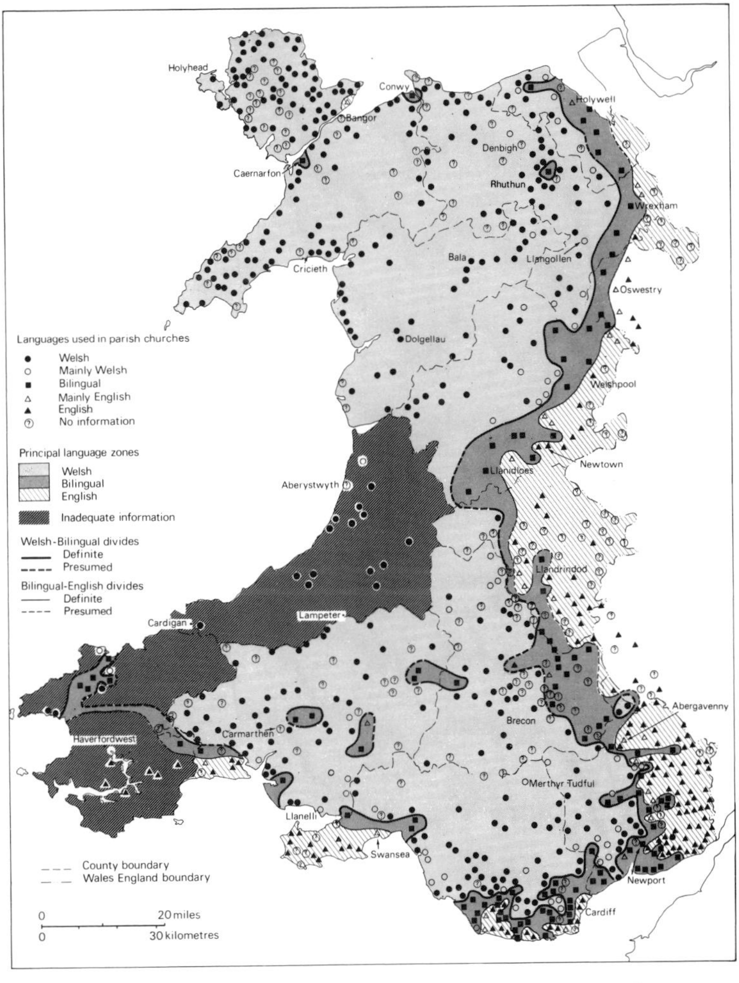

Figure 13: Principal language zones in the mid-eighteenth century.

the border with England there occur frequent references to an incipient invasion of the English language. Typical of such returns is that received from the rural dean when he reported on the parish of Llanrhaeadr-ym-Mochnant in southeast Denbighshire:

> . . . The service is performed all in Welsh except the second service & sermon once a month in English.

Elsewhere from northern counties came reports that English was occasionally introduced for official purposes or to meet the whims of the gentry:

> LLANYCIL (near Bala). Services are 'altogether Welsh except when the Judges come to Church when the Assizes are at Bala. Then we have the Service and Sermon all in English'.
>
> RUG CHAPEL (near Corwen). '. . . When the Family is at home, most part of the Service is read in English; and when not, all in Welsh'.

Further south, in Montgomeryshire, Welsh was often the dominant language but occasionally the rural deans reported adversely on arrangements then existing in specific churches. Thus, for example, English and Welsh were used on alternate occasions at Llangynog and the rural dean was not convinced that this was appropriate:

> . . . But ye Natives who are intirely Welsh, grumble as they have not Welsh Service & Sermon oftener. English was first introduced here on ye Acct. of a great Nbr. of Engl. People who work'd formerly at a great lead Work belonging to Ld. Powis. But that Work being now exhausted & mostly of ye English gone, the Natives ought certainly to have more Welsh.

Similarly, at Llanllwchhaearn (now part of Newtown) and at Aberhafesb on the flanks of the upper Severn the rural dean felt that a greater amount of Welsh was needed in public worship. His recommendations at Betws Cedewain did not go unheeded for he reported to the bishop that here '. . . the Vicar promises to do more Duty in Welsh it being agreeable to the majority of his parishioners'.[29] It is clear that all these parishes were then an integral part of the Welsh-speaking heartland. Nevertheless, it is equally clear that these reports reflected their regional location in the shadow of the language divide between Welsh and the predominantly English-speaking communities of eastern Montgomeryshire.

Although only the upland parishes in the vicinity of St. Harmon retained Welsh in the county of Radnor, in Brecknockshire, despite its border location, the great majority of the western districts can be regarded as having been monoglot Welsh in the mid-eighteenth century. Thus, at Trallong (Llywel) immediately west of the town of Brecon itself the two Sunday services were always conducted in Welsh. Signs of change, however, can be detected in the working policy adopted by the local clergy:

> Young persons repeat their catechism in English most [Sunday] afternoons & I expound it to them in English and Welsh.

Yet, in the upland fastness of Ystradfellte, Welsh retained its role as the only language of worship and the sole medium for the instruction of the young.[30]

In southeast Wales the Welsh-speaking heartland extended right through the western half of the county of Monmouth to reach the River Usk. Moreover, the greater part of Glamorganshire was then an integral part of Welsh Wales. Eventually, very considerable language changes were to occur in these locations but in the pre-industrial era they remained sparsely populated and intensely Welsh in speech.

From place to place, however, minor differences in the intensity of Welsh did arise and these are reflected in unsolicited comments which were sent in to the bishops on the actual visitation returns. At Bedwas (Mon.) all services were in Welsh except for the psalms and lessons at morning worship which were always read in English: from Betws (then a chapelry of Newport parish) it was reported that so few understood English that it was necessary to appoint a Welsh-speaking curate to assist the vicar. Conversely, at Newport itself all services were in English 'because the congregation best understood the language'.[31]

All the services at Merthyr Tudful were in Welsh but, significantly, in what is now regarded as the first industrial town in Wales, it was recorded,

> . . . of late there is an English Sermon every other Sunday evening at the request of the Englishmen belonging to the Iron Works lately erected in this Parish.

Welsh seems to have been the principal language used by the peasantry throughout much of lowland Glamorgan. Even at this early date, however, some of the clergy were keen to introduce English into the services of the church as at St. Lythan's near Cardiff:

> . . . the duty is sometimes Welsh and sometimes English. Welsh for the Ignorant—English however for the catechism generally.

Similar arrangements stood at Llantrisant where there was an English sermon every fourth Sunday. In contrast, the services at Peterston-super-montem (north of Cowbridge) were always held in Welsh and it was the local curate in this particular parish who pinned his own failures on the illiteracy of the peasants:

> . . . no children to catechize by Reason that I believe that there is not one can read his mother tongue.

Further west still, it is clear that Welsh was the most popular language for the great mass of the poeple. Thus we find that at Cadoxton in the Vale of Neath best attendances at the catechism classes were made when they were conducted in Welsh rather than in English.[32]

Only very few eighteenth-century visitation returns relating to Cardiganshire and the county of Pembroke now exist. However, subsequent surveys suggest that, apart from south Pembrokeshire, all these areas can be regarded as having been monoglot Welsh. And they were to remain virtually so for the next four generations. With the exception of castle towns such as Caernarfon, Conwy and Rhuthun, the same was to be the linguistic situation throughout a very large number of parishes in the northern counties.

The bilingual zone

Normally the word 'bilingual' refers to a person who is able to speak two languages but, in the context of this present study, the term 'bilingual zone' is used to describe *communities* where Welsh and English co-existed. This implies that within the bilingual zone there must have been large numbers of Welsh as well as English monoglots. Thus, depending on their ratios, some communities would have been 'more Welsh' or 'more English' than others. The Anglican clergy, in having to decide the extent to which each of the two languages should be used in religious worship were obliged to weigh up the local situation and then to institute arrangements appropriate to the potential needs of *all* their parishioners. From surveys of their evaluations an unmistakable zone can be identified in the culture transition between Wales and England where the two languages enjoyed roughly equal status.

We find, therefore, that starting at Trelawnyd (Newmarket) in northeast Wales the zone of bilingualism can be traced throughout the borderland parishes, to Newport in Gwent before swinging west to skirt the Vale of Glamorgan. Outliers occurred in Gower and in south Pembrokeshire where, according to returns made in 1807, the bilingual zone echoed the location of the historic Landsker.[33] As we shall see, this bilingual zone constitutes a spatial phenomenon of the utmost significance in understanding dynamic aspects of the culture region model.

Very considerable evidence that the linguistic character of the bilingual zone was determined by varying admixtures of Welsh and English monoglot populations occur in the remarks sent in to the bishops. Thus, for example, from the small borough of Llanfyllin (Co. Montgomery), the services were described as 'partly English' and 'partly Welsh'. The rural dean approved of the local arrangements, adding that '. . . most of ye Town People understand Engl. well enough & some of ym. rather better than W'. Likewise, while in 1749 Llanfair Caereinion itself was an integral part of Welsh-speaking Wales, the adjacent village of Castell Caereinion (four miles to the east) lay within the bilingual territories. Here the rural dean observed that Welsh and English were used on alternate Sundays.[34] Many observations and comments were received from churches in Brecknockshire, Monmouthshire and Glamorganshire, and these are of considerable value when it comes to idetifying the location of the transitional bilingual zone in the southeast region. From Boughrood, a parish straddling the boundary between the counties of Radnor and Brecknock, we are informed that two services were held each Sunday and in these Welsh and English were used alternately 'according to the custom of the place'.[35] Similarly concerning the one Sunday service held regularly at Tredynog (Tredunnock) in the county of Monmouth it was reported 'both the English and Welsh Languages are used equally here',[36] and from the joint livings of Llandough, Cogan and Leckwith (now Penarth, Co. Glamorgan), which were to become overwhelmingly English in language in consequence of urban growth in the late-nineteenth century, the arrangements were that services would be conducted 'either in English by the vicar or Welsh by the curate'.[37]

It was in the older borough towns and in centres which were to grow in stature as urban centres that the clergy had already begun to use more English. This occurred long before the many changes which were to be imported with industrialization, especially in south Wales. Caerleon, Trevethin (Pontypool), Cowbridge and Llanblethian, Roath (later incorporated in Cardiff), Neath, Loughor and Cydweli are prominent as reception points for English within the bilingual zone. Subsequently, these were to serve, along with all the larger towns, as springboards from which English could penetrate the interior Welsh-speaking core of the country. Although there must be some doubt as to their reliability, returns from parishes in the vicinity of Abergwili (the seat of the Bishops of St. David's), Llandybie and Llandeilo in Carmarthenshire indicate the first signs that the bilingual zone had begun its invasion of the core in the late eighteenth century. The same features are evident in northern Wales but here the small enclaves of bilingualism reflected merely the long-standing use of English in the vicinity of castle towns and their planted urban settlements.

The English-speaking territories

In the county of Radnor, east Monmouthshire, Gower and south Pembrokeshire, even in the mid-eighteenth century, English had long been the sole language of the people for many generations. Nevertheless, although forming such distinct cultural entities, throughout written history all these communities have been tied up inextricably with the rest of Wales. Industrialism, urbanization and the social revolutions of the nineteenth century meant that, in many respects, their symbiotic relationships were to be deepened. Outside these long-standing Englishries it is only in one or two border parishes that the English language was able to command such dominance.[38]

Evidence can be drawn from the visitation returns to show that parts of the English zone had, at some previous date, been much more Welsh than they were in the mid-eighteenth century. All these parishes are designated as 'mainly English' on Figure 13. From their location in very close proximity to the bilingual-English language divide it seems clear that these were places that formerly had been within the bilingual zone. Much evidence of the lingering of Welsh in otherwise overwhelmingly English-speaking communities occurs in specific circumstances. Sometimes this occurs in contradictory circumstances. Thus, while the language of worship at Pool (Welshpool) in the Severn valley was uncompromisingly returned as 'altogether English', in the market town and borough of Oswestry (actually located in England) some Welsh was still used even as late as 1749:

> ... Welsh Sermon & Service in the morning every second Sunday otherwise the Service is English on Sundays & weekdays.[39]

The growth of what was eventually to become the small but temporarily significant spa resort at Llandrindod is reported in its Englishness, even at this early date: services were 'always *English* ... to oblige the Gentry'. Conversely, nearby in the ancient parish of Diserth (Betws Diserth) where there was an English sermon every Sunday the second lesson and communion was still in Welsh and there was '... a Welsh sermon twice or thrice in the year if required'.[40] Visitation surveys confirm Bradney's own interpretations[41] of the retreat of Welsh from many parishes in the eastern and lowlands parishes of Gwent. At Llanwytherin (Llanvetherine), northeast of the town of Abergavenny, the two Sunday services were in English, but it was felt that a Welsh sermon was still needed on the first Sunday of the month. Here, however, the virtual banishment of Welsh may have reflected an absentee incumbent for, in completing his return, J. Lewis, who signed himself as 'Curate', observed rather acidly

> ... There is a good deal of Welch Duty performed in our Parish & our Rector being an Englishman, he resides in Sussex.

Although surrounded by English-speaking communities Welsh was retained as the principal language of worship at Llanofer (three miles southeast of Abergavenny) whilst nearby at Cemais Comawndwr (Kemeys Commander) the minister wrote, somewhat ambiguously

> ... I Preach ... often in Welsh but oftener in English [!]

Yet, in the regional context in which it was made, the meaning is quite clear for it indicated the way in which the older, native language was experiencing a lingering death in a countryside which already had gone through the processes of Anglicization.[42]

Industrialization and the Patterns of Change

Because of the need to appreciate the nature of our source data and what they mean in the context of the culture region model, considerable space has been devoted in the previous section to language zones in Wales before industrialization. The nineteenth century was to bring very fundamental changes in the territorial relationships between Welsh, bilingual and English-speaking communities. Many of these changes underpin significant developments in the cultural and political life of our country at the present time.

All these are summarized in Figure 14. As in the previous map the shaded areas indicate the regional location of the principal language zones but as they existed in the early 1900s. However, it should be noted that the point symbols now record long-term situations and, where they occur, the specific nature of changes. The trends refer to specific locations and they have been derived from the scanning of returns which are nearest in date to the four intergenerational stadials centered on 1750, 1800, 1850 and 1900.

From this map it can be seen that, by the early 1900s, the Welsh-speaking core had retreated westward under pressure from the encroaching bilingual zone. In the past, bilingualism has often marked a generational stage within families in the change from the use of Welsh to the English language. Similar stages in the process of change can be recognized in territorial terms. Influxes of Irish and English workers meant that the 'new' industrial communities, especially in southeast Wales, were forced to adopt English as the popular means of communication: once a comnity moved towards a bilingual status then almost inevitably English was to gain overwhelming dominance in the next generation. So we find that in southeast Wales where the impact of industrial growth was to be most profound, a very large number of churches experienced

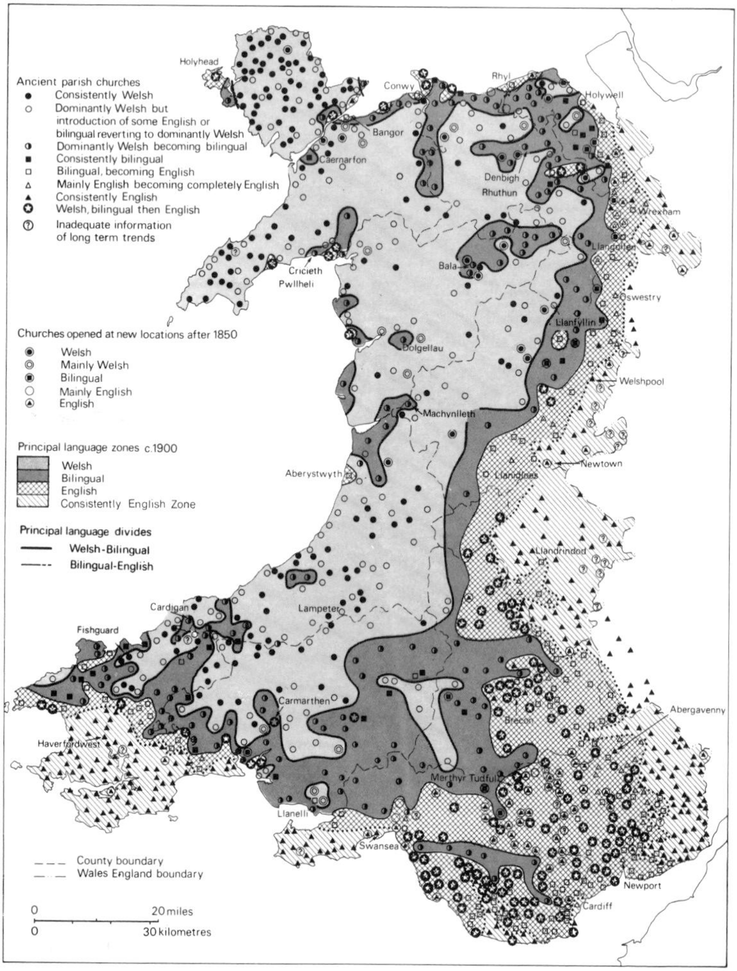

Figure 14. Long-term changes at specific locations c. 1750-1900 and the principal language zones in 1900.

the full cycle of change from being monoglot Welsh in the pre-industrial era to becoming monoglot Engish by the early 1900s. Conversely, in the middle borderland and in northeast Wales where the initial impact of industrialism was soon spent, it seems that many parishes were to be held back at the intermediate stage. In consequence they have maintained their bilingual status into our own time. Similar events seem to have occurred in southwest Wales where English seems to have extended northwards along the valley routes to create extrusions of the bilingual zone in north Pembrokeshire and Teifiside. Nevertheless, with the exception of a few bilingual parishes located on the Landsker itself which ceased to use any Welsh whatsoever between 1750 and 1900, there were no territorial advances comparable to the changes in the southeast.

The mechanisms underlying all these changes must have been of very great complexity. In part they were shaped by the movements of peoples: initially the migration of families from the rural counties of central Wales helped to reinforce and sustain the 'new' Welsh-speaking communities of the iron works and the coalfield, especially along the northern rim of the coalfield and later in Rhondda and mid-Glamorgan. Later, however, increasing labour needs and a vastly expanded scale of production meant the in-migration of a non-Welsh speaking population and these have never been fully absorbed by the receiving communities.[43]

The English zone

In Figure 14 the English zone has been subdivided into those districts which can be regarded as having been consistently English in language between 1750 and 1900 and the wider belt of country which had *become* English during this time. Some parishes, particularly rural ones in close proximity to long-standing Englishries, soon ceased to use any Welsh in their public services. Thus, for example, from Guilsfield (near Welshpool, Co. Montgomery) in 1809 the rector stated that there were two services each Sunday but '. . . of late entirely in English'.[44] Yet in southeast Wales at this time while English was the main vehicle of worship, even at Roath (then a country parish just outside of the small market town of Cardiff) and at Penarth, Welsh was still occasionally used. In east

Monmouthshire, however, Welsh was now virtually unknown as at Widston where English was the language 'by custom'.[45]

By the mid-nineteenth century it seems that here and there attitudes were hardening against the use of any Welsh in church activities: at St. Hilary (Co. Glamorgan) 'no Welsh [was] allowed to be spoken' in the services of the parish church or amongst the younger generation attending the catechism classes.[46] In Gwent, however, the occasional use of what had been the native language was tolerated, presumably because Welsh was needed in order to communicate with the older generations when the clergy visited their parishioners.[47] Fifty years later, however, it is clear that even faint memories of the use of Welsh had all disappeared from parishes who had recorded some use of the language in the early 1800s. Thus, from Boughrood (Co. Radnor) the bishop was informed 'no Welsh is spoken in the county'. Similar reports were received from Bryngwyn, Cascob, Clyro and Cefnllys (Llandrindod) where it was stated, incorrectly, 'Welsh died out 200 years ago'. From numerous locations in Brecknockshire came reports which were now openly hostile to the very idea of using any Welsh in public services: 'The children's parents *want* English'! At Builth Wells, Welsh services had been organized for the benefit of visitors who, presumably, would have included subantial numbers from mining valleys in the south. The local clergy soon abandoned these because '. . . too few came to encourage me to continue'.[48] In southwest Wales visitation returns from the parishes of south Pembrokeshire offered very few comments beyond the factual confirmation that English continued to be the only language of worship there. Two remarks received in 1900 probably epitomized prevailing conditions:

> BOSHERSTON PARISH: Welsh is unknown in the parish practically and instruction in the language would be impossible.

UZMASTON PARISH: Parish absolutely English, except a few who have migrated into it and perhaps use Welsh in private.[49]

Conditions in Gower were very similar although from the parish of Llanrhidian where the church services were returned as 'mainly English' the following candid remarks were received:

> . . . Children can converse but certainly none can read W. All the intelligent W. folk are Nonconformists—practically without exception.[50]

The bilingual zone

In 1900 the bilingual zone was much more extensive in territorial terms than it had been 150 years earlier, before the Industrial Revolution and the growth of towns. Moreover, numerous protrusions and extensions from it into what had been previously the dominantly Welsh-speaking communities of the west, particularly in the vicinity of towns and holiday resorts, now indicated that a cultural invasion of the heartland core was in progress: Outer Wales was beginning to make very significant inroads into the territories of Inner Wales.

As we have seen, pressures for change were often linked with the idea that it was in the interests of the young that they should gain a working knowledge of the English language. Thus, in the parish of Manafon (Co. Montgomery), which was later to drop the use of Welsh altogether, English was introduced in 1809 'for encouraging the Sunday scholars to respond to the psalms'.[51] By this time, too, it seems that the two languages were of roughly equal status in east Brecknockshire for at Llangors Welsh or English was adopted without notice and according to the needs of the congregation that had managed to turn up![52] Similarly, Welsh and English alternated at Llangatwg Dyffryn Wysg (Llangattock nigh Usk) '. . . by agreement of the Parishioners at a Parish meeting'.[53] By the mid-nineteenth century it was necessary for the clergy in what had been hitherto either dominantly Welsh or overwhelmingly English parishes to be sensitive to changing needs. Thus, in 1848 we are informed by the Rector of Llanywern in the county of Brecknock that '... of late owing to an influx of English to the Parish I preach in both languages'.[54] Conversely, in the mushrooming urban settlements of the Glamorgan coalfield it was necessary to re-introduce Welsh at St. Martin's Church, Eglwysilan (Caerffili).[55] All these observations, comments and explanations provide most useful insights in the clergy's perceptions of local situations and how they themselves attempted to respond to changing conditions within the bilingual zone.

The Welsh-speaking core

The inner Welsh areas of Figures 13 and 14 represented survivals of the 'old' way of life where the country people, like their forefathers of many generations, were all monoglot, not able to speak any other language than Welsh. Recognition of this very fact is fundamental to a proper understanding of the nature of the changes manifest in the territorial shrinkage of the core between 1750 and the early 1900s.

In Figure 11 we saw that by 1901 half the population in the ancient counties of Anglesey, Caernarfon, Merioneth and Cardigan—which can be regarded as the core of Bowen's Inner Wales—were returned as unable to speak English. This very large number (some 130,000 people in just these counties alone) was to be reduced very considerably in subsequent censuses. In these respects the 1901 census figures themselves portrayed a residual situation of what had been Welsh Wales. Using the 1971 census returns Bowen and Carter have demonstrated the continued erosion of the Welsh heartland. Now the overwhelming majority of the population of these inner zones are bilingual. Modern Wales still has distinctively Welsh communities in Llŷn, central Anglesey, Meirionnydd and Dyfed. These can properly be regarded as the last bastions of the very essence of Welshness.[56] Nevertheless, throughout much of Inner Wales a whole series of far-reaching changes have taken place and these have given rise to a considerable degree of linguistic and cultural pluralism.

This is a very different situation from the nature of Inner Wales in the early-nineteenth century when numerous unsolicited comments in the visitation returns emphasized a deep, intense, inherent Welshness. From Troedyraur in the rural fastness of south Cardiganshire the local cleric remarked 'My congregation are chiefly Welsh and therefore I seldom read it [Divine Service] to them in English';[57] from Llanbedrycennin in the Vale of Conwy it was reported simply that church services were 'always in the language of the Country'; from the ancient parish of Llandudno where the isolated church on Great Ormes Head served some 400 inhabitants in the district the bishop received the following retort to his question on whether English or Welsh was used in the divine services:

> . . . Welsh most assuredly, as in Wales it is a Mockery to read the Service in English where the Congregation don't understand it or indeed don't wish to have the Language of their Forefathers abolished'.[58]

Competition for numbers in the sparsely-populated countryside also meant that in the early nineteenth century the Anglican church could not afford to neglect any parishioners. Thus, at Trelawnyd (Newmarket) in north Flintshire it was considered unwise to introduce too much use of English

> . . . it wd. be quite sufficient to introduce English into the Service once a month only—There are only two persons in the Parish who do not understand Welsh; but there are many who, because they do not understand English sufficiently, change the Church for the Dissenters' meeting every other Sunday.[59]

Despite the commonly held view that the Established Church was itself a most formidable anglicizing agent, Welsh remained the sole language of worship in the north and in the west. Even as late as 1900, services at Llanfair Pwllgwyngyll and Llandysilio in Anglesey retained Welsh as the principal means of public worship because 'Welsh services are much better attended'.[60]

Yet, on the other hand, sometimes Welsh and the needs of the country people were ignored in order to fit in with the desires of the gentry and other small minorities. These often represented the first attempts to introduce English to what had been essentially monoglot Welsh communities. In 1809, for instance, the clergy sent in a return from Tremeirchion (north Flintshire) stating that all services continued to be taken in the Welsh language but that an English sermon was given '. . . when Mrs. Piozzi is in the Country'; at Llandysilio-yn-Iâl in the Vale of Llangollen an English lesson was read '. . . when the Family of Llantysilio Hall may be in Church';[61] in Caernarfonshire the gentry sometimes were able to introduce English by means of special payments to the clergy as at Llandygai in 1811;[62] and from Anglesey there is at least one rather resentful remark directed against obligations to pamper the gentry:

> . . . Since I came here the Family of Llwydiarth is *indulged* with English Service the first Sunday in the Month . . .[63]

Modifications to the services in the interests of English-speaking minorities were reported frequently from parishes in the south. In 1848 from Pendeulwyn in the Vale of Glamorgan the minister stated:

> . . . I read a part of the Service in English, the Litany & I also give out the text in English and sometimes the introductory part of my Sermon for the benefit of an English family . . .[64]

Similarly, the bishop was informed that in the church at Llansamlet (near Swansea) 'leading subjects of [the] sermon [are] given in English'; at Llangorwen, just north of Aberystwyth, Welsh was always the language of worship but each service included 'a post epitome of the Sermon in English'.[65] At the outset these innovations had been made to accommodate, perhaps temporarily, the needs of a handful of people in each locality: tourists, holiday makers, house guests of the gentry, business people in shops and the growing service industries or government officials such as the coast guard stationed at Dinas in north Pembrokeshire.[66] It seems that the introduction of the English language was made with the full support and good will of the Welsh-speaking majority. After all, English was now regarded widely as the language of commerce, trade and internationalism: therefore, it was widely felt to be in the interests of everyone to promote its usage.

Yet, the great majority of these arrangements turned out to be of a transient nature. Moreover, specific reports indicate that, as at Llanerfyl (Co. Montgomery) in 1809, attempts to introduce English sometimes failed miserably:

> . . . It has been usual to preach an English Sermon on the second Sunday in every month but I have been obliged of late to discontinue that custom or to have a very small or scarcely any congregation . . .[67]

Railway building meant that some English had been introduced by the mid-nineteenth century at churches in Anglesey. However, soon afterwards its use was abandoned on the completion of the railway and the departure of the labour force which had been essential for the construction work.[68] Conversely, from south Cardiganshire reports were received that in 1845 English settlers had left for quite different reasons!

> . . . the Rebecca riots drove away most of the English. Since [then] I have regularly [in] Welch two services where I have no English attendants [*sic*].[69]

All these observations illustrate the capacity of Inner Wales to accommodate alien intrusions when they were of a temporary nature and when the incoming influences were not of sufficient strength and persistence to bring about fundamental changes in the host community. Clearly, Inner Wales was maintained essentially as

Welsh-speaking Wales during the nineteenth century. Nevertheless, changes in intensity had occurred so that in the early 1900s it was no longer a network of intensely Welsh monoglot communities as it had been four or five generations earlier.

Core and Periphery 1750-1971

In this paper we have drawn on a very large number of parochial returns in order to delineate principal language zones in Wales and their changes since the pre-industrial conditions of the eighteenth century. Despite some initial criticisms which tended to play down their historical significance,[70] E. G. Bowen's characterization of Wales with its distinctive Inner and Outer zones still has much validity. At the most basic level his ideas provide a most useful and appropriate framework in which the long-term evolution of Wales may be interpreted. Beyond this, in the basic polarities of his model, we can identify features inherent to the culture region as postulated by D. W. Meinig. Inner Wales corresponds to what is popularly known today as *Cymru Gymraeg*, the Heartland or, in some circles, as 'Y Fro Gymraeg'. This can be equated with the 'core' of Meinig's Mormon culture region but in Wales its retreating nature over time and the implications of this for the very survival of the Welsh language have made it a central and vital issue in present-day politics. Outer Wales can be equated with *Cymru ddi-Gymraeg* or the anglicized territories and in these we see reflected many of the features of Meinig's 'sphere'.

In Wales, the 'domain' of Meinig's model is expressed in terms of the bilingual zone as identified in this paper. Occupying the transitional territories between inner and outer regions this can be regarded as the zone of active engagement with external forces. Although more detailed, local studies are needed before all its complexities can be unravelled, it is already clear that this functioned as the zone of change. In some places, as in the central borderland and Pembrokeshire, until very recently the bilingual zone had remained fixed in location for many gener-

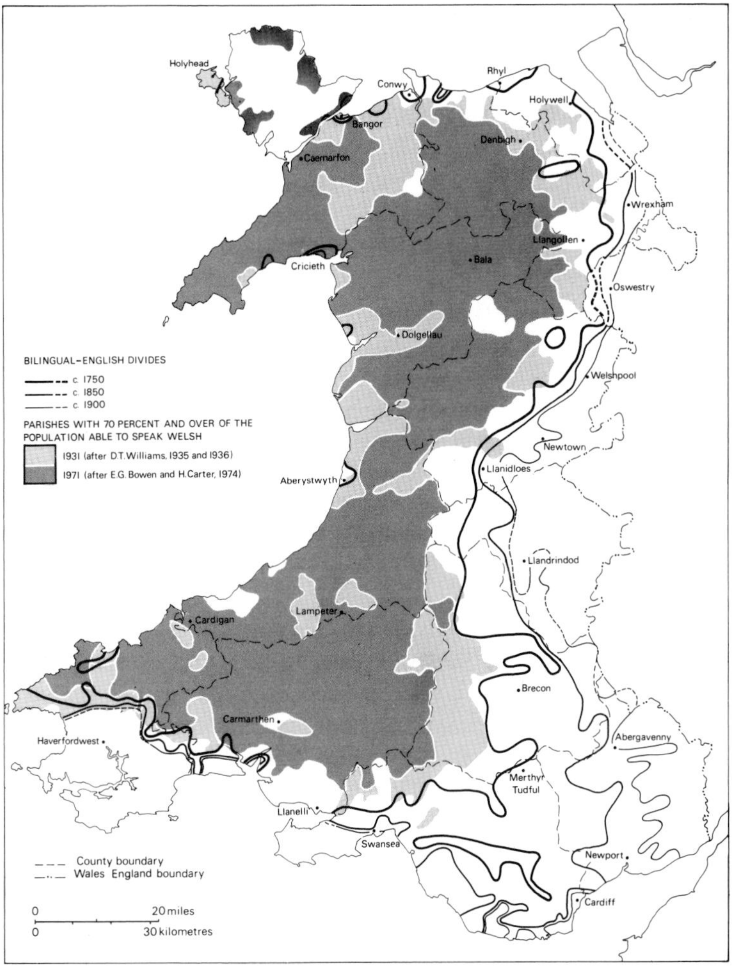

Figure 15. The territorial shrinkage of *Cymru Gymraeg*, c.1750-1971.

ations. Yet elsewhere, as in the northeast and in the southeast, through contact and encroachment it was to be the means by which English was diffused into the Welsh-speaking core. Moreover, in the context of nineteenth-century conditions and attitudes, the bilingual zone seems to have functioned as a socializing agency and a mechanism for English acculturation.[71] In these respects its very existence is of the highest significance in understanding the processes of change.

Long-term changes and their ultimate effects on Wales as a culture region are summarized in Figure 15. Since the mid-eighteenth century the outermost principal language divide between bilingual and English-speaking communities has been pushed back. Even in 1931 the processes of change were so far advanced that it was then evident that the core would eventually break into two subregions, a northerly one based on Gwynedd and a southerly one centred in what is now Dyfed.[72] As the proportion of Welsh speakers has continued to decline it became apparent in the 1970s that a second language front originating in the small urban communities of the Cardigan Bay coastline is advancing eastwards into the core. The final break-up of the core is now imminent.[73]

Policies and the Balance of Numbers

Although each generation may settle on new symbols, above all others language has remained the essential badge of nationality for Welshmen.[74] When the future viability of Welsh is threatened, it seems that the whole question of their nationhood is at stake. In consequence there exist today numerous movements for the retention of Welsh and its promotion through democratic means. Since 1901 the population of Wales has increased considerably while at the same time the number of Welsh speakers has continued to decline. Compared with Outer Wales, proportions of Welsh speakers in the counties of Inner Wales have remained high despite a slackening in their intensity (Fig. 16, cols. 2 and 3). However, the changing balance of numbers between counties is of equal significance. Figure 16 (cols. 4 and 5) indicates that by 1971 virtually all the counties of Inner Wales had increased their share of the total number of Welsh speakers. Yet it is important to recognize that this derives from a contracting situation where the decline in numbers in Outer Wales is substantially greater than within Inner Wales. In 1901 37 per cent

Figure 16. The distribution of Welsh speakers, 1901 and 1971

(1)	(2) INTENSITY Welsh speakers as a percentage of the population in each county	(3)	(4) DISTRIBUTION Welsh speakers in each county as a percentage of the total in Wales	(5)
	1901	*1971*	*1901*	*1971*
INNER WALES*				
Anglesey................	91.7	65.7	4.7	6.8
Caernarfon............	89.5	62.0	11.3	13.5
Cardigan................	93.0	67.6**	5.8	6.6
Carmarthen	90.3	66.5	12.3	19.1
Merioneth	93.7	73.5**	4.6	4.6
OUTER WALES				
Brecknock	45.9	22.9	2.5	2.2
Denbigh	61.9	28.0	8.1	9.1
Flint	49.1	14.7	4.0	4.5
Glamorgan.............	43.6	11.8	37.1	26.0
Monmouth	13.0	2.1	3.8	1.7
Montgomery	47.4	28.1**	2.6	2.1
Pembroke	34.5	20.7	3.0	3.6
Radnor	6.3	3.7	0.1	0.1
WALES				
Welsh speakers.......	—	—	929,824	542,420
Total population.....	1,864,696	2,602,960	—	—

* Defined as counties where 80 per cent and over of the population was returned as able to speak Welsh in 1901.

** These counties enumerated smaller populations in 1971 than in 1901.

of Welsh speakers were enumerated in the old county of Glamorgan and even in 1971 still over one quarter were to be found there. Despite declining numbers this very fact must remain an important consideration for promoters of the language today. Policies directed at the maintenance of Welsh solely within designated zones such as 'Y Fro Gymraeg' may lead to a situation where the needs of a very substantial number of Welsh speakers now living in Outer Wales become neglected.[75]

Conclusion

Since the onset of the Industrial Revolution, Wales has evolved into a complex culture area in its own right with distinctive regional components. This chapter has demonstrated that the culture region model serves as a most useful framework in which comparative studies can be given context and a new meaning. Moreover, in the understanding of present-day problems, this particular approach allows the adoption of a much more theoretical stance than hitherto, not least in the difficult question as to whether differential regional policies for the maintenance of Welshness are appropriate. In the recent past Wales evolved a cultural pluralism which was manifested in terms of distinctive language zones. Now, however, there are undoubted signs that new dimensions are being added. In these Welshness is but one of several components in a new complexity of social structures which, increasingly, do not always seem to be related to questions of place or geographical location.

References

1 The substance of this paper was delivered as a lecture to the Honourable Society of Cymmrodorion in London on Wednesday, December 14th. 1977, with Dr. Gwynfor Evans, M.P., as the Chairman. This version was first published in the *Transactions* of the Society, Session 1978, pp. 229-61.

2 This view is adopted in M. Hechter, *Internal colonialism—the Celtic fringe in British national development, 1536-1966*, London: Routledge & Kegan Paul 1975. See Chapter 9 of this book.

3 H. Carter, 'The growth and decline of Welsh towns' in D. Moore (ed.), *Wales in the eighteenth century*, Swansea: Christopher Davies, 1976, 47-62.

4 H. Carter, *The towns of Wales*, Cardiff: University of Wales Press 1965, 69-75. H. Carter, *The growth of the Welsh city system*, Cardiff: University of Wales Press 1969.

5 W. T. R. Pryce, 'Welsh and English in Wales: a spatial analysis based on the linguistic affiliation of parochial communities', *Bulletin of the Board of Celtic Studies*, 28 (1978), 1-36.

6 E. G. Ravenstein, 'On the Celtic languages in the British Isles: a statistical survey', *Journal of the Royal Statistical Society*, 42 (1879), 580, 636.

7 Office of Population Censuses and Surveys, *Census 1971: Report on the Welsh language in Wales*, Cardiff: H.M.S.O. 1973, 83.

8 Local changes in the prorportions of Welsh speakers can be presented only at the level of the ancient administrative county since these are the sole

territorial units for which the language returns have been published consistently from 1901 to 1971. Problems of data as well as areal comparability and the reliability of the census enumeration rule out the use of the first language returns relating to 1891 in this study.

9 Some commentators regret the loss of monoglot Welshmen. See, for example, Iorwerth C. Peate, *Tradition and folk life: a Welsh view*, London: Faber & Faber Ltd. 1972, 134-9.

10 Successive education policies in Wales have been built around the recognition of the need to establish 'Welsh' (that is, explicitly bilingual) schools in areas where English is overwhelmingly the dominant language. In Welsh-speaking Wales the assumption has been that Welshness could be maintained through the 'natural' influence of the pupils' home background.

11 This classification is derived from plotting (1) Welsh gains/losses and (2) population gains/losses on a cartesian graph and subdividing the four fields of the graticule into uniform divisions. The method has been adapted from J. W. Webb, 'The natural and migrational components of population change in England and Wales, 1921-31', *Economic Geography*, 39 (1963), 130-48.

12 A. L. Kroeber and C. Kluckhohn, 'Culture, a critical review of concepts and definitions', *Papers of the Peabody Museum of American Archaeology and Ethnology*, no. 47, 1952.

13 W. Zelinsky, *The cultural geography of the United States*, Englewood Cliffs, N.J.: Prentice-Hall Inc. 1973, 70.

14 Board of Education Departmental Committee, *Welsh in Education and life*, London: H.M.S.O. 1927; Ministry of Education, *The place of Welsh and English in the schools of Wales*, London: H.M.S.O. 1953; Department of Education and Science, *Primary Education in Wales* (The Gittins Report), London: H.M.S.O. 1967.

15 Ministry of Education, *The place of Welsh and English in the schools of Wales*, 50.

16 ibid.

17 E. Jones, 'Some aspects of cultural change in an American Welsh community', *Transactions of the Honourable Society of Cymmrodorion*, 1952, 16-17.

18 D. W. Meinig, 'The Mormon culture region: strategies and patterns in the geography of the American West, 1847-1964', *Annals of the Association of American Geographers*, 55 (1965), 191-220. See, also, D. W. Meinig *Imperial Texas: an interpretative essay in cultural geography*, Austin and London: University of Texas 1969, 92-124. The culture region has enjoyed a long history of application to problems in anthropology and human geography. For recent criticism of its validity as a working concept see J. C. Hudson, *Geographical diffusion theory*, Evanston, Illinois: Department of Geography, Northwestern University, 1972.

19 E. G. Bowen 'Le Pays de Galles', *Transactions of the Institute of British Geographers*, 26 (1959), 1-23.

20 E. G. Bowen, *Daearyddiaeth Cymru fel cefndir i'w hanes*, London: BBC 1964. The English version of this important radio lecture has been reprinted as Chapter 3 of this volume. The map illustrating Inner and Outer Wales did not appear until much later, see E. G. Bowen, 'Early settlement' in D. Thomas (ed.) *Wales, a new study*, Newton Abbot: David & Charles 1977, 70-93.

21 Census 1891 *General report*, London: H.M.S.O. 1893, 81-3 and *Division XI: Monmouthshire and Wales*, London: H.M.S.O., 226-7.

22 Council for Wales and Monmouthshire, *Report on the Welsh language today*, London: H.M.S.O. reprinted 1969, 13.
23 W. T. R. Pryce, 'Approaches to the linguistic geography of northeast Wales, 1750-1846', *National library of Wales Journal*, 17 (1972), 343-63.
24 N.L.W. MS. SA/RD/26.
25 N.L.W. MSS. SA/QA/15, Year 1809.
26 N.L.W. MSS. SA/RD/52, *c.* 1844.
27 N.L.W. MSS. SA/QA/28, 1902.
28 For a fuller evaluation of these sources and classificatory considerations see W. T. R. Pryce, 'Welsh & English in Wales: a spatial analysis based on the linguistic affiliation of parochial communities', *Bulletin of the Board of Celtic Studies*, 28 (1978), 1-36. The problems of standardization are discussed in W. T. R. Pryce, 'Approaches to the linguistic geography of northeast Wales 1750-1846', *National Library of Wales Journal*, 17 (1972), 343-63.
29 N.L.W. M.S. SA/RD/26, 1749. Rug Chapel was a private place of worship intended for the family, workers and tenants on the Rug Estate.
30 ibid., SD/QA/181, 1762.
31 ibid., LL/QA/5, 1771.
32 ibid., LL/QA/4, 1771.
33 ibid., SD/QA/124-5, 1807. B. S. John 'The linguistic significance of the Pembrokeshire Landsker', *Pembrokeshire Historian*, 4, 7-29.
34 N.L.W. MS. SA/RD/26, 1749.
35 ibid., SD/QA/181/1762.
36 ibid., LL/QA/5, 1771.
37 ibid., LL/QA/5, 1771.
38 I. James, *The Welsh language in the 16th and 17th centuries.* Cardiff: Daniel Owen & Co. Ltd. 1887 (reprinted from *The Red Dragon*).
39 N.L.W. MS. SA/RD/26, 1749.
40 ibid., SD/QA/181, 1762.
41 J. Bradney, *A memorandum, being an attempt to give a chronology of the decay of the Welsh language in the eastern part of the county of Monmouth.* Abergavenny: Minerva Press, 1926.
42 N.L.W. MS. LL/QA/5, 1771.
43 P. N. Jones, 'Some aspects of immigration into the Glamorgan coalfield between 1881 and 1911', *Transactions of the Honourable Society of Cymmrodorion*, 1969, 82-98.
44 N.L.W. MS. SA/QA/15, 1809.
45 ibid., LL/QA/22, 1809.
46 ibid., LL/QA/35, 1848.
47 ibid., LL/QA/36, 1848 Llanelen return.
48 ibid., SD/QA/248, 1900, Llanfihangel Abergwesyn return.
49 ibid., SD/QA/175, 1900.
50 ibid., SD/QA/114,1900.
51 ibid., SA/QA/15, 1809.
52 ibid., SD/QA/187, 1807.
53 ibid., LL/QA/23, 1809.
54 ibid., SD/QA/206, 1848.
55 ibid., LL/QA/35, 1848.
56 E. G. Bowen and H. Carter, 'The distribution of the Welsh language in 1971: an analysis', *Geography* 60 (1975), 1-15. In 1901 280,900 Welsh monoglots were returned in a population (aged 3 years and over) of 1.8 millions; in 1971

only 32,700 Welsh monoglots were returned in the 2.6 millions enumerated in the country of Wales.

57 N.L.W. MS. SD/QA/16, 1807.

58 ibid., B/QA/19, 1811.

59 ibid., SA/QA/15, 1809.

60 ibid., B/QA/33, 1900.

61 ibid., SA/QA/15, 1809.

62 ibid., B/QA/19, 1811.

63 ibid., B/QA/20, 1811. Llanerch-y-medd return.

64 ibid., LL/QA/35, 1848.

65 ibid., SD/QA/17, 1845 and SD/QA/77, 1848.

66 ibid., SA/QA/15, 1809 Abergele return; SD/QA/77, 1845 Dinas return; B/QA/27, *c.*1850 Llanfaes, Llangadwaladr, Llandysilio and Rhoscolyn (Anglesey) returns.

67 ibid., SA/QA/15, 1809.

68 ibid., B/QA/27, *c.*1850, Aberffro and Llanfaelog returns.

69 ibid., SD/QA/17, 1845, Troedyraur return.

70 See, for example, G. Williams, 'Geography and Welsh history', *Welsh History Review*, 2 (1965), 275-8.

71 W. T. R. Pryce, 'Migration and the evolution of culture areas: cultural and linguistic frontiers in north-east Wales, 1750 and 1851', *Transactions of the Institute of British Geographers*, 65 (1975), 79-107.

72 D. T. Williams, 'Linguistic divides in south Wales', *Archaeologia Cambrensis*, 90 (1935), 239-66 and 'Linguistic divides in north Wales', *Archaeologia Cambrensis*, 91 (1936), 194-29.

73 E. G. Bowen and H. Carter, 'Preliminary observations on the distribution of the Welsh language in the 1971 census', *The Geographical Journal*, 140 (1974), 432-40.

74 P. T. J. Morgan, 'The character of Welsh society' in D. Thomas (ed.), *Wales, a new study*, Newton Abbot: David & Charles 1977, 272-90.

75 See E. Llewelyn, *Adfer a'r Fro Gymraeg*, Pontypridd a Lerpwl: Cyhoeddiadau Modern Cymraeg Cyf. 1976; and C. Betts, *Culture in crisis: the future of the Welsh language*, Upton, Wirral: The Ffynnon Press, 1976. Chapter 10 of this book is a representative extract from E. Llewelyn (1976).

Chapter Three

The Geography of Wales as a Background to its History*

E. G. Bowen

Reference to a general relief map of Wales, such as can be found in a school atlas, will greatly assist the reader in following the themes developed in this chapter.

In this lecture I will deal with the relationships between geography and history. This is no new theme, for in the days of the Greeks, Herodotus and Thucydidus speculated on the relationship between people and their environment. To some extent men lost sight of this theme in the Middle Ages, but it was resurrected like many other classical ideas during the Renaissance. In 1621 the issue was raised again by Peter Heylyn in his *Microcosmos or a little Description of the Great World.* He said that 'Geography without History seemeth a carkusse without motion, so History without Geography wandereth as a vagrant without a certaine habitation'. Two hundred and fifty years later Jules Michelet in one of his introductions to his famous book *Histoire de France* said almost the same thing, in language equally impressive, suggesting as did the Greeks that there was causal relationship between the two subjects—'Without a geographical foundation the makers of history would appear to be walking on air, as in those Chinese pictures where the Earth is lacking. As is the Nest, so is the Bird; there is a Likeness between the Land and the People'. It is obvious that Michelet thought,

* Originally broadcast in Welsh as the Annual Radio Lecture on BBC Wales Radio 14 May 1964, 7.30-8.15 pm and published as E. G. Bowen *Daearyddiaeth Cymru fel cefndir i'w hanes*, Llundain: BBC 1964. Subsequently translated by the author and republished in English with the above title in H. Carter and W. K. D. Davies (eds) *Geography, culture and habitat: selected essays (1925-1975) of E. G. Bowen*, Llandysul: Gomer Press 1976, pp. 11-30.

like many other writers on this theme, that there was a geographical basis to history and that this basis was a help in explaining the course of events. The great Scottish divine Sir George Adam Smith made his opinion perfectly clear in his famous book *The historical geography of the Holy Land*, which was first published in 1894, and subsequently reprinted twenty-five times, when he said that his purpose in writing the work was 'to discover from the lay of the land why the history of Palestine took a special course'. Sir George Adam Smith and Michelet were historians and their treatment of the relationship between geography and history was much less rigid that that of the geographers in the nineteenth century. Alexander von Humboldt and Karl Ritter, the men who laid the foundations of modern geography in the first half of the nineteenth century, believed that everything on the face of the earth, the hills and the valleys, the climate and the natural vegetation, the peoples and their cultures were the direct result of Divine Providence. With the scientific revolution in the mid-nineteenth century and associated in Britain with the names of Lyell and Darwin, it became necessary to reconsider these matters which were formerly thought to be ordained by Providence and provide a rational explanation for them. In their enthusiasm, the human geographers put forward exceedingly ambitious claims seeking to explain human history everywhere in terms of one overriding influence, that of the physical environment. This standpoint was developed by Friedrick Ratzel (1844-1904) Professor of Geography at Leipzig and by his followers in Britain and the United States. In the end they sought to explain all history through geography and we had statements like the following: 'History is controlled by Geography'; 'History is Geography in action'; 'History is Geography accumulating with interest'. Such statements are unreasonable and easy to disprove. On the other hand, no one will maintain that the people of the past adopted their way of life, or their way of working, without some consideration of the natural and human potentialities of the country in which they dwelt. As a result the geographers have chosen a middle way between those who maintain that history represents a series of happenings in a vacuum, with the geographical features of the country exerting no influence whatsoever on events, and those who believe that the geography of a country determines the course of its history. It is the middle way that is usually accepted today and this is the point of view that will be adopted in this lecture. It will be argued that any territory or country, such as Wales, presents to its inhabitants an opportunity of choosing how to act within limits, in light of their needs, powers and aspirations at any given time. This viewpoint is usually termed 'The Possibilist Viewpoint' and it was strongly supported by the French school of historical geographers in the present century. The clearest presentation is that of Lucien Febvre in his well known book *A Geographical Introduction to History* which was translated into English in 1925. We can now turn to the problem of Wales.

The essential features of the physical geography of Wales are its rectangular shape with the high ground in the centre and the low ground around the edges; the high aggregate of rainfall particularly on the high ground; and the extensive areas of high moorland with their cold, clayey damp soils.

Briefly one can say that the highland reaches from north-north-west to south-south-east. In the extreme north west are the mountains of Eryri, then come the Arenig mountains with the Hiraethog lowlands on one side of them and the Harlech Dome on the other. Then come the Cadair Idris mountains and south-south-eastwards the Pumlumon moorlands and the central Wales uplands with the Brecon Beacons and the coalfield uplands at the south-eastern corner of the mountain core of Wales. The highest points of these uplands reach to over two thousand feet and from this high land the chief rivers of the country derive. They present a long list of radial streams, beginning with the Seiont in the north-west followed by the Peris, Conwy, Clwyd, Alun, Dyfrdwy, Tanat, Fyrnwy, Severn (Hafren), Usk (Wysg), Wye (Gwy),

Rhymni, Ebwy, Taf, Sirhowy, Rhondda Fach and Fawr, Ogwr, Nedd, Tawe, Llwchwr, Lliedi, Gwendraeth Fach and Fawr, Tywi, Cleddau Wen, Cleddau Ddu, Nefern, Gwaun, Teifi, Aeron, Wyre, Ystwyth, Rheidiol, Leri, Dyfi, Dysynni, Wnion, Dwyfor, Glaslyn and Dwyfach. These rivers drain into the lower land which is fairly extensive on the eastern side of Wales forming the lowlands of the Dee, the Vale of Powys and those of the rivers Usk and Wye. The lowlands are also extensive along the southern coastal plain. Bro Morgannwg is not really a lowland area, as it is formed of a series of relatively high plateau surfaces, one above the other, but it is so different in character from the highlands of Wales, that it is necessary to classify it with the lowlands. It is usual to group the land forming the Gower peninsula and that around the mouths of the Gwendraeth Fach and Fawr, the Tywi and the Taf, together with the whole of south Pembrokeshire as lowland. On the western seaboard the lowland is much narrower and in parts of Merioneth the high lands come down almost to the waters' edge. More low-lying land exists in the north-west beyond the highest mountains. Llŷn, Arfon and the Isle of Anglesey fall into the group. Then, in eastern Caernarfonshire and western Denbighshire the highland once again reaches to the waters' edge, before the wide Vale of Clwyd opens in the north east to add to the amount of lowland around the coast.

The first thing to note is that the physical geography of Wales, including its mild, damp, sunless climate proved no obstacle to Early Iron Age settlers, who brought to this country, two or three hundred years before Christ, some elements of culture that have remained a feature of Welsh life up to the present time, not least of which was the fact that they introduced those dialects of Celtic speech that are ancestral to modern Welsh. It is worth emphasizing that not only was the physical geography of Wales no hindrance to these Iron Age settlers, but it helped to consolidate the economic patters of the Welsh way of life which, with little change, has remained down to the present time—the physical conditions favoured pastoralism and the pastoral tradition is deeply rooted in Welsh life and culture. It would appear that these Early Iron Age settlers came from western Gaul and used the sea routes of the west to reach western Britain. The western uplands of Britain at that time were very much like they are today, apart of course from the roads and the small villages and towns that are a part of the present landscape. The most significant difference was that the valleys and most of the lowlying land we have referred to was covered with a damp oak forest with thick undergrowth. It would appear from modern research that this forested land reached up to about 600 ft. The climate was much like it is today; damp, windy, mild and sunless. The experts think that, if anything, these 'Atlantic' features in the climate were more marked than they are today. The Iron Age B conquerors (as they are termed by the archaeologists) built their camps on hillforts on the spurs of the high ground above the 600 ft. level, that is above the forest limits. It was on the high ground, therefore, that the pastoral economy was based, but we must be careful not to over emphasize the pastoral side for modern scholars are showing that there was more arable cultivation in the economy than was previously thought. It is well known, also, that the newcomers hunted freely in the forested valleys below their homes.

While we know that this type of economy was characteristic of the territory now called Wales, and indeed extended far beyond it, we have to await until the immediate post-Roman centuries before we can think of Wales as a geographical unit. Under strong Anglo-Saxon pressure the inhabitants of this part of the western highlands became conscious of their unity. We see a reflection of this feeling in the very name *Cymry*, indicating people of the same country, or comrades. The Saxons called them Wallas (The Welsh), the strange people or the strangers. By the Saxon victory at Deorham in Gloucestershire in 577 the Welsh of Wales were cast off from their fellow Celts in Cornwall and the southwest, and in 616 from the Celts of Cumbria, when they were conquered in the Battle of Chester. In the next century King Offa of Mercia succeeded in establishing a boundary line which gave Wales an eastern frontier from sea to sea. The dyke is still clearly traceable and known as Offa's Dyke. By this time the free tribesmen in Wales had already left their hill forts and come down to the valleys where they lived in clusters of single homesteads in forest clearings. The physical conditions suited their economy of mixed farming, sheep and cattle pastoralism with crops of barley and oats. With the passage of time the cluster of farmsteads spread out associated with common inheritance of land in the male line. In this way the scattered habitat so common in Wales probably came into being. It would appear that the only nucleated settlements were the villages of the bond men who did services for the free tribesmen. These bond villages were found around the home of a chieftain or possibly around a Celtic church. The important point to emphasize is that it is in association with these scattered farms of the free Welsh tribesmen that the Welsh way of life continued to grow and develop its special features. It was in the isolation of these farms that so much emphasis was placed on the non-material culture, music, poetry, philosophy and religion, to say nothing of their interest in later times in eisteddfodau, singing festivals, and the religious revivals of the eighteenth and nineteenth cenuries. There developed at the same time a very high standard of craftsmanship and many of the farmers combined their work on the land with one of these crafts, such as furniture making, boot making and clock making and basketry. They were possibly very poor in their material resources but indeed very rich in the things of the mind and the spirit. The most important element in their culture was their language and the usage closest to hand was the spoken word. Indeed Welsh culture is largely a literary and linguistic culture and the language has played the most important part in its perpetuation. It is no wonder, therefore, that the word *iaith* (language) was used in the Middle Ages to denote 'nation'. Therefore, in the centuries following the Middle Ages (and indeed today) it was customary to confine the word *Cymro* (Welshman) to someone who spoke Welsh.

It is interesting to compare the richness of Irish life in this formative period with its fine stone crosses and illuminated manuscripts and the general poverty of Welsh society at this time. Wales has little to show at this early stage but the poetry of Llywarch Hen and Taliesin and the Tales of the *Mabinogion*. Many scholars would seek the source of this material in the far north, in southern Scotland rather than in Wales itself. This is not the place, however, for a comparative study. We must pass on to consider a later stage in Welsh life and culture.

While, as we have seen, there was much in the physical endowment of Wales that helped to develop not only a strong pastoral tradition but also a strong sense of national feeling, yet nevertheless it must not be forgotten that the geographical shape of Wales and the location of the central mountain core proved entirely unsuited to the development of political unity. The physical geography of Wales offered no natural focal point or centre for administration. As a result centrifugal rather than centripetal forces dominated the Welsh scene throughout the ages. This is nowhere more clearly seen than in matters political and administrative and the failure of Wales to develop from being a nation into a state in the political sense. When we have our first glimpse of Wales after Offa's boundary line was set up, we see it composed of a number of small Kingdoms, as in contemporary England. The peoples' loyalty was to the local chieftain and there arose no London or Winchester and no political unit as achieved in England with the Norman Conquest. The idea of a Welsh state grew up much later and only when Wales had already lost her independence. There is no doubt that this special feature of Welsh history is a reflection of the physical background and indeed it is so fundamental as to deserve further consideration.

In order that the country should have achieved political unity it was necessary for one area within the territory known as Wales to develop as a central or core area. Such an area should be the most suitable area by virtue of its location and geographical potential. As we have seen the overall physical geography of Wales made this difficult, but, nevertheless, there were several possibilities when the Normans came. There were four petty kingdoms within the boundary laid down by Offa and each one had possibilities in this direction. Powys possessed the broad valleys that faced eastwards and was thus endowed well with lowlying rich territory. Indeed, it would have been possible for the richest area, namely the mid-Severn valley, to have developed as a central focus, had it not been for the fact that these rich valleys were entirely defenceless in the military sense. This was specially true of the Vale of Powys which was completely open to invasions from the east, a very easy route for enemies to enter Wales. Another possible nucleus for a Welsh state would have been Glamorgan in the south-east of Glywysing. The latter comprised in the eighth century most of the country between the Nedd and the Usk. Geographically this included the high ground (later called Blaenau Morgannwg) and further south the border vale, and still further south, beyond the present trunk road, Bro Morgannwg (The Vale of Glamorgan). In the eighth century Morgan, grandson of Meurig ap Tewdrig became King of Glywysing and the ruler of all the land between the Nedd and the Usk, and Glamorgan took its name from him. He took for himself that southern part of his overlordship known as Gwlad Morgan (Morgan's Land or Glamorgan) and divided the remainder among his followers. Basically the Land of Morgan represented a third of the vast territory of Glywysing, but definitely the richest third, and it could have developed as a focus for a much larger area than Glamorgan itself. Yet here again it suffered from the same disadvantages as Powys, it lay wide open to influences from the east as was clear in Roman and even pre-Roman times. We remember, too, that it was easily overrun by the Normans under Fitzhamon. It is in this part of Glamorgan that we find the most intensive Normanization. Deheubarth forms the third kingdom. At its maximum extent in its prime it included most of the territory that now forms Pembrokeshire, Cardiganshire and Carmarthenshire, together with Gower and Breconshire. The natural centres here were the Vale of Tywi and Vale of Teifi and there was considerable agricultural potential based on these areas also. The Teifi valley is well protected from eastern influences, although south Pembrokeshire with its wonderful harbours (the bases used by the Normans for their conquest of Ireland) made the southern parts of Deheubarth, and especially the Vale of Tywi around Carmarthen, territories firmly held by the English Crown (Fig. 17). When Deheubarth began to develop as a focal area for the nation it was not its geographical background that was responsible for its primacy, but the outstanding influence and power of its able prince, Rhys ap Gruffydd, better known as the Lord Rhys. This was at the close of the twelfth century. But the death of the strong ruler and the disagreement among his successors gave the Normans the opportunity of regaining their hold on the territory so that with the passage of time the little Kingdom was greatly depleted in size. Of the four petty kingdoms mentioned at the outset, Gwynedd came nearer than any of the others to being the nuclear area around which a Welsh state could have developed in time. There were real prospects that this might have happened in the thirteenth century. By virtue of its position Gwynedd was far removed from English influences, and its natural defences made it more difficult to conquer than any other native principality in Wales. Its natural defences (or if you wish, the protection which the nature of the relief of the land, afforded) were excellent. Three rings of high mountains afforded defence in depth and at the terminals of each there were wide estuarine areas providing real hazards for the heavily armoured Norman knights. The outer ring of natural defences comprised the Cadair Idris mountains, the Berwyns and the Clwydian hills, with the estuaries of the Dyfi in the south-west and of the Dee in the north-east. The second ring of mountains comprised the Harlech Dome and the Arenigs and the Hiraethog moorlands, with the Mawddach estuary on one

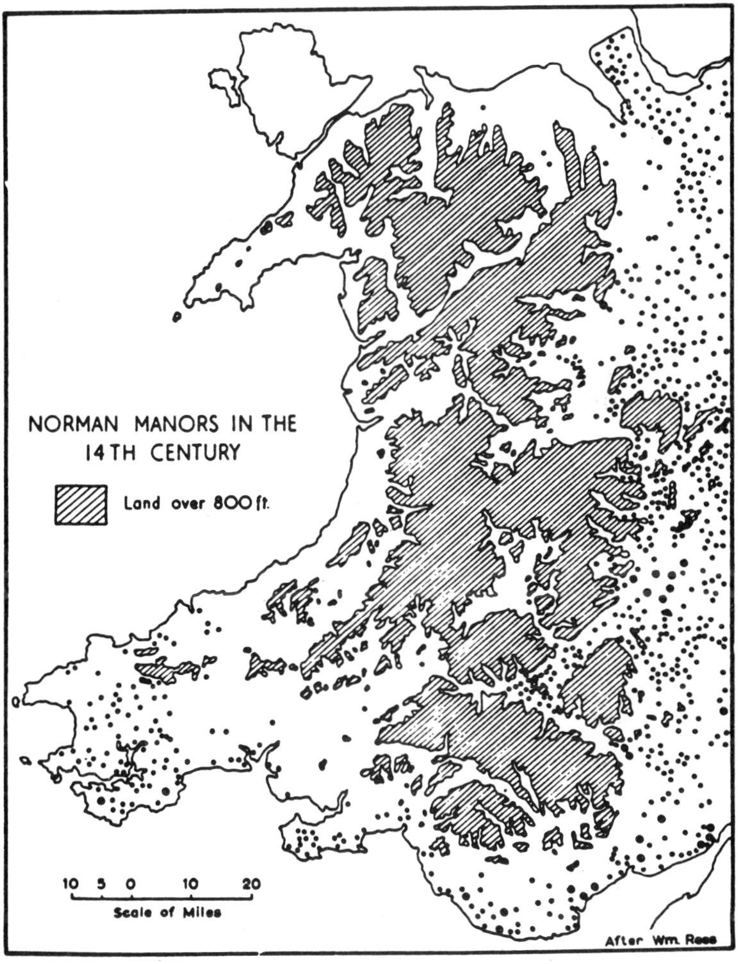

Figure 17. Wales: Norman manors in the fourteenth century

side and that of the Clwyd on the other. The third and inner ring of defence was formed by the Snowdon range, with the Traeth Mawr (a great estuarine area before it was drained by Mr Maddocks in the eighteenth century) in the southwest and the estuary of the Conwy on the northern coast. Behind these great natural defences lay a rich terrain capable of producing an abundance of food and grain for the whole of Wales. Here lay the Plain of Arfon, and the Isle of Anglesey (*Môn Mam Cymru*—Anglesey the Mother of Wales). In the thirteenth century Llywelyn Fawr and his family showed that they had the power and the drive that is necessary for good government and gradually they conquered surrounding lands, so that much of west and north Wales came under their domination. Llywelyn the Last was able to sign himself *Princeps Wallia* and it appeared as if a real Welsh feudal state was about to materialize and to all intents and purposes the problem of a Welsh state was settled. Unfortunately, however, the sea provided an easy route for a conqueror to penetrate into Gwynedd. The Normans had command of the sea and it was, therefore, possible for them to outflank the strong defences of Gwynedd and reach the nuclear area beyond the Conwy. In this way the last defences of native Wales were overcome. Nevertheless, the feeling of national identity was not diminished, but the gap between national consciousness and political unity widened. Political unity or statehood in the full sense of the term would imply a nation with national buildings, a recognized centre as the capital city, and all the other trappings of statehood. For thirteenth century Wales this was not to be and, indeed, this has not been achieved even in our own time. This situation is very apparent in the Glyn Dŵr revolt at the beginning of the fifteenth century. Glyn Dŵr succeeded in rekindling national feeling at a favourable time, namely during the Wars of the Roses. He proved himself to be a military leader of exceptional ability, and by 1403 the greater part of the country was under his authority and it became necessary for the English settlers to seek safety in their large castles and fortified towns. After his victories in the field, Glyn Dŵr began setting up national institutions and creating a Welsh state. A Welsh parliament met on several occasions and it included representatives from all areas. He wanted to establish a Welsh archbishopric that would be independent of Canterbury. He desired to obtain a University for Wales and he signed treaties and agreements with foreign Kings. Glyn Dŵr, however, was a national leader without an administrative centre. His Parliaments met at Machynlleth, Dolgellau and even at Pennal in Merioneth. He intended his Archbishopric to be located at St. Davids and he desired to have two universities, one in the north and the other in the south. There was, however, no single centre where he could place all these things together and where a powerful, central government could draw up laws for the people and be the centre of an effective administration. In a strict geometrical sense the location of a centre of this kind should be on the slopes of Pumlumon but geography has decreed that it would have been impossible to set up some medieval Canberra at such a site. So Glyn Dŵr himself would appear to be 'a vagrant without a certain habitation'. The national spirit arose many times after this, especially after the Tudors came to the Throne and raised the Red Dragon of Cadwaladr on the field of Bosworth. The Venetian Ambassador in London at the time said 'It can be said that the Welsh people have regained their independence for that wise and fortunate prince Henry the Seventh is a Welshman'. In spite of all this the Tudors did nothing to create an independent Wales. The idea never received any consideration by them. It is clear that they drew up the Acts of Union of 1536 and 1542 to give Wales a uniform pattern of local government and to make it similar in this matter to the English pattern. The Act of Union had very important results for both countries, for this was the first step aimed at bringing Britain as a whole under a central government in London. While these great changes were in progress we must not forget that Henry the Seventh revived the idea of a Council for Wales and the Marches which became quite powerful in the hands of Rowland Lee. The Act of 1542 gave the council legal status. For the geographer it is an interesting reflection that this administrative body, which dealt with Wales and the Border, operated not in Wales at all, but in Ludlow which was geographically convenient for all parts of Wales. In this way, therefore, beyond the geographical frontier of the nation was to be found that which Wales did not possess, namely a centre which could unite the territory politically.

In spite of all these changes national feeling lived on and at times it expressed itself powerfully. The desires of Glyn Dŵr were kept alive for many thought him to have been born before his time. Indeed, there was a story current that one morning in the early dawn, while he was walking over the hills he met by chance the Abbot of Aberconwy. He greeted him with the words 'My Lord, you have risen very early this morning'. It is said that the Abbot replied 'It is you who have risen six hundred years too soon'. It is not even now too late for the prophecy to come true, for it is significant that part of Glyn Dŵr's vision has indeed materialized. For example, with the resurgence of national feeling in the nineteenth century and a great effort by the common people, a University of Wales was established, but even so it was scattered around the mountain core, namely at Aberystwyth, Bangor, Cardiff and Swansea. Many of the administrative meetings of the University (including the University Court and the Higher and Honorary Degree ceremonies) migrate from one centre to another and we find other administrative meetings of the University held at either Shrewsbury or London. The twentieth century saw the disestablishment and disendowment of the Church and Wales had its own Archbishop independent of Canterbury. But the Archbishop did not have a fixed episcopal seat as Glyn Dŵr would have wished, the Archbishop's see once again 'wandereth as a vagrant without a certain habitation'. Since 1920 the Archbishop has had a home at St. Asaph, Bangor, St. David's, Llandaf and Monmouth, thereby almost completing the circuit of the central mountain mass. The major nonconformist bodies, of whose existence Glyn Dŵr never dreamt, are not in any way better off. The Baptist Union of Wales shifts its centre every year, and the same applies to the *Cymdeithasfa* (or *Sasiwn*) as the Calvinistic Methodists and the Union of the Independents. This is equally true of the chief national festival, the National

Eisteddfod. Ever since the Eisteddfod was established in its present form in the middle of last century it has moved from place to place every year, sometimes in the north and sometimes in the south, then in mid-Wales and sometimes again in the west. The present rule is for the Eisteddfod to be held one year in the north and the next year in the south. Therefore, we see the chief gathering of the nation housed in a pavilion that can be taken down and set up again in different parts of the country. It could appear, therefore, that geography has won the day at the expense of history in Wales in so far that the nation has failed to create a centre where the idea of political unity as distinct from national feelings can take root. The matter was in no way settled when in 1955 a city of quarter of a million people (created by the Industrial Revolution, but possessing several fine civic buildings) was officially recognized as the capital of Wales. But Cardiff has little in the way of historical or cultural claims for this particular honour. Besides, the location of the capital is hardly ideal from a geographical point of view. We do not look to south-east Wales for a centre to serve the Principality as a whole. We should rememeber, however, that the coming of modern rapid communications (like the motor ways, radio and television) makes this requirement less essential today than it would have been in the past. Thus we have seen from 'the lie of the land', as Sir George Adam Smith expressed it, why the history of Wales has followed the course it has and why, in particular, Wales failed to become (like other nations in Western Europe) a full nation-state.

On the one hand we find that the physical geography of Wales prevents the creation of a centre wherein a national government could be established, but on the other hand it is equally clear that the physical geography of Wales permits two cultures to exist, one in Inner Wales and the other in Outer Wales. The first involves the north and west of the country and the second the south and east. This dualism is made possible because the valleys and lowlands that face the east and south are open to English influences while the country which faces north and west is protected from foreign influences by the highlands of Central Wales. This theme is worthy of further consideration in relation to special periods in the history of Wales.

With the English penetration of the south-east in the Middle Ages, the territories speaking Celtic languages became restricted in area, a position that became more marked with the Anglo-Norman conquest in the subsequent centuries. From their bases at Chester, Shrewsbury, Hereford and Gloucester the Norman lords penetrated into Wales. This was, perhaps, less marked in the north than it was in the south. In the north the mountains which faced the English lowlands were steeper and more difficult to cross than those in the centre. In addition the entries to the coastal lowlands of the north were narrower than those giving access to the southern coastal plain. The Anglo-Norman penetration of the mid-Severn valley was rapid and complete, while the penetration of the Wye and Usk valleys reached its full strength with the early establishment of the lordship of Brecon. The fact that Fitzhamon conquered Glamorgan so easily and quickly from his base at Gloucester indicates how wide open were the lowlands of Gwent and Morganwg to the onslaughts of the enemy. In like manner Gower fell rapidly into Norman hands. In several of these conquered zones the land was divided into Englishries and Welshries, where English and Welsh law operated respectively. The former were composed most often of lowlying lands and the latter of upland territory. Welsh customs and Welsh speech survived in the Welshries which were, nevertheless, under Norman supervision. A number of permanent Englishries, however, were established by installing foreigners and Anglo-Normans around the newly established castles. The permanent Englishry established by Henry I in south Pembrokeshire is a good example of this type of settlement. The overall effect in the thirteenth century is the juxtaposition of an Inner and Outer Wales. Inner Wales is clearly represented by the lands over which Llywelyn the Great ruled either directly or through the

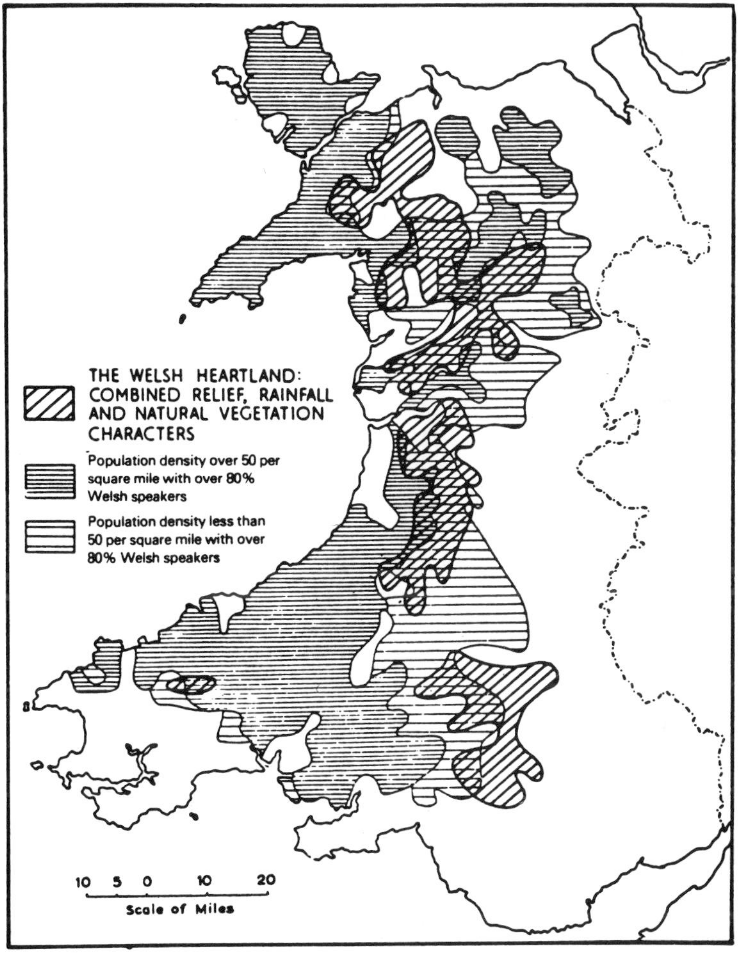

Figure 18. The Welsh Heartland: combined relief, rainfall and natural vegetation characters

help of minor princes. The remainder of the country, which was in the hands of the Anglo-Normans, comprised Outer Wales (Fig. 17). In greater detail we see that Llywelyn's lands were made up of most of Anglesey, Caernarfon, Denbigh, Flint, central and western Montgomery, Cardigan, western Radnor and in addition Cartref

Mawr and Cartref Bychan in the north and east of Carmarthenshire. On the other hand the lands of the Anglo-Normans stretched across the south-east of Montgomeryshire, eastern and central Radnorshire, most of Brecknockshire, Glamorgan, Monmouth and the southern fortress of Carmarthenshire and Pembrokeshire.

A similar dualism is found if we compare the agriculture practices in Inner and Outer Wales in the Middle Ages. Outer Wales was the province of the Norman manorial system. This was a special economic system with its open fields tilled in rotation annually. It was essential that this system had the appropriate type of territory in which to function, namely relatively low lying land with fairly good soils, an equable climate without too high a rainfall aggregate and with a fairly high hourage of bright sunshine (Fig. 18). These conditions appertain on the whole in Outer Wales where the Norman manorial system is found, while it is clear that there is less arable and more pasture to be found in the lands that remained under native control.

A similar dualism is seen in the religious situation in Wales in the period following the Protestant Reformation. The Welsh Puritanism of the seventeenth and eighteenth centuries is English in origin and like the Anglo-Norman penetration that preceded it, spread over most of the lowlands of the east and south, leaving that part of the Principality that once formed independent Wales more or less in the hands of the Established Church with strong leanings towards Rome (Fig. 19). The little market towns that had gathered beneath the great Norman castles became in later centuries centres of local industry (especially the woollen industry). Many of these towns also had their Edwardian or Elizabethan grammar schools. The Independents became deeply rooted on the eastern borderland from Llanfaches, in Monmouthshire (where their first church was established in 1639), to Brecon in the Usk Valley and to the westward they reached into Llanbrynmair in Montgomeryshire and north-eastwards to Llanfyllin and Wrexham. In a similar manner their

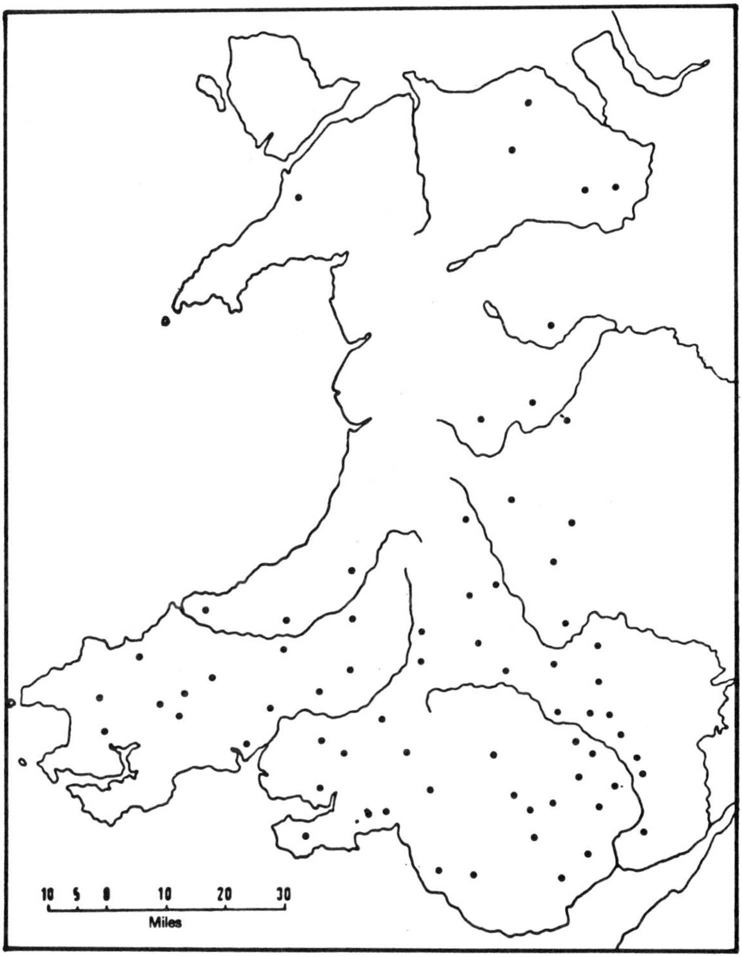

Figure 19. Distribution of Puritan churches c. 1715 (after the list of Dr. John Evans)

denominational college (where the ministers are trained) moved in course of its long history backwards and forwards along the eastern borderlands. It began its existence at Brecon and then moved to Oswestry and from there to Wrexham, afterwards to Llanfyllin and from there to Newtown, establishing itself finally at Brecon until

1960 when it was decided to move to Swansea to be nearer to the University College there. Another early centre of the Independents was at Carmarthen in the southern part of Outer Wales. This town also had an early non-conformist college, half Independent and half Unitarian, until its doors closed only two years ago. Almost similar is the history of the Baptists. Their centres were Pen-y-bont and Nantmel in Radnorshire, Olchon on the borders between Brecon and Herefordshire, Ilston in Gower and, away to the westward, Rhydwilym on the Pembrokeshire-Carmarthenshire border. It was from this important church established in 1668 that the Baptists spread markedly into north Pembrokeshire. The history of the Baptists and Independents is very similar and in the early days of Puritanism in Wales we find the Quakers in almost the same areas as the Independents and Baptists as well.

A whole century passed before any religious awakening affected Inner Wales or Welsh Wales. When it came it was known as the Methodist Revival of the Eighteenth Century, a movement in which the leaders appealed to the people in their own language. This was a native movement and not an external movement as its fires were lit within Welsh Wales at Llangeitho and Pantycelyn, in Trefecca and Bala and in Anglesey. This is the territory that kept alive old traditions. It was here that the Calvinism of the Middle Ages was brought again to life. It is true, however, that the power of the Revival was too strong to be confined within the frontiers of any single geographical unit and by spreading to the rest of Wales many of the older Puritan sects were changed and indeed made more 'Methodist' in character. Nevertheless, the contrast between the older Puritanism of Outer Wales, foreign and English in tradition, and the Methodism of Inner Wales, that was native to Wales, is to be seen quite as clearly as the contrast between the lands of Llywelyn Fawr and those of the Anglo-Norman six hundred years before. The stage remained but the actors were new.

At this stage another geographical factor enters the field, a factor that had been dormant for man did not possess the technological 'know how' to develop it. Many would argue that the presence of the Welsh coalfields is a geological rather than a geographical factor, but it is clear that the presence of the two most important coalfields in Wales, one in the north-east and the other in the south is both a geological and a geographical factor. The northern coalfield follows the margins of the highland from the Point of Ayr through western Flintshire into Denbighshire and then as far south as Chirk. The south Wales coalfield is not so much a feature of the lowlands of the south and east, as it is really a coalfield of the uplands found on the southern flanks of the mountain country that forms the central massif of Wales, and extending to the westward below Carmarthen Bay and into Pembrokeshire. We must not forget, however, that the narrow valleys that cut across the hills of Glamorgan and Monmouth open out onto the lowlands of the coastal plain, where the chief coal ports are found. The irony of the location of the Welsh coalfields is that they occur in Outer Wales, with the result that they have made this outer zone, after the Industrial Revolution, more populous than Inner Wales, and at the same time more English and cosmopolitan in character than the quieter valleys of Inner Wales that face the western seas.

As in the case of the Anglo-Normans and the Puritans, in earlier centuries the Industrial Revolution in Wales was the result of ideas in technical matters that had first developed in England. The use of coked coal to smelt iron proved to be an invention of the highest order and increased production ten fold. This discovery which in fact initiated the Industrial Revolution was made by Abraham Darby in Coalbrookdale in Shropshire at the beginning of the eighteenth century. He was afraid of the consequences of his discovery as far as it affected the armament industry so he kept the whole thing a secret and his discoveries did not spread abroad until the days of his son Abraham Darby the Second. John Guest brought the idea to Dowlais about 1749 and thirty years later John Wilkinson was using coke to smelt iron in Bersham on the north Wales coalfield. At first, the increase in population was inconsiderable, and indeed, many of the unskilled workers in the coal mines and in the iron industry worked in the winter-time and returned to their farms in the summer season to look after the harvest. When, however, the deeper coal seams of the south Wales coalfield were opened up in the nineteenth century, people flocked into the area and with them, of course, a strong non-Welsh element which the earlier inhabitants failed to absorb into the existing social structure. In parts of Merthyr Tudful the two communities lived apart and we have, for example, a street called *Row y Saeson*, 'the English People's Row'. The cosmopolitan nature of the population on the nothern coalfields was made all the more complicated by the large number of Irish workman, that were driven out of their own country by the Great Famine in the forties of the nineteenth century. With the coming of the railways, people migrated to the coalfields from places further afield and we see from an examination of the 1851 census that in the borough of Merthyr Tydfil alone there was in that year at least one person who had been born in each of the counties of England, Wales, Scotland and Ireland. The fact that the new industrial population was so mixed and that so many of them were unskilled labourers and that more people were arriving all the time, made it extremely difficult to unite them into a consolidated community. In its turn this was one of the most important factors that delayed the beginnings of the labour movement in south Wales. These great movements were not really effective until the election of Keir Hardie as Member of Parliament for Merthyr Tudful as late as 1900. More marked still was the influence of local geographical conditions on the social life of the community. As we have seen, the south Wales coalfield was located on land which at the beginning of the Industrial Revolution was open moorland, desolate country with deep narrow valleys, heavily forested. When the deep coal pits were opened in the valleys that had to be deforested, it was essential to make rapid progress in building houses for the new workers. There were, of course, no shops, no towns, no public buildings and, therefore, it was necessary for the iron masters and coal owners to set up shops, and the workers, of course, were forced to buy their food and other necessities in them. They paid for them not in ready cash but by tickets, or coupons, which were given in exchange for goods and commodities 'purchased' in these truck shops. In this way the owners had not only control of the market but also a powerful weapon to prevent industrial unrest, because they could cut off the miners' food supply or turn them out of their houses if trouble arose. Later on, when more and more houses were built they were arranged row above row on the steep mountain sides and there was very little truly nucleated settlements as in the traditional town or village. As a result, public or civic buildings were few and the traditions of urban life had little opportunity of developing.

The conditions in north Wales were less pronounced for the reason that the geographical conditions were simpler and everything was on a smaller scale. Merthyr Tudful grew into a county borough with a population of 70,000, while the population of Wrexham was only 5,000 in 1901.

In the end it is the culture of Inner Wales that has given Wales its personality, its language, its religion and song. These survive into the modern epoch and represent the real Wales. These characteristic features were either common to the whole of Wales at one time, or have spread from the Inner zone to the Outer in recent centuries, with the Outer zone always more exposed to influences from outside Wales. The theme put forward in this lecture is that the continuation of Welsh life and culture in the Inner Zone depends to a very large extent on the ability of the mountains to defend the culture of valleys facing the west and north. We are, however, living in an age that can override geographical obstacles with ease. What was begun by the railways and carried forward by the trunk roads and the motor car, is completed with the coming of radio and television (Fig. 20). Geographical factors are losing their potency, for at the present time mountains, as

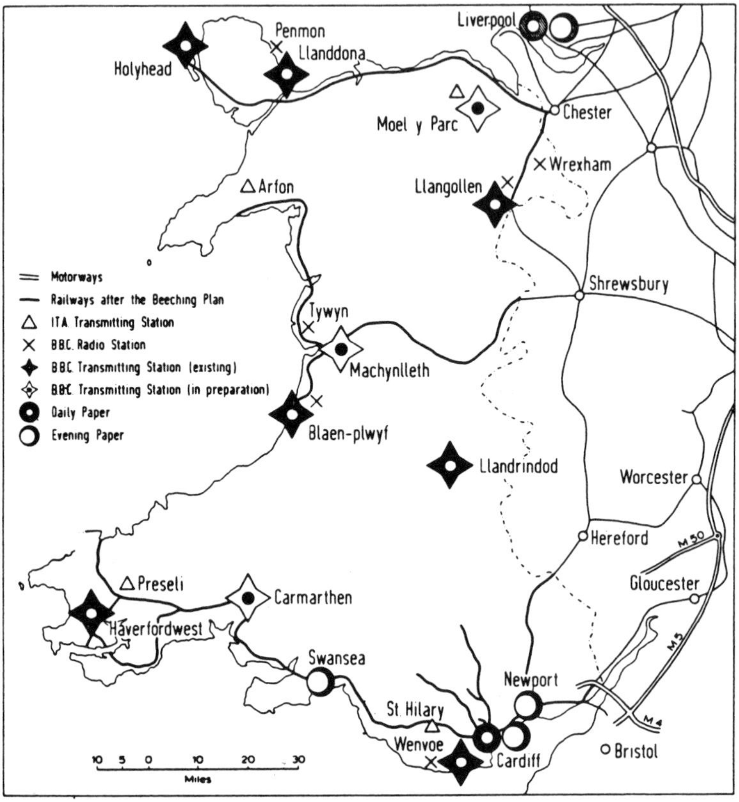

Figure 20 Modern mass communications in Wales

EDITOR'S NOTE

Since 1964 the M4 motorway has been extended into south Wales as far west as Pont Abraham, northwest of Swansea. Similarly, in north Wales the A55 trunk road has been improved up to near motorway standards, so bringing Bangor and the coastal resort towns closer to northeast Wales and linking into the motorway system of northern England. Broadcasting in all its forms has been extended throughout Wales. New local radio stations have been established on a commercial basis at Swansea, Cardiff, Newport and Wrexham. In addition, Wrexham now has an evening newspaper.

such, provide neither shelter nor protection. These obstructions have been surmounted. Our cosmopolitan civilization can now reach into the farthest west. Is there a danger that the old inner stronghold of Welsh life and culture can be overrun by modern cosmopolitan culture?

This is the problem that faces Wales today. The fact that the mountains can no longer offer shelter and security for Welsh life and culture does not make the situation impossible. We must return to the philosophy of the 'Possibilist School' which we mentioned at the beginning. Every human geographer has, at some time or other, quoted the famous saying of Lucien Febvre concerning the relationship of geography and history: 'There are nowhere necessities, but everywhere possibilities, and Man as the master of these possibilities is the judge of their use'. No situation is incapable of resolution, Man chooses what action to take; Man and not mountains determines.

PART II

THE TRADITIONAL SOCIETY

Chapter Four

Community Studies in Wales: An Overview*

Trefor M. Owen

The community study approach is no longer in favour among sociologists working in Britain. Despite its obvious early attraction as an economical research method capable of being undertaken by a single investigator—the equivalent of taking the subway to the ethnic quarter—it has fallen into disuse, if not disrepute, during recent years. Community has come to be regarded as a somewhat intractable concept despite the sociologist's obvious concern with social bonds in everyday life. George Hillery's identification of no fewer than ninety-four different sociological definitions of community, sharing the vague assertion that community has to do with people and places, has discouraged not only sociologists but also historians, who are less preoccupied with theoretical matters, from using the concept (Hillery 1955, Macfarlane 1977). Some sociologists, like Stacey, emphasising the discipline's preoccupation with the study of social relations and institutions, have minimized the importance of the geographical dimension. In its place 'local social system' has been put forward as a more fruitful alternative to the mythical 'community', thus allowing both the replicable investigation and systematic comparison which are necessary for the cumulative building of theoretical knowledge expected of a scientific discipline (Stacey 1969). Community studies, it has been alleged, are too idiosyncratic and subjective in character and, therefore, nearer the art-form of the novel than the scientific treatise. Other soci-

* Based on an earlier version first published in M. Firestone (ed.) *Anthropological studies in Great Britain and Ireland.* Arizona State University Anthropological Research Papers no. 27 (1982), 54-82.

ologists such as Carter and Newby have rejected the inadequacies of the community study in favour of approaches which emphasise the analysis of the social relations of agricultural production and the class structure of the countryside, respectively (Carter 1976, Newby 1977). Even anthropologists who have not disparaged or forsaken the community study recognise the need 'to attempt to move beyond the community, beyond the rather ahistorical, village-focussed studies which have characterised much of European anthropology to date' in order to 'deal with the effects of such familiar processes as increasing industrialization, geographical mobility and urbanisation' (Boissevain and Friedl 1975).

The Welsh community studies discussed in this paper belong to the period before this disillusionment with the approach, and any discussion of their methodology is, perforce, historical in character. Their publication occurred between 1950 and 1971 but, for the most part, the fieldwork on which they were based was carried out during the 1940's and 1950's with the result that they were historical in content also (A. D. Rees 1950, Davies and Rees 1960, Frankenberg 1957, Emmett 1964, Jenkins 1971). As they were all essentially studies of rural communities they relate to social conditions which prevailed during the years of agricultural prosperity which came in the wake of the Second World War. The exception is David Jenkins's second study which deliberately set out to deal with an even earlier period, the social life and culture of a rural area at the turn of the present century, a time, as it happens, during which the first contribution was made to the sociology of the Welsh countryside.

This early contribution took the form of a government report by the Royal Commission on the Agricultural Labourer prepared by Daniel Lleufer Thomas and published in 1893 (Royal Commission on Labour). This was the first attempt to describe systematically the social conditions of rural Wales. For the purposes of the Report eight Poor Law Unions were visited. The units selected each had a population of about 20,000 and were fairly evenly distributed throughout the country. In each district witnesses were examined, submissions received and a certain amount of statistical data assembled. Each Poor Law Union was dealt with in a separately written report covering such topics as the supply of labour, conditions of engagement, wages, accommodation (in cottages and farm buildings), trade unions and benefit societies. In a general summary Thomas drew attention to several differences between the districts visited, for example, the scarcity of labour in the vicinity of the south Wales coalfield and the consequent influx of farm labourers from Somerset, in-migrants who, in their turn, left the farms of the Vale of Glamorgan for the mining valleys. He also noted the migration of harvest labour in northern and western parts of Wales, the varying degree of specialization in farm work in different localities, as well as regional differences in social distinction between farmers and their servants. Lleufer Thomas was subsequently Secretary of the Royal Commission on Land in Wales which dealt with agrarian problems such as land tenure, depopulation, housing conditions etc., and whose report was published in 1895, together with five large volumes of the evidence received by the Commission during its meetings in various parts of the country (Royal Commission on Land 1894-96). These two government reports are a key to the rural life of nineteenth-century Wales and contain a vast amount of information, much of it miscellaneous, about social conditions. Despite their importance, however, they were compilations rather than studies, collections of facts rather than analyses of processes. However, it is interesting to note that two members of the Royal Commission on Land, Sir John Rhŷs, Principal of Jesus College, Oxford, and Professor of Celtic at Oxford, and David Brynmor-Jones, a barrister and Member of Parliament, published a volume entitled *The Welsh people* in 1900, incorporating five chapters originally drafted by the authors for the Commission's Report and a chapter on the history of land tenure in Wales by another eminent member of the Commission, Frederic Seebohm (Rhŷs and Brynmor-Jones 1900). Six new chapters, mainly on archaeology and legal history, were added by the two authors, and the resulting book may, in some ways be regarded as an early precursor of the Welsh community studies published after the Second World War.

The first academic study of Welsh rural society was Alwyn D. Rees's *Life in a Welsh countryside* which appeared in 1950. Rees was a student of C. Daryll Forde who was, for several years, Gregynog Professor of Geography and Anthropology in the University College of Wales, Aberystwyth. Rees's book described both as a 'social study' and 'a survey', was essentially an attempt to adapt the approach of the anthropologist to the study of contemporary Welsh life. The chapter headings—the economy, house and hearth, farmsteads, family, kindred, religion, status and prestige, etc.—could equally well have occurred in an anthropological monograph on a primitive society published in the inter-war period. The work was carried out with no particular methodological approach in mind and is an example of what Daryll Forde described in another context as 'integrated description'. Few ethnographical studies of Western rural life had been published hitherto, and it is apparent from the citations in the text that Rees was familiar with the pioneering work of Arensberg and Kimball in County Clare, George C. Homans on *English villagers of the thirteenth century* and Horace Miner's study of a French Canadian parish, all of which appeared between 1937 and 1943 (Arensberg 1937, Arensberg and Kimball 1940, Homans 1942, Miner 1939). None of these, however, served directly as a model for Rees's study, although certain influences may perhaps be discerned. Arensberg's *The Irish countryman* was probably the volume which appealed most to Rees's deep interest in Celtic folklore. There is a general similarity of approach, but with the important difference that Rees's work contains far more statistical information about the community which he studied. Unlike any of these predecessors, too, Rees used questionnaires completed by every household in the parish for the collection of the data which he subsequently employed in his discussions of the economy, the family farm and demography generally. Since he did not adopt any form of sampling the complete data which he had assembled could be presented in the form of both maps and statistical tables. Moreover, the selection of a parish as a suitable unit for his study enabled him to draw upon census data, agricultural returns and historical documents, such as the 1842 Tithe Survey, in order to give an historical perspective to his work which, in these respects, is very much in the tradition of the social survey.

One of the major difficulties in applying an anthropological approach to the study of Western society related to the unit which was to be studied by the recognized methods of participant-observation. The Andaman Islands, the Trobriand Islands, Tikopia and other subjects of the classical monographs of the formative period of modern anthropology were all small-scale societies clearly delineated by physical features. Even where the units studied were not so small and not so well-defined, they were at least not unmanageable and did not present insuperable difficulties. The problem of adapting the intensive methods and holistic approach developed in such small-scale entities to the study of large-scale societies was overcome, but only in part, by the adoption of the community study. An obvious factor in the use of this approach was the choice of a suitable community which was, in some way, representative of a larger unit or of a particular complex of social phenomena. Arensberg, in his Irish studies, wished to deal with the smaller farmer and his social life and chose the two small communities of Luogh and Rynamona in Co. Clare where he could study in direct detail what he had also observed in a more general manner over a larger region. Alwyn Rees's choice of Llanfihangel-yng-Ngwynfa was partly for reasons of personal convenience—he was a University Extra-Mural Tutor in the same county—and partly because it was 'a relatively secluded and entirely Welsh-speaking area which could be expected to have retained many features of the traditional way of life' (A. D. Rees 1950:v). One is reminded of Arensberg's statement to the same effect: 'when I first came to Luogh I knew only that in this remote little community of small farms I should find something of the old tradition still alive' (Arensberg 1937:22). Like Arensberg, Alwyn Rees was faced with the problem of typicalness: 'This book,' he wrote in his Introduction, 'is a survey of Welsh life as it exists in Llanfihangel-yng-Ngwynfa', suggesting that here was a microcosm of Welsh society open to the anthropologist to interpret. Further on he added 'the social organisation of the area remains fairly representative of the Welsh uplands generally', suggesting that Llanfihangel was not typical of Wales as a whole but, nevertheless, represented something more than Llanfihangel itself (A. D. Rees 1950). This dual standard of relevance helps to explain some of the characteristics of his study. As was suggested above, the statistics which he assembled, and many of the illustrative examples which occur in the book, were drawn from Llanfihangel parish and had a valuable particularity, but the discussion itself was framed in more general terms and based on a familiarity with a much larger geographical area. The dualism was reflected, on the one hand, in the intensiveness and geographical limitation of the statistical and factual material and, on the other, in the much broader area of north Wales for which the generalized discussion was valid. The distinctiveness of the individual community and the vividness of its life, despite adequate documentation, did not fully emerge, as they did, for example, in the Welsh community studies by Frankenberg and Emmett. One feels that these two latter authors, because they did not possess a general background knowledge of Welsh life when they embarked upon their field work, based their analysis more exclusively on their direct observations in '*Pentrediwaith*' and '*Llan*' respectively.

It is important to realize that Alwyn Rees's 'social study' dealt not only with social life and social structure—although admittedly not in a most intensive way—but also with Welsh culture, in the normal anthropological use of that word, as that culture was exemplified in the parish of Llanfihangel. He thus included a description of the material culture as something of intrinsic interest, and not merely to elucidate social relationships. Sociologists have naturally placed less emphasis on this aspect of his ethnography and it is frequently forgotten that Alwyn Rees's study was the first serious treatment of the material culture of a community in the British Isles. The houses of the parish were classified into distinct, if rather crude, morphological types, consisting of the various categories of 'oblong' and 'square' houses and of cottages. Rees's was also the first description of the layout of farm buildings which, characteristically, he saw mainly in terms of agricultural functions. Llanfihangel farmsteads, he pointed out, were arranged in a particular way because that was the most convenient and labour-saving way which had evolved by local tradition. Similarly, in describing houses and cottages his ultimate concern was with the material culture as the setting for social behaviour. He recognised that the parish was too small a unit for dealing satisfactorily with building types and their evolution and pointed out that 'the history and distribution of house-types in Britain requires much more detailed study before any definitive conclusions can be drawn as to the antecedents of those which characterise Llanfihangel today' (1950:38). He turned to the use of the various rooms by the family and, in particular, the layout of the *cegin*, or living room, dominated by the hearth and typified in the larger farmhouses by the two tables for the family and the servants respectively. This practice he saw, following E. Estyn Evans, as belonging to the 'open hearth' tradition of western Europe as distinct from the 'oven tradition' of central Europe where the social centre was the table and not the hearth. Again, he was interested in the settlement pattern of the parish not for its own sake, as a geographer might be, but because the dispersed nature of farmhouses and cottages was to him a dominating feature of social life in the parish. What he was really interested in was the absence of a focus and of a village tradition on the English pattern. Here, he said, was a tradition which actually thrived on the absence of an organizing centre, a tradition in which funerals and weddings were more important than villages in bringing people together. Characteristically, he saw the significance of the diffuse quality found in Llanfihangel for Welsh life in a more general sense. Nonconformity thrived on this antipathy to the parish church, and even the traditional ecclesiastical centres of Wales, its four cathedral cities, were in the past little more than villages. Welsh national institutions were either shared out geographically, as in the case of University, the Library and Museum, or else became peripatetic, as in the case of the Eisteddfod, the Agricultural Show (until recently) or the administrative assemblies, courts and committees of various public and church bodies (1950: 108). The history of Wales, we are made to feel, bore out Alwyn Rees's findings in his analysis of this little community.

History, or more particularly the awareness of history, was, in certain other respects, a characteristic of Alwyn Rees's study—and this at a time when such prominent anthropologists as A. R. Radcliffe-Brown were disputing the relevance of history to the study of society. Put in crude and simplified terms, this argument, which is now out of fahsion, went as follows: primitive societies had no historical records; therefore, our knowledge of their past was conjectural and unreliable. In any case, anthropologists had been able to understand primitive societies as going concerns without having recourse to their histories, so history was an irrelevant and unnecessary complication which we could do without, even where historical records existed. In contrast to this view, which was fairly prevalent at the time, Alwyn Rees, who was, after all, working in a society whose history was documented, was very much aware of the past and its influence on the contemporary social life of Llanfihangel. Just as in a geographical dimension his study of the parish led him to a discussion of Welsh rural life in general, so in a historical dimension he was led to consider the vital part an age-old historical tradition had played in the creation of the community he was studying. There is hardly a chapter in the book which does not take one back to the eighteenth century, if not to the Middle Ages, to throw light on present-day conditions. 'Like the solidarity of the family', we are told 'loyalty to relatives is a heritage from the tribal past. A tribal organisation of life continued in modified form in Wales throughout the Middle Ages in contrast to the feudal system of rural England' (1950:81). One important source of information on this distant past used by Rees, as by other scholars working in cognate disciplines, was the body of legal codes and texts dating in substance from the twelfth century. Rees noted the tolerant attitude towards illegitimacy expressed in the Welsh laws in relation to succession and saw an obvious similarity in contemporary attitudes in Llanfihangel. The evidence of seventeenth and eighteenth century parish registers was seen as supporting this view, as was the general testimony of the twelfth-century writer Giraldus Cambrensis. The discussion was widened to take account of trothplight in sixteenth-century England and a brief comparison of Welsh and English marriage customs in terms of historical survival. Indeed, Rees's approach here, and in other historical discussions, was that of the ethnologist rather than the community sociologist. However, he was not driven by any strong urge to record vanishing customs in detail for their own sake in the manner of the folklife researcher. His description of *y blygain fawr*, the traditional carol service, at one time held before dawn on Christmas Day but latterly on the second Sunday in January, was couched in very general terms. He was not tempted to investigate the history of this regional practice and to deal with its distinctive carols. The carol service was presented in the context of a general ethnographic account of church and chapel services (1950:126 cf.). In other words, his standard of relevance here and throughout the book was the Llanfihangel he visited and saw with his own eyes. For this reason he refrained from discussing wedding customs which were extinct in Llanfihangel, in spite of their historical significance.

As an example of Alwyn Rees's general approach his treatment of what he regarded as a central feature of Welsh rural sociology, namely the family farm and its perpetuation, might be cited (1950: Chapter 5). Llanfihangel farms were small, less than half of them were over fifty acres. The ideal unit of production for the small farm was a family of father, mother, and two or three sons and daughters who were old enough to work. On some farms the children were too young and outside labour was required. This was supplied by farm families which had a surplus, lending, as it were, a son or, less often, a daughter, as a servant. Most servants lived in, and were treated as members of the family. In all probability the farmer employing labour in this way had, at one time, been a servant himself. The servant he employed also had every chance of becoming a farmer in his own right in due course. Thus even the employment of farm labour, after the decrease in the agricultural labour force since 1900 or so, operated within the framework of the family farm system. Given such conditions as these it is easy to understand why there was little social distinction between farmer and servant, and Alwyn Rees made this point, as well as giving a sound statistical basis for the account just summarized. He was, however, also concerned to see how this system operated over a period of time and how the tenancy of the family farm, and the control of resources, were transmitted from one generation to another.

Once the sons were old enough to work at home, the money hitherto paid out in wages could be set aside for the future. The son who stayed at home was unpaid. Those sons who worked out had to save their wages to provide for their futures, and if the farmer could afford it he would contribute towards their farm stock when the time came. But his chief responsibility was towards the son or sons who remained at home.

The son who was to succeed to the farm could not marry while there were brothers at home or while his mother was alive. Those who married were set up as farmers elsewhere and automatically eliminated themselves from the succession. Usually it was the eldest who went in this way, leaving the youngest son at home to help his ageing parents until the day finally came when he could take over the farm and get married. Alwyn Rees showed how this influenced the age of marriage and how the ideal pattern outlined above could be upset or short-circuited by the premature death of the father when the youngest son was too young to take over and his elder brothers had not yet been set up on their own.

Rees thus showed the prevalence of the succession of the youngest son, a feature, incidentally, which had been noted outside Llanfihangel, and suggested it might be accounted for by the operation of the family farm system and contingencies which might effect its cyclical development. However, to explain the origin of the system he turned to the social system of medieval Wales. The Welshman of the early Middle Ages, on the evidence of the native laws, retained control of his share of the land of the kindred until his death. His sons received equal shares of moveable property as they left the hearth, and, after their father's death, inherited equal shares in the land itself; but on the final division of the inheritance the paternal homestead and the remaining moveable property went to the youngest son.

In a similar manner Rees's historical orientation was revealed when he saw a correspondence between the twentieth-century practice of allowing the farmwife a completely free hand in the housekeeping expenditure financed out of the sale of eggs, butter and poultry—her sphere of economic activity on the farm—and the right of the wife of a free man under medieval Welsh law to dispose of her clothing, meal, cheese, butter and milk without the advice of her husband (1950:63).

Rees's emphasis on historical continuity, it should be noted, was couched in general rather than particular terms.

The medieval conditions to which Rees referred were true of Wales in general rather than of Llanfihangel in particular, of which, in any case, we know very little; and as previously noted, the present-day conditions to which Rees referred are true also of other districts besides Llanfihangel. In fact, one of the fundamental criticisms which can be levelled at Rees's book is this lack of particularity—the failure to concentrate sufficiently on the local situation and on the significance of the ways in which it is different from other surrounding parishes. Rees's preoccupation with the representative character of Llanfihangel's community and its relevance to Welsh life in general precluded a more penetrating sociological analysis. His awareness of history, too, helped to deflect him from such a course and led him to useful but perhaps less pertinent generalities.

Alwyn Rees's final chapter sought to place his study in a wider context. His 'ethnographic description', had given prominence 'to those elements which distinguish the rural culture of Wales from that of rural England and still more from that of modern urban communities' (1950: 162). Beyond this modest aim he made no attempt to relate his work to sociological theory, a field which was, in any case, quite under-developed in this country. Not until Ronald Frankenberg's study of *Communities in Britain*, published in 1966, was any serious attempt made to place the findings of British community studies in any kind of sociological framework. Rees concentrated instead on cultural-historical differences between England and Wales, again in a very general discussion. The diffuse pastoral and tribal heritage of Wales, and its dispersed settlement pattern, were contrasted with England's village-centred culture and its weak blood ties, which prepared the English for modern urban standards in a manner which the Welsh did not experience. Out of Wales's detribalised society emerged a landowning class increasingly estranged in language, religion and politics from the rest of Welsh society, in such a way as to prevent it from performing the normal functions of a local aristocracy. Out of this situation, fired by religion, there emerged the popular synthesis exemplified in contemporary Llanfihangel and precariously dependent on direct religious experience. The greater society of England and Wales was poised to engulf the local community as this synthesis dissolved, its effects exacerbated by the pervasive results of industrialisation imported into Wales through England. Llanfihangel, furthermore, was on the verge of a dramatic social transformation with the disappearance of the historically important and dominating local landlord as tenants became owner-occupiers. Paradoxically, a class solidarity which first appeared among English farmers was spreading in the Welsh hills but remaining 'unintegrated with the wider complex of traditional culture'. The 'completeness of the traditional rural society . . . and its capacity to give the individual a sense of belonging, . . . phenomena that might well be pondered by all who seek a better social order' were threatened by an insufficient urbanism with its 'disintegration into formless masses of rootless nonentities' (1950: 170). The note of pessimism and subjective judgement introduced in the final pages of the book reflected Rees's refusal to remain academically aloof from the object of his studies, although scrupulously restricting his views until his summing-up. A small polemical book published in Welsh in 1943, at the time when he was working upon his study of Llanfihangel, made evident his pessimistic view in wartime of modern civilization with its lost ideals and materialistic attitudes. The book's title, *Adfeilion* ('Ruins'), reflected his disillusion with contemporary thought and his search for a new spiritual answer to the problems of society. His final sentences in that book and the deep feeling which they express are worth quoting in translation:

> No new inspiration will come unless there is a yearning for it, and in order to deepen that yearning we must completely despair of deliverance from the Old Regime and shake ourselves from the grip of its dead hand. If this little book succeeds in doing something to create this kind of despair it will have achieved its purpose. We must, as a society, go

> through the darkness of a kind of 'Pass of Convincement' now, or face a long period in the purgatory of fascist totalitarianism before reaching a New World (A. D. Rees 1943:54).

What was remarkable was not the briefly expressed anti-urban and anti-industrial sentiment of the 'Epilogue', but the fact that feelings so strongly felt at that time were so successfully curbed in the study itself. Later on Rees became deeply involved in Welsh political life as an influential social commentator and editor of the Welsh language journal *Barn*. His polemical articles on Welsh affairs, and especially on the Welsh language and its official recognition, were collected and published in 1976 shortly after his death (R. M. Jones 1976). He was not to return to the field of community studies, except indirectly through his students. By the time *Life in a Welsh countryside* was receiving international recognition as a pioneer study Rees had returned to his earlier love of folklore and mythology and published in 1961, with his brother Brinley Rees, a substantial work on that subject which constitutes a major contribution to Celtic studies (Rees and Rees 1961). In many ways *Life in a Welsh countryside* may be regarded as an anthropological interlude which, despite its limitations (which are more recognisable now than in 1950) constituted a major achievement. It is difficult to find a better introduction to the rural life of Wales as a whole in the first half of the twentieth century.

Rees's study, as planned in 1938, was intended to be the first in a series of such studies of selected communities in various parts of Wales to be carried out by the Department of Geography and Anthropology at the University College of Wales, Aberystwyth. The original scheme was delayed by the War, and the four studies subsequently published in abbreviated form under the editorship of Elwyn Davies and Alwyn D. Rees in 1960 belong to the immediate post-war years. Although the studies in the form in which they appeared in the volume *Welsh rural communities* were largely complementary in approach and coverage, they were unfortunately not planned as a co-ordinated project of research. The absence of an overall plan meant that there was no controlled investigation on comparative lines of significant variations in the pattern of Welsh rural life as revealed in the study of Llanfihangel. Two of the studies—those of Aberdaron and Tregaron—dealt with the functions of a rural neighbourhood and a small market town and, as the editors pointed out, were to a large extent complementary.

T. Jones Hughes's (1960) contribution on Aberdaron, situated at the tip of the Llŷn peninsula in south Caernarfonshire, was subtitled 'The social geography of a small region' and had a somewhat different emphasis from that of Alwyn Rees. Geography was concerned with spatial relationships rather than social relationships, or, at least, with social relationships in their spatial dimension, if it dealt with them at all. Geography was also interested in man's adaptation to his environment—in how farming, settlement, housing, social groups and so on, were related to the physical setting in which they were found: i.e., to the nature of the earth's surface, to climate and vegetation. Professor Hughes approached Aberdaron from this broadly ecological viewpoint. To use a comparison drawn from the world of the theatre, he was especially interested in the layout of the stage and in the scenery among which the action of the play took place. He was also interested in the plot and in the roles of the participants, but only to the extent it was necessary to invoke their assistance to account for the existence of particular kinds of stage props and to explain why the action took place in one part of the stage rather than another. The vicissitudes of the farming economy and demography were dealt with in accordance with this approach. In the author's words, 'The emphasis has been laid wherever possible on the distribution of the material and non-material elements of the culture' (1960:123). In this study local topography featured more prominently than in Rees's book. One gets the impression that there was a more frequent use of place-names, for example, and micro-geographical divisions loom large: individual neighbourhoods were described in a fair amount of detail, the emphasis being placed on the differences between them in very concrete terms. One neighbourhood had two chapels belonging to different denominations, the smallholders supporting one, the other being the affair of a single family; a corrugated shed near one of the chapels had become a general stores serving the neighbourhood. In this instance the chapel was the first manifestation of the existence of the neighbourhood; the shop came later and gave it a further nucleus. Another neighbourhood was the village of Aberdaron itself which was growing at the expense of the surrounding country-side; villagers were tenants and there was no continuous occupation by village families; Wesleyan methodists predominated. Geographical variations within the parish, in terms of what appeared to be rather superficial social categories, were chronicled at length, and one feels that the author was asserting that even the parish, which we usually take for granted as a basic unit, was a world in itself and had its own divisions and diversity which were important at a local level.

To give another example, within this small region six miles long by five miles across, Hughes saw a dichotomy between the eastern and western parts in terms of nineteenth-century tenurial conditions which he is able to trace back to medieval times. In the east there were compact and continuous farms on the sites of earlier hamlets bearing the same names, for example, one farm which many centuries ago consisted of a group of small holdings with intermingled fields. In the west these medieval conditions survived in part: there were still small holdings of a few scattered acres providing a meagre livelihood. This division was significant in terms of social geography, but although Hughes referred to the near-peasant nature of small-farming in Llŷn, and to its almost scavenging economy, he did not describe the ramifications of these features in the community's social life. How did the small farmer co-exist with the large farmer and what economic relationships were there between them; how were these reflected, for example, in stratification, prestige and leadership? Hughes stopped short of presenting an analysis of the community beginning with its ecological basis in the land and, to a lesser extent, the sea. He would probably have argued that this would take him beyond the limits of social geography and away from his legitimate preoccupation with the micro-region.

Emrys Jones (1960), in his contribution to the volume, dealt with the small town of Tregaron in central Cardiganshire. His analysis of the functions of this market town in many ways complemented Hughes's study of a country neighbourhood. Tregaron had a population of only six hundred, but was essentially urban in function. 'In rural Wales', we are told, 'size is not an important criterion' in defining a town (1960:87). Rural Wales in this respect resembled Ireland rather than England. Even in industrial Wales many of the populous settlements were hardly towns in the usual sense, and geographers not surprisingly found it difficult to classify Welsh urban settlements with hierarchical arrangements worked out on the basis of English criteria. Emrys Jones in this study did not seek to see Tregaron in relation to any hypothetical urban hierarchy as other geographers had done; instead, he concentrated on the life of this little market town and asked himself what kind of social differentiation existed in what he emphasised was an urban settlement, despite its small size.

He distinguished four neighbourhoods in the town and was able to correlate these with periods in the economic development of the settlement. First, there was the *llan*, the old village around the church, which from the thirteenth century had a right to a yearly fair and subsequently to other fairs and markets. Because of a toll-free route leading eastwards, cattle droving to the fairs of Barnet, Banbury and Kent added to the importance of the little village in the eighteenth century. Blacksmiths and innkeepers flourished, and a new neighbourhood around Chapel Street emerged. A third neighbourhood of small cottages built on a drained common came into existence in the mid-nineteenth century with the establishment of a hosiery trade, and Station Road, with its air of suburbia, came into being with the coming of the railway in 1866. The cattle now went by train, but the link with London established by the drovers survived the change from cattle trading to milk selling, hence the traditional mid-Cardiganshire predominance among London Welshmen, including millionaires and multi-millionaires. With this change Tregaron reverted to a small market town serving the surrounding countryside in a manner described in detail by Jones, its existence based on the inflow and outflow of goods, services and people. Within the community there was surprising differentiation in terms of occupational groups. Forty-five percent of all employed persons were in administrative, professional, managerial and proprietorial jobs. Fifteen percent were craftsmen and specialized workers, thirty-nine percent were unskilled workers and labourers. Yet any stratification was restricted by the smallness of the community, by the face-to-face character of social relationships, and by the sectarian organisation which cut across other divisions. Family connections were important, for example, in local elections, the results of which, in terms of the votes cast for each candidate, could be calculated by any one with a sound knowledge of local families. Emrys Jones did not pursue the implications of its small size on the social structure of Tregaron beyond citing interesting examples. His aim, rather, was to present a comprehensive portrait of the town's social characteristics which could be compared in general terms with other portraits of communities.

The contribution by the present writer to *Welsh rural communities* (Owen 1960) dealt with a single aspect of the life of a community, Glan-llyn, located only fifteen miles northwest of Llanfihangel but separated from it by the geographical barrier of the high moorlands of the Berwyn. Much of the formal social life of Glan-llyn in 1949 took place in the fifteen small neighbourhood chapels: there was one chapel for every sixty-three inhabitants in this overwhelmingly nonconformist community, and each chapel was a centre for meetings on week nights as well as on Sundays. I found myself asking why it was that these nonconformist chapels which had been expressly founded to house congregations which had turned their backs on the world had become the scene of so much of the community's formal social life. One way of answering this question, it seemed to me, was to turn to the history of Llanuwchllyn, for which, as it happens, there exists a fair amount of relevant documentary material. In the eighteenth century and later the district was well known for its stocking industry which was carried on in the farmhouses during the winter evenings. Neighbours assembled on the hearth, each bringing his or her needles—men knitted, too, in those days—to knit stockings and to enjoy a sociable evening spent in singing impromptu verses, gossiping and telling stories. These informal meetings were held in different houses on different evenings and were an important part of the social life of the community. The eighteenth-century nonconformists took advantage of these 'knitting nights' and turned them into preaching meetings and prayer meetings. This proved extremely successful, and in the early nineteenth century numerous small chapels were built in the various neighbourhoods to house the growing congregations and the increasingly frequent activities. But it was not only the religious meetings that were transferred from the isolated farmstead. Some of the harmless competitive entertainments found on the hearth were also transferred and incorporated in the secular side of chapel life where they took root. Thus it is possible to explain in historical terms how the situation in Glan-llyn came about; but this, of course, tells us nothing about the significance of this alignment of formal secular activities with religious organisation, nor, for that matter, does it help to explain why, in the first place—and quite paradoxically—an originally puritanical system came to embrace such worldly activities. These features called for a sociological explanation which took account of the nature of religious sects and their transformation over a period of time.

It was possible to compare the situation in Glan-llyn with that in a Hebridean community which resembled it in many ways but which did not have the same close connection between religious and secular social life (Owen 1956). In fact, so far as it is possible to judge, the Hebridean community, in this respect, resembled the Glan-llyn of the early nineteenth century. The social rift between church and world was basic to the Hebridean situation. Secular entertainment remained wholly outside the influence of the church, and the continued existence of traditional forms such as folk-dancing, story-telling, and bagpipe-playing was largely to be understood in terms of this factor. In Glan-llyn, where secular entertainment had been brought within the sphere of the chapel's activities, these forms had been eliminated a century ago. Since church leaders in Glan-llyn actually organized entertainment their control over its content was much greater than that of the Presbyterian elders of the Hebrides who condemned something which they were powerless to influence. Even in wider terms the leaders of the Hebridean churches had less influence in the life of the community at large, whereas Glan-llyn's county and local councillors were all deacons or elders in their local chapels. Perhaps most important of all, in Glan-llyn and similar communities denominationalism was a far stronger element in social life, probably because of the way in which the original religious cleavage had been re-emphasised by the alignment of week-day secular activities on sectarian lines: one tended to vote for a fellow Methodist, to buy from a fellow Methodist, to canvass for a fellow Methodist, to let a farm or a house to a fellow Methodist—other things being equal. In Glan-llyn, the lines denoting significant differentiation in the community in this respect were vertical: they separated parallel social systems each of which had a balanced pattern of social relations covering both religious and secular activities. In the Hebridean community, while vertical lines existed, they were less important than the horizontal line which cut across each of the social systems separating church members from mere adherents. Within each social system the relationships above the line (that is, among members) were much more intensive, and those below it much less intensive than in the corresponding social systems in Glan-llyn. Secular recreation, in fact, was incorporated in the social life of the chapels at a time when, in the mid-nineteenth century, the religious organisation of Glan-llyn was changing from that of the Hebridean pattern to that of modern Wales. At this particular stage, now that the doctrinal 'charter' of the religious groups no longer emphasised the separateness of sacred and secular, the new alignment emerged.

David Jenkins's (1960) study of Aberporth, a coastal village in south Cardiganshire, touched on a similar aspect of social life, but he found a rift in the community, not on denominational grounds, but on lines not unlike those found in the Hebridean community. Whereas the cleavage there was in formal terms between members and non-members of churches, the cleavage in Aberporth existed within a social pattern similar to that in Glan-llyn. Jenkins began by examining the terms used by the inhabitants of Aberporth to describe categories of people in their midst. A classification based on the sociological convention of dividing people into upper, middle and lower classes, he suggested, was unreal and unrecognized in the behaviour of local people. The categories used locally were quite different and had distinct moral overtones: on the one hand there was *pobl y capel* ('chapel people') and, on the other, *bois y pop* ('the pop boys') and *pobl y dafarn* ('pub people'). To describe these two contrasting groups he used the terms *buchedd A* and *buchedd B*, *'buchedd'* being a Welsh word denoting behaviour and, more particularly, a 'life-style' with certain moral overtones.

The two *buchedd* groups were differentiated on the basis of social interaction, but Jenkins stressed that the common interests originate in the group and not vice versa. *Buchedd A* people tended to be regular chapel-goers, teetotallers and thrifty. Here it was the pattern of expenditure and not of income which was significant. 'Thrift', said Jenkins, 'is compatible with high or low earnings' (1960:15). House ownership statistics did not correlate simply with earnings, but also with values and attitudes governing how the earnings were spent. Eighty-four percent of *buchedd A* members were owners of the houses they occupied as compared with only forty-six percent of group 'B'. *Buchedd A* people, too, respected education both for its own sake and as a means of 'getting on in the world'. *Buchedd B* had the reverse of these features: *buchedd B* people were neither sabbatarian nor tee-totallers; they spent more on immediate pleasure and wanted their children to go out to work so that they could earn money. The distinctions between the two groups were rather more subtle than suggested here, but David Jenkins—who, unlike his co-authors, was a native of the area he studied—knew the inhabitants sufficiently well to classify them all into these two categories. Sixty percent of them were in the *buchedd A*, forty percent in *buchedd B*. What is more, whole families lay within each of these two categories and tended to marry within their approp-riate *buchedd* groups. Kinship thus did not cut across these groupings, creating conflicting allegiances, although it did provide an element of differentiation within the groups. Occupation, however, was tied up with the *buchedd* structure, but not in a straightforward manner: *buchedd A* people attached importance to prestige oc-cupations, though these were not necessarily thought of in simple financial terms. But of the *buchedd A* people only a third were in such prestige jobs, the remaining two-thirds being what Jenkins described as the most character-istic Welsh group—i.e., manual workers who were also Sunday school teachers and deacons and whose ambitions for their children were that they should find jobs in such prestige occupations as the professions, teaching and banking. Among the *buchedd B* people nearly all were in non-prestige jobs, and their children usually followed suit. Jenkins cleverly showed how the system of values rep-resented by the *buchedd* structure influenced the pattern of emigration from that area. *Buchedd A* people, he pointed out, could usually satisfy their ambition to put children in prestige jobs only by sending them outside the community, especially now that the Merchant Navy connection—and the possibility of becoming a captain which this once offered—had declined. The rural exodus, he suggested, was proportionately a far heavier drain on the intelligentsia than on other groups. It was the potential leaders, the potential supporters of the whole pattern of activities of *buchedd A* ideals—the debating society, the local eisteddfod, etc., who were drained away, ironically because of the ideals themselves. The *buchedd A* ideology, one might say, contained the seeds of its own impoverishment, if not of its own destruction.

Turning from the present to the past, David Jenkins sought an explanation of the *buchedd A* group and its ideals in the nonconformist movement of the last century, and stressed the importance of the religious 'society' (*seiat*) created by the Methodist revival. The *buchedd A* group, he suggested, was a much secularized modern descendant of the religious society—the society of believers which kept itself aloof from the world. There had been no religious revival since 1904, but the *buchedd* pattern had perpetuated itself beyond the original religious impetus, despite its indirect encouragement of emigration to get on in the world. The *buchedd B* group was the old 'world' in the theological sense, leavened to some degree by the yeast of the Elect. In 1949, both *buchedd* groups existed within an environment of Christian values—the chapel was still there in the background even if one did not attend regularly. In terms of a social hierarchy, Jenkins suggested that nonconformist values provided a status system of its own, based on a *buchedd* or partly moral style of life, which operated quite apart from that of the society at large. Beneath the landowning gentry in the accepted social class hierarchy there was the *buchedd* status group arrangement which, in Jenkins's view, submerged disnctions based on other grounds (such as occupation) although it did not obliterate them. In Aberporth, he concluded, the latter constituted secondary differences within the overall *buchedd* group structure.

Of the studies included in *Welsh rural communities* David Jenkins's Aberporth, particularly his treatment of the *buchedd* division, has attracted most attention among British sociologists. On the one hand, it has seemed to other writers with an intimate knowledge of Wales to possess a wider application to the study of Welsh society in general. In an interesting discussion of the 'Folk of Wales: myth and reality' Dr. Prys Morgan (1967; reprinted in Chapter 5) suggested that in other areas of Wales the consistency of the status group might vary internally, giving a *buchedd A* minus or a *buchedd B* plus, as it were, as well as in the relative strength of the two groups. Jenkins's estimate that sixty percent of the people of Aberporth belonged to group 'A' and forty percent to group 'B' might well not hold for other communities where the local 'mix' reflected different historical developments and circumstances. In an industrial setting no doubt the class differences underemphasised in Jenkins's study would come to the fore. In relating the Aberporth evidence to social stratification in British society as a whole, Graham Day and Martin Fitton (1975) made the important point that the people of Aberporth existed within the class structure of the engulfing society, even though that structure might not be observable.

Ronald Frankenberg's study *Village on the border* was published in 1957 and thus appeared before *Welsh rural communities* although the fieldwork was actually carried out in 1953-54. The village in question, Glyn Ceiriog, Denbighshire, was concealed under the name *'Pentre-diwaith'*, literally 'village without work', pointing to the fact that the community had lost the economic basis of its existence when its slate quarries were closed before the Second World War. This was central to Frankenberg's analysis, but we are not told whether the choice of Glyn Ceiriog was governed by it or whether it was a pure accident which came to light during the field investigation. Glyn Ceiriog was not typical of rural Wales, but the selection of a representative community was far from being Frankenberg's purpose. His concern was with the study of social processes observable in a single place studied over a single year although the findings might have a wider relevance.

Frankenberg was strongly influenced in his approach by the work of Professor Max Gluckam of Manchester who contributed an introduction to the book. Gluckman's theoretical leanings are apparent in all his published work, the best known and most accessible of his books being *Custom and conflict in Africa* published in 1955. As the title suggests, Gluckman (1955:2) emphasises conflict as a fundamental process in social life:

> Men quarrel in terms of certain of their customary allegiances but are restrained from violence through other conflicting allegiances which are also enjoined on them by custom. . . . Conflicts are a part of social life, and custom appears to exacerbate these conflicts, but in so doing custom also restrains the conflicts from destroying the wider social order.

Even the conflicts conflict and, paradoxiaclly, lead to cohesion.

The emphasis in this approach lies in a dynamic view of social life: decisions taken in actual situations, or behaviour observed in the course of a sequence of events, are capable of being analysed in terms of the relative strength of conflicting allegiances. One anthropologist, J. A. Barnes (1959:13-15), described Frankenberg's book as the observation and analysis of politics round the village pump, politics being used here in the sense of action seeking to influence the decision of policy, or actions associated with competition in terms of power. These topics, in fact, were Frankenberg's main preoccupation, and he found his raw material in his own direct and detailed observation of events which took place in Glyn Ceiriog during his year of residence there. His descriptions of the culture of Glyn Ceiriog were minimal, attitudes were described because they helped to explain the moves made by people on committees in terms of contrasting allegiances, and even social structure in formal terms was not followed up in detail. To use Barnes's words 'we can see a community in action and not merely a set of role-playing, norm-oriented persons going through their paces' (1959: 13-15). The cultural detail was left out because it was either familiar—e.g. the rules of football or of committee procedure—or because it had been dealt with in general terms by writers such as Alwyn Rees and did not need to be repeated, since it was not of direct concern to the anthropologist's purpose as he saw it. Studying a community with a known history and environment enabled him to dispense with much of the introductory material on ecology and general background which normally prefaced social anthropological analyses (Frankenberg 1957: 148). His main interest was in the social processes stripped of their cultural idiom and reduced to functional terms.

Glyn Ceiriog, as was noted briefly, could not offer any work to its menfolk who therefore had to make a daily journey down the valley to miscellaneous jobs in nearby towns and on building sites. Thus Glyn Ceiriog women who remained at home interacted with each other more than did the menfolk, and there was a rift in the village between the sexes. This was reflected in several ways: the womenfolk could discuss local affairs together and come to a decision as a group much more easily than could the men; such organisations as the British Legion and the Football Club had separate women's sections which were powerful; pubs were the men's territory, the women had their sewing classes; women's organisations on the whole flourished, men's did not. In peasant societies the division of sex roles forges the family into an organic unit because of the complementary nature of the male and female roles, a point emphasised in Arensberg's study of the Irish Countryman. In Glyn Ceiriog this division had extended outside the elementary family and created a real division within the community. Apart from this, Frankenberg saw further divisions on class and economic lines, for example, between local people and outsiders who had moved in—

this had a key significance as we shall see—between church and chapel, and between English speakers and Welsh speakers. These, however, were bequeathed to Glyn Ceiriog by divisions derived from its past and from the larger society in which it existed, i.e., they were national divisions found locally. All these divisions, of course, cut across each other, and conflict balanced conflict to produce order rather than chaos. However,

> despite such cross-linkages between groups there is always a danger that their mutual hostility may awaken. The attempt to avoid such open conflicts which disrupt social relations within the village is a very marked feature of the social life of Pentrediwaith. This has several minor effects on the day-to-day behaviour of villagers. Thus Pentre people rarely give the lie direct to statements made in public, or even to those made in private by people with whom they are not on very intimate terms. Villagers rarely refuse a request, but delay indefinitely fulfilling one of which they disapprove. Committee minutes often leave out names and details, for committees of the village, like the village itself, must maintain an appearance of impersonal, unanimous even leaderless unity (Frankenberg 1957:18).

To avoid awakening dormant hostilities, 'strangers' were brought into an activity to take the responsibility for decisions and withstand the unpopularity of leadership. 'Stranger' was a shifting concept, and a 'stranger' in one context was not a 'stranger' in another. Even Frankenberg was not a stranger in certain situations. A local person who was not actually born in the village might be a stranger in certain other situations, but outsiders, of course, made ideal 'strangers' in this sense, and were often made scapegoats.

In this view of community life as a perpetual state of concealed hostility combined with an obsession to prevent, at almost any cost, an open breach, two aspects of social activity were of great significance: first, committee practice, when participants did their utmost to avoid committing themselves in situations of almost open conflict; and second, gossip, which was informal and which both united and divided the community. 'Gossip', said Frankenberg (1957:21) 'was used as a vehicle through which criticism and conflict could be expressed without ripening into open hostility. Private gossip was, in a sense, a licensed method of airing public grievances in private'. 'Gossip, and even scandal', said Gluckman in an article on these two features, 'unite a group within a larger society, or against another group.' 'By gossiping,' he added, 'we maintain our membership of a group and exclude outsiders: there is no such thing as 'idle gossip.' Disputes, quarrels, gossip and scandals have the effect of maintaining the village as a village and of preventing it from becoming a collection of houses like a housing estate. 'Town planners', wrote Gluckman, 'are very anxious to turn housing states into communities: they should develop scandal in them. Perhaps it is their duty to provide cause for it' (Gluckman 1963;307-16). Gossip, as a social process, was far more central to Frankenberg's analysis than in Alwyn Rees's book, where it was described in much more general terms.

Frankenberg's investigations involved looking for the way in which such social processes operated in the activities which were prominent during his period of residence in the community. In one chapter he dealt with the role of the parish council in its attempts to bring work to the village and to oppose the alteration of a scheme for a bilateral secondary school (1957: Chapter 3). In relation to the outside world the parish council was impotent; nevertheless, its members were drawn from among the village's working population and could fairly be said to represent it. The rural district council and county council which possessed power consisted of partial outsiders who had an ambivalent position, explaining the community's wishes to the council and vice versa. The squabble over the new school described by Frankenberg, incidentally, brought into prominence the dormant church/chapel division.

One of the most fascinating features of *Village on the border* is the detailed study of the significance of recreation for the villagers. The Football Club and the Carnival, Frankenberg felt, affirmed the existence of Glyn Ceiriog as a community in the eyes of the outside world and to the villagers themselves, despite the loss of the community's economic basis. The internal rifts and conflicts, however, proved too powerful, and the people of Glyn Ceiriog had to abandon their Football Club and their Carnival during his stay and shortly afterwards. Frankenberg gathered this had also happened in the past when they had dispensed with their brass band and their choir. Efforts were made to avoid conflict, but once the breach was made patent it spread through the village. The face-to-face nature of social contacts, and the multiplicity of ties which close residence in an 'isolated' unit brings about, made this spread inevitable. After a period, the village became so divided that particular activities could not continue. Unfortunately, conflicts were carried over from one form of recreational activity to another, and new conflicts engendered in disputes over football and carnivals extended back into everyday life and caused further division within the village.

No attempt has been made to summarize Frankenberg's detailed treatment of the committee meetings and the attendance and manoeuvres of members, and consequent repercussions on the community. The chapter on 'The politics of recreation' is well worth reading if only as an example of intensive sociological reporting and analysis. In contrast to the dualism in Alwyn Rees's work between local detail and the general validity of his conclusions, Frankenberg's analysis contains a rather different kind of dualism. This is between the underlying social realities—the divisions and the processes of conflict—and the first-hand material, based on minute observation, which brings these to light. the fight for work, the squabble over a school, the football club and carnival episodes were all ephemeral phenomena thrown up by these processes and, in turn, exemplifying them. Had Frankenberg visited Pentre during a General Election, or during a local election year, or when the Sunday Opening battle was in full spate, or during a chapel split, then his material of observation would have been quite different. Each, however, would have presented a social drama capable of being used as a unit of social analysis. Frankenberg in another work, quotes Victor Turner's view of this concept:

> The social drama is a limited area of transparency in the otherwise opaque surface of regular, uneventful social life. Through it, we are enabled to observe the crucial principles of the social structure in their operation and their relative dominance at different points in time (1966a: 143).

His study may be said to be a vindication of this approach.

Isabel Emmet's book *A north Wales village* which appeared in 1964, is, like Frankenberg's, a study in depth with much illustrative anecdotal material. For the same reason the identity of '*Llan*', the parish in question, was concealed. It is not difficult, however, to identify the community as Llanfrothen situated in the foothills of Snowdonia in the old county of Merioneth. The choice of the area of study was governed by purely personal reasons, Emmett, who had been trained as a social anthropologist at the London School of Economics, having married into the community. Her fieldwork was carried out as a full participant in local life over the four years 1958-62. Having little faith in the usefulness of information gleaned by questionnaires as a means of understanding social behaviour, she forsook 'the door-to-door method because taking the role of house canvasser would have clashed with my desire to participate in parish activities as much as possible'. Her new information was gathered 'primarily in the hope that it will lead to insight rather than for the purposes of comparison', although it might be 'usable for comparisons with similarly intensive studies'. The 'isolated facts of the kind collected by a team of technique-laden surveyors' are not only dull, they are not true in any important sense unless they are related to each other in a general analysis of the social situation. Furthermore, as an unfamiliar society (to her) north Wales was not amenable to survey methods; instead she sought to gain insight into it. The difficulty, of course, is that it is often impossible to test the validity of knowledge gained through insight. One can feel that it is true, just as one can feel that a poem, novel or painting is true. One of the main tasks of social anthropology, she felt, was to make meaningful to other people the apparently senseless or mischievous or strange activity of any group. To be an outsider (at the outset, at least) has the virtue of possessing an external standard of relevance to provoke insight. To Emmett such a comparison presented three paradoxes which her book set out to explain, namely the absence of class distinction, the importance of salmon-poaching which had no apparent motive, least of all economic, and the high rate of illegitimacy in a chapel-dominated society (Emmett 1964: preface).

Emmett's analysis of the first paradox led her to identify a social hierarchy in which, beneath the apex represented by the local landowners, there existed a basic Welsh/English opposition manifesting itself in the two parallel status systems or opposing prestige ladders. The English system, that of the larger engulfing society, was the familiar arrangement based on the social grading of occupations. The Welsh system was conceived in terms of Welshness, that is, climbing the Welsh ladder led one to assert Welshness and to identify oneself with native tradition—towards which Emmett, incidentally, was particularly sympathetic. It was the Welsh prestige ladder which unified the parish, and Emmett felt that her analysis of this feature might have a wider application to other parts of the world in their attempts to resist Anglo-Americanisation. Young people differed in their response to the attractions of these opposing prestige ladders: there were those who had become anglicised in order to be in the swim; there were others who were influenced by the new ways; yet others were 'resisters' who felt that to emigrate was to betray one's roots; while another category consisted of the 'regretters' who had become anglicised and who, in their search for their roots, often became politically conscious.

In putting forward her concept of two opposing value systems Emmett rejected the *buchedd A/B* division of David Jenkins. The Welsh value system, she maintained, was a relatively coherent mixture of chapel and all that chapel was against. In fact, by emphasising the English/Welsh conflict she appeared to telescope the two *buchedd* groups into one paradoxical group united only by the stress laid on Welshness. Her emphasis on the English/Welsh conflict may have resulted from the fortuitous choice of Llanfrothen which had a sizeable colony of English people living at least part of the year in the cottages left empty by depopulation, a feature which became more prominent throughout the whole of northwest Wales in subsequent years. In Llanfrothen, the landowner, Sir Clough Williams-Ellis had encouraged the settlement of a colony of English intelligentsia, thus giving the area the nickname of 'the Greenwich Village of Wales'. The constant emphasis on partisanship which Emmett made in her analysis would appear to have been exacerbated by the chance occurrence of an 'Englishry' and a 'Welshry', to use historical terms, in what was, at the time, a rather exceptional village. In wider terms one can argue that the sociology of '*Llan*' as depicted by Emmett was the sociology of plantation.

Emmett's analysis of the second paradox, namely the prevalence of salmon-poaching without economic incentive, depended very much on her insight. These observations are difficult to contradict but equally difficult to find totally convincing. Poaching, which took place largely out of season when the fish could not be sold, was part of the partisan battle against officialdom. All the menfolk went poaching during the five or six weeks in late Autumn when the fish came upstream to spawn. Because it was illegal, and because both police and bailiffs were on the look-out, it became a battle of wits between outside authority and the local grapevine which involved almost everybody in the local community. '*Llan* people' won few open battles with English officialdom in the class suggested, but this was one battle which they did win. Poaching, she suggested was part of being Welsh, and the conspiracy which it brought about activated the community and drew people together, cutting across village quarrels and differences in income, religion, sex and age; it symbolized unity, fellowship and solidarity.

> The motives in the people's minds as they engage in the action which brings them together are non-economic. The result of their fusion is that their mutual co-operation in economic affairs is helped, and I do not think the poaching conspiracy would continue in its present strength if those involved in it needed each other's support and service less (1964:76).

Motives, however, were not her primary concern as an anthropologist: it was the outcome of the activity to which she felt she should devote her attention, that is, solidarity. Formerly the chapel was the central symbol of Welshness which brought people together. This was no longer the case, according to Emmett; participation in the salmon poaching conspiracy and in the anti-English feeling generally had become a much more important and general badge of Welshness than the chapel.

Emmett's third paradox was that of illegitimacy in a chapel-dominated society, which she hinted, was part of the coherent mixture of all that chapel stood for and all that it was against. The incongruousness of ideal and actual behaviour was, of course, nothing new, and she suggested that where it existed people had to pretend not to know half of what they actually knew about each other if they were to live together harmoniously in a small community. We are back again on the subject of gossip, not in its active form, as in the grapevine connected with poaching, but in the negative form of feigned ignorance and avoidance. 'Gossip is the commodity which is exchanged most in country life: it is the currency of social relationships and the *Llan* man saves it up to help himself and his relatives' (Emmett 1964:117). Withholding gossip, she emphasised, kept dangerous situations from breaking out and helped to reconcile the verbal adherence of the chapel and the frequent breaches of it in practice. As in Frankenberg's study, gossip had a central place in the social life of the little community.

Emmett's book, although avowedly idiosyncratic in its reliance on insight, had the virtue of relating the author's findings to other known studies, as in her treatment of Jenkins's *buchedd A/B* findings in the analysis of *Llan's* prestige ladders. She also examined Frankenberg's ideas about the role of the 'outsider' in Glyn Ceiriog and found that in Llanfrothen the outsider was not made a scapegoat, largely because the language difference was more prominent and because there was no threat of obliteration of the community's identity. Outsiders in Llanfrothen were intermediaries rather than scapegoats. The operation of the scapegoat principle took place on a higher level: it was England and the English—and not individual Englishmen—who were blamed for major ills. Like Frankenberg, Emmett identified one of the features of social change which were to become significant in the nineteen-sixties and seventies. The polarisation which she discerned in Llanfrothen later manifested itself in the spread of such organisations as the Welsh-speaking women's movement *Merched y Wawr* and the Welsh Language Society in response to the spread of second homes and retirement in-migration, just as the economic decline, the consequences of which Frankenberg investigated in his 'village without work', was to become true of other villages transformed into commuter settlements.

The final work to be considered in this chapter is David Jenkins's *The agricultural community in south-west Wales at the turn of the twentieth century*, published in 1971 and based on fieldwork carried out in 1958-61, but relating, as the title indicates, to a much earlier period. The volume cannot properly be regarded as a continuation of the author's earlier study of Aberporth, although it deals with an adjoining district. The historical emphasis is dominant and the scope of the work is much broader. In some respects it may be described as a sequel to Alwyn Rees's pioneer contribution but relating to an earlier 'ethnographic present' and drawing in considerable detail on oral history. The approach is broadly ecological with the aim of showing 'how the form of the society was related to the needs of working the land' (1971:) but includes a detailed analysis of religion, including the religious revivial of 1904-5, the last of the great religious upheavals of the nineteenth century, which exerted a powerful influence on south Cardiganshire. The volume is a major contribution to the historical anthropology of Wales in which the author succeeds in his aim, namely 'to study the structure of the society, and the changes in that structure during the lifetime of those who are now aged' (1971:5). It is not a community study in the strictest sense, being concerned 'with the structure of a society that does not consist of discrete communities' (1971:9). However, just as Alwyn Rees used data relating to Llanfihangel-yng-Ngwynfa to provide a statistical basis for a discussion of wider application, so David Jenkins chose one parish, Troed-yr-aur, for detailed investigation while stressing the broader relevance of the work.

In his work on Aberporth Jenkins contributed his important analysis of the *buchedd A* and *B* status groups in a largely egalitarian local community in which the holders of authority and owners of property were generally absent. In the broader-based historical study the land-owning gentry came in within the author's purview, together with the landlord-tenant system as it existed in south Cardiganshire. One of the most interesting sections of the book, however, is that which deals with ecologically-based relationships beneath the social stratum of the local gentry before the widespread introduction of harvesting machinery (1971:Chapter 2).

In south Cardiganshire the mild climate and plentiful rain gave a prolific growth of grass during the summer months. This was used by local farmers to feed and fatten calves born in the previous spring, the surplus milk being made into salted butter to be sold in tubs to merchants in the small market towns. When the grass stopped growing in the autumn the young cattle were sold off in local fairs, but for those which were retained on the farm, fodder had to be provided locally in the form of hay, root crops and barley. To obtain these the farmer had, of course, to plough his land, and thus needed horses. These also required fodder, and so the farmer needed to grow oats to feed his horses as well as for human consumption in the form of traditional foods such as porridge, oatmeal and other milk and buttermilk based 'spoon foods'. Since there was little money to buy artificial fertilizers, the farmyard manure which had accumulated over the winter months was the only means used to keep the cultivated land fertile, apart from the rotation of crops. Such was the ecological basis of the tenant farmers' operations.

In this local economy thirty to thirty-five acres were needed to support a married couple without a supplementary income, and a farm of this size would have had one pair of horses worked by an unmarried farm servant who was hired annually and lived with the family. Larger farms of up to 150 to 200 acres, of which there were but a few, might have had two pairs of horses and two farm servants. Such farms also employed labourers on a weekly or daily basis for hedging and ditching. However, only one-fifth of the households in Troed-yr-aur parish fell into these two classes. There were far more smaller farms of fifteen to twenty acres which could maintain only one horse, as well as even smaller holdings of under fifteen acres which could only manage to keep a single cow. Below them came the cottagers, 'the people of the little houses', who had only a garden and a pig and who usually supplemented their income with earnings from labouring or from a craft. In the course of his investigations Jenkins found that four-fifths of the households, those with under thirty acres of land, depended in one way or another on the remaining one-fifth. Even farms of between thirty and sixty acres depended on the larger farms for the services of a bull, which was an expensive but vital animal to keep in this cattle-rearing economy. This dependence was, indeed, better described as interdependence, since the farms, including the larger farms, in turn, had to rely on the small holders and cottagers for essential help during the hay, corn and potato harvests. In fact, a network of symbiotic relationships existed in the district which was basic to its social structure at the turn of the century.

This symbiosis was to be seen in many forms. All the farms and smallholdings which required the services of the bull incurred a debt which was paid in the form of free labour during the hay harvest in most cases, one day for each cow served. Similarly, small farms with only one horse needed to borrow another horse from a larger farm in order to plough, and thus owed obligations which were again repaid at harvest time. But the most significant form of interdependence involved the cottagers and the farmers, and centred on the potato field on the farm. In Jenkins's words, 'The practice of setting out potatoes can properly be said to constitute a linkage between the social and agricultural systems' (1971:54).

The form this co-operation took can best be illustrated by selecting as an example, one of the largest farms which was 220 acres in size, and which had forty acres under corn that had to be cut by scythe and bound. This required seventy-five working days, with a further twenty-five working days for stooking and stacking. The staff of the farm itself, which numbered eight, could not hope to cope with this work, especially as ordinary farm routine needed attention as well. The additional labour required was, in this case, supplied by twenty-four cottager families in the district in return for the right to grow potatoes in the potato field on the farm. The arrangement was this: for each row of about 100 to 120 yards in length which was ploughed, manured, closed and weeded by the farmer in his potato field, each cottager had to provide one day's free labour in the corn harvest, as well as planting and harvesting the farmer's potatoes. The twenty-four cottager families had an average of four rows of potatoes, depending on their requirements, and therefore provided ninety-six working days' labour during the critical period of the corn harvest in September. In addition, the farmer applied most of the farmyard manure to his potato field, which was changed from year to year, the land being kept in good tilth in this way. The smallholder, in particular the cottager, needed his potatoes not only for household purposes, but also to feed his pigs which were kept both for his own consumption and for selling to pay the rent. Furthermore, on the basis of this form of co-operation between farmer and cottager, other links were established over the whole year and not merely during the active working season. Cottagers were invited to a meal on the farm on New Year's day; small gifts of buttermilk, butter or bread were made and rights of gleaning and gathering firewood were enjoyed. Carriage of coal was often arranged by the farmer, and in August, between the hay and corn harvests, the farmers used to run a trip to the seaside in their carts for their potato-setting groups of cottagers.

This institution was, then, an important feature of the local society until the coming of the self-binder toward the end of the nineteenth century, which meant that the reaping party was no longer necessary on the same scale. Previously, a larger farmer, Jenkins pointed out, would be in a position to direct the labour of more than a hundred people, including the cottagers' children, not only during the corn and potato harvests but during the potato-planting as well—a reflection of his standing in the local community. The arrangement amounted to an almost feudal relationship, or an economic patron-client relationship, which had its origin in a period much earlier than that with which Jenkins was concerned, for the connection between farm and cottage was one which was continued over the generations. As Jenkins suggested, the system was probably older than the introduction of the potato, which became a staple food in the eighteenth century, and was an elaboration and regional development of earlier feudal-like harvest arrangements.

David Jenkins's volume on south west Wales at the turn of the century marked the end of a brief tradition of community studies in Wales extending over two decades. In some ways it marked a return to the earlier pattern established by *Life in a Welsh countryside* with its dual emphasis on parish and region and its comprehensive coverage (with the notable exceptions of status and politics). Like Rees, Jenkins is concerned with an historical set-up, but at a greater distance in time. His search for earlier social conditions arose not from an idealized view of the past, but from a realization that the far-reaching changes brought by technological innovation at the end of the nineteenth century could still be studied through the oral evidence of survivors of that period. Despite the significance of the historical stance adopted by Jenkins at a time when other writers, notably George Ewart Evans (1956, 1960) were exploring the possibilities of oral history in recording rural life, his work remained squarely within the social anthropological tradition. Jenkins, in fact, made no use of the tape recorder and there are few direct quotations from informants in his book. His treatment of oral evidence, however, was meticulous and involved numerous visits to his historical witnesses before using their testimony alongside that of other contemporary evidence. His informants were not 'tradition-bearers' in the sense in which that term is used in folklife studies, the knowledge which they imparted was based on direct participation: they were delayed eyewitnesses rather than passive transmitters of an old tradition.

Conclusions

The community studies carried out in Wales and published between 1950 and 1971 showed few signs of a systematic development of theory. Those carried out by Welsh researchers reflected their basic grounding in human geography and anthropology rather than sociology, the academic development of which in Wales came too late to influence their approach. The 'outsiders', who brought with them a freshness of perception, saw the social processes, especially gossip, rather than the formal social structure, as central to community life. With the growth of sociology as an academic discipline in the University of Wales, interest extended beyond a community study method of limited application to a sociology of

Wales as a whole, including studies of limited areas of social life, such as family organisation, religion and politics, carried out within local or regional communities (Rosser and Harris 1957; D. Ben Rees 1975; Madgwick, Griffiths and Walker 1973), as well as studies of language ethnicity, second homes and other social characteristics of sparsely inhabited areas (Williams 1978, Bollom 1978, Wenger 1980), hints of which were to be discerned in the earlier community studies.

References

Arensberg, C. M.
1937 *The Irish countryman.* London: Macmillan.

Arensberg, C. M. and S. T. Kimball
1940 *Family and community in Ireland.* Glouster, Mass. Peter Smith.

Barnes, J. A.
1959 'Politics without parties', *Man* 1959: 13-15.

Boissevain, J. and J. Friedl (eds.)
1975 *Beyond the community: social process in Europe.* The Hague: Dept. of Education Science of the Netherlands.

Bollom, C.
1978 *Attitudes and second homes in rural Wales.* Cardiff: University of Wales Press.

Carter, Ian
1976 'The peasantry of northeast Scotland', *Journal of peasant studies*, 3, 151-191.

Davies, Elwyn and Alwyn D. Rees (eds.)
1960 *Welsh rural communities.* Cardiff: University of Wales Press.

Day, Graham and Martin Fitton
1975 'Religion and social status in rural Wales: *buchedd* and its lessons for concepts of stratification in community studies, *Sociological review*, 23, 867-91.

Emmett, Isabel
1964 *A north Wales village.* London: Routledge and Kegan Paul.

Evans, George Ewart
1956 *Ask the fellows who cut the hay.* London: Faber and Faber.
1960 *The horse in the furrow.* London: Faber and Faber.

Frankenberg, Ronald
1957 *Village on the border.* London: Cohen and West.
1966a 'British community studies: problems of synthesis' in *The social anthropology of complex societies.* Edited by M. Banton. London: Tavistock.
1966b *Communities in Britain.* London: Penguin.

Gluckman, Max
1955 *Custom and conflict in Africa.* London: Blackwell.
1963 'Gossip and scandal', *Current anthropology,* 4, 307-16.

Hillery, G. A. Jr.
1955 'Definitions of community: areas of agreement', *Rural sociology,* 20, 111-23.

Homans, George C.
1942 *English villagers of the thirteenth century.* Cambridge: Harvard University Press.

Hughes, T. Jones
1960 'Aberdaron: the social geography of a small region in the Llŷn Peninsula' in *Welsh rural communities.* Edited by Elwyn Davies and Alwyn D. Rees. Cardiff: University of Wales Press.

Jenkins, David
1960 'Aber-porth: a study of a coastal village in south Cardiganshire' in *Welsh rural communites.* Edited by Elwyn Davies and Alwyn D. Rees. Cardiff: University of Wales Press.
1971 *The agricultural community in southwest Wales at the turn of the twentieth century.* Cardiff: University of Wales Press.

Jones, Emrys
1960 'Tregaron: the sociology of a market town in central Cardiganshire' in *Welsh rural communities.* Edited by Elwyn Davies and Alwyn D. Rees. Cardiff: University of Wales Press.

Jones, R. M. (ed.)
1976 *Ym marn Alwyn D. Rees.* Abertawe: Christopher Davies.

Macfarlane, Alan
1977 'History, anthropology and the study of communities', *Social history*, 5, 631-52.
Madgwick, P., N. Griffiths and V. Walker
1973 *The politics of rural Wales: a study of Cardiganshire.* London: Hutchinson
Miner, Horace C.
1939 *St. Denis: a French Canadian parish.* Chicago: University of Chicago Press.
Morgan, Prys
1967 'Gwerin Cymru—y ffaith a'r ddelfryd', *Transactions of the Honourable Society of Cymmrodorion*, Session 1967, 117-31.
Newby, Howard
1977 *The deferential worker.* London: A. Lane.
Owen, Trefor M.
1956 'The communion season and Presbyterianism in a Hebridean community', *Gwerin*, 1, 53-66.
1960 'Chapel and community in Glan-llyn, Merioneth' in *Welsh rural communities.* Edited by Elwyn Davies and Alwyn D. Rees. Cardiff: University of Wales Press.
Rees, Alwyn D.
1943 *Adfeilion.* Llandybie: Llyfrau'r Dryw.
1950 *Life in a Welsh countryside.* Cardiff: University of Wales Press.
Rees, Alwyn and Brinley Rees
1961 *Celtic heritage.* London: Thames and Hudson.
Rees, D. Ben
1975 *Chapels in the valley.* Upton: Ffynnon Press.
Rhys, John and D. Brynmor-Jones
1900 *The Welsh people.* London: T. F. Unwin.
Rosser, C. and C. C. Harris
1957 *The family and social change.* London: Routledge and Kegan Paul.
Royal Commission on Labour
1893 *The agricultural labourer, II Wales.* London.
Royal Commission on Land in Wales and Monmouthshire
1894-95 *Minutes of evidence* (5 vols.) and *Report* (1896). London.
Stacey, M.
1969 'The myth of community studies', *British journal of sociology*, 20, 134-47.

Wenger, G. C.
1980 *Mid Wales: deprivation or development.* Cardiff: University of Wales Press.

Williams, G. (ed.)
1978 *Social and cultural change in contemporary Wales.* London: Routledge and Kegan Paul.

Chapter Five

The *Gwerin* of Wales—Myth and Reality*

Prys Morgan

The point of this essay is to try to translate the untranslatable. One single word cannot convey *gwerin* into English. Since the 1890s the word has gathered about itself a richness of meaning, sonorous with ambiguous overtones, because of its use as a myth or generalisation about Welsh society. Although for decades it has lived in Welsh-speaking society, it has recently appeared in English as 'the gwerin' or (because of the mutated form in Welsh) as 'the werin'. This essay attempts to trace the origin of the word in its ordinary literal meaning, then its mythical meaning in the work of Welsh authors from the 1890s to the 1930s. It traces the origin of this elaborate concept back to the crisis in Welsh society in the 1830s and 40s, and asks why the concept should be turned into a form of propaganda from the 1890s onwards, and how it could survive as a myth about Welsh society right up to the present day.[1]

Gwerin is a feminine singular noun, with a collective meaning. Words similar to it appear in the other Celtic tongues, and the older signification seems to be 'host' or 'force', 'band of warriors' or 'rank and file of an army'. By the sixteenth century (e.g. in the Bible of 1588) it had come to mean the common folk as opposed to the nobility, that is, the lower orders or the masses. Indeed it remained until recently in several south Welsh dialects with the meaning of a 'mass' of anything, not just of people. A diminutive of *gwerin* was the word *gwerinos* and this

* This is a revised and updated version of the original paper first published as P. Morgan 'Gwerin Cymru, y ffaith a'r ddelfryd' in the *Transactions of the Honourable Society of Cymmrodorion*, Session 1967, 117-31.

meant rabble or mob, or could be used in a more sympathetic way as a term of pity, thus Thomas Roberts of Llwynrhudol in his *Cwyn yn erbyn Gorthrymder* ['Complaint against Oppression'] said in 1798 that he wrote it for the *gwerinos* of Wales as a radical protest. The word *gwerin* or more fully *gwerin-bobol*, literally the 'mass of the people', is used quite commonly in current Welsh in a matter-of-fact or literal way.[2]

The problem does not arise with this common usage, but with its symbolic usage since the 1880s or 90s, often with the capital letters *Y Werin*, as one of those generalisations about the Welsh people which gather all sorts of overtones and undertones about them, and which, whatever reality lay behind them long ago, seem to take on a life of their own even when that reality disappears. Most Welsh-language writers, with some notable exceptions, have referred to the Gwerin, but in order to analyse what the characteristics or virtues of the Gwerin are it would be best to concentrate on the work of four of them: John Morris Jones in his poetry, Owen M. Edwards in his numerous prose writings up to his death in 1920, Crwys Williams (the Archdruid Crwys), especially his poetry written before 1920, and Professor W. J. Gruffydd in his essays written before 1939. The first three writers show the ideal as it was formed and developed from 1890 to 1914, the last shows a strong sense that the age of that ideal Gwerin had passed by the 1920s and 30s.[3]

For these writers the word could not be translated simply as 'working-class', it was a term of cultural nationalism and not of class conflict or class struggle. It was an optimistic term referring to the progress of the common folk of Wales coming to the fore in the 1840s and 1850s, after centuries of passivity and mute obedience to Welsh squire and parson.[4] It excluded the Tory squirearchy and Anglican clergy, it is true, from the Welsh people, but included middle and lower classes. It looked back for its origins to the religious upheavals of the eighteenth, and the political and social upheavals of the early nineteenth centuries, paid respect to the heroes of an earlier generation, Welsh radical propagandists or publicists such as Samuel Roberts of Llanbrynmair, William Rees (Gwilym Hiraethog), David Rees of Llanelli, the 'Agitator', R. J. Derfel, Evan Jones (Ieuan Gwynedd), Henry Richard M.P. and Michael D. Jones of Bala. It also looked back in another sense to the rural pre-industrial, though recent, past of Wales. Although Owen M. Edwards as a leader of Welsh education could see in the early twentieth century the need for technical and industrial education, in his writings his Gwerin is largely rural, mountain peasantry based on memories of his childhood home Llanuwchllyn in the 1860s. Crwys came from a craftsman's family in the coal-mining village of Graig-cefn-parc near Swansea but his long poem on the Gwerin, the prize-winning poem of the National Eisteddfod of 1911, largely idealises a rural peasantry. This reflects one of the general tendencies of European art towards the pastoral rather than the industrial, but also it refers to one feature of Welsh life which made Wales a very different country from England, and that was the turning of the country folk towards radical politics from the 1850s and 60s onwards. Some Welsh historians have observed a tendency of Welsh nonconformity in general in the nineteenth century to hark back to the rural past, the pre-industrial Wales in which their movements originated.[5]

Despite this tendency to pastoral romanticism, the ideal Gwerin comprised the whole of the Welsh people, all those who counted, that is the middle and lower classes. Gwyn A. Williams in a recent work has put it precisely:

'A whole people did indeed form along this line [Nonconformist Radicalism]; like the Czechs, they came to think of themselves as classless, a *gwerin*, to use the popular term. Everything outside them came to seem only half-Welsh, they were the *real* Welsh. As they became more radical in their politics, they came to feel that they, as a Nonconformist people, *were* the Welsh nation. Henry Richard, one of their leading spokesmen, put it in so many words, echoed by Gladstone himself, "The Nonconformists of Wales are the people of Wales"'.[6] The Gwerin were also the people who had always been in Wales down the ages, through thick and thin, refusing to budge in the ebb and flow of conquests and oppressions. Their steadfast toil on the land of Wales gave them a moral right to own that land, but they were never the proprietors. Down the ages Saxon and Norman conquerors had come, Roman Catholic Bishops and Scottish stewards and land-agents had oppressed the workers of the soil, but the Gwerin were still there, biding their time. John Morris Jones, scholar, poet and friend of O. M. Edwards, expresses this well in his long poem *Cymru Rydd* ['Free Wales']:[7]

> Tis true that her *gwerin*
> Owns not an inch of the land,
> The Welsh are only pilgrims
> Upon the earth of beloved Wales,
> The arrogant conquered her,
> How often has she groaned!—
> The people which dwelled in her
> Live in dark deep captivity!

Not only were the Gwerin strongly rural in background and steadfast in the face of conquerors, stoic under their long oppression, but they were also faithful to Welsh culture in the teeth of desertion by the squirearchy and the scorn of the English. Like many Welsh intellectuals of the period Owen M. Edwards was amazed that colleagues in other nations expressed disdain for the peasantry and common people: for him the Gwerin was faithful to the finest traditions of Wales and represented the greatest strength of the nation.[8] John Morris-Jones in his long poem *Toriad y dydd* ['Break of day'], a characteristic poem of the end of the nineteenth century, portrays the Welsh language as a victim of the aristocracy—driven, bruised and broken from manors and halls; lords and proud ladies simpering in the Saxon tongue, while the Gwerin nurtured the old language in its time of injury, keeping it on their tongues and in their hearts.[9]

The Gwerin also were the guardian of truly Welsh religion. For Crwys in his poem *Gwerin Cymru* the cottage of the humble peasant outlasts the now-ruined Norman castle, the humble meeting-house triumphs over the ruined papist priory. Religious revivals had uplifted and sanctified the Gwerin:[10]

> The ruddy blush of great revivals
> Burning on her threshing-floors
> Leaves a mark on the faces of the Gwerin
> Like that of a heavenly dawn.

For Crwys even Christ himself, son of a carpenter, is a man of the Gwerin (a *gwerinwr*). Christianity was the appropriate faith for the Gwerin, and Nonconformist Christianity had made the Welsh Gwerin both godly and moral and an example to other European peoples. Alun Llywelyn-Williams has studied many of the 'bard-preachers' of the turn of the century and dubs this part of the movement 'Chapel Romanticism'.[11] The Gwerin of Wales had become moralistic, respectable: they respected the things of the mind and the struggle for education. The great progress had begun with the Griffith Jones's Circulating Schools in the eighteenth century, then went on through the Sunday Schools to the movement for colleges and the University in the mid-nineteenth century. For Crwys the University of Wales was the college of the Gwerin:[12]

> The Gwerin's college stands on the shore,
> Workmen of the land chiselled its stone,
> The Gwerin of talent dug its foundations,
> Minds never schooled put slates on its roof.
>
> Here in the cottage was the earliest desire,
> The most earnest prayer for that day to dawn,
> Here the readiest penny was offered,
> For a debt-free college and a free education.

Despite the advance of Gwerin education, the Gwerin still retained a native simplicity, innocence, closeness to nature and to the soil. If there was a roughness or lack of sophistication, then that was a virtue. Although the

Gwerin had slaved away on the land for centuries, they were the creation of fairly recent movements in Welsh religion, education and politics. W. J. Gruffydd in his biography of Owen M. Edwards said that Welsh tradition was really a recent tradition, and Professor Caerwyn-Williams in his study of the ideals of Owen M. Edwards has stated that for all his apparent childlike innocence, Owen M. Edwards realised that his Gwerin was a recent creation, the figment of the imagination of preachers and reformers.[13] This echoes the view stated by Sir John Rhŷs and Sir David Brynmor Jones in 1900 that the Welsh people were in many ways the creation of the Methodist Revival.[14]

By 1900 the common folk of Wales had become a remarkable phenomenon: according to this ideal, a classless society, progressing rapidly yet retaining a closeness to the soil, educated, religious, cultured, keen to own its own land and property, hard-working and methodical, law-abiding, temperate in drink, respecting the Sabbath, and an example to the world. An optimistic picture, worthy of the expansive spirit of Wales in the halcyon days of the British empire, but there was in it a sense of danger, fragility, and fear, implicit. Crwys said in a famous phrase 'Wales'll not be Wales, with her crown trampled underfoot' [*'Nid Cymru fydd Cymru a'i choron dan draed'*]. Even before 1900 Owen M. Edwards was aware that things were not as they used to be: the Sunday School was not developing, fewer Welsh books were being produced; the censuses were showing, if not an absolute decline, then a relative decline in Welsh-speakers; a middle class was emerging which turned its back on the older Gwerin virtues. In *Er mwyn Cymru* he prayed that the sons and grandsons of the old Gwerin would not be beguiled by the siren voices of alien power and *mores.* Crwys was also aware (as he must have been for example when he lived in the industrial settlement of Brynmawr on the borders of Breconshire and Monmouthshire) that popular culture in south Wales was undergoing a vast upheaval in his time. W. J. Gruffydd was writing after

1918 and was deeply conscious of the development of the Gwerin, and the distance of the ideal from the present reality. In many ways his writings are an elegy for a society which he believed had existed and was now passed or passing away. Gruffydd, in his life of Owen M. Edwards, said that all his life Edwards was sustained by the vision of his native village of Llanuwchllyn; the same could be said of Gruffydd that all his life he was sustained by the vision of the slate-quarrying village of Bethel, near Caernarfon, where he was born. Gruffydd belonged to the first generation of working-class children to go to the new 'County Schools'. He and his parents were sustained by the ideal that the Gwerin, if only its potential could be realised, through education and political participation, would create a wonderful world. As far as Gruffydd was concerned, the period after 1918 was one of disappointment, and the heirs of the old Gwerin seemed to him to be pettifogging, parochial and pedantic, in local and central government, in Welsh cultural and educational institutions, mere *epigoni* after an age of giants. He was too intelligent a man to believe that the great age of the Gwerin had been a happy one. He grew up in the age of the Penrhyn lock-out and in a milieu of suffering from diseases such as tuberculosis, but the Gwerin of that age had been sustained in its struggles by noble, even heroic, ideals. A pessimist, he held up the ideal of the Gwerin of the past in order to enliven a Wales that had become stagnant.[15]

An attempt has been made here to sketch in a few characteristics of the Gwerin as idealised by some Welsh-language writers from the 1890s to the 1930s, some of whom were aware that their Gwerin was the result of a fairly recent tradition. Where had these writers come by their image of Welsh society? Had the ideal Gwerin been a reality in any sense in the previous generations? As we have mentioned the notion of a common people (*gwerin*) separated from the gentry (*bonedd*) is to be found as far back as the sixteenth century in Welsh writing. Such a separation was not very significant in a society such as Wales, say in the sixteenth century, where people lived their lives in small tightly-knit communities with an infinite gradation of ranks from lowest to highest, from cot to castle. Eighteenth-century observers however do note that Wales (outside a few favoured areas like Glamorgan) was a poor country, with a small rich gentry class lording it over a desperately poor peasantry, some of them adding that Wales was remarkably lacking in a middle class. The gulf between rich and poor was accentuated by the coming of industry, for Wales was a country of heavy extractive industries from the 1780s onwards, its industrial development relatively lacking in commercial enterprises, crafts, service or light industries which might create a substantial middle class.

The gulf between rich and poor was also accentuated by cultural changes. In Wales right up to the middle of the nineteenth century political power was in the hands of a small class of mainly Tory landowners, becoming steadily more anglicised in language and customs, and steadfastly Anglican in religion. The life of the common people was changed by a series of religious revivals which made the Welsh, in the words of Rhŷs and Brynmor Jones, 'the most earnest and religious people in the whole kingdom'.[16] But such a cultural revolution was not easily accomplished: throughout the eighteenth and early nineteenth centuries groups of evangelical Anglicans, Methodists, and Dissenters, all struggled to raise the religious consciousness of the dim and backward Welsh people, and to raise their moral and spiritual tone. As in other Protestant countries, two sets of values appeared. One was based on the older popular culture of the Welsh: artless, childlike, irregular, feckless, uneconomical, merry and colourful, a culture of alehouse and churchyard sports, of ballad and dance, harp and fiddle and folktale, colourful customs, often violent sports and carousals. Despite all the toil and grinding poverty this was, in the words of the Welsh cliché, the '*Werin gyffredin ffraeth*' ('merry old common folk'). To Welsh scholars and romanticists at the end of the eighteenth century this was the true Welsh way of life, although now under threat from an alien set of values. William

Jones of Llangadfan, radical country doctor and folkdance collector, thought the tyranny of the landowners and Methodists had brought darkness to Wales. The stonemason and bard Iolo Morganwg said the north was becoming as methodistical as the south, and the south was as methodistical as Hell. The folklorist and royal harpist Edward Jones said that Wales hitherto had been the merriest of countries and was now, because of Methodism, becoming the dullest.[17]

The other set of values emerging by the end of the eighteenth century was a serious religious culture, which patriots at first thought was a grim importation from England (ultimately from Geneva). At first the new culture was exclusive, cut off from the world of the squire, parson and peasantry, older dissent appealing to the independent-minded farmer and craftsman whilst newer Methodism appealed to the young thoughtful individualist who wished to give some shape, methodicality and purpose, to his or her life. Until the second quarter of the nineteenth century—that is, for about a hundred years—this was the culture of a growing minority, marked by intense seriousness, sobriety, hard work, cultivation of the soul (and sometimes cultivation of the mind), decency of conduct and quietness of manner, and sometimes (as in the case of the old dissenters) involvement with radical politics. Meeting-house culture certainly had great dynamic, but it could not (yet) be called 'The Welsh way of life'.[18]

Meanwhile, all around the hordes of rural peasantry and the exclusive people of the meeting-houses, there occurred great upheavals in Welsh life, the coming of Agrarian and Industrial Revolutions, the impinging of political events, all drawing the half-isolated communities of Wales into contact with each other and the wider world, and also there occurred a great revival or renewal of Welsh cultural patriotism, just at the time when the Welsh were drawn inexorably into the orbit of English industrial society at the height of its world power and prosperity. The crisis years were the 1830s and 1840s, decades of strife between the religious bodies in Wales, between the sacred and secular elements in Welsh society and between the Welsh and the English. The high point of the crisis years was the rumpus known as the 'Treason of the Blue Books, 1846-7'.[19]

The reports of the government commission on Welsh education, the Blue Books of 1847, turned out to be an indictment of Welsh backwardness, ignorance, squalor, isolation, poverty, incompetence. They castigated the Welsh language for this isolation and backwardness, so that Welsh patriots of all groups and parties were hurt and moved to react. But indirectly, the reports implied that, in the period since about 1815, the enormous advance of the chapels, dissenters and Methodists alike, contributed greatly to this lamentable state of affairs. Dissenters and Methodists felt for the first time that they must make common cause against the alien Anglican commissioners and defend each other against an attack on nonconformity in general. All things Welsh appeared to be under attack as well, and so the nonconformists for the first time made common cause with Welsh patriots to try to defend the honour of the Welsh. Even before 1847 the older dissenters (such as the Independents) had begun to involve themselves in political radicalism, in such semi-political forms as Liberationism (freeing the state from the control of the state Church). Moreover, Dissenters and Methodists alike had begun to involve themselves from the 1830s onwards in social causes such as temperance and total abstinence, and all forms of public education.[20] The religious census of 1851 showed that in Wales the great majority of those attending places of worship were dissenters and Methodists, the Anglicans a small minority.[21] The census only confirmed what the nonconformists already knew, but it gave them a sense of great public responsibility, that they were truly the people of Wales. They themselves were fond of using the expression 'going through the narrow defile of conviction' ('*bwlch yr argyhoeddiad*'), and in this period they had to go through the difficult defile separating their position as a minority: and in coming to act as the majority, they convinced themselves that they represented all the people and that they were the guardians of Welshness, of all that was best in Welsh life.

The rumpus over the Blue Books was called 'The Treason of the Blue Books' after a play satirising the government commissioners by R. J. Derfel and published in 1854.[22] In the play the Welsh nation has become a nonconformist Gwerin, they in turn have become a godly, pious people, chapel-going but also intensely public-spirited, self-consciously Welsh, with a sense of responsibility for Welsh culture as well. The Welsh people in the play are set upon by a horde of demons, in the form of bishops, politicians, Englishmen and so on, and the turning-point is where the Welsh people come to realise their plight, a sudden heightening of consciousness, which then leads them to rout their attackers and finally to create a new and better Wales. The Welsh bard takes his place alongside the representatives of the nonconformists in turning the tables in the play. The Wales of the future envisaged in the play of 1854 is uncannily similar to that of the Welsh radical movement of the 1880s and 1890s, *Cymru Fydd*: freedom from religious and landlord oppression, improvement of housing for the workers, fine monuments for Welsh national heroes, a good school system crowned by a national university.

The Treason of the Blue Books controversy, however, had other effects on Welsh nonconformity. Not only did Welsh nonconformity try to take over Welsh culture and Welsh patriotism, for example institutions like the eisteddfod,[23] it also began to try to take over the whole of Welsh society. The nonconformists were aware that in the religious census of 1851 about half the Welsh population were recorded as attending no place of worship at all. But the nonconformists did their best to behave from now on as if they were an overwhelming majority. The Blue Books of 1847, if their contentious attacks on the language and the chapels were ignored, were an indictment of Welsh backwardness, and the Welsh nonconformist leaders were acutely conscious of the isolation and weakness of their nation when face to face with the colossal power of English commerce and industry. It has been said more than once that the effect of the Blue Books was to produce in the Welsh an aggresive nonconformist nationality and at the same time a desire to adopt the values of the English commercial middle classes. Thus, from 1847 onwards the leaders and publicists of Welsh nonconformity, who had long ago taken on board the values of the older English Puritanism, now added to their cargo the values of the Victorian middle class. Through example or the precept of the numerous nonconformist journals, the people of Wales had to be made hard-working, methodical, economical, keen on good education, to learn English for business success, to save money to buy land or improve homes, to elevate the tone of family and public life, through chapels, mutual improvement societies, benefit clubs, and a host of other means. The nonconformist leadership, David Rees of Llanelli, Henry Richard, Hugh Owen, Dr. Thomas Nicholas, Dr. Thomas Rees of Swansea, and a host of others like them, in the 1850s and 1860s had a growing sense of responsibility for the whole of the common folk, inside and outside the chapels, hence their sense of mission that they must press their version of Welsh nationality upon the whole, a strange amalgam of the virtues of Puritanism, middle class business ethic, together with a modernised version of Welsh native culture. By the 1850s and 1860s the army of propagandists for the nonconformists had not yet evolved the ideal of the Gwerin, in so many words, but all the elements of the ideal were there, and used to press a new way of life upon the whole people. Writers such as Ieuan Gwynedd Jones have shown that it was possible to make this amalgam of middle class and working class cultures at this stage in Wales because on so many questions their interest was the same, as for example in the improvement of housing and public health, or in Welsh literary and musical culture, or in religious matters.[24] Kenneth O. Morgan has defined it well as 'Nonconformist populism'.[25] Gwyn A. Williams has seen it as a powerful synthesis of middle and working class movements making for this populism, but criticises it as 'the pseudo-nation of Welsh Dissent'.[26] Gwyn A. Williams also states that while the ethos of the Gwerin is a wonderful example of the 'superstructure' arising out of a 'base', in its turn coming back to reshape that 'base', it is nevertheless a process in the 1850s and 1860s in which the middle classes and nonconformity combined to take over the leadership of the Welsh working classes, so that the latter simply 'lost their memory' of their struggles in the period from 1780 to 1840. The Welsh nonconformist leaders evolved a set of values for Welsh society: they took over the running of Welsh culture, and began to influence political life. Thus, it can be seen that Welsh Radicalism from 1868 to 1922 bears many of the marks of their influence. Welsh middle and working classes had become bound together against their bogeymen, the anglicised landlords and stewards, the bishops and parsons, the Tory brewers and many others.

By the 1890s it seemed as if the leaders of nonconformity had a hegemony over Welsh life. But strains were already beginning to appear. Kenneth O. Morgan has recently drawn attention to the conflict of rural and industrial ideals to be found among the Welsh radicals in the 1880s even in the work of Owen M. Edwards, a conflict which comes into the open in the rise and failure of the *Cymru Fydd* or 'Young Wales' movement inside Welsh Radicalism in the 1880s and 1890s.[27] In industrial Wales, a challenge was beginning to emerge to the world of William Abraham 'Mabon', the world of 'Lib-Labbism', the world where the harmony of interest of middle and working classes reigned, the world of the classic Gwerin. It was a period also when Wales was becoming steadily less Welsh as, from 1870 onwards, there was a compulsory education for all through the medium of English, and vast numbers of English, Scots and Irish poured into the industrial areas of Wales to find work. All this contributed to the general secularisation of Welsh life, the great expansion in this period of sports and secular entertainments, theatres and music-halls, and the like. Within Welsh nonconformity, too, there occurred signs of dissatisfaction in this period. The Flintshire novels of Daniel Owen were read by all the Welsh-speaking Gwerin, but they contain much criticism of chapel leadership. The recent massive work on Welsh religion from 1890 to 1914 by Principal R. Tudur Jones spotlights these strains and stresses in Welsh religion. The world of the Gwerin was under pressure.[28] Of course it is in this period, the 1880s and 1890s and the decades immediately following, that writers like Owen M. Edwards, John Morris-Jones, and Crwys, raised the ideals of the Welsh Gwerin to their greatest height and romanticised them most successfully. They cannot have been unaware of the failure of the *Cymru Fydd* movement to bridge the gap between the declining rural Welshness and the thrusting industrialism of the south Wales coastal belt, or the fears of the older Radicalism of Lib-Labbism in the face of new Trade unionism and the rise of the I.L.P. (Independent Labour Party). Although Owen M. Edwards in *Er Mwyn Cymru* ['For the sake of Wales'] writes of the poor mountain cottages as 'the finest source of our national life', he knew very well that, by that time, the great majority of the Welsh lived in urban and industrial areas.[29] The writers were also aware that, as they wrote of their idealised Gwerin, the life of the common folk was being rapidly secularised and anglicised all around them. One may suggest that it was precisely an awareness of these changes—frightening changes to traditionalists, Liberal or Radical leaders, bards and preachers, Welsh-language journalists and publicists—that urged them to formulate the myth of the idealised Gwerin in Wales in this period.

W. J. Gruffydd, pessimist though he was, looked back from the 1920s and 1930s into the nineteenth century, and believed that the Gwerin had once been a reality but that the First World War, the decline of Liberalism and Welshness, had killed it. What evidence is there that the Gwerin had ever been something of a reality in Welsh communities? This must be the final part of our inquiry. An echo of what had once been the reality or partial-reality of the Gwerin may be gained from the research studies reviewed in Chapter Four dealing with Welsh-speaking rural communities as they existed in the 1950s and 1960s. All these dealt with communities in the north and west, that is in those areas which geographers refer to as the 'Welsh heartland'.[30] In these areas there survived up until the mid-twentieth century a vigorous community life, united and harmonious and yet divided into what the sociologists have termed two 'ways of life' using the Welsh word *buchedd* [moral life or ethic], *Buchedd A* and *Buchedd B*. Buchedd A comprises the chapel folk, 'pop-drinkers' as opposed to 'tavern-drinkers', earnest and respectable, keen to build up business, to own property, keen for their children's education, leaders of local committees, deacons and elders, chairmen of the literary societies or *eisteddfodau*, or folk who support such ventures or aim to do so in the future. Buchedd B comprises the 'people of the world', unconcerned about the future, perhaps feckless, never bothering much about money, property, business, or taking causes or culture or religion seriously, 'tavern-drinkers' not 'pop-drinkers', merry happy folk who are prepared to accept the leadership of the others in the varied activities of life. It should be emphasised that Buchedd A and Buchedd B coexist harmoniously in the community, the latter gladly accepting the drive, resourcefulness and leadership of the former. Moreover, the earnest chapel-folk of Buchedd A do not turn away from the world—as the Methodists had done before the 1840s—but turn towards it to influence it. In a local eisteddfod, for example, the chairman of the eisteddfod might be from Buchedd A but the bard winning the prizes might be a wayward bohemian sot—definitely Buchedd B. This harmony of the two *Bucheddau* could even occur in the same household, husband and wife possibly differing in their scale of values. The rural sociologists also observed that the Buchedd A values had succeeded in some areas to such an extent that when the surveys were made, Buchedd A represented the ethic and values of the majority of the community; for example in

Aberporth (Dyfed) 60 per cent of the village was Buchedd A, only 40 per cent Buchedd B. Other sociologists have seen the Gwerin differently, the ethical distinctiveness of Buchedd A and Buchedd B being subordinated to other differences or antagonisms: the Gwerin being the country folk against the townsfolk, the common man in the street against the official, the Welshman against the Englishman. In such communities the older nonconformist Gwerin has been eroded, whilst the patriotic or nationalistic Gwerin elements we have mentioned earlier have taken over.[31]

Such rural communities of course are not representative of contemporary Wales, nor of industrial Wales, but, as recorded in the middle of the twentieth century, they are close in mood and spirit to the Wales of the Gwerin writers that we have been considering. It is interesting that such communities do not see their conflicts and antagonisms in terms of class-conflict, but rather as differences of culture, or religion, moral, or sometimes ethnic nature. It is striking, too, that the idealised Gwerin of writers such as Owen M. Edwards, Crwys, and others, is close to the virtues and values of the Buchedd A group of the rural sociologists, and that for the sake of propaganda such writers assumed that the whole of the Welsh nation, not merely an influential section of it, was Buchedd A, or, to use a more common phrase, followed 'The Welsh way of life'. Consciously or unconsciously, they had made a part stand for the whole—they had, as it were, turned the whole pint of milk into cream.

Writing in the 1920s and 1930s W. J. Gruffydd felt that, since the common folk were no longer interested in the finer things or the things of the mind, the Gwerin had largely disappeared. But the myth of the Gwerin, once created, could not so easily disappear, and from time to time, socialists and nationalists have claimed to be the heirs of the older Gwerin: in fact in the 1930s there was a *Gwerin* movement representing left wing Welsh patriotism. Today, with a strong challenge to the Labour hegemony from a revived Conservatism, the Wales of

Labour hegemony from the 1920s to 1970s now seems, in retrospect, to represent a harmony of interests in the local community, intensely Welsh and *gwerinol* compared to that of the 1980s—the older Wales of James Griffiths and his brother the bard Amanwy.[32]

But that is to argue that there is some sort of exactitude or reality belonging to the myth of the Gwerin. What we have argued here is that the Gwerin was a useful myth, based, like all successful myths, on a certain amount of realism, but a little bit too good to be true.[33] Wales likewise is going to be called the 'Land of Song' even if not every single Welshman can sing like Sir Geraint Evans. Not every American is a cowboy or a frontiersman, very few can answer to such descriptions, and yet they loom large in the American imagination as myths, and may influence American behaviour. The myth of the Gwerin is particularly interesting for historians and social scientists, because it is made up partly of real elements, partly of ideals and propaganda, and because it comes into existence first of all in a simplified way in the 1840s when the Welsh are challenged by English progressives and when they need confidence and backbone and when the chapel way of life needs to be upheld against outside rivals, and because it subsequently appears in an elaborate romanticised form in the 1880s and 1890s when that way of life is challenged by rival elements inside Welsh society. In each case Welsh society was forced to defend itself by defining itself, and the myth created was so attractive, so pervasive, that it has lived on to colour modern Welsh life. The Gwerin is still a cliché influencing our mode of thinking long after the last *gwerinwr* has disappeared.

References

1 P. Morgan 'Gwerin Cymru, y ffaith a'r ddelfryd', *Trans. Hon. Soc. Cymmrodorion*, 1967 (1), 117-31; F. P. Jones 'Gwerin Cymru', *Traethodydd* xxxiii (1965), 12-22; A. Llywelyn-Williams *Y nos, y niwl a'r ynys* (Cardiff 1960), 16-25, 141-61, 181-2.

2 *Geiriadur Prifysgol Cymru, s.nn* 'Gwerin', 'gwerinol', 'gwerinos'.

3 Biographical details of J. Morris-Jones and O. M. Edwards in *Dict. Welsh Biog., s.nn.* See also J. Morris-Jones *Caniadau* (Oxford 1900); Crwys Williams *Cerddi Crwys* (Llanelli 1920); and W. J. Gruffydd *Hen Atgofion* (Aberystwyth 1936), *O. M. Edwards Cofiant* (Aberystwyth 1937), and *Y Tro Olaf ac ysgrifau eraill* (Welsh Book Club 1939).

4 T. Evans *Background to modern Welsh politics 1789-1846* (Cardiff 1936), *passim*; D. Williams *Modern Wales* (London 1950), 246-8, 269-85; R. T. Jenkins, *Hanes Cymru yn y bedwaredd ganrif ar bymtheg, i.*, (Cardiff 1933), v and 154-5.

5 R. T. Jenkins op.cit., 52-3; D. Williams op.cit., 235-6.

6 G. A. Williams *When was Wales?* (Harmondsworth 1984), 204.

7 J. Morris-Jones op.cit., 2, and in general see D. W. Howell *Land and people in nineteenth century Wales* (London 1977).

8 O. M. Edwards *Er mwyn Cymru* (Wrexham ed. 1927), 64.

9 J. Morris-Jones, op.cit., 3.

10 Crwys, op.cit., 18.

11 A. Llywelyn-Williams op.cit., 149-51. .

12 Crwys op.cit., 22. Cf. O. M. Edwards op.cit., 80.

13 J. E. Caerwyn-Williams 'Gweledigaeth Owen Edwards', *Taliesin* iv, 4-29; W. J. Gruffydd, *O. M. Edwards*, 8-9; R. T. Jenkins *Ar ymyl y ddalen* (Wrexham, ?1957), 38-9; A. Llywelyn-Williams, op.cit., 159; and Wynne Lloyd 'Owen M. Edwards' in C. Gittins ed., *Pioneers of Welsh education* (Swansea 1962), 93.

14 J. Rhys and D. Brynmor Jones *The Welsh people* (London 1906 ed.), 472-4.

15 T. J. Morgan *W. J. Gruffydd* (Cardiff 1970) *passim*.

16 Rhys and Brynmor Jones, op.cit., 472.

17 P. Morgan *The eighteenth-century Renaissance* (Llandybie 1981) *passim*.

18 E. T. Davies *Religion in the industrial revolution in south Wales* (Cardiff 1965); *Religion and society in nineteenth century Wales* (Llandybie 1981); I. G. Jones *Explorations and explanations: essays in the social history of Victorian Wales* (Llandysul 1981).

19 F. P. Jones 'Effaith Brad y Llyfrau Gleision', *Traethodydd* xxxi (1963), 49-65, also reprinted in his *Radicaliaeth a'r werin Gymreig yn y bedwaredd ganrif ar bymtheg* (Cardiff 1977); P. Morgan 'From long knives to Blue Books', in R. R. Davies et.al. (eds.), *Welsh society and nationhood* (Cardiff 1984), 199-215; D. Salmon 'The story of a Welsh education commission' *Y Cymmrodor* xxiv (1913), 189-237; J. L. Williams and G. R. Hughes, eds., *The history of Welsh education* (Swansea 1979).

20 W. R. Lambert *Drink and sobriety in Victorian Wales c 1820-1895* (Cardiff 1983).

21 I. G. Jones and D. Williams, eds. *The religious census of 1851, returns for Wales.i.S.Wales* (Cardiff 1977), and *Returns for N. Wales* (ed. by I. G. Jones) (Cardiff 1981).

22 R. J. Derfel *Brad y Llyfrau Gleision* (Rhuthun 1854).

23 H. T. Edwards *Gŵyl Gwalia—yr eisteddfod genedlaethol yn oes aur Victoria 1858-1868* (Llandysul 1980).
24 I. G. Jones 'The people's health in mid-Victorian Wales', *Trans. Hon. Soc. Cymmrodorion* 1984, 115-47, and idem. *Health, wealth and politics* (Swansea 1979).
25 K. O. Morgan *Rebirth of a nation, Wales 1880-1980* (Oxford 1982), 16.
26 G. A. Williams *The Welsh in their history* (London 1982), 88, and cf. D. Smith (ed.) *A people and a proletariat, essays in the history of Wales 1780-1980* (London 1980).
27 K. O. Morgan, op.cit., 87-8 and cf. idem. *Wales in British politics 1868-1922* (3rd ed. Cardiff. 1980).
28 R. T. Jones *Ffydd ac argyfwng cenedl. Crefydd Cymru 1890-1914* (2 vols. Swansea 1981, 1982).
29 *Er mwyn Cymru*, 41.
30 A. D. Rees *Life in a Welsh countryside* (Cardiff 1950) 142-53; A. D. Rees and E. Davies eds., *Welsh rural communities* (Cardiff 1960) *passim*; and D. Jenkins *The agricultural community in south west Wales at the turn of the twentieth century* (Cardiff 1971), *passim*.
31 I. Emmett *A north Wales village* (London 1964), esp. 1-14.
32 P. Morgan and D. Thomas *Wales—the shaping of a nation* (Newton Abbot 1984), 150-2.
33 P. Morgan 'From a death to a view—the hunt for the Welsh past in the romantic period', in E. Hobsbawm and T. Ranger *The Invention of tradition* (Cambridge 1983), 43-100.

Chapter Six

The Sociology of Wales: Issues and Prospects, 1979 and 1985*

Graham Day

ISSUES AND PROSPECTS, 1979

The political successes of nationalist parties in the 1970s, and the ensuing debate about devolution, gave new confidence to those working in the periphery of Britain that their contribution to social science need not automatically be relegated to the category of the quaint and parochial. Britain has been shown to display obstinately persistent regional differentiation, and this has been related in turn to the perceived threat to the vaunted unity of the British state.[1] It is a propitious time to consider the condition of sociology with regard to peripheral areas, and the publication of a collection of research papers affords the opportunity to do so for Wales.[2] On this evidence current research consists of apparently haphazardly chosen topics, narrow in focus and limited in aspiration, showing little overall consistency of direction.

There is more to this question than the fortuitous circumstances of individual research programmes. In particular, one notes a dearth of material relating to industrial Wales, to the Welsh economic structure, and to stratification. In all probability this stems from a problem in identification: those working in rural areas, in north and west Wales, most readily regard themselves as students of Wales, whereas those working in the south are more centrally concerned with industrial, urban, or political sociology which simply happens to be carried out within Wales, but is not intended greatly to increase our understanding of Wales as such. If so, this tells us a great deal

* Based on an earlier version which first appeared in *The Sociological Review*, 27 (1979), 447-74.

about how the sociology of Wales is currently defined,[3] and suggests that the ominous silences will be filled only given some attempt to think theoretically about Wales, so that in the light of theory we know better where to concentrate our attention.

Orthodoxies

Many of the current weaknesses are similar to, if not directly rooted in, much earlier work and one of the tasks of a new Welsh sociology must be to come to terms with and critically scrutinize the legacy of an indigenous 'school' of sociology, the Aberystwyth group headed by Alwyn D. Rees which produced a series of Welsh community studies before and immediately after the Second World War (see Chapter 4). While this patently dates the work, the general assumptions exercise a continuing sway over many discussions. The work of these writers resonates certain 'domain assumptions'[4] of political and social thought in Wales, contributing to something approaching a dominant account of Welsh society.[5]

Their products were reticent concerning theoretical origins. While they appear to have debts to functionalist anthropology, particularly Lloyd Warner and his students, Arensberg and Kimball,[6] explicit mention of other sociologists was rare, and the most direct influence was an institutional background of cultural geography.[7] The object of interest was the 'community', viewed as a virtually self-contained phenomenon bearing little relation either to a wider society or to history. The drift was functionalist in the sense that most, if not all, aspects of life could be shown to contribute to a coherent, stable pattern with few internal tensions, which Rees refers to as 'the completeness of traditional rural society'.[8] Having emerged gradually over a long period of time, this could be regarded as in effect timeless, so that we are presented with the image of a static, ahistorical past, marked only by the eruption of a few events—the rise of Nonconformity, periodic religious revivals—which are themselves unexplained, but at once absorbed into the steady flow of 'tradition'. There is a limited sense of process and, more importantly, no examination of internal contradictions or tensions which might fuel or amplify future change. With one exception, where divisions and rivalries could be seen to exist—between communities, generations, chapels—they were viewed as essentially positive, since they contributed to a romantic solidarity which gave individuals roots and added to the interest of communal existence. In any case, they were overridden by much deeper attachments to certain core values: the 'Welsh way of life', centred on the cultural configurations of Nonconformity and the chapel, the language, a literary tradition, was almost bred in the bones of the Welshman, and traceable back over many centuries:

> Wales has no civic heritage. The essentially rural culture of Wales, like that of the Balkans, had crystallized before the introduction of towns by aliens, and after the conquest the distinction between country and town became largely a distinction between English and Welsh.[9]

Given the predominant emphasis, when change occurred it was held to be exogenous, imposed, and detrimental: in fact, treated as the 'urban' creation of the English, whose influence brought into the situation new elements which were quite out of keeping with the realities of Welsh life. These would include: industry; new organizational forms;[10] new values, of secularism and materialism; and new social divisions, especially class. These influences were felt in the remoter upland regions, but were concentrated in the industrializing centres of south and north Wales; they were seen as destructive of Welsh values, religion and language. Yet, and this is a crucial consideration for present purposes, since the urban-industrial centres were alien, they could, in a sense, be ignored, treated as 'foreign' territory. A great deal of attention came to be paid to the exact delineation of what was variously referred to as 'Inner Wales', 'Welsh Wales' or '*Y Fro Gymraeg*',[11] a distinct zone containing 'the traditional Welsh culture complex'.[12]

The major impact in the rural areas came through, first, the diffusion of Anglicizing influences, in which the one avowed division in Welsh society, that between gentry and the 'ordinary people' (*gwerin*), played a crucial mediating role: however, the gentry were not 'of' Welsh society since they were—it did not appear to matter which—themselves either English or 'Anglicized'; secondly, through the depopulating pull to the towns, undermining the vitality and ultimately the fabric of rural society. These appeared however as recent impacts on the particular communities studied: invariably, the studies contrived to catch society just on the turn, as the old pattern was weakening, and Welsh society was facing its most severe test, being pulled (finally?) into the wider, English-dominated, context.

There was on offer then a species of 'dual-society' thesis, in which the traditional, long-established, and previously autonomous (or uncontaminated) hinterland retained a degree of independence, albeit decreasing, from the dynamic 'enclave'. But the value attached to these two sectors was the reverse of what is usual: the situation was viewed unequivocally from within rural society and seen in terms of threat. For these writers, 'modernization' was in no sense a benefit, but a destruction; ideologically they lined up not with the modernizing theorists of the industrial society but with the anti-urban sentiments of much British sociology—tradition stood for the good life, the new was bad. The Welsh sociologists took on the mantle of defenders of the faith, apologists for a particular kind of cultural nationalism, and so lent academic respectability to views which, by virtue of background, education, and place in society they shared with other spokesmen—ministers of religion, schoolmasters, poets. When the spirit moved them, they even wrote as if from the pulpit.[13]

While there were indications of a different story, these were not developed: evidence of social class divisions within Welsh rural society and small towns was discounted, as alien borrowings, out of place even in language; thus a closure was effected so far as discussion of certain topics was concerned—in particular, the emergence and assimilation into Welsh society of new patterns of class relations corresponding to new modes of production. The limited definition of Welsh society—the 'real' or 'essential' Wales—had the effect of excluding the vast bulk of the Welsh population, more than 70 per cent of whom lived in the industrial areas, ruling out the probability that an equally 'Welsh' urban culture might be found there:

> Whatever culture there has been in the mining valleys of south Wales has been the remnant of the social life of the countryside, and has been Welsh in speech. The extension of English has everywhere accompanied the decay of that culture, the loss of social traditions . . . It has produced no richness of idioms.[14]

Once this perspective is adopted, it is a simple matter to treat industrial/urban society as a one-dimensional phenomenon, and so arrive at Rees's dismissal of urban people as 'formless masses of rootless nonentities'.[15] Subsequent discussion has often taken this direction: witness Mayo's 'explanation' of nationalist resurgence as 'a desire to recapture a lost identity and a sense of belonging' in the face of urban and centralist rootlessness and uniformity.[16] Often in place of the serious study of history we are offered arguments in terms of collective psychology or racial memory—for example, that before English encroachment, Wales

> . . . if not classless, lacked the sharp class distinctions of England, and was marked by a lively intellectual activity and a powerful concern for things of the mind and spirit. A political characteristic was a passion for social justice which gave Wales her radical bent.[17]

Here history serves to precipitate certain timeless values which then continue to be revealed in diverse and changing expressions. Obviously, history can be used as a source of values, and as a means through which people might construct certain 'identities' that they then seek to accomplish; but this is a different matter altogether from supposing those identities were once 'theirs' and have to be recaptured. The account of Wales as having once consisted (entirely?) of 'a society of warm, intimate, radical communities'[18] may serve as a powerful political and ideological weapon: it will not do as sociology.

We need an historically informed sociology of Welsh *ways* of life, and the transformations of communities. So far as the dominant account is concerned, there is a strong probability that this was a reading backwards of selected elements of the recent past and that the composition of the Welsh community, apparently on the verge of cataclysmic change, had to be regarded itself as a product of the history of long-standing relations with a wider society: both urban and rural Wales had been engaged in such relations for centuries. Instead what we are given is the *informant's* perspective on change, an idealized past contrasted with a crisis-ridden present; the sociologist is captivated by 'local subjective models'.[19]

Continuities

In a distorted way, the views briefly considered do pose a real question, namely, the social reality of Wales. The attempt to preserve a specific view of Wales, past and future, at the cost of severing large areas of Welsh life as secondary and unimportant. This is patently unacceptable insofar as the two 'sectors' so created are in no sense separate. We must, however, face the problem that by taking as our object of interest an entity which is empirically defined, in terms of administration, political decision, and certain historical events, we are uncertain of its sociological unity (our 'theoretical' object). In some respects, which are as awkward for nationalists as they are for sociologists, the problems and orientations of different sections of Welsh society are widely diverse. Thus the everyday concerns of people in Mid-Wales—depopulation, decay of social provision, tourism, second homes, the struggle to preserve a language—do not find straightforward correspondences in the valleys and cities of south

Wales, or, indeed, on Deeside where issues of decision-making in nationalized industries, the role of multinationals and large-scale movements of capital, urbanization and suburbanization, bulk larger.

To the extent that we believe the real problems have been posed already by earlier work, we will find the first set of issues in some way closer to Welsh sociology than the second; research assumes a culturalist bias, and the focus is on language use and change, identity, ethnicity, nationalism. Yet these important questions are likely to be far more fruitfully pursued if related clearly and firmly to the structural context in which they occur. As sociologists, we must surely accept Riddell's ruling, that 'Methodologically, structural considerations are prior to cultural ones',[20] and approach Wales with the same principles we would apply to any other society (or part-society). Nairn indicates where emphasis should lie, with his appeal for 'A materialist theory focus[ed] primarily upon . . . real location in the modern process of socio-economic development.'[21]

Insofar as any society consists of numerous competing groups, engaged in processes of conflict, struggle, competition, employing whatever means come to hand to further their particular interests and goals, making and breaking alliances, but doing so usually within boundaries set by broad and deep-seated constraints of social location, then Wales is exceptionally rich in possibilities, since alongside the normal relations of class, and town and country, there exist divisions between the 'Welsh Welsh' (*Cymry Cymraeg*), 'Anglo-Welsh', and the English. How alignments develop along these various axes is of great interest, but these need to be seen against the adage that politics (and group relations) concern 'Who gets what, when, how'.

At present only the barest outlines of a political sociology of Wales and Welsh nationalism exist. The existence of a Welsh ruling class has not been examined, while very little is known about the nature of Welsh elites, the articulation of elite groups, its bearing on the practice of government or wielding of economic power, and the management of opposition. In one particularly interesting passage, Alan Butt-Philip compares the long struggle of *Cymdeithas yr Iaith* (the Welsh Language Society) for bilingual road signs with the short, sharp engagement fought by *Barn*[22] to secure bilingual road-fund discs: 'venerable and prestigious' individuals were mobilized to convert the Welsh Office, within eight weeks, from the view that these were 'impossible' to their issue. Of 642 people eventually involved in the campaign, 40 per cent were schoolteachers, a further 28 per cent clergy and university staff.[23] Here is clear evidence of the effectiveness of a specific correlation between language interests and quite particular occupational/status levels. Action by such interests is only part of the question: there is also the 'mobilization of bias', which keeps certain issues on the agenda, and others off it; how are issues defined, where is cultural and idealogical hegemony exercised and by whom? Too often, the tone of discussion militates against adequate analysis; to the uninitiated, Welsh politics seems to consist of a plethora of names; this lends to political movements the appearance of bands of sturdy individualists united around shared values. Reasons can be suggested for this: the smallness of Wales, the intimacy of leading circles, the excellence of channels of communication; but the personalization of political life allows to fall from view the existence of underlying interests, better handled in sociological categories. The lack of any overarching perspective dissolves the question of power in Welsh society, while conjectures about the motives of rank-and-file activists are poorly grounded.

New directions

More interesting possibilities have been opened up recently that approach Wales in a comparative framework, make no reference to the community study tradition, but take up perspectives for analysis which are very much wider. The basic innovation is to situate Wales in the sociology of development, using conceptual and methodological tools produced in studies of the Third World. Michael Hechter, in particular, has wrenched Wales into the mainstream of sociology (see Chapter 9).[24] The principal value of such approaches lies in their assertion that the characteristics and problems of less developed areas are not simply intrinsic to them, effects of their 'failure' to keep pace with industrial and technological change, inadequacies of local institutional arrangements, or weak motivation among their populations, but to be understood as a relationship between them and the surrounding society, taking place over time. The many precursors of such views would include the Scottish nationalist who wrote in 1945 of 'outlying regions (being) increasingly subjected to exploitation and impoverishment by centralised authority';[25] but the position has become familiar following the impact of the work of A. G. Frank.[26] Development theory in general, and Frank in particular, has inspired new interests in the study of regional disparity as an historical and structural reality, to elucidate the insight that advanced societies also consist of 'overdeveloped, overindustrialized and overurbanized areas, together with areas of increasing underdevelopment'.[27] A number of British studies have shared this general orientation.

At the same time, certain critical objections which have been directed at Frank's conceptualization of the problem preclude the literal transfer of his framework to the analysis of peripheral regions within advanced societies. His account of underdevelopment as the direct correlative of development, the 'other side of the same coin', has been challenged for its lack of specificity: the reference to the 'ubiquity' of the relationship indicates a universality which is confirmed in the loose description of all colonial development as 'capitalist'. Similarly, the necessity of either stagnation or regression in underdeveloped societies has been challenged and the concept of 'dependence' has been formulated so as to allow for the possibility of limited forms of development occurring, subject to conditioning external factors. While Frank has often stated the necessity for considering class relationships as central to the analysis of development, his definition of the problem as one of the extension of market relations has prevented him from paying the attention given by other dependency theorists to the internal class structuring of dependent formations, which should rightly figure among the conditions of development or underdevelopment. In fact, 'structural dependence' can be interpreted to signify the articulation of internal and external stratification systems and the extent to which it perpetuates underdevelopment. In other words, it has to be remembered that 'the exploitation of one area by another is only another expression of the relationship between classes in any class society';[28] in the final analysis terms like 'metropolis' and 'satellite' are no more than metaphors for relationships between classes. This has a definite relevance for recent work on Wales.

Underdeveloped Wales

An underdeveloped social formation is not characterized by the total absence of development, but by its one-sidedness. Integration into a larger system implies that the conditions of existence for a satellite, or peripheral region, are largely determined elsewhere, in movements of capital, political decisions and social policies directed from the centre. Whether these are planned or unplanned (left to the free flow of market forces) they are formulated in terms of a whole in which the satellite is only a part: its needs and interests are 'balanced' against others, some of which are far more powerful and salient for the decision-makers. Local ruling interests will tend to identify with the wider system, since it affords larger opportunities than can be found 'at home'; collusion with dominant external interests will bring greater rewards than competition with them. Autonomous movement from within is liable to co-optation and incorporation; if it threatens existing interests, it is more likely to be choked off, leaving evidence of a variety of false starts. Consequently the economic and industrial base is unbalanced: certain industries, functioning chiefly as exporters, are built up at the expense of more rounded development. They are vulnerable to shifts of demand, which may leave them high and dry; crises begin sooner, last longer, and bite deeper than in areas of greater diversity. Backwardness in key sectors, where progress is possible, is part of the wider inability to make self-generated, self-perpetuating growth. The shaping of social and political structure around previous developments sets a whole range of barriers to breakout in new directions: population structures, economic infrastructure, built environment, communications, all act as fetters on new movement. When new development occurs it tends to deepen dependence, because it is complementary to the wider economy; external aid, increasingly sponsored and administered by the State, has similar effects. Despite the appearance of subsidy and investment flowing into the area, the net transfer is often outward, local capital formation is difficult, and there is progressive subjection to external control.

Nairn has suggested that 'In the Welsh knot the usual forces of uneven development have been tied together unusually closely and graphically'.[29] This has achieved a partial, formal recognition since for forty years, in common, it must be stressed, with several other parts of the United Kingdom, Wales has been regarded as a 'problem' area, granted development status, and has had a series of public bodies created to find answers to persisting economic and social distress. This is the legacy of an economic history during which the main role of Wales has been to act as supplier of raw materials, basic products, and labour to the wider system. The resulting pattern has been one in which a succession of industries has been intensively exploited and then abandoned in the face of falling demand, rising costs or growing competition, producing a series of transformations of social and community structures. Usually, although not invariably, this has involved external investment and control, and the profits have been creamed off and realized elsewhere. Cattle and wool were early examples in which Welsh production was oriented to English markets and the more profitable aspects of trade monopolized elsewhere (Shrewsbury, London). Much later, it could be noted that while Wales was virtually the sole producer of tinplate and sheet steel in Britain, only 11 per cent of the former and 4 per cent of the latter were processed for finished products within Wales.[30] Natural resources—lead, slate, iron, coal, water—have been worked in turn, yet no self-sustaining industrial base has been created around them. Thus, areas of dereliction: the lead mines of mid-Wales; the slate quarries of Caernarfonshire; the woollen mills of the upper Severn; each in turn foreshadowed the fate of the south Wales coalfield. In each instance, the creation and destruction of local social life has to be explained in terms of 'the history of capital in that area, its ownership and origins, its profitability and its decline or transfer out of the area'.[31]

Until the 1920s, there was sufficient dynamic to prevent Wales experiencing the mass emigration undergone by Ireland and Scotland. At the peak of expansion on the coalfields the problem was quite different: the assimilation of masses of imported labour. Since the countryside acted as a reservoir of labour, internal shifts were also huge: the condition of the rural areas was intrinsically bound up with the growth of industries elsewhere, which came progressively to mean the concentrated relative over-development of south Wales. At the turn of the century, when between 1901 and 1911 the coalfield required almost 100,000 in-migrants from beyond Wales, there was every appearance of a developing economy. The chickens of over-specialization came home to roost in the 1920s, when Wales paid the price for development which throughout had been complementary to the needs and interests of a wider economy, and geared primarily to Britain's export trade. Unemployment at the worst point reached 38 per cent, and between 1921 and 1939 almost half a million people left Wales, over fifty per cent of them young people aged 15-29. At the start of World War II, Wales looked set for prolonged impoverishment as the penalty of over-specialization:[32] a depopulated, moribund countryside coupled with heavy long-term unemployment in the industrial areas, both interrelated phenomena of the dependence of the Welsh economy.

Some will argue that the War, and post-war policy, have been the salvation of Wales, economically and socially. The War stimulated strategic decentralization of industry, which for the first time brought substantial manufacturing employment to Wales and drew large numbers of women into paid employment. Since then the state has intervened to redress the regional balance and attend to the social costs of grossly uneven development between the midlands and south east regions of England and most of the rest of Britain. Action has included nationalization, subsidization and directive planning, and in Wales such policies have had at least a limited success: manufacturing employment has been greatly increased (its share of occupied persons increased from 17 per cent in 1921 to 29 per cent in 1971); coal, steel, and farming are no longer the basis of the economy. Yet it is doubtful whether an adequate mix for autonomous development has been created. The effectiveness of regional policy has been greatest in deflecting market forces by preventing further expansion at the centre: the relocation of industry is, in many cases, a second-best solution, in which Wales must compete, in terms of proximity to markets, adequacy of communications, and cheapness of labour, with other areas also able to provide grants, cheap capital and favoured treatment. In common with these other underdeveloped areas, Wales faces the prospect of dominance by branch establishments and by reluctant employers who view their presence as to some extent a marginal commitment and who may therefore choose to 'rationalize' in the event of serious recession. At the fringes, it attracts fly-by-night operators whose chief consideration is precisely the low costs that Wales offers. More centrally, Wales can be regarded as participating, along with other European peripheries, in a re-appropriation of marginal areas which, because they offer adequate supplies of poorly organized labour, become attractive as sites for sections of advanced enterprises handling basically semi-skilled assembly work. Despite the expansion of manufacturing activity, and the contribution made by foreign (non-UK) firms towards raising the technological level of Welsh industry, it remains true that Wales is relatively starved of the more progressive functions, such as scientific research and development.

Thus, development continues in a dependent mode. While state employment goes some way towards correcting the regional imbalance, cut-backs in coal and steel in recent years underline the extent to which Wales is subject to decisions made elsewhere. In general terms, there is little reason to doubt the description of Wales as an underdeveloped, dependent social formation, beset with major problems of unevenness. Unemployment levels remain obdurately higher than the British average, and the economy is still disproportionately vulnerable to fluctuations. Activity rates and income levels are low, and deprivation can be seen across the whole range of amenities and services;[33] out-migration continues, more or less, to cancel natural population growth, while urbanization and concentration entails continuing transfers of people from the countryside and mining valleys to the coast.

The tenor of the argument so far has been to convey that it makes little sense to think of state intervention or the arrival of the multinationals as bringing 'closer' integration: the problems of Wales have not been the consequences of isolation, but of the particular forms taken by integration with England, and with 'the Atlantic economy', in the past. This conclusion is a central tenet of, by far, the most ambitious attempt at a sociology of Wales, Michael Hechter's *Internal colonialism*.

The 'internal colony'?

Hechter has done a major reworking of a mass of historical and sociological literature on what he refers to as 'Britain's Celtic periphery', subjecting it to an intensely theoretical scrutiny. Yet in certain crucial respects his approach is flawed by weaknesses of the kind already disclosed. Although he has been criticized for economic determinism, the problem in reality is quite different, as is evident from his choice of central analytical constructs: 'internal colonialism' and 'cultural division of labour'. Hechter presents the problem in terms of an unnecessarily stark opposition: either one accepts the diffusionist 'model' of progressive assimilation and acculturation through modernization, in which case regional distinctions in Britain should by now be negligible; or one notes the stubbornness of these distinctions, and adopts an internal colonial model. What distinguishes an internal colony from a peripheral region is the treatment meted out to its culture: 'the existence of a culture of low prestige within a peripheral region is justification enough for the establishment of an internal colonial category: without it, there can be no cultural division of labour'.[34] The acceptability of this latter concept is absolutely central to the cogency of Hechter's discussion.

His argument is as follows. Aggregate economic differences between 'core' and periphery are causally related to cultural differentiation; thus an account of the basis of regional inequality will also provide an explanation for the persistence of cultural and ethnic variation. The direction of causation is not always consistently stated: at times, cultural variables are merely 'superimposed' on economic inequalities; but elsewhere regional disadvantage is said to 'result from' ethnic stereotypes, and stratification to be 'based upon' observable cultural differences. However, the general thesis is clear: cultural factors occur independently of relations to the means of production and distribution and assume priority; initial states of advantage and disadvantage arising fortuitously from the uneven development of industry are perpetuated through the manipulation of cultural boundaries. The regional imbalance effectively excludes the great majority of the Welsh (and other 'Celts') from access to command positions in the key institutional orders:

> To the extent that the region is materially deprived, the average Welshman competes with the average Englishman at a disadvantage in many free market situations. When such long-term differences in aggregate rates of development are the result of ethnic stereotypes, it is appropriate to speak of institutional racism.[35]

As defined by Hechter, internal colonialism combines political incorporation, economic dependence, and cultural exclusion. The last of these assumes a decisive importance in that it produces effects, such as residential segregation, which intersect occupational levels so that ethnic boundaries are more salient, less abstract, than class divisions. The existence of a cultural division of labour affords a permanent basis for resurgence centred on ethnic/national aspirations, and hence in reality there has been no 'national' integration of Britain, for this is found only where there exists 'one all-encompassing cultural system to which all members of the society have primary identification and loyalty'.[36]

It might be objected that national integration is thereby precluded in any class society. Hechter informs us however that the question of the incorporation of excluded social classes is analytically distinct, a point which is a little easier to understand when we consider his comment that the English bourgeoisie and proletariat are 'culturally similar' groups. This is just one aspect of a general tendency to attach minor significance to the class nature of British (and Welsh) society. The account of class provided by Hechter is decidedly weak: class and status are counterposed as alternative bases of stratification. Class, which is referred to as a 'structural' phenomenon, is a matter solely of orientation to the market, hence of rational individual self-interest, or 'looking out for number one'. Consciousness of class appears to consist of making decisions about voting which are appropriate to one's structural position. Status, by comparison, is non-structural, a residual category which includes every specific attribute around which some degree of closure may be possible to override market interests and divert action from pure class lines. Membership of a status group implies solidarity; this is not necessarily the case with class.

By definition, this approach rules out the vital issue of the interaction between class alignments and status group formation; in particular, it does not countenance the possibility that status distinctions are an expression of class, even though they bear a complex and ambiguous relation to class position, or that the practices of exclusion and ideologies of social honour which demarcate status groupings are bound up with the promotion of class interests. By seeing class as a matter of orientation to the market, Hechter minimizes the role of classes as collectivities, and allows the question of relationships betwen classes to disappear from view, and with it the fact that England and Wales are internally differentiated societies. Thereafter only two actors are allowed on to the stage at any one time: core and periphery; England and Wales. Hechter therefore falls into the same trap as Frank; by uncoupling internal and external class relations he is led to construct a model in which nations, or regions, oppress one another.

Assigning cultural factors the leading role accounts for Hechter being taken up with some enthusiasm inside Wales, for here is a more sophisticated, densely argued version of the familiar story: cultural oppression of the Welsh by the English. Unfortunately the crux of the case, the cultural division of labour, is sketchily argued, and frequently rests on ungrounded assertions about the significance of ethnocentricity, the cumulative impact of individual decisions built upon an anti-Celtic racist ideology, and discriminatory policies pursued by the State. The relative deprivation of Wales is made to depend upon the ability of the English ethnically to stigmatize the Welsh and confine them to undesirable occupations. Yet it is perfectly possible to accept that the industrialization of Wales meant the importation of technical and managerial labour, indeed that such labour is still imported, and that many controlling interests lie outside Wales, without thereby committing oneself to the view that

Wales is a colony or even that Welshness is a main consideration in recruitment to roles. An adequate explanation would be provided by the general association of elite positions with geographical mobility, or 'spiralism'.

This is a sharp reminder of the need for comparative research which does not stop at the 'Celtic fringe'. Hechter is uneasily aware of this when, for example, he says that a cultural division of labour exists in any society to a greater or lesser degree, and warns of the danger that 'internal colonialism' might be so unspecific conceptually as to embrace almost any instance of stratification. Without very much stretching of concepts, one could place large parts of England in the same category, especially given that Hechter's definition of objective cultural differences upon which a division of labour might be built already extends to accent, dialect, and life style, as well as religion and language. Certainly a great deal of interest attaches to the part played by cultural barriers in the allocation of occupations, and the use made of ethnic distinctions to limit access; the questions of motivation and perception which Hechter deliberately puts to one side need to be explored, if only to strengthen the largely speculative history he employs. Differences in the pattern of regional development cannot however be reduced to the subjective motivations and prejudices of the actors concerned.

Conclusion

The potential of a sociology of Wales is lifted to a qualitatively new level by the bringing together of the themes of economic development and cultural distinctiveness: thus, a comprehensive approach to Wales begins to seem possible. However, the most influential available treatment of the question obscures at least as much as it illuminates, and in the end has to be rejected for its continuation of major distortions. Like earlier approaches, it fails to take a sufficiently critical stance towards certain prevalent conceptions, whose function is ideological. Cultural factors are given pride of place, and Wales is treated as an unproblematic, homogeneous reality, the problems of which are reducible to the imposition of external power. Questions about the distribution and use of power within Welsh society are shelved, along with examination of its internal structure, in favour of a crude opposition between 'Anglo-Saxons' and 'Celts'.

There are features of society in Wales which are not replicated in other parts of Britain: the existence of a substantial, and often militant, linguistic minority; historical grounds of appeal to a separate national identity; consciousness of an ethnic division. These can hardly be ignored. This, however, is not where analysis should begin (and often end). Rather than concentrating on what Wales has which is special, these factors are more likely to be given their proper weight when put into context through approaching Wales in the same terms as other parts of Britain. The fundamental questions about past underdevelopment and prospects for future development in Wales are most likely to be clarified by analysis of the economic structure as it is affected by changing productive relationships: central to this is a much closer study of the class framework within which the current and past dependence of Wales has been produced than has so far been undertaken.

POSTSCRIPT, 1985

To a considerable extent, recent developments in the sociology of Wales have followed the path sketched out above. Whereas before the tendency had been to approach Wales as if it presented problems that were unique, and could be understood only in their own terms, increasingly the attention of both sociologists and historians has turned to providing a more thoroughly worked out analysis of the distinctiveness of Wales. A remarkable flowering of interest has brought progress towards a more convincing account of the social and economic structure of contemporary Wales. British sociology has also begun more generally to show greater sensitivity to the kinds of regional and cultural differentiation that Wales displays.

Approaches from the sociology of development were helpful in situating the condition of Wales as a problem worthy of investigation and in indicating some of the broad areas that required examination. For a while the entire enterprise became too closely identified with the work of Hechter, and therefore with the particular shortcomings of his 'internal colonialism' thesis, and with the political conclusions to which they appeared to lead. Welsh historians were especially prone to treat Hechter's contribution as the definitive sociological statement on Wales, and to refuse to engage further with sociological concepts. Nevertheless, despite the mutual suspicions between the two disciplines, it has been possible to detect considerable convergence between them with regard to the features they now single out for emphasis.

What remains central is a stress on the unevenness of economic and social development, and its basis within the organization of production. Spatial variations assume great importance once it is recognized that unevenness is a routine and inevitable feature of modern capitalist society. There is now a substantial body of literature addressing the 'regional problem' in these terms, treating regional development as the outcome of the movement through space of successive stages of the division of labour.[37] As yet, the analysis is more complete with regard to economic relations than it is at the level of their social and political repercussions. This can encourage a form of economism in which deductions are made from abstract laws of economics with no more than the odd gesture towards the political and ideological constraints on their realization. At its worst, this produces a kind of functionalism in which little attention is given to the conflicts and struggles between interests that help determine the precise outcomes which will be observed. This is understandable, however, given that the difficulties met in grasping the inter-relationship of the economic with other aspects and levels of society continues to be one of the most highly contested problem areas in current sociology.

It is in clarifying just these kinds of problem that the sociologists of Wales, although still thin on the ground, have been able to make significant contributions. A serious start has been made on the job of tracing, through detailed empirical work, the specific implications for Wales of the general processes of de-industrialization, new forms of division of labour, and occupational change that have transformed British society in the post-war period.[38] The patterns which are uncovered will be of decisive importance for understanding group formation within Wales, including the shape taken by local class structures. The growing recognition that many of the questions about the interaction of different social variables can be resolved best through the study of their workings within particular localities has also produced a renewal of interest in the community study style of work, in which Welsh sociologists once played such a leading role, even if such research carried out now would be built upon very different theoretical and value assumptions. The sociology of Wales has been a relatively late developer, and the study of Welsh society still suffers somewhat from the implicit centralism of mainstream sociology: but there has been a qualitative shift in the level of interest over a short period and we can look forward to the fruits of what has been an exciting period of theoretical re-orientation.

References

1 For example, M. Hechter: 'Regional inequality and national integration: the case of the British Isles', *Journal of Social History*, vol. 5, no. 1, 1971, pp. 96-117; R. Rose: 'The United Kingdom as a multi-national regime', reprinted as ch. 11 in *Governing without consensus: an Irish perspective*, Faber and Faber, London, 1971, pp. 42-73; T. Nairn: *The break-up of Britain: crisis and neo-nationalism*, New Left Books, London, 1977; and P. M. Rawkins: 'Outsiders as insiders: the implications of minority nationalism in Scotland and Wales', *Comparative Politics*, 1978.

2 G. Williams (ed.): *Social and cultural change in contemporary Wales*, Routledge and Kegan Paul, London, 1978. The papers result from an SSRC Conference in September, 1976.

3 For similar observations with respect to Scotland see I. Carter: 'The Highlands of Scotland as an underdeveloped region' in E. De Kadt and G. Williams (eds.): *Sociology and development*, Tavistock, London, pp. 279-311; A. Maclaren: 'An open society', in Maclaren (ed.): *Social class in Scotland: past and present*, John Donaldson, Edinburgh, 1976, pp. 1-11.

4 A. W. Gouldner: *The coming crisis of western sociology*, Heinemann, London, 1971, pp. 30-35.

5 This passes over as proven fact into further education: see Prys Morgan: *Background to Wales: a course of studies on modern Welsh life*, Christopher Davies, Swansea, 1967, pp. 35-39.

6 C. M. Arensberg and S. T. Kimball: *Family and community in Ireland*, Peter Smith, London, 1940.

7 See C. D. Forde: *Habitat, economy and society: a geographical introduction*, Methuen, London, 1934; H. J. Fleure: *A natural history of man in Britain*, Collins, London, 1951. Forde and Fleure were both professors of geography at the University College of Wales, Aberystwyth. For a brief discussion of the background to the Aberystwyth studies, see H. Carter and W. K. D. Davies: 'Introduction' to their edition of *Geography, culture and habitat: selected essays (1925-1975) of E. G. Bowen*, Gomer Press, Llandysul, 1976, pp. xxiv-xxxiii.

8 A. D. Rees: *Life in a Welsh countryside*, University of Wales Press, Cardiff, 1950, p. 170.

9 Ibid., p. 108.

10 Even such resolutely Welsh bodies as *Urdd Gobaith Cymru* (Welsh League of Youth) and *Merched y Wawr* (the Welsh language equivalent of the Women's Institute) can be represented as in a deep sense 'Anglicizing', since they have no natural place in Welsh tradition. See T. Jones Hughes: 'Aberdaron, the social geography of a small region in the Llŷn Peninsula', in E. Davies and A. D. Rees (eds.): *Welsh rural communities*, University of Wales Press, Cardiff, 1962, pp. 174-176.

11 The classic text is E. G. Bowen's essay: 'Le Pays de Galles', 1959, reprinted in Carter and Davies, op. cit., pp. 244-271. For a recent example, see H. Carter and S. Williams: 'Aggregate studies of language and culture change in Wales' in G. Williams (ed.): op. cit., pp. 143-165. See also E. J. Hobsbawm: *Industry and empire*, Penguin, Harmondsworth, 1969, p. 298.

12 Carter and Williams: op. cit., p. 150. Bowen specifies this complex as 'love of music, poetry, philosophy and religion': op. cit., p. 259.

13 A. D. Rees: op. cit., ch.X., 'Religion', opens with what is described as 'a short statement from within the culture', p. 112.

14 Saunders Lewis, cited in D. Tecwyn Lloyd: 'Wales—see England', *Planet*, 34, 1976, p. 37.
15 A. D. Rees: op. cit., p. 170. The sentiment was repeated in Rees's 'Introduction' to L. Kohr: *Is Wales viable?*, Christopher Davies, Swansea, 1971.
16 P. E. Mayo: *The roots of identity*, Allen Lane, The Penguin Press, Harmondsworth, 1974, p. 81. For a more serious treatment of this theme, see J. Osmond: *Creative conflict: the politics of Welsh devolution*, Routledge and Kegan Paul, London, 1978.
17 Gwynfor Evans, cited in K. Buchanan: 'The revolt against satellization in Scotland and Wales', *Monthly Review*, vol. 19, no. 10, 1968, p. 43.
18 R. Tanner: 'National identity and the one-Wales model', *Planet*, 17, 1973, pp. 31-34; see also I. Bowen Rees: *Government and community*, Charles Knight, London, 1971, ch. 9.
19 C. Bell and H. Newby: *Community studies*, Allen and Unwin, London, 1971, p. 187.
20 D. Riddell: 'Towards a structuralist sociology of development', *Sociology*, 6, No. 1, 1972, p. 90.
21 T. Nairn: 'Scotland and Wales: notes on nationalist pre-history', *Planet*, 34, 1976, pp. 1-11: reprinted as Chapter 8 of this volume.
22 The leading Welsh intellectual periodical, edited until his death in 1974 by Alwyn D. Rees.
23 A. Butt-Philip: *The Welsh question*, University of Wales Press, Cardiff, 1975, pp. 246-247.
24 M. Hechter: *Internal colonialism: the Celtic fringe in British national development, 1536-1966*, Routledge and Kegan Paul, London, 1975.
25 Archie Lamont, cited in Buchanan: op. cit., p. 42.
26 A. G. Frank: *Sociology of development and underdevelopment of sociology*, Pluto Press, London, 1971.
27 H. Lefebvre, cited in J. Carney *et al*: 'Regional underdevelopment in late capitalism: a study of the north east of England', in I. Masser (ed.): *Theory and practice in regional science*, Pion, London, 1976, p. 12.
28 J. Carney *et al:* op. cit., p. 14.
29 T. Nairn: op. cit., p. 8.
30 K. Buchanan: op. cit., p. 42.
31 T. Davies: 'The Arfon quarries', *Planet*, 30, 1976, p. 11.
32 B. Thomas: 'Wales and the Atlantic economy', reprinted in B. Thomas: *The Welsh economy: studies in expansion*, University of Wales Press, Cardiff, 1962, pp. 1-29.
33 P. Wilding: *Poverty: the facts in Wales*, Child Poverty Action Group, London, 1977.
34 Hechter: *Internal colonialism*, p. 349.
35 Ibid., p. 133.
36 Ibid., p. 5.
37 D. Massey: *Spatial divisions of labour*, Macmillan, 1984.
38 See, for example, the work of the Wales Regionalism Group, based in the University of Wales Institute of Science and Technology (UWIST), at Cardiff.

Chapter Seven

Recent Trends in the Sociology of Wales*

Glyn Williams

For many years the growth of sociology as an academic discipline in Britain focused upon a few universities in England. When the teaching of sociology expanded during the 1960s there remained a tendency for the new centres to reflect the perspectives of the early centres. Thus the establishment of sociology departments within the University of Wales did not generate an immediate interest in the sociology of Wales. On the contrary the tendency was to bring sociological method and theory to bear upon social problems in Wales with little reference to the fact that the work was undertaken in Wales. Furthermore, little of the teaching of sociology focused upon Wales and the organisation of the profession in the form of the British Sociological Association was administered from England with the activities of the Association being almost exclusively English. Little wonder that the contents of the various courses titled 'The social structure of modern Britain' and the textbooks which served them contained virtually no mention of anywhere outside of England.

An exception to this unfortunate disciplinary ethnocentrism was the anthropological perspective developed by workers such as Daryll Forde, Alwyn D. Rees, Dafydd Jenkins, Trefor M. Owen, Emrys Jones and others at Aberystwyth and one or two of Max Gluckman's students at Manchester, most notably Isobel Emmett and Ronald Frankenberg. These workers made important contributions to the community study tradition of the 1940s and 1950s.[1] Unfortunately this interest at Aberystwyth

* This chapter is an updated version of G. Williams 'Towards a sociology of Wales' which first appeared in *Planet*, 40 (1977), 30-37.

appears to have disappeared at the beginning of the 1950s when the focus of the joint Department of Geography and Anthropology shifted almost exclusively to the study of geography.

By the beginning of the 1970s, partly as a result of the expansion in the teaching of sociology and partly as a result of the increasing interest in Welsh affairs in general, the number of people working on issues relevant to the sociology of Wales was on the increase. There is little doubt that the interest in Wales shown by North American social scientists lent an air of respectability to such studies, especially among those who had undertaken research in Wales which bore little relevance to the place of study. Many such people were incensed by the work of Michael Hechter who described Wales as an internal colony of England. This antagonism promoted a critical scrutiny of Welsh society and culture.

Since 1978 three collections of essays on Welsh society and culture have been published in addition to numerous other publications.[2] Much of this activity derived from the funding of a conference and a series of research seminars by the former Social Science Research Council (now known as the Economic and Social Studies Research Council (E.S.R.C.)) and the various meetings of the Sociology of Wales Study Group (British Sociological Association). There is little doubt that these forums have stimulated considerable discussion and that those involved have learnt a great deal from one another. While the main thrust of this activity has involved sociology, other disciplines, including planning, geography, psychology, anthropology and social administration have also contributed.

It is not surprising that the early work showed little theoretical or thematic integration. Neither is it surprising that the self-conscious nature of the work on Wales led to an emphasis on the study of language and ethnicity. This may account for the relatively small attention that was given to industrial Wales. There was an emphasis on the relative economic deprivation of Wales within the

British context and also of the inability of the state to extend its compensatory services to many areas. In addition there was a concern about the denigrading effect of the neo-evolutionary modernisation thesis, with the emphasis on class as the exclusive dimension of inequality and with the prevailing attempts to analyse language shift and maintenance. Yet it was not easy to come to terms with the causal explanations of what ultimately can be regarded as very complex problems.

Perhaps the most rewarding part of this early work involved the re-evaluation of preceding work on Welsh society and culture. The ensuing debate brought contrasting theoretical and political perspectives into focus. It is little wonder that subsequent work has adopted a much more uniform orientation on topics which were to become the focus of research as a consequence of this discussion. Although it is inconceivable that such an exercise would be undertaken with reference to the sociology of England, it would certainly be beneficial.

For a long time the emphasis on the community studies of the Aberystwyth school obscured the false nature of the rural-urban dichotomy and the manner in which it inhibited the analysis of society *per se*. This should not be surprising given that the work derived from the theoretical perspective of structural functionalism and also that the prevailing modernisation theme depends upon such dichotomies.[3] The limitations of structural functionalism were evident in these community studies. Thus Rees was criticised for treating communities as homogeneous, holistic and harmonious entities unarticulated to the wider society. The associated 'Welsh way of life' was claimed to represent a romantic solidarity. The absence of a dynamic theory resulted in the development of a view of society as a central dominant core, perilously surrounded by a diverse periphery, both attracted by the prospects of assimilation and repelled by the uneasy and humiliating—but perhaps rewarding—prospects of accommodation. Rees's failure was held to involve a failure to locate the mechanism by which this uneasy balance between centre and periphery was settled or unsettled, and more specifically the question of legitimacy. It is only recently that an alternative conception of community has been drawn from quite a different theoretical perspective. This suggests that such a reconceptualisation involves a rejection of the emphasis of space, institution and interaction as the defining criterion of community. In its place it is suggested that, as in the feudal/capitalist distinction or, indeed, the anarchist perspective, the community should be placed in opposition to the state. Thus the forms of social practice which the various community studies identified should be seen as a form of resistance to the power of the state.

While it is difficult not to disagree with this criticism it is perhaps unfair to single out Alwyn D. Rees for special attention and to isolate his work from the more general trend of anthropological studies of that period. Indeed, the argument is reminiscent of that between Robert Redfield and Oscar Lewis during the 1960s following the restudy of Tepozlan by Lewis.[4] It does not seem that Rees was somehow wrong but that he presented and answered questions which were not only different in particulars but also in kind to those which his critics found of interest and relevance. This is the inevitable consequence of the ability and inability of different problematics to confront specific issues. The structural functionalist problematic assumed by Rees and British social anthropologists of the time did tend to portray a 'Welsh way of life' as a single, homogenised entity under threat from external forces. Nonetheless the work of Rees and his associates did constitute a valuable background for subsequent study and many social scientists would do well to consult the work of Rees which focuses on issues other than community studies. It contains much that is topical.

One of the most obvious issues associated with the criticism of the Aberystwyth school involves the centrality of social class in the analysis of society and culture. This is an issue which has plagued Marxism since Lukacs introduced the issue of false consciousness with its claim that any form of consciousness other than class consciousness constituted a false consciousness since class awareness was the only 'real' form of consciousness. It has been evident to many students of Wales that it is essential to reject this argument but it has taken the feminist movement to persuade most social scientists that such a perspective is, indeed, tenable. Recent developments in French social science involve the rejection of the idea that society consists of rational actors and its displacement by the idea that the subject is formed in, and not outside of, discourse. This means that individuals are drawn into a variety of discourses where they are brought into existence. Thus ethnic, gender or any other form of discourse is as relevant for interpellation[5] as the class discourse. Indeed, part of the class struggle involves the struggle to establish the salience of the class discourse.

Criticisms of community studies *per se* and of the rural nature of these studies led to an emphasis on the increasing relationship of Wales to Britain and on the relationship between economy and society. The forerunner in this reorientation was Hechter.[6] His work constituted a break with the previous diffusionist orientation of modernisation theory. Hechter's objective was to test the proposition that ethnic salience is to be explained by reference to a model of uneven economic development. He claims that socio-cultural differentiation is not, of itself, a sufficient reason for the resurgence of ethnic nationalism. Yet there is an element of continuity with previous work for it reflects the manner in which the concept of culture is operationalised in terms of cultural relativism.[7] Its basis is a belief in the essential equality in principle of all cultures and sub-cultures. This idea of culture is expressed in terms of the colonial analogy where the culture of the oppressed people or group being held to represent the 'true' aspirations for the liberation of the oppressed. Thus, national liberation involves the rediscovery and reinforcement of their 'own' culture by individual members of the oppressed. Culture is a given feature which the individual can grasp rather than a dynamic, constantly produced, entity. Hechter's reactive theory suggests that ethnic solidarity will increase in stratified social systems when individuals are assigned to specific types of occupations on the basis of observable cultural traits. This generates a hierarchical division of labour which in conceptual terms, can be contrasted with a segmented division of labour where certain occupational sectors are monopolised by ethnic groups to the exclusion of others. As modernisation continues ethnic division will increase since the colonised group 'reactively asserts its own culture as equal or superior to that of the relatively advantaged core'.

Hechter's work was subject to numerous criticisms which included the question of the validity of his empirical 'proof', the inadequacy of his analysis of socio-economic diferentiation and the limitations of his theoretical assumptions. One fundamental weakness of his work seems to be the epistemological confusion which derives from attempting to integrate concepts drawn from different theoretical perspectives. Thus, while he draws upon the Marxist concept of uneven capitalist development, his discussion of class is unambiguously Weberian, involving the individual in the market place. Many of the contradictions in the study derive from this inconsistency.

Hechter claims to have produced a 'theory of ethnic change'. He claims that *given* a system of stratification and *given* that the system is based upon a cultural division of labour, then we can expect opposition to domination and exploitation to assume an ethnic dimension. What is undertaken in the study is to suggest that ethnicity on the part of the dominated group is a product of ethnicity on the part of the dominant group. Ethnicity is therefore already given in the situation: it is part and parcel of an original assumption—the cultural division of labour. Furthermore there is a sense of conspiracy involved in the emergence of this important concept. This is manifest in terms of a failure to explain ethnicity while raising a different question of under what conditions a cultural division of labour emerges.

It is evident that Hechter did raise numerous hackles in claiming that Wales constituted a colony of England. This in itself was beneficial in that it led some to question their own assumptions about the relationship between the two countries. More important, perhaps, it led to a focus on the issue of uneven development and its relationship to Marxist theory. Where ethnicity was discussed within Marxism there existed the inevitable functionalism of Marxist reductionism in which superstructural forces are held to 'function' in order to sustain an infrastructure. The state is presented as functioning as the general factor of social cohesion with ideology existing as a function of its role in legitimising capitalist relations of production. Thus the 'cause' of reactive nationalism lies at the infrastructural level. Similarly ethnicity is treated as an ideology which is 'explained' by reducing it to some hidden infrastructure that logically precedes it. The integration of actors along ethnic dimensions derives from the way in which the economic and political generates a structure which 'needs' an ideological support. Ethnicity then becomes superstructural, imaginary or epiphenomenal. Only to a limited extent does this reductionism treat ethnicity as a feature of an autonomous or semi-autonomous superstructure. Moreover, it is conceivable that ethnicity is an aspect of ideology that is irreducible to the economic base, having its own separate historicity. This would mean that ideology has its own internal law of development. While this means that reducing ideology to the economic base is impossible it also means that ethnicity is explained in terms of itself which is to reify ethnicity and to proffer on it its own internal laws of development. By rejecting the reductionism of the orthodox position with the idea of a correspondence of levels also being rejected it was possible to recognise that substantial transformation could be affected in one level without having implications for the other levels. This development had profound repercussions for both gender and ethnicity but it has yet to be systematically absorbed into the sociology of Wales.

It is this theme of relative deprivation within the Marxist context of uneven economic development which has been the predominant issue in more recent sociological discussions on Wales. Some have taken a broad perspective, relating the situation in Wales to developments in the capitalist world economy while others have resorted to locality studies.[8] It is held that the increasing integration of the world economy and the concentration of economic power in the form of multi-national corporations is having an effect upon the internal economies of several states. The world economy is conventionally divided into core, peripheral and semi-peripheral space. It is claimed that Britain has moved from being part of the core to being part of the semi-periphery, being exploited by the more powerful states while itself exploiting the peripheral states. These changes in the world economy mean that the terms of economic competition have changed for the British economy and especially so for peripheral locations within Britain. These developments are forcing an internal restructuring of the economy.

Competition on a global scale involves both producer and consumer markets and obliges these sectors to reorganise, relocate or even to close their production facilities. Some have treated this as a new phase of the capitalist mode of production. This view means that it is possible to focus attention on the social formation, that is, features of social organisation belonging to more than one phase are seen in conjunction rather than as in a relationship of historical disjunction.

Some of the earlier work focused upon the uneven development of capitalism in explaining 'regional' inequalities,[9] an orientation which, if focused exclusively on economic factors or even on social classes merely as empirical forces, lost sight of any unique features of the Welsh experience. There was also a tendency to treat this unevenness as a static phenomenon. The shift to a discussion of economic restructuring as a cause of uneven development has emphasised the dynamic nature of the process. Indeed, studies of electronic enterprises in Wales indicate that the training period for the workers is no longer than two weeks while the continuing shift in production machinery is also evident. This means that if the relative advantage a firm recognises vis-à-vis other competitors is lost, there will be no difficulty in relocating either to a competing area where the state offers higher incentives or, indeed, to any other part of the globe. The study of individual enterprises is one of the most time consuming and yet one of the more rewarding aspects of this type of study. Yet this focus cannot be taken in isolation from the consequences of such developments for the spatial division of labour.

The new pattern of economic investment means that earlier patterns are being undermined with consequences for enterprises and the nature of the workforce. This development should not be seen in terms of succeeding phases which can be explained within an evolutionary scheme by superimposing history and a dichotomous earlier/present or traditional/modern dichotomy. Both exist at the same moment in time and must be explained in terms of their relationship to one another. The role of the state in stimulating such developments must also be recognised. The focus on uneven development emphasised the role of the state in channelling public funds to private enterprises in order to generate relocation. Evidence suggests that such incentives were unnecessary since most such firms were seeking advantages in terms of cheap labour and/or new markets. This has had consequences for the established enterprises who are in direct competition with the beneficiaries of the new developments and in the resultant competition with the beneficiaries of the new developments and in the resultant competition many of them are liquidated. Neither should we lose sight of the fact that the reorientation is not simply a 'regional' reorientation but invariably involves growth-pole concentrations within each 'region'. As a consequence there is a marginalisation[10] of both space and people.

Economic restructuring has profound implications for the local social structure. It is no coincidence that much of the work that has been undertaken in Wales has concentrated on the nature of change in the occupational structure for it is the kind of work which requires least resources. Data on occupational change are readily available but there is a need to conduct funded research in order to investigate the consequences and precise nature of such changes. It is disarming to say the least that, once again, the main funding body for sociological research, the E.S.R.C., in funding work on restructuring has given all of its resources to projects on English localities to the exclusion of Wales, Scotland and the north of Ireland. This merely underlines the ethnocentrism of English academics.

Prior to 1939 the economy of Wales was orientated towards primary production, being dominated in terms of employment by coal, agriculture and steel production. One of the most obvious features of the restructuring has been the manner in which employment has shifted away from these sectors. The undermining of the heavy industries and agriculture which, in terms of occupational emphasis, was heavily male dominated, means that new forms of employment involving females have been introduced. The explanatory argument within the restructuring thesis is that this is a consequence of the unorganised nature of female employment which is capable of underpricing male labour whilst, at the same time, also being willing to work part time. This does not have to be a conspiratorial argument if the dynamics of capital accumulation are recognised. However there is a tendency to equate this development with a conscious attempt on the part of the state to dismantle trade union activity. This argument does a grave disservice to women and fails to recognise that much of the resistance to the organisation of female labour derives from the male chauvinism of the trade union movement. Alongside the feminisation of the labour force is a deskilling of the labour force, a development which allows constant replacement of labour. Thus the demand for young female labour in the electronics industry partly relates to the strain of this type of work on the eyesight and the associated high turn over of personnel.

Given that different localities have different occupational characteristics as a consequence of the reshuffling it is clear that the first task involved identifying the nature of the local labour markets within Wales. Such work has identified how previously under-industrialised locations

Figure 21. Over and under representation of Welsh speakers and the population born outside Wales, Gwynedd 1981.

Socio-economic groups	*Welsh speakers** (1)	*Extent of over/under representation* (2)	*population born outside Wales** (2)
		(per cent)	
1. Employers/managers: large establishments	–	10.8	+
2. Employer/managers: small establishments	–	21.6	+
3. Professional workers: self employed	–	12.6	+
4. Professional workers: employers	–	29.2	+
5.1 Ancillary workers and artists	–	0.6	+
5.2 Foreman/supervisors non-manual	–	10.9	+
6. Junior non-manual	–	4.6	+
7. Personal service workers	+	2.1	–
8. Foreman/supervisors: manual	–	4.3	+
9. Skilled manual:	+	9.3	–
10. Semi-skilled:	+	4.7	–
11. Unskilled manual:	+	12.2	–
12. Own account: non-professional	–	10.1	+
13. Farmers: employers/managers	+	20.7	–
14. Farmers: own account	+	25.3	–
15. Agricultural workers	+	13.4	–
16. Armed forces:	–	45.7	+
Percentage totals	66.9%	—	33.1%

* Under representation: –
Over representation: +

SOURCE: Unpublished census date, 1981, (10% sample).

have experienced the entry of decentralised branch plants and small independent or sub-contracting firms while conurbations have become de-industrialised and converted into predominantly service economies. Thus different forms of local concentrations can be identified and the next stage is the obvious one of linking these concentrations to occupational and, if possible, class configurations. This line of analysis has yet to be developed.

The pace of the restructing process has been so rapid that it would appear a mistake to look for adjustment processes associated with occupational restructuring within the localities. Thus the most obvious conclusion is that the new circulation of capital has been related to a circulation of labour. Thus migration is one essential feature of any analysis. Again there is some scope for drawing upon published official data. The argument focusing on the cultural division of labour can be substantiated by looking, for example, at an area such as the county of Gwynedd where there have been profound developments of branch plant and new manufacturing industries. The most obvious feature of such development is that if the employment decisions for both manufacturing and retail are made outside of Wales, at head office, then most of the higher-level managerial or professional posts will be held by in-migrants. On the other hand, if the objective is the search for cheap labour, the proletarian labour will be local. That is, we envisage two different labour markets for different class locations. A comparison of Welsh speakers and residents born outside Wales in Gwynedd indicates clearly that this line of argument is correct (Fig. 21). There is a heavy over-representation of non-Welsh born and an under-representation of Welsh-speakers in the top four official socio-economic groups used in the census tabulations. There seems to be little room for capital accumulation by indigenous, non-oligarchic entrepreneurs. The data merely show an acceleration of the tendency for most industry in Wales to be non-Welsh owned. Furthermore it is absurd for officials of the Welsh Development Agency to push the culturalist explanation that whatever is unique to the Welsh inhibits such developments. This merely displays a naivety about the nature of capitalist dynamics.

We are here beginning to witness the next stage in the development of research on social restructuring: what is the precise nature of the change in social structure and how does this relate to specific forms of struggle? Thus far this work has been limited to analyses of the struggle over the language, nationalism and local politics.[11] Conspicuously absent is the study of gender struggle. There are a few exceptions to this predominant trend but the study of men and women in the workforce in terms of the sex typing of jobs and seniority have been few. It is here that we can identify the social, historical and cultural variations which are specific and the manner in which they become an integral part of struggle. The most obvious example of this involves language. As suggested above, the labour market for the higher classes has expanded considerably as a consequence of restructuring, encompassing, in some cases, an international dimension although state closure places a constraint on such developments. Whilst this section of the labour market was essentially local it involved *burgher mobility* (upward mobility linking local involvement and occupational involvement), as opposed to *spiralism* (the link between social and geographical mobility within careers). The emphasis on spiralism generated a reaction on the part of the local bourgeoisie and petit-bourgeosie and an attempt was made to close parts of the labour market by emphasising that certain occupations required a Welsh language qualification. This is not unlike the manner in which professionalisation generates closure. However, since most of the private sector was externally owned and controlled, it was limited to the public sector.

The restructuring process and the associated mobility of labour has generated profound repercussions for Welsh language production and reproduction. The reproduction concept is essential if we are to avoid the consensus limitations of structural functionalism which remains the main theoretical perspective of sociolinguistics and the sociology of language. Historically the reproduction of the language was limited to the family, community and religious domains. Increased in-migration has resulted in substantial language group exogamy which means that the family is no longer able to reproduce the language to the extent that it once did. Furthermore in-migration also undermines the ability of community institutions to serve this function while secularisation derives from the advent of the welfare state and undermines the language reproduction role of the chapels. The subsequent rapid erosion of the language has resulted in a language movement which, while not clearly understanding the nature of these changes, has fought to redress their effect. This involved relegitimising and reinstitutionalisation of Welsh language reproduction in new domains, most notably education and the media. Unlike the previous situation these domains are central to social reproduction and, as a consequence, we begin to see the emergence of class varieties of Welsh—a feature which hitherto was absent. This in turn leads to a struggle within language, a struggle over language purity, a struggle with clear class dimensions.

This form of analysis has been extended to encompass nationalism—another phenomenon which has fascinated observers of Wales. There is an unfortunate tendency in much analysis of Welsh politics to treat nationalism as a residual unrelated to the 'natural' class basis of politics in general. In consequence nationalism is claimed to have a different form of rationalism from 'real' politics, this rationality deriving from some feature of cultural uniqueness be it language, religious nonconformity or some other feature. The consequence of this perspective is the denigration of nationalist voters who are either treated as non-rational or possessing an outmoded rationalism associated with 'tradition'.[12] This perspective shares with the restructuring thesis the weakness of the centred actor: that is, most theories of society conceive of people as rational actors who consciously construct reality. Inevitably, this view leads to conspiratorial perspectives and to a competition between alternative forms of consciousness or rationality. In order to escape these limitations there is a need to decenter the actor. This can be achieved by recognising that there is no reality outside of discourse and that the human subject is not outside of discourse but rather is created through discourse.

This in turn, means that the human actor is created through language. Thus 'Wales' or 'nation' can have quite different meanings depending upon the discursive formation in which they are located and it is a matter of struggle to locate them in the symbolic where they achieve their 'true' meaning. Thus class, gender and ethnicity can be competing or overlapping forms of interpellation none of which has any necessary predominance. It means that political orientation is no longer a simple matter of establishing the relationsip between class configuration deriving from restructuring and voting behaviour as the restructuring thesis implies. Rather, it involves a careful analysis of discursive formation and the relationship between capitalist contradiction and interpellation. The analysis of Welsh politics is very slowly moving in this direction.

In conclusion it should be clear that the past ten years have seen a pronounced shift of emphasis in the analysis of Welsh society and culture. From a critical scrutiny of earlier work through the analysis of on-going theoretical perspectives the research has progressed slowly towards a more integrated materialist approach which encompasses recent theoretical developments. The empircial facets of these theoretical developments await full and proper development.

References

1. Rees, A. D. *Life in a Welsh countryside.* University of Wales Press, Cardiff, 1950. Frankenberg, R. *Village on the border.* Cohen and West, London, 1957. Emmett, I. *A north Wales village.* Routledge and Kegan Paul, London, 1964. Rees, A. D. and E. Davies (eds.) *Welsh rural communities.* University of Wales Press, Cardiff, 1960.
2. Williams, G. (ed.) *Social and cultural change in contemporary Wales.* Routledge and Kegan Paul, London, 1978. Rees, G. and T. Rees (eds.) *Poverty and social inequality in Wales.* Croom Helm, London, 1980. Williams, G. (ed.) *Crisis of economy and ideology: essays on Welsh society, 1840-1980.* B.S.A. Sociology of Wales Study Group, Bangor, 1983.
3. Structural functionalism is a theoretical perspective which draws upon a biological analogy, seeing society as a series of interlocking parts. Change in one part inevitably obliges the other parts to adapt in order to reassume a harmonious integration. Consequently continuous conflict is inconceivable. It was the main perspective of Anglo-American sociology during the 1950s and 1960s, its main theoretician being Talcott Parsons.
4. Redfield, R. *The folk culture of the Yucatan.* University of Chicago Press, Chicago, 1941. Lewis, O. *Life in a Mexican village: Tepozlan restudied.* University of Illinois Press, Urbana, 1951.
5. Interpellation refers to the manner in which a person is hailed or drawn into a discourse by key features of that discourse. A Welsh person in New York will respond to the word 'Taff' whereas it will be disregarded by others.
6. Hechter, M. *Internal colonialism: the Celtic fringe in British national development 1536-1966.* Routledge and Kegan Paul, London, 1975. Parts of Hechter's original text are reprinted in Chapter 9 of this book.
7. Cultural relativism involves the belief that all sociocultural systems are inherently of equal value.
8. See Rawkins, P. 'The global corporation, ethno-nationalism and the changing face of the European state'. *World Affairs.* November, 1978. Cooke, P. 'Dependency development in UK regions with particular reference to Wales', *Progress in Planning.* vol. 15, no. 1, 1980, pp. 1-62. Cooke, P. 'Local class structure in Wales', *Papers in Planning Research.* No. 31, University of Wales Institute of Science and Technology, Cardiff, Department of Town Planning. Morgan, K. 'State regional interventions and industrial reconstruction in post-war Britain: the case of Wales', *Urban and Regional Studies Working Papers.* No. 16, University of Sussex, 1980. Rees, G. and J. Lambert 'Nationalism as legitimation? notes towards a political economy of regional development in south Wales'. In M. Harlowe (ed.) *New perspectives in urban change and conflict.* Heineman, London, 1981, pp. 122-137.
9. See Lovering, J. *Gwynedd a county in crisis.* Occasional Paper no. 2, Coleg Harlech.
10. Marginalisation refers to the manner in which specific forms of economic change generate a cleavage between the dynamic features of new developments and the stagnating features of the pre-existent forms. See Quijano Obregon, A.; Redefinición de la dependencia y proceso de marginalizacion en America Latina. In C. Weffort and A. Quijano Obregon (eds.) *Populismo, marginalisacion, y dependencia.* Editorial Universitaria Centroamericana, San Jose, Costa Rica, 1973, pp. 171-229.

11. See Williams, G. (ed.) *The sociology of Welsh.* Mouton, The Hague, forthcoming. Willams, G. 'The political economy of contemporary nationalism in Wales', in R. Rogowski and E. Tiryakin (eds.) *New nationalisms of the developed West.* Allen and Unwin, London, 1985, pp. 315-337. Rawkins, P. 'Living in the house of power: Welsh nationalism and the dilemma of antisystem politics' in R. Rogowski and E. Tiryakin (eds.) *New nationalism of the developed West.* Allen and Unwin, London, 1985, pp. 294-315. Williams, G. 'What is Wales? The discourse of devolution', *Journal of Ethnic and Racial Studies*, vol 7, no. 1, 1984, pp. 138-159. Cooke, P. 'Recent theories of political regionalism: a critique and an alternative proposal', *International Journal of Urban and Regional Research*, vol 8, no. 4, 1984, pp. 549-571. Williams, G. and C. Roberts 'Language, education and reproduction in Wales', in B. Bain (ed.) *The sociogenesis of language and human conduct.* Plenum, New York, 1983, pp. 497-517.
12. Political scientists seem to insist on persevering with this theme. See, for example, some of the papers in Osmond, J. (ed.) *The national question again.* Gomer, Llandysul, 1985.

SECTION 3

IDEOLOGIES

Chapter Eight

Culture and Politics in Wales*

Tom Nairn

I

> People talk of the betrayal by the Tudors, of the decline of the Welsh nobility; of the disappearance of the bardic profession; of the beginning of the middle class and wealthy merchants who saw nothing in Welsh culture; of the wrong done to the Welsh language; of the Anglicizing of education . . . All these are secondary causes. There was a deeper cause: the thing that destroyed the civilization of Wales and ruined Welsh culture, that brought about the dire plight of Wales today, was—nationalism . . .'

It is fifty years since Saunders Lewis electrified the audience at Plaid Cymru's first Summer School with these words. He was of course warning it against the perils of a merely political, power-hungry nationalism—against a development in any way like what he imagined the course of modern English history to have been. And the warning was accompanied by his plea for a distinctively Welsh development; for a spiritual and cultural nationalism founded on native tradition and looking back to the Middle Ages.

It is about fifty years, too, since Scottish nationalism first assumed an embryo yet vaguely recognisable shape with John MacCormick's National Party of Scotland, in 1928. This broad and already moderate political movement was only one ancestor of today's SNP; but it had begun to lead the way out of what one pioneer, Lewis Spence, saw as the giddy confusion of the cultural nationalists in Scotland. On that side, he wrote, the movement in favour of a national rebirth has attracted ' . . . many of the

* Originally published as T. Nairn 'Wales and Scotland: notes on nationalist pre-history', in *Planet*, 34, 1976, 1-11.

greatest cranks in Christendom . . . a maelstrom bubbling with the cross-currents of rival and frequently fantastic theories, schemes and notion, riotous with tumultuous personality and convulsive with petulant individual predilection . . . There is not chart, no plan, nothing approaching a serious, practical Scotsman-like policy in either art or politics.'[1] Within a short time the serious and Scotsman-like trend was to emerge triumphant, expelling the culture-heads and *littérateurs* to a Celtic outer darkness.[2]

Although not many would now swallow Lewis's mediaevalism, or denounce the Scottish literary renaissance quite so sharply, the two images are still quite familiar. They reflect, respectively, a nationalism in which cultural issues have been predominant, and one in which culture has occupied a very secondary place. It would be exaggerated to say that Welsh nationalism was culturist in outlook while Scottish nationalism was philistine. But few would fail to recognise some truth in the contrast.

This contrast is linked to many others, and to a great deal of mutual misunderstanding. Few Scots easily understand or sympathise with the anguishing dilemmas of the language-problem here: on the other hand, Welshmen are often puzzled by the very existence of a nationalist movement without a language of its own. The Scot perceives a colossal fuss being made about nothing: the Welsh nationalist is intrigued by a country where there seems nothing to make a fuss about. Welsh nationalism has always been strikingly internationalist in outlook, finding a natural affinity in many movements and personalities on continental Europe. Scottish nationalism has tended to be somewhat solitary, with only its Gaelic fringe seeking actively for such contacts. Although sometimes voicing the proper sentiments about repressed nationalities and minorities, the SNP mainstream shows distinctly greater enthusiasm for bourgeois Scandinavia than for the Bretons or the Basques.

And so on. We still do not understand each other very well. After fifty years, we ought to understand one another better. It has become practically and politically important to do so, as well as culturally desirable. The pre-history of Welsh and Scottish nationalism is over, and we are now launched into the irreversible process of the history of these movements—a history in which Wales and Scotland will have many more common interests and struggles than when they were tame provinces of empire.

However, it is not so easy. Although it is high time we advanced beyond the base-line of sonorous sermons about solidarity and common foes, it is actually difficult to work out a line of march. The trouble is that we still lack reliable charts.

A mere point-by-point comparison between two national movements—or between two nations—will not reveal or explain very much. Anyone can see that Wales and Scotland are remarkably different countries: but in itself, such observation will remain superficial and a matter for anecdotes rather than analysis. To get farther we have to have some kind of theory that embraces both of them, a theory which deals with places like Wales and Scotland and situates them in an intelligible historical context. Only then, surely, will we be able to determine more realistically where we stand, and what we can do together or hope to learn from one another.

II

> The small-state concept . . . seems not only a matter of expediency but of divine plan, and on this account makes everything soluble. It constitutes, in fact, nothing but the political application of the most basic organizing and balancing device of nature . . . social blessings are concomitants of social size—small size (Leopold Kohr, *The breakdown of nations* (1957), pp. 97-8).

We do not yet have a theoretical framework which will let us do this properly. But this is not all. The trouble is that a phoney theory has arisen, a framework which to some extent actively misleads us in the quest. Were we merely in the normal condition of being in the dark, this would be bad enough. As it is, a lurid light falls across the landscape, and conveys a grossly over-simplified technicolor image.

The theory I have in mind may be called for purposes of argument that of 'cultural colonialism'. Its key notions are those of cultural identity and cultural oppression. The identity it focuses on is that of the smaller peripheral communities and regions of Western Europe; the oppression lies in the way they have been treated by the politically dominant nationalities, the 'core areas'. Metropolitan domination has of course assumed economic form. It has extracted what it needed from these regions, in labour power and other resources; and such development as it has fostered there has been typically lopsided and transitory. However, the theory characteristically emphasises cultural robbery rather than economic. Large-scale, over-centralised capitalism has eroded or destroyed old community identity. It is through a battle for the recovery of their culture that these regions are reviving today—a struggle primarily against 'alienation', and the brontosaural bureaucracy epitomised by the Swansea Licensing Centre.

In *The centralist enemy* John Osmond has summed up many elements of the view as follows: 'The road of the Corporate State leads to a dead end . . . The only rational alternative is a view of life that gives precedence to the concept of community. This requires a new philosophy: one that will put community interests first, even at the expense of economic interests . . . The first requirement of a community is that it be given a human scale in which people can reasonably seek a sense of purpose, responsibility and identity'.[3] Naturally, communities can fight for this philosophy best when they have a strong ethnic and linguistic basis. So these particular vehicles of nationality are seen as especially significant.

I am well aware of the powerful Welsh stake in this new European *Weltanschauung*. Twenty years ago Leopold Kohr produced an advance philosophical benediction of it, in the shape of *The breakdown of nations*. More recently, as well as John Osmond, Ned Thomas's *Planet*, Patricia Mayo, and a number of others, have played a part in formulating it.[4] It fits many aspects of Welsh experience rather well, obviously. And as an ideology it probably appeals particularly to the strong cultural dimension of the Welsh national movement.

The taproot of this new smallness-and-beauty world-view may lie in Vienna, like so many others. However, the stirrings of the last decade have produced many new versions of it. Apart from Wales, it is probably most influential now in regions like Occitania and Brittany. Outside Europe it has a certain importance in Canada, in the more anarchist form given it by George Woodcock and his school. From North America also have come two recent *tours de force* on the subject, Michael Zwerin's breathless travelogue of neonationalism, *A case for the balkanization of practically everyone*, and Michael Hechter's imposing study of *Internal colonialism*.[5]

The latter is particularly important. It represents a definitive academic anointment of the thesis, complete with Ph.D.-worthy tables of figures, prodigious variety of arcane references, and a style of argumentation tortuous to the point of illegibility. Underneath the armour, though, the idea is the same. British capitalist development produced a set of 'internal colonies' in its Celtic fringe, for basically the same reasons as it created external colonisation all over the globe. It is the contradictory nature of capitalist growth to do so. After external decolonisation the liberation movements of the interior colonies have begun. 'The most recent crystallisation of Celtic nationalism may ultimately be understood as a trenchant critique of the principle of bureaucratic centralism', he writes. Alas (he continues in characteristic vein) 'Bureaucratic administration seldom seems to enable less advantaged groups to achieve resources equal to those of dominant groups', and the under-advantaged finally tumble to this and demand something better.

Their demand has to be couched in cultural terms. This is why Hechter takes such a kindly view of Wales, and such a chilly one of Scotland. Unable throughout his argument to cope with the fundamental error of locating

Scotland in the 'Celtic fringe' at all, he ends by chastising us for our addiction to GNP and input-output tables. Still recovering from the shock of being told they were really colonized Celts, most SNP-ers would be even more disconcerted to lean that their party's 'lack of a strong appeal to the separate cultural identity of Scotland' means that the SNP 'tacitly admits the cultural indistinguishability of Scotland and England', and is therefore a form of nationalism 'available for cooptation with appropriate ceremony and rewards' by Mother England.[6]

Something is wrong here. It is not merely that the author fails to realise that there might be another sort of 'cultural identity' altogether, one having little to do with literature or emblems, which Scottish nationalists fail to appeal to only because they feel so secure in it. Nor is it the absurd confusion about the Celtic and the non-Celtic in Scottish history. There is also something more deeply amiss on the plane of theory.

This theory is wrong because it lumps too many different things together. Both in analysing the causes and in considering the effects of new nationalism in Europe, it is too superficial. It may be effective ideology, but it rests on rather poor history. Both the causes and the results and the probable future of these movements are more various than it allows for. In spite of Professor Hechter's massive attempt at legitimation, the theory remains too abstract, and too neat.

The acid test of this and similar generalizations is the comparison betwen Wales and Scotland. Although parts of the same geographical island and ruled by the same state, they are possibly the most different of the emerging countries, above all in a deeper historical sense. As I said, we need a theoretical framework to put them together; and they in turn should be the main proving ground of such a theory.

III

> In most respects Wales and Scotland are very different countries. Scotland is, to use 19th century terminology, a 'historic nation' ... Wales on the other hand was a typical 'non-historic nation ...' Eric Hobsbawm. *The attitude of popular classes towards national movements for independence* (1966).[7]

The new political romanticism perceives Wales and Corsica, Scotland and Galicia, Friesland and the Basque Country as so many detachments of the same army, fighting broadly the same battle. No doubt they do have certain things in common. But the only way of being sure what these are is to take full account, at the same time, of the remarkable differences among these territories and situations.

There is one such difference which we ought to concentrate on. More than any other, I think it may help us to grasp the differential location of Scotland and Wales within the larger process. There are at least two contrasting sorts of problem at work. One might define these, in an admittedly crude way, as the problem of relative under-development and the problem of relative over-development.

'Under-development' in this context is of course relative to the general conditions of the 'metropolitan' area of Western Europe. It does not imply any wider identification with third World under-development (an analogy that has frequently been taken much too literally). Here, it refers to those predominantly agrarian regions—usually of peasants or small cultivators—which were exploited as sources of manpower and food or raw materials during the first century and a half of the industrial revolution. They were also typically exploited in a political sense, as the basis for political conservatism in the core areas. And nowadays they have usually become zones of summer holiday development or tourism. Corsica, Occitania, Brittany, Galicia, the Highland region of Scotland,

Friesland—these are some among many examples of this situation.

In all these cases uneven development has simply thrust back regions and peoples. It has induced depopulation, cultural impoverishment, a psychology of powerlessness and dependency, and fostered particularly fragmentary or distorted kinds of economic growth. The 'regional policies' of the big states and the Common Market were intended to counteract this pattern, but were probably too little and far too late to do so.

But there are also a number of regions whose key problem has been determined in a wholly different fashion. They occupy a different location altogether in the general history of the economic development process. These are the areas whose problem is that they develop more rapidly and successfully than the territory surrounding them. They have never been 'relatively over-developed' in relation to the European core-area of industrialisation, of course—the Ruhr, the English Midlands, and so on. But they have been so in relation to the larger states dominating them politically. They became dynamic, middle-class enclaves in a more backward country—capitalist societies struggling to be free, as it were.

Naturally, there are fewer stories of this kind than of the other. Yet there are considerably more of them than one would think, and their importance is greater than most writers on nationalism have realised. Western Europe contains four such zones: Catalonia and the Basque Country in Southern Europe, and Protestant Ulster and Scotland in Northern Europe.

Three of these are notorious problems of European history. In Spain the industrial revolution took place mainly in the periphery of the state, and in countries with strongly marked separate identities. As a consequence, strong bourgeois societies developed around great urban centres like Bilbao and Barcelona, and constituted a permanent threat to the backward and parasitic state centred on Madrid (a state whose social supports lay, incidentally, in under-developed provinces like those just referred to, such as Andalusia, Estremadura, and others). The Civil War was fought partly to solve this problem—or rather, as far as the Spanish Conservatives were concerned, to liquidate it. But as we know, it is still there, rendered more acute by forty years of reaction.

In Ireland the industrial revolution also occurred mainly in an ethnic periphery, creating the large Protestant 'city-state' of Belfast. Here, too, uneven development worked to separate the successful middle-class enclave from the more backward land-mass around it. When that southern region managed to constitute its own political state, the relatively over-developed north refused assimilation, and of course it continues to reject it today. It does so, in spite of the archaic religious dimension of the conflict, essentially as a more advanced ('civilised' is the ideology for this) social formation fearful of being dragged down and preyed upon.

The fourth case, Scotland, has only recently entered the category. Although an old industrial society like Catalonia, with its own cities and native capitalist class, it previously developed at approximately the same rate and with the same cadences as the larger society it was linked to, industrial England. Only with the dramatic decline of the latter, and the sudden differential impetus given to the Scottish middle class by North Sea oil production, has a crisis of uneven development arisen. Although recent, this fissure is growing extremely rapidly, and creating a political situation basically similar to the others. Even more clearly, the outlook of the previously rather quiescent Scottish bourgeoisie is one of restive impatience with English 'backwardness', London muddle, economic incompetence, state parasitism, and so forth.

Obviously, in any categorisation of this kind there are bound to be many qualifications and exceptions. But let us ignore these for the moment, for the sake of the argument. The two types of nationalist dilemma in Western Europe are, respectively; under-developed or pillaged regions that have finally begun to react against this treatment; and quite highly-developed epicentres of industrialisation, middle-class cultures who are for one reason or another out of phase with the ruling nation-state, and want separate development to get ahead faster.[8]

Not only are there more of the former than of the latter. They are also much more visible intellectually. In the usual theoretical perspectives they have had a high profile. This is mainly for an interesting reason, very relevant to the comparison between Wales and Scotland. In the general history of nationalism material under-development has always had ideological and cultural over-development as its companion. Faced with the culture of deprivation and enforced ruralism, rebels have always had to compensate with forms of militant idealism. They want to redeem lands devoid of the real powers of redemption—lands without the institutions of self-defence and change, countries by definition robbed of a normally constituted civil society, and so of the normal motor of development. So they have to lay correspondingly extreme emphasis on the ideal society the national movement want to will into existence, often in a very romantic and dream-like fashion.

The intellectual dominance of ideas reflecting this sort of nationalism is not peculiar to present-day Western Europe, of course. Quite the opposite: their salience in the theory of neo-nationalism is due to the world climate already fostered by extra-European national and anti-colonial movements. Those are the mountain-ranges whose influence leads us to look for and find the same shapes in our native hills. If the shapes are not there, we may even be led to invent them (like Professor Hechter).

So far I have made this typology purely in developmental terms. However, there is another important set of co-ordinates we should consider, since they are again very pertinent to the Scotland-Wales contrast. This is the notorious scheme of 'historic' versus 'non-historic' countries.

The notoriety derives from the original misuse: Hegel and Friedrich Engels employed the distinction mainly to discredit the smaller and more backward peoples whom they found a nuisance on the map of Europe. The Slavs, in particular, regularly had this poison served up to them. 'The ruins of peoples', snorted Engels, 'still found here and there and which are no longer capable of a national existence, and are absorbed by the larger nations, or maintain themselves as ethnographic monuments without political significance'.[9] With the exception of Southern Ireland, the ethnographic monuments of Western Europe were not noticeable enough to be worth dismissing.

However—as is usually the case with such thinkers—the basic concept is stronger than its polemical misuse. All it means is that among the great scatter of territories and peoples who had not managed to form their own modern state, some had previous experience of existence as a state and others (the great majority) had not. This state history is very important, although certainly not all-important, as they imagined. The inheritance it leaves behind, both institutionally and psychologically, is an enormous asset to any later political movement, even if the institutions are destroyed, the recollection of such a past remains prominent in national consciousness. In the 19th century the story of the re-emergence of the two nationalities which had been awarded the 'historic nation' accolade, Poland and Hungary, demonstrates this very well.

Among the reviving nationalities of Western Europe at present, two seem clearly to be 'historic nations' in this sense: Scotland and Catalonia. These were states whose independent existence ended at about the same moment, in the early 18th century, and then suffered different forms of assimilation by a larger unit. Of course the destruction of the Old Catalan state was much more total; but on the other hand it was dramatically revived by the experience of the short-lived Catalan Republic in the 1930s—an experience which has now itself become something like the 'historic nation' to which the contemporary independence movement looks back.

The other two industrially developed areas I mentioned, Euzkadi and Ulster, were not historic entitites in the Hegelian sense. They are 19th and 20th century creations.

Yet as they now are they do have at least certain aspects of this character. They have both been semi-independent states in living memory: the Basques at the same time as the Catalans, under the liberal Republic of the 1930s, and Northern Ireland from 1922 and 1972. And in quite different ways this recent state existence will remain the crucial factor in the eventual transition to self-rule.

So, of the four relatively developed countries, it would perhaps be fair to say that the Scots have retained an astonishing amount of the structure of their 'historic nationality'; the Catalans recovered it; the Basques acquired it; and the Ulster Protestants had it thrust upon them. Although the political parabolas of these state histories are wildly divergent, what they have in common is some relation to industrialisation and bourgeois development; it is the more 'middle-class' societies which kept or got some kind of statehood. To them that had was it given (and will be given again).

The other, more numerous under-developed countries in Western Europe are 'non-historic' ones whose contemporary efforts to stop being ethnographic monuments mainly take the cultural form mentioned above: the idealist nationalism of compensation against their history of forced transformation into 'ruins of peoples'.

IV

> Recently Professor Brinley Thomas has been showing that it was the industrial revolution which kept the Welsh language alive in the second half of the last century. Were it not for the coal-mining valleys and the industrial undertaking of the South the drift of people from rural Wales would have been the death of Welsh . . . Saunders Lewis, *The fate of the language* (1962)

Returning now to the Wales-Scotland comparison, it is clear where Scotland is located according to the coordinates we have traced out. It is one of the most evolved societies among the buried nationalities, in the sense of industrial and social-class development; and it is easily the most intact of the historic nations. A constellation of national institutions was left in existence by the peculiar contract of 1707, and is mostly still there. The separate legal system and courts, with the substantial middle class which serves them, the educational system, the Church of Scotland, and administrative apparatus slowly built up through a whole series of devolutionary concessions over the last century—these famous bulwarks are little diminished. They are surrounded by an interminable and growing list of associations, societies, museums, institutes, clubs, foundations, all as 'Scottish' as their titles, and all concerned with this or that national interest.

So the survival of Scotland's 'identity' has never been primarily a question of literature or of a cultivated self-consciousness. The culture it rests on is a deeper, more articulated social structure, and one not necessarily visible on superficial acquaintance. It is like a set of rock formations, which may be almost underwater reefs from many points of view. It is certainly not to be met with while strolling down Princes Street (or even at the annual conferences of the SNP). Indeed, any displays one is likely to encounter on Princes Street—in the shape of tartan performances in the garden, pipe bands or 'Highland' restaurants—are guaranteed to be 99 per cent unrelated to these realities.

So Scotland might be depicted as high up on the right-hand corner of the graph, with a high developmental and 'historic-nation' quotient. Where does Wales fit in? I believe that its position could be symbolically depicted as dead centre.

Wales does not belong neatly to either of the first two categories I outlined. This is perhaps its peculiarity in the wider European context: perhaps its peculiar importance as well. Historically Wales shares many of the features of forced under-development: depopulation, cultural oppression, fragmentary and distorted development, and so on. These features are strongly evident in the Welsh national movement too, insofar as it has been a battle for the defence and revival of rural-based community and traditional identity—an identity evoked overwhelmingly by literary and musical culture, and having as its mainspring the language question. But of course in another key respect Wales is more akin to the relatively over-developed group: like them, it is a great secondary centre of the European industrial revolution.

This ambiguous, midway location is explained by the nature of Welsh industrialisation. It was unlike the sort of economic development normally inflicted on backward provinces in being massive and in transforming (eventually) the conditions of life of most of the population. Speaking of the Heads of the Valleys, the Plaid Cymru *Economic Plan* states: 'Somewhere on Blackrock, between Gilwern and Brynmawr, there should be a notice; ''Welcome to the birthplace of the modern world''—the birthplace of modern industry. Here the early ironmasters established industry on a scale never before seen throughout the world. South Wales became the centre of the iron and steel industry and the techniques developed were copied in every developing country . . . For once, Wales led the world'.[10] Nothing remotely comparable could be said of any of the other European countries whose nationalisms superficially resemble that of Wales.

However, this industrialisation *was* like that of such periphery regions in being overwhelmingly guided from outside: it was not the work of a native entrepreneurial bourgeoisie accumulating capital for itself (as in Scotland or the Basque Country) but much more like an invasion from outside. Previously without the main motor of effective separate development, an urban middle class, Wales now acquired an English or at least highly Anglicised bourgeoisie.[11] This combination, an industrialisation at once enormous and decentred, was probably unique to Wales.

If we turn now to the other broad distinction made earlier, that between so-called historic and non-historic nationalities, the position of Wales is again less clear-cut than might appear at firsty glance. Although not an example of 'historic' nationhood in the sense of Poland,

Scotland ot Catalonia, it is not a straightforward case of the 'non-historic' either.

The non-historic features of the Welsh past are very well known: 'a territory inhabited by an agrarian population united by . . . a primitive social and economic structure and by the fact of not speaking English', as Eric Hobsbawm has put it, without much urban development until the industrial revolution, and without an indigenous aristocracy or bourgeoisie. None the less, even in the form which it assumed, the South Wales industrial revolution could not help altering the meaning of these conditions. We saw before how ethnic-linguistic nationalism had been usually a compensatory reaction to retardation. But what is striking about the Welsh reaction in this comparative view is its size and success.

None of these other European regions knew an institutionalised culture movement comparable to the Welsh one of the 19th century—a movement which, on the foundation of 18th century Welsh Nonconformity, extended from the renewed *Eisteddfod* to the University Colleges of Wales, from the Welsh National Library to the great museums of Cardiff. Although still in the narrower sense 'cultural'—concerned primarily with *Kultur*—here is a movement which from the beginning passed beyond simple poetic protest or the dreams of small intellectual coteries. It created something like the cultural form, the tracery of a nation where no state had existed. It became a substantial force in the new civil society of nineteenth and twentieth century Wales, even without political, legal and other institutions.

The movement was in reaction against the Anglicising invasion of the South—yet also to some extent based upon it. It sought to defend the language and traditional life—yet also to adapt the nation to a more modern existence. As Saunders Lewis recognised in his famous 1962 broadcast, the industrial revolution which so threatened Welsh language and life also gave it a new chance of life—indeed, the only chance of surviving permanently and avoiding the fate of Cornish, Irish and Scottish Gaelic. By becoming the language of the industrial Valleys, Welsh had come part of the way towards the condition of Catalan, in Western Europe, or Czech or Slovene among the smaller ex-Hapsburg countries, of Eastern Europe.[12]

To say that the Welsh situation is unusually central, or suspended between the standard alternatives of European neo-nationalism, is of course to say that it is unusually divided. It is not necessary here to comment on the strong antagonisms and dilemmas built into the national movement by this history: Welsh versus Anglo-Welsh, Adfer versus bi-lingualism, ethnic traditionalists versus South-Eastern modernisers, and so on. All that should be stressed is that this internal conflict has a wider comparative significance. It reflects, within Wales and Welsh nationalism, certain deeper dilemmas of choice which can be seen operating everywhere else. In the Welsh knot the usual forces of uneven development have been tied together unusually closely and graphically.

V

> Q *Do you believe that a 'sense of Welsh nationhood' is more consistent with one particular attitude to life and affairs than any other?*
>
> A If I catch the drift of the question, I would say that I do not feel that the Welsh national spirit has had to bank itself up in the Welsh language for want of being able to express itself politically . . .
>
> John Cowper Powys 'Answer to *Wales* questionnaire, 1939,' *Obstinate Cymric* (1947).

What happens to Scotland on the road to self-government has some significance for other countries. But less than might appear superficially. It would be principally through a general demonstration-effect, by which the constitution of any new state in the West of Europe will encourage the rest. The paradox of Scotland's strong 'historic-nation' status is that it makes the country less relevant and weaker as an example, above all in relation to the more typical countries where cultural nationalism prevails.

What happens to Wales is likely to be far more influential in the long run. This is the point of the Welsh centrality in the nationalist spectrum which I have tried to analyse. All Western Europe's deprived and re-awakened peoples want and need stronger economic development, for example. Given the condition they start from, such development is bound to be in large measure from outside, whether by multinationals or by investment and aid from other countries. Wales has already gone through this, in the most violent and chaotic fashion: such de-centred, invasive industrialisation created the whole problem of modern nationalism in Wales. Hence, how the Welsh national movement—or a future Welsh political state—copes with the question is directly relevant in all these places.

If Welsh nationalism can arrive at a viable political integration of its contending elements, then many others can hope to. If the ideal, 'cultural' nation can be reconciled with the industrial one here, then the formula may eventually be copiable elsewhere. Nationalism has always been a struggle to connect romantically-conceived tradition and culture with the need for modern social and economic development. In modern Welsh history these two things are thrust together with special intensity, imposing a duty of political leadership on the nationalist movement.

The romantic theory of cultural colonialism described earlier sees all the resurgent nationalities as essentially the same (and all are of course also 'unique' in the same way). The less idealist account I have tried to begin here perceives them as different, even opposed, and certainly classifiable in a number of interesting ways. A materialist theory focuses primarily upon their real location in the modern process of socio-economic development—it sees them as real places, in this sense, no less real and diverse than the bigger nation-states they are still attached to. But I am conscious of having done little more than suggest the starting-point of a theory of this kind. There are many things we have not looked at at all here.

For example, the question of the causation of the wave of new nationalist movements in Western Europe. It seems very unlikely that these have arisen out of a general protest against impersonal centralism, or against the synthetic culture of bureaucracy and multinational business. Presumably there are deep economic changes behind the new climate. But why are they especially operative in three of the old states—the United Kingdom, Spain and France—and unimportant or non-existent in others? Why should the new forms of inter-dependence promoted by multi-nationals have undermined these ex-imperial nations but—e.g.—left the Netherlands largely unaffected? Why should Italy, a country marked by gross and long-standing uneven development, have been untroubled by separatism in the recent past?

These are all questions that seem to call for much more discriminating and realistic answers than the ones nationalists are at present tending to give. The same might be said of attempts to prospect a nationalist future. The results, as well as the causes, of new nationalist success are not easy to see. There will be a new map of Europe. But it is not likely to resemble the diagrams of a sub-divided, small-nation continent which became fashionable a few years ago.[13]

Returning—in conclusion—to the Scotland-Wales direct comparison, what farther inferences can be drawn from the argument so far? I have chosen to emphasise our differences, and to plead for a more cautious sceptical approach to inter-nationalist relations. The aim of this is to reinforce such relations—on the assumption that realism ought to balance ideology, and will preserve what is positive in the latter by doing so.

Like other movements, these ones have the strengths of their weaknesses (or vice-versa). The great Welsh cultural movement, with which Welsh nationalism is so closely associated, may have led to a certain over-emphasis upon these factors. There is a great deal both in Welsh history and in current ideology that underwrites this emphasis. Looking back again to that address of fifty years ago, one cannot help being struck by the extreme prudence—even fear—with which political authority is regarded. 'The Welsh civilizing concept is the only worthwhile argument for self-government', said Lewis, '. . . that being so, we must have self-government. Not independence. Not even unconditional freedom. But just as much freedom as may be necessary to establish and safeguard civilization in Wales'.[14] A political state not one hundred-and-one per cent sanctified by cultural needs and values is, frankly, the work of the Devil of Materialism. Cultural nationality and power-hungry nationalism are conceived as real antitheses.

Unless I am greatly mistaken, this underlying attitude is still quite strongly felt in Wales. It must be the only country where one regularly hears nationalists denouncing nationalism. Since Saunders Lewis's antithesis is not a real one, and no state institutions can ever exist purely and solely to cultivate cultural traditions in that sense, I suppose this is a kind of weakness. I suppose therefore that the Welsh national movement ought to give the Devil his due more than it has done in times past, and try to adopt a mildly more Machiavellian attitude to the state and the other non-cultural institutions of power. But it is hardly for me to make recommendations about that.

As far as the Scots are concerned, I feel on stronger ground. The weakness of the Scottish national movement is the contrary of the Welsh one: it is the consistent, canny philistinism of the movement from its earliest days, and the chronic divorce between what Lewis Spence called the 'practical, Scotsman-like' policy and the somewhat erratic flight of the intelligentsia. The Scottish movement benefits from the existence of a powerful middle class: but one of the traits of that class is a powerful distrust of culture in any spectacular form. Along with the seriousness and practicality, there is of course a dreadful conceit buried in this outlook. One might describe it as the unjustified conceit of a once 'historic nation' which deep down still feels itself to be such. Nor should one forget that, while in Wales Calvinism figures as a creed of prolonged popular opposition to the high and mighty, in Scotland it has been mainly a creed *of* the high and mighty. The Welsh may be too apprehensive about state power; the Scots are not apprehensive enough. Authority appears to them naturally dressed in a Minister's gown and a halo.

With the imminence of self-government, this Scotsman-like weakness has become a more tangible threat. Never having imagined an ideal nation with the visionary enthusiasm found in so many other nationalist movements they are at a loss. There is a sudden, rather belated rush to invent actual things to do. The SNP has produced a philosophy, or something like a philosophy, bearing some distinct resemblances to the radical ideology of other European nationalist movements (I refer to the newly-published volume, *The radical approach: papers on an independent Scotland*). In deference to the new mood, one or two intellectuals were seen openly circulating at the recent party conference in Motherwell.

Satire apart, Scottish nationalism desperately needs to counter this malformation, by integrating politics and culture more deliberately than in the past. We need new institutions to do this—new means of forging links between practical politics and cultural ideas, between the institutions of power and the imagination of a new nation. I have myself been involved in recent months in the formation of such a body, an International Institute specifically concerned with the problem. It is intended as a centre to foster just that interaction between the political and cultural movements which has been lacking in the past.

The title 'International' is itself a recognition that we cannot accomplish such a task by ourselves, or with our own resources. We are compelled to look outwards to tackle it seriously. To study the culture of a nation inwardly demands, in today's circumstances, that one look at it comparatively. A realistic international perspective is not only ethically desirable but intellectually—and, increaingly, practically—necessary. A cultural nationalism that fails to make this effort will end up drowned in its own mythology.

Given the evident complementarity of Welsh and Scottish problems, Wales is one of the places to which we look with the keenest sense of useful difference. Countries so different can never become 'like each other' in a merely imitative sense. This need not matter. What matters is to learn to change, inevitably in one's own way, through the constant stimulus of contact and studied comparison. This is, for us, the new internationalism which ought to arise out of Europe's new wave of national movements.

References

1. H. J. Hanham, *Scottish nationalism* (1969), pp. 154-5.
2. Ibid., p. 160: 'The purge of 1933 (sinister date) gave control of the National Party to those whose aim was . . . Home Rule within the British Commonwealth, and who eschewed romantic literary flourishes. There was now no place in the National Party either for Erskine of Marr and the Gaelic militants of the Scots National League, or for most of the wild young literary men. They were driven into the wilderness . . .'
3. John Osmond, 'Centralism or democracy', in *The centralist enemy* (1974), p. 13.
4. P. E. Mayo, *The roots of identity: three national movements in contemporary European politics* (1974)—on Wales, Euzkadi and Brittany; the Plaid Cymru pamphlet *Culture and politics (Oct. 1975) with contributions by* Raymond Williams, Ned Thomas, John Osmond and Phil Wiliams.
5. *Les temps modernes*, special issue, 'Les minoritès nationales en France', August-September 1973; the Canadian debate can be studied in the volume *Nationalism or local control: responses to George Woodcock* (1973), edited by V. Nelles and A. Rotstein; Michael Zwerin, *A case for the balkanization of practically everyone . . . the new nationalism* (London, 1976); Michael Hechter, *Internal colonialism: the Celtic fringe in British national development, 1536-1966* (1975); Sergio Salvi, *Le nazioni proibite*)Florence, 1974).
6. Hechter, op. cit. Chapter 9, '20th century Celtic nationalism', pp. 307-8.
7. E. J. Hobsbawm, 'Parties Celtiques de la Grande-Bretagne', in *Mouvements nationaux d'indépendance et classe populaires* (1965) edited E. Labrousse, 2 vols.
8. There are examples in Eastern Europe, like Bohemia and Croatia; and examples outside Europe, like Eastern Nigeria (Biafra), Singapore and Kurdistan.
9 F. Engels, *Po und Rhein (1859), Marx-Engels werke*, XIII, p. 267; a résumé of the theory is given in Anthony D. Smith, *Theories of nationalism* (1971), pp. 72-75; an interesting example of resurrection of this dead theory in relation to Wales is the British & Irish Communist Organisation's 1972 pamphlet, *Is Wales a nation?* (unsigned).

10. Plaid Cymru, *Economic plan* (1969), Vol. 2, pp. 119-20.
11. Sir Reginald Coupland, *Welsh and Scottish nationalism: a study* (1954), pp. 169-75.
12. Glanville Price 'Minority languages in western Europe', in *The Welsh language today*, edited by Meic Stephens (1973), especially pp. 8-9, on Catalan.
13. Again Leopold Kohr ranks as a forerunner—see the Appendices to *The breakdown of nations.* 'The principle of federation in maps'.
14. Saunders Lewis, *Principles of nationalism* (1926), pp. 15-16.

Chapter Nine

Towards a Theory of Ethnic Change*

Michael Hechter

An Alternative Model: The Periphery as an Internal Colony

Common to both the structural and cultural diffusion theories is a unilateral conception of social and economic development. This type of development, as indicated by such measures as labor diversification indices and urbanization statistics, is assumed to spread from one locality to another though the mechanism of this diffusion is somewhat mysterious. However, an important distinction can be made between development which occurs as a result of factors endogenous to a specific society and that which is the result of basically exogenous forces. The second type of development—that usually associated with certain sectors of Third World societies—arose out of what Georges Balandier has termed the 'colonial situation'. Typically this involves domination by a 'racially' and culturally different foreign conquering group, imposed in the name of a dogmatically asserted racial, ethnic, or cultural superiority, on a materially inferior indigenous people. There is contact between the different cultures. The dominated society is condemned to an instrumental role by the metropolis. Finally, there is a recourse not only to force, to maintain political stability, but also to a complex of racial or cultural stereotypes, to legitimate metropolitan superordination.

* An extract from Chapter 2 of M. Hechter *Internal colonialsm: the Celtic fringe in British national development 1536-1966*, London, Routledge and Kegan Paul (1975), 15-43. Footnotes which are not directly relevant to the purposes of this volume have been omitted.

The pattern of development characterizing the colonial situation is markedly different in these respects from that which emerged from endogenous development in Western Europe and Japan. First, colonial development produces a cultural division of labor: a system of stratification where objective cultural distinctions are superimposed upon class lines. High status occupations tend to be reserved for those of metropolitan culture; while those of indigenous culture cluster at the bottom of the stratification system. The ecological pattern of development differs in the colonial situation, leading to what has been termed economic and social dualism. Since the colony's role is designed to be instrumental, development tends to be complementary to that of the metropolis. The colonial economy often specializes in the production of a narrow range of primary commodities or raw materials for export. Whereas cities arose to fulfill central place functions in societies having had endogenous development, the ecological distribution of cities looks very different in colonies, where they serve as way stations in the trade between colonial hinterlands and metropolitan ports. Hence cities tend to be located on coasts with direct access to the metropolis. Similarly, transportation systems arise not to spur colonial development—they are seldom built to interconnect the various regions of the colony—but to facilitate the movement of commodities from the hinterland to the coastal cities.

Thus, the cultural contact engendered in the colonial situation did not lead to a type of social and economic development in the colony which was recognizably similar to that of the metropolis. Andre Gunder Frank has characterized the fruits of such contact as 'the development of underdevelopment.[1] It must not, however, be assumed that this colonial type of development is to be found only in those areas subjected to nineteenth-century overseas imperialism.

Simultaneous to the overseas expansion of western European states in the fifteenth and sixteenth centuries were similar thrusts into peripheral hinterlands:[2]

> The prime aim of the new rulers in their expansionist efforts was to bring under sway all territory not already theirs within the 'natural frontiers' dimly coming to be perceived ... small nationalities which had failed to develop as States were now swallowed up: Brittany (1491), Granada (1492), Navarre (1512), Ireland. Their languages and cultures persisted nevertheless and none of the governments succeeded fully in its program of unification. England strove in vain to absorb Scotland; Spain was only briefly able to absorb a reluctant Portugal. Frontiers thus surviving helped by mutual irritation to generate a corporate sentiment on both sides. By the seventeenth century an Englishman who did not look down on a Scotsman would have been only half an Englishman; a Scotsman who did not hate an Englishman would not have been a Scotsman at all.

These internal campaigns were not in any sense coincidental to overseas colonization. There is reason to believe that both movements were the result of the same social forces in these states, among which the search for new sources of foodstuffs may have been of primary importance. Fernand Braudel has referred to this territorial expansion of the Western European states as a quest for 'internal Americans'.

This bears a striking resemblance to the description of internal colonialism which has emerged from consideration of the situation of Amerindian regions in several Latin American societies. This conception focuses on political conflict between core and peripheral groups as mediated by the central government. From this perspective the 'backwardness' of peripheral groups can only be aggravated by a systematic increase in transactions with the core. The peripheral collectivity is seen to be already suffused with exploitative connections to the core, such that it can be deemed to be an internal colony. The core collectivity practices discrimination against the culturally distinct peoples who have been forced onto less accessible inferior lands.

Some aspects of internal colonialism have been sketched, though not yet systematically demonstrated. These bear many similarities to descriptions of the overseas colonial situation. Commerce and trade among members of the periphery tend to be monopolized by members of the core. Credit is similarly monopolized. When commercial prospects emerge, bankers, managers, and entrepreneurs tend to be recruited from the core. The peripheral economy is forced into complementary development to the core, and thus becomes dependent on external markets. Generally, this economy rests on a single primary export, either agricultural or mineral. The movement of peripheral labor is determined largely by forces exogenous to the periphery. Typically there is great migration and mobility of peripheral workers in response to price fluctuations of exported primary products. Economic dependence is reinforced through juridical, political, and military measures. There is a relative lack of services, lower standard of living and higher level of frustration, measured by such indicators as alcoholism, among members of the peripheral group. There is national discrimination on the basis of language, religion or other cultural forms.[3] Thus the aggregate economic differences between core and periphery are causally linked to their cultural differences.

In this description national development has less to do with automatic social structural or economic processes, and more with the exercise of control over government policies concerning the allocation of resources. Since increased contact between core and periphery does not tend to narrow the economic gap between the groups, national development will best be served by strengthening the political power of the peripheral group so that it may change the distribution of resources to its greater advantage. Ultimately this power must be based on political organization. One of the foundations upon which such organization might rest is, of course, cultural similarity, or the perception of a distinctive *ethnic identity* in the peripheral group. The obstacle to national development suggested by the internal colonial model analogy, therefore, relates not to a failure of peripheral integration with the core but to a malintegration established on terms increasingly regarded as unjust and illegitimate.

Thus the internal colonial model would appear to account for the persistence of backwardness in the midst of industrial society, as well as the apparent volatility of political integration. Further, by linking economic and occupational differences between groups to their cultural differences, this model has an additional advantage in that it suggests an explanation for the resiliency of peripheral culture.

On the Cause of Cultural Differences Between Collectivities

The antecedent causes of cultural differentiation between groups sharing close geographical proximity have seldom been satisfactorily explored by social scientists from a theoretical perspective. Partly this may be due to the extraordinary slipperiness of the concept of culture, which at base must refer to the prism through which groups ascribe meaning to the physical and social world around them. While it is relatively easy to specify the content of a particular culture by observing such phenomena as socialization processes, it is a problem of a different order to ask *why* a child is nursed for five years in one society, or taught to mumble reverences to an inanimate flag in another. The participant's answer to this question will be of the form: 'But that is the way it is customarily done.' The sociologist of Durkheimian persuasion will hasten to illustrate the ways in which such practices simultaneously reflect and contribute to the solidarity of the group. But generally the specific form of the culture—whether it is animist or totemist, Catholic or Protestant—is regarded as of incidental significance when compared with the functions the culture performs towards the maintenance of the social order. It is much simpler to assume that a group's culture is an attribute of the social system rather than a variable to be explained. Thus the group may be defined as having a certain set of cultural traits which, when aggregated, make up its 'ethnicity'.

This may be a valid assumption in those few societies which are largely self-enclosed and have only sporadic contacts with other societies. For instance it is clear that cultural differences between proximate groups may be a function of their mutual isolation. If these groups are suddenly brought into contact they will manifest these cultural differences to a greater or lesser extent. These initial differences may well result in different institutional arrangements in the two groups.[4]

> What do we mean by a cultural explanation? When a people has lived together generation after generation, sharing a common history, answering often to a common name, it tends to develop distinctive institutions, a distinctive way of life, adapted of course to its physical environment and technology. When faced with new circumstances, the people may well adjust its institutions to meet them, but the adjustment will start from the old traditions, and a recognizable continuity will be maintained . . . When we find two people practicing different sets of institutions—even though the differences may not be great, and even though they live in somewhat similar environments and employ a similar technology—we are apt, quite rightly, to explain the facts by saying that the two practice different cultures, the precipitates of different past histories.

For the purpose of cross-sectional analysis at a single point in time the assumption of the givenness of a particular set of cultural traits may well be justified. But if the investigator is interested in the longitudinal process of social change and exchange, then the maintenance of cultural differences over time may be an important clue as to the nature of their interrelationship, particularly in so far as dominance and subordination are concerned.

The cultural theory is really no theory at all. It merely refers back to an antecedent period when the specific group in question fashioned its culture in an unspecified way. In the attempt to progress beyond 'the fruitless assumption that culture comes from culture', the notion of cultural ecology was devised by Julian Steward.[5] For Steward a group's culture emerges from particular characteristics of its social structure, which in turn is adapted to a specific physical environment. Culture, in this view, is largely responsive to changes in a core element of the social structure which is defined as:[6]

> the constellation of features which are most closely related to subsistence activities and economic arrangements. The core includes such social, political, and religious patterns as are empirically determined to be closely connected with these arrangements.

While accepting the logic of this search for explanatory variables in cultural differentiation, Clifford Geertz cautions that 'there is no *a priori* reason why the adaptive realities a given sociocultural system faces have greater or lesser control over its general pattern of development than various other realities with which it is also faced.'[7] Geertz's objection seems true *a fortiori* in developed societies, where groups are much less constrained by the purely ecological considerations of how food and shelter are to be provided in the face of a hostile environment. For development typically offers several types of alternative life-styles to individuals. First, there are very many different ways to provide for sustenance through participation in the primary, secondary, or tertiary sectors of the economy. Thus the individual is liberated from crude ecological constraints. But secondarily, in developed societies some individuals are allowed choices about the kind of culture they will adhere to. Individuals may choose to be Protestant or Catholic, Ga or Ashanti, in certain settings.[8] Frederik Barth has emphasized that ethnicity must be considered to be a boundary phenomenon. What ultimately separates one ethnic group from another is that it 'has a membership which identifies itself, and is identified by others, as constituting a category distinguishable from other categories of the same order.'[9] The subjective element in ethnic identity in complex society has been illustrated in a different way by Ernest Gellner.[10]

> If a man is not firmly set in a social niche, he is obliged to carry his identity with him, in his whole style of conduct and expression: in other words, his 'culture' becomes his identity. And the classification of men by 'culture' is of course the classification by 'nationality'. It is for this reason that it now

> seems inherent in the very nature of things, that to be human means to have some nationality. In our particular social context, it *is* inherent in the nature of things.

In an age of bureaucratic organization and mass literacy, cultural distinctions, particularly those involving language, assume great importance since education has an important place in allocating occupational and social status in the society at large. All of these considerations imply a different type of core element to account for cultural particularity than that which is tied to the ecological situation. *What is problematic in complex society are the social conditions under which individuals band together as members of an ethnic group.*

It is clear that culture maintenance in the periphery can be regarded as a weapon in that it provides the possibility of socialization, as well as political mobilization, contrary to state ends. Max Weber termed those collectivities having distinctive life-styles and cultures status groups (*Stände*), each of which is allocated a different ranking on a hierarchy of social honour, or prestige.[11] In effect, the difference between the type of social solidarity predominating in the core and that in the periphery is akin to the distinction Weber made between classes and status groups. Class solidarity is consonant with a high level of modernization and tends to be organized functionally in occupational groups. Trade unions, for instance, unite men in narrowly defined occupations at the primary, shop level, and confederations of unions tend to be much less solidary than constituent locals. Class solidarity assumes an individual orientation towards the market place, whereas status group solidarity involves a group, or collective orientation. The important question, of course, is to come to an understanding of the dynamics between class and status group solidarity. Why does status group solidarity appear to be stronger in the periphery than in the core?

The persistence of objective cultural distinctiveness in the periphery must itself be the function of the maintenance of an unequal distribution of resources between core and peripheral groups. Initially, individuals in the disadvantaged peripheral group are not permitted to become acculturated in the core. For Barth,[12]

> the persistence of ethnic groups in contact implies not only criteria and signals for identification, but also a structuring of interaction which allows the persistence of cultural differences ... a set of prescriptions governing situations of contact, and allowing for articulation in some sectors or domains of activity, and a set of proscriptions on social situations preventing inter-ethnic interactions in other sectors, and thus insulating parts of the cultures from confrontation and modification.

Such boundaries are maintained by the differential allocation of social roles with the society:[13]

> Common to all these systems is the principle that ethnic identity implies a series of constraints on the kinds of roles an individual is allowed to play, and the partners he may choose for different kinds of transaction. ... The persistence of stratified polyethnic systems thus entails the presence of factors that generate and maintain a categorically different distribution of assets: state controls, as in some modern plural and racist systems; marked differences in evaluation that canalize the efforts of actors in different directions, as in systems with polluting occupations; or differences in culture that generate marked differences in political organization, economic organization, or individual skills.

This system of stratification is, in effect, a *cultural division of labor.*

Gellner sees the initial advantage to one cultural group rather than another as an historical accident caused by the uneven spread of industrialization through territorial space. 'The wave creates acute cleavages of interest between sets of people hit by it at differing times—in other words the more and less advanced.'[14] This accounts for the ability of the superordinate group to impose the kinds of role restraints to which Barth makes reference. However, if the unequal distribution of resources is based on observable cultural differences there is always the possibility that the disadvantaged group in time will reactively assert its own culture as equal or superior to that of the advantaged group.[15]

> This cleavage and hostility can express itself with particular sharpness if the more and the less advanced populations can easily distinguish each other, by genetic or rigid cultural traits. These aid discrimination and humiliation, and thus further exacerbate the conflict. If such differentiae are lacking, nothing happens: the 'backward' area becomes depopulated, or a depressed area within a large unit, or an object of communal charity and assistance. If, however, the differentiating marks are available—whether through distance, 'race', or cultural traits such as religion, they provide a strong incentive and a means for the backward region or population to start conceiving of itself as a separate 'nation' and to seek independence.

Hence, if at some initial point acculturation did not occur because the advantaged group would not permit it, at a later time acculturation may be inhibited by the desires of the disadvantaged group for independence from a situation increasingly regarded as oppressive. This accounts for the cultural 'rebirths' so characteristic of societies undergoing nationalistic ferment. It is not that these groups actually uncover evidence of their ancient cultural past as an independent people; most often such culture is created contemporaneously to legitimate demands for the present-day goal of independence, or the achievement of economic equality.[16]

Conclusion: The Politics of Ethnic Change

The internal colonial model would therefore seem to provide a more adequate explanation of the persistence of ethnic identity among peripheral groups in complex societies than do diffusion theories portraying the periphery as culturally and economically isolated from the core. In general, relations between core and peripheral groups may be schematized as follows:

The uneven wave of industrialization over territorial space creates relatively advanced and less advanced groups, and therefore acute cleavages of interest arise between these groups. As a consequence of this initial fortuitous advantage there is a crystallization of the unequal distribution of resources and power between the two groups.

The superordinate group, now ensconced as the core, seeks to stabilize and monopolize its advantages through policies aiming at the institutionalization and perpetuation of the existing stratification system. Ultimately, it seeks to regulate the allocation of social roles such that those roles commonly defined as having high status are generally reserved for its members. Conversely, individuals from the less advanced group tend to be denied access to these roles. Let this stratification system be termed the cultural division of labor: it assigns individuals to specific roles in the social structure on the basis of objective cultural distinctions.

The cultural division of labour may be enforced *de jure*, when the individual from the disadvantaged collectivity is denied certain roles by the active intervention of the state. This is the racist solution to the maintenance of the *status quo*. The cultural division of labor may, alternatively, be preserved *de facto*, through policies providing differential access to institutions conferring status in the society at large, such as the education, military, or ecclesiastical systems. This is the institutional racist solution to the maintenance of the *status quo*.[17] Both types of policies insure that the character of the cultural division of labor remains intact.

The existence of a cultural division of labor contributes to the development of distinctive ethnic identity in each of the two cultural groups. Actors come to categorize themselves and others according to the range of roles each may be expected to play. They are aided in this categorization by the presence of visible signs—distinctive life-styles, language, or religious practices—which are seen to characterize both groups. Such visible signals allow for intergroup interaction, necessarily involving a certain commonality of definitions on the part of interacting partners, in the face of objective cultural differences between groups. Acculturation need not occur because each individual can adjust his behaviour in accordance with the other's status (which can be perceived visually) even before interaction takes place.[18]

> Regarded as a status, ethnic identity is superordinate to most other statuses, and defines the permissible constellations of statuses or social personalities, which an individual with that identity may assume. In this respect ethnic identity is similar to sex and rank, in that it constrains the incumbent in all his activities, not only in some defined social situations.

The political position of the peripheral group within the society is likely to be feeble given this situation. This is so even in the most formally democratic polities since the peripheral collectivity is likely to be resource-poor relative to all other social groups. If the peripheral group is also a numerical minority its political situation is far worse. As a minority group it cannot independently force changes in central government policies, such as those which might provide a reallocation of income from the core group, on the strength of votes alone. This often results in politics of 'stable unrepresentation'.[19]

In most developed societies the above considerations hold only in a probabilistic sense. That is to say it is statistically possible for an individual of low ethnic status to achieve, for instance, high-status occupational roles, though of course it is very improbable. The realization of these conventionally forbidden roles makes it possible for statistically deviant individuals to reconsider their ethnic identity. They may have several types of options. By identifying with the advantaged group, these individuals may attempt to 'pass', and thus undergo a subjective re-identification of their ethnic identity.[20] Alternatively, they may attempt to maximize their individual power by acting as brokers between the two groups. As 'ethnic leaders' they may seek to incrementally narrow the material differences between the groups by appealing to the universalistic norms which many industrial societies aspire to. Or they may reactively assert the equal or superior value of their culture, claim the separateness of their nation and seek independence.

The first option, basically one of selective co-optation, serves to remove potentially divisive leadership from the peripheral group and thereby ensures stabilization of the cultural division of labor. The ultimate consequences of the second choice are somewhat less clear, except for the probability that should any change occur it will be gradual. The slowness of actual economic integration in the face of larger expectations will most likely insure that a more militant group will form in the name of the ethnic nationalist position. In general, the probability of achieving economic integration within the society, as against other outcomes, such as actual secession or relative stasis, will be determined by factors such as the relative numbers of both groups, the indispensability of the periphery's role in the national economy, and the kinds of policies adopted by the central government.

The existence of ethnic solidarity in a given group should therefore be regarded as a special instance of the general phenomenon of political mobilization. Hence, ethnic change facilitating political integration cannot be expected to result in the periphery until there is widespread satisfaction that the cultural division of labor has largely been eliminated. Once placed in this framework, it is easy to see the reason for the frequency of political demands along ethnic grounds in industrial society. The Marxian discussion of political mobilization points to two fundamental conditions for the emergence of group solidarity. Substantial economic inequalities must exist between individuals, such that these individuals may come to see this inequality as part of a pattern of collective oppression.

However, the aggregation of individual perception of economic inequality alone is insufficient for the development of collective solidarity. There must be an accompanying social awareness and definition of the situation as being unjust and illegitimate. Oppression by itself can, of course, if severe enough, precipitate random violence against the social system, as in the many instances of peasant *jacqueries* throughout history; but this is not the result of the attainment of group consciousness and hence lacks the organization and purposefulness to achieve effective ends.

Thus another vital condition for the advent of collective solidarity is adequate communication among members of the oppressed group.[21] Communication within collectivities generally occurs within the context of social institutions: neighbourhoods, workplaces, schools, churches, social and recreational clubs, and the host of voluntary associations to which individuals may typically belong. To the extent that these contexts for social interaction are limited to members of a group sharing the social definition of an ethnic minority, the possibilities for intercommunication will be maximized. This is so because in the periphery there tends to be not only segregation in the workplace but also residential segregation as well. The concatenation of residential and occupational segregation gives a decisive advantage to the development of ethnic rather than class solidarity. Since the concept of social class seeks to deny the salience of cultural and residential differences among members of similar occupational groups, to the extent that such differences actually exist, class is ultimately more abstracted from the reality of everyday social life than is ethnicity.

Finally, the very economic backwardness of the periphery contributes to the inevitability of such residential and occupational segregation. As an impoverished and culturally alien region there is little incentive for members of the core group to migrate there in force. Typically the periphery has a declining population, an over-abundance of the elderly, and a disproportionate number of females, all of which reflect the lack of adequate employment opportunity which is both a result of peripheral backwardness and a case of further economic disadvantages.[22]

From these general observations it is possible to make three propositions concerning the prospects for the political integration of peripheral collectivities into the society as a whole:

1 The greater the economic inequalities between collectivities the greater the probability that the less advantaged collectivity will be status solidary, and hence, will resist political integration.
2 The greater the frequency of intra-collectivity communication, the greater the status solidarity of the peripheral collectivity.
3 The greater the intergroup differences of culture, particularly in so far as identifiability is concerned, the greater the probability that the culturally distinct peripheral collectivity will be status solidary. Identifiable cultural differences include: language (accent), distinctive religious practices, and life-style.

It should be underlined that when objective cultural differences are superimposed[23] upon economic inequalities, forming a cultural division of labor, and when adequate communications exist as a facilitating factor, the chances for successful political integration of the peripheral collectivity into the national society are minimized. The internal colonial model predicts, and to some extent explains, the emergence of just such a cultural division in labor.

Notes

1. Andre Gunder Frank, *Capitalism and underdevelopment in Latin America* (New York: 1969).
2. V. G. Kiernan, 'State and nation in Western Europe' *Past and Present*, 31 (1965), pp. 21-2.
3. There does not seem to be a general consensus on a small number of essential defining features of internal colonialism. Since the concept evolved from the study of ethnic conflict in Latin American societies, the above list is particularly applicable to societies with a similar history, especially with regard to Spanish and Portuguese patterns of colonialism. However, with certain modification, the notion of material colonialism may be much more general in scope. What if all but one or two conditions seem to be met? The danger, of course, is to so relax the meaning of internal colonialism that almost any instance of stratification may fall somewhere within its boundaries.

   Let me give an example. A strict case study of internal colonialism should probably include *administrative differentiation*, such that there are both citizens and subjects, as dictated by the colonial analogy. This qualification is easily met by many Third World societies, but probably by only one developed society, the Republic of South Africa. Are we therefore to conclude that internal colonialism is an inappropriate concept in modern European history? Ireland is a perfect example of an internal colony under the old United Kingdom until 1829, when Catholics were nearly granted full civic and political rights. But it would be folly to consider that this legislation ended the essentially colonial status of the island. Are we then to refer to post-1829 Ireland as an instance of internal neo-colonialism?

   Similarly, is *territoriality* a necessary condition, or can American Blacks be considered an internal colony as Robert Blauner ('Internal colonization and ghetto revolt', *Social Problems*, 16, 4 (1969), pp. 393-408) and others have suggested? These are some of the problems that remain to be worked out if internal colonialism is indeed to become a useful concept.
4. George C. Homans, 'The explanation of English regional differences', *Past and Present*, 42 (1969), p. 29.
5. Julian Steward, *Theory of culture change* (Urbana. 1963), p. 36.
6. Ibid., p. 37.
7. Geertz, *Agricultural involution*, (Berkeley: 1963), pp. 10-11.
8. Such subjective 'tribal' re-identification has been described by Immanuel Wallerstein in 'Ethnicity and national integration in West Africa', *Cahiers d'études Africaines*, 1, 3 (1960), pp. 129-39.
9. Frederik Barth, 'Introduction' in F. Barth, ed., *Ethnic groups and boundaries* (Boston: 1969), p. 11.
10. Ernest Gellner, 'Nationalism' in *Thought and change* (London: 1969), p. 157.
11. Max Weber, *Economy and society*, eds. Guenther Roth and Claus Wittich (New York: 1968), vol. II, pp. 926-40.
12. Barth, *op. cit.*, p. 16.
13. Barth, *op. cit.*, p. 17.
14. Gellner, *op. cit.*, p. 171.
15. *Ibid.*, pp. 171-2.

16. David C. Gordon, *History and self-determination in the Third World* (Princeton: 1971).
17. Stokely Carmichael and Charles V. Hamilton, *Black power* (New York: 1967), pp. 3-4. The failure of national educational institutions to provide equal training for members of all status groups is now well recognized, and has generated an exhaustive literature.
18. Barth, *op. cit.*, p. 17.
19. This may be said to occur when the 'political system normally operates to prevent incipient competitors from achieving full entry into the political arena. Far from there being built-in mechanisms which keep the system responsive, such groups win entry only through the breakdown of the normal operation of the system or through demonstration on the part of challenging groups of a willingness to violate the "rules of the game" by resorting to illegitimate means carrying on political conflict'. William A. Gamson, 'Stable unrepresentation in American society', *American Behavioural Scientist*, 12, 2 (1968), p. 18.
20. It need hardly be added that to the extent that different ethnicity is symbolized by phenotypical differences between groups such an option is correspondingly limited.
21. Karl Marx, *The Eighteenth Brumaire of Louis Bonaparte* (New York: 1926), p. 109.
22. This vicious circle of regional underdevelopment is lucidly discussed in Gunnar Myrdal, *Rich lands and poor* (New York: 1957), pp. 23-38.
23. For a parallel discussion of the effects of such superimposition on the intensity of class conflict, see Ralf Dahrendorf, *Class and class conflict in industrial society* (Stanford: 1959), pp. 213-18.

Chapter Ten

The Shadow of the Swastika?*

R. Tudur Jones

This is a strange and very frightening book. On page 93 the author states 'Only what is correct in accordance with our tradition and history is acceptable to a Citizen of *Y Fro Gymraeg* (the Welsh-speaking region)'. Yet this book is full of echoes of continental philosophies—those of the Frenchman Comte and of the Germans Hegel, Fichte, Schelling and Alfred Rosenberg. The author has not seen fit to enlighten his readers about his doctrine's literary sources, but the similarity between his thought patterns and the philosophical tradition which reached its horrendous climax in the tyranny practised by the Third Reich is too obvious to be accidental. And if it is, indeed, accidental, the author's intellectual innocence is inexplicable.

The most revealing chapter is the last, *Dinasyddiaeth y Fro Gymraeg* (Citizenship of the Welsh region), a speech delivered in August 1975. We may therefore infer that it represents the author's most mature thinking. Emyr Llewelyn's basic principle is that the nation is the ultimate entity 'a society which has given meaning to its existence and found guidelines for its life . . .'. In particular, a nation is the social form which creates and sustains mankind. The significance of the individual's life arises from the fact that the Spirit of the People (the *Volksgeist* in German) flows through him.

Fritz Stern expresses the Nazi conviction on this point like this: 'the individual soul has significance to the extent to which it has been linked with the soul of the race; only through the perpetuation of the race itself can the individual soul survive the death of the body which

* A review of *Adfer a'r Fro Gymraeg* by Emyr Llywelyn (Cyhoeddiadau Modern Cymreig 1976) published originally in two parts in *Tafod y ddraig*, January and February 1977. Translated from the Welsh by Eirian E. Edwards and B. P. Jones.

EDITORIAL STATEMENT

After the publication of Dr. R. Tudur Jones's review in 1977; Mr. Emyr Llywelyn composed a reply which was circulated and stated that Dr. Jones was incorrect as to the sources of Mr. Llywelyn's ideas. The editors of this book were unaware of these facts at the time of publication when about 200 copies of *The Welsh and their country* were circulated in February, 1986. Subsequently, Dr. R. Tudur Jones has formally accepted Mr. Emyr Llywelyn's view that Chapter 10 in the book was not based on a correct interpretation and that the conclusions drawn were incorrect. It is planned, therefore, that a second edition of *The Welsh and their country* should appear at an early date with revised and updated chapters, with emphasis on Chapter 10.

Ian Hume
Dr. W. T. R. Pryce

The Open University in Wales
Cardiff

30th July, 1986.

has been its home'. Emyr Llewelyn places no emphasis on race, and in this respect his doctrine differs from one layer of Nazi thought. But for him also the fate of the individual soul rests in its being at one with society, in this case the nation. 'Wales is this spirit which flowed through men before I was born and which will speak through others when my body has turned to dust' (p. 88).

The philosopher who accorded a considerable position in his system to this mystical emphasis on society was Auguste Comte (1798-1857), the father of modern Positivism, who taught that man's dignity rests wholly on his being an inseparable part of a social circle such as a nation. This society is the *grande être*, the supreme being which gives man a meaningful existence and invites him to respond creatively to its wealth. Indeed, it is the mystic's duty to channel each thought and action towards perfecting this 'supreme being'. And Society—whether a Nation or Mankind—grips man emotionally rather than intellectually. It is spiritual, mystical and indefinable.

In Emyr Llewelyn's words, 'this moulding on the deepest levels of our subconcious is more important than the development of our thought and reason . . .'. The connection between man and the society which gives his life value and meaning is a mystical one in the realms of the irrational. The Spirit of his People takes possession of him in a way that cannot be comprehended, only experienced. And this gives Emyr Llewelyn a great advantage in argument because argument is a logical process and when thorny questions are raised about the details of his philosophical system, he can flee to the illogical world of emotions.

His word for *Volksgeist* is *eneidfaeth*. It is a spiritual substance which 'feeds man's soul'. It is also the 'product of the spirits of those who have been here before us' and is passed on to each one by his society, the society which 'creates man's personality'. But what does it consist of? It seems to be completely pure and good. Indeed, this 'is the most valuable of man's treasures' (pp. 87-88). It is of key importance in the author's argument. The *eneidfaeth* is the medium by which one may separate the bogus Welshman from the real one. It is the medium of grace which 'gives our souls rest', (p. 89) and is the standard which enables us to recognize justice (p. 90). This is to be found in its full force in Wales in *Y Fro Gymraeg*.

It is, therefore, vitally important for us to know the composition of the *eneidfaeth*. But one asks in vain. The secret is not revealed. Only Emyr Llewelyn knows its precise composition. It's too mystical to be expressed in words. We have, however, heard about it in other contexts. Alfred Rosenberg, one of the Nazi philosophers, stated 'religion is something between a man and his own soul or, if he is lucky to be a German, something between himself and the souls of his people'. Replace 'German' with *Cymro* in this quotation and you will see that knowledge of the *eneidfaeth* is a matter of luck. And unless you know about it you are unlucky, you are not a Welshman [*Cymro*].

One other point. One of the book's themes is that true Welsh culture can only be found among country people. Here again we hear the echoes of the fascist past. As Hitler said in 1935, 'the Germany of the future cannot but be a state of smallholders . . . We can overcome all the blows of fate and every crisis if the country people will be a solid foundation for our People'. Emyr Llewelyn is of the same opinion. 'The more pure and basic Welshness which belongs to the Welsh people must be safeguarded' (p. 91). Professor A. Brady in his book on the organization of Germany under Hitler sums up Nazi ideas on this subject with these words: 'The urban way of life has its particular values, its characteristic thought processes and its own particular outlook. They are completely opposed to those of the country people. The outlook and the values of country folk are those considered worthwhile by the Nazi government. So, to the extent that the countryman's perception deteriorates, the values of the Nazi order face on barren ground'.

The Nazi belief that some special virtue belonged to country people emanated from the Romantic movement. Such people lived closer to Nature and so were more aware than townspeople of the eternal spirit which pervades everything. And on the basis of this belief, the Nazi government tried to arrange to move people to the German areas in order to draw on their people's age-old *eneidfaeth* or *Volksgeist*. As one of their officials, M. Gardner, explained in 1935, students should spend some of their time working manually in fields and orchards. 'Thus', he said, 'they draw nearer their own people's thoughts and the roots of the German people'. Or, as Emyr Llewelyn puts it, those who live in towns should draw nearer to the country people because the latter are 'the true inheritors of the Welsh *eneidfaeth*, and anyone who wishes to receive and partake of it must live amongst them' (p. 94). The Third Reich arranged for schoolchildren to spend some months on farms in the truly German regions so as to 'mould the rhythm of town children's lives according to the rural pattern, thus enabling them to absorb a great deal of the *Volksgeist*'. In 1935, the first year of the scheme's operation, 35,000 children were sent off to the farms, and laws were passed compelling people to move from the towns to live permanently in the German areas. Emyr Llewelyn advocates the same thing when he states that '(the people) must return from their exile in English cities and settle in *Y Fro Gymraeg*' (p. 93).

For the Nazis, only the culture acceptable to the 'spirit of the nation' (and by its anointed spokesman—the leaders of the Nazi Party) could be allowed. Goebbels, the head of Germany's Propaganda Ministry, put it in a nutshell when he told the National Chamber of Culture in 1935 that 'artists had to receive their inspiration from the complete nature character alone'. Every other source was poisonous and unacceptable. Emyr Llewelyn echoes these words. 'Only that which is correct and in accordance with our history and traditions is acceptable in *Y Fro Gymraeg*' (p. 93). The *eneidfaeth* is what separates the acceptable from the unacceptable. And who will tell us whether a film, a book, a novel or a painting is 'in accordance with our tradition?' As the secret of the exact make-up of the *eneidfaeth* belongs to Emyr Llewelyn, we cannot hope to receive an objective description of it. Yet the answer appears on p. 96. Until the day dawns when *Y Fro Gymraeg* is an independent state, '*Mudiad Adfer* [the Restoration Movement] will guard and defend the civilization of the Welsh people, and will act as the Protecting Government of *Y Fro Gymraeg*'. This is logical enough. And those who possess the mystical link with the *eneidfaeth* can interpret the mysteries of the acceptable and the unacceptable—the exact argument used by Hitler and his followers in relation to Germany's *Volksgeist*.

How on earth is it possible to reconcile this horrendous philosophy with our nation's traditions?

But this is not all, by any means. This doctrine offers us ideas about the law which challenge all we know about justice. It also strikes a blow to the very heart of Christianity.

On pp. 96-99, Emyr Llewelyn discusses the law. Anyone who has studied law will know that it is no easy matter to formulate a satisfactory system of philosophy on this subject. Emyr Llewelyn has decided to join what is known as the Historical School. The father of this school of philosophers among the German professors of law was Friedrich Karl von Savigny (1779-1861). Von Savigny and his disciples laid great stress on historical development as a natural growth and held that this development was legitimized by the power of the national spirit, the *Volksgeist*. As a result, his followers (though not von Savigny himself) opposed the adoption of Roman Law because it was foreign to the National Spirit and, as such, interfered with the continuing development of the nation's own law. Emyr Llewelyn aligns himself with this school of thought.

No such thing as general justice exists and 'it is not possible for one nation's law to be just if applied to another nation' (p. 97). He believes, like von Savigny, that the nation's traditions shape its law and thus defines justice. 'Where law springs from the people's traditions, the duty of each member of that nation towards it is something personal and sacrosanct: and an individual will obey laws out of respect to the spirit of the elders who formulated them' (p. 97). This last sentence deserves careful analysis. It is a duty to respect this law not because of any conviction that the law is just—that it is an expression of justice—but for an historical reason: that it was the elders who formulated it. Law is the mystical product of the national spirit down the centuries. It follows, therefore, that the laws of any national elders apart from our own are not to be respected. 'What legality has any law which has not been rooted in the customs of the people it serves?' (p. 97). It follows logically from this that English law has no legality whatsoever in Wales. Could it not be argued, however, that there are many elements, even in English law, that are fair and just? Does not the Habeas Corpus Act of 1679, for example, give an excellent legal expression to the Christian emphasis on the value and dignity of the individual and his right to freedom? No, it does not, says Emyr Llewelyn. Unless such a law develops directly from our 'age-old tradition', it is not just. All English laws are similarly condemned because each and every one is the result of Wales's conquest by England. Law is not based on any general concept of justice—even the Christian concept—but on the will of the Welsh people through the ages. And the law is definitely not there to protect the rights of the individual. 'English law is unsocial in that it fails to see man in relation to his fellow men . . . '. It places too great an emphasis on the individual, says Emyr Llewelyn—rightly or wrongly. For him, 'The function of law is to defend and preserve society's values'. If it does that, it cannot be challenged. Another way of putting this would be to say that the purpose of the law is to confirm and consolidate the work of politicians. If the leaders of *Y Fro Gymraeg* pass a law which is, in their minds, consistent with the 'age-old tradition', it must be unquestioningly obeyed no matter how unjust some people may believe it to be. For there is no justice superior to the justice which develops historically from the national tradition. If it is the natural tradition to execute everyone on his or her eightieth birthday, it's no use complaining. That is what the *eneidfaeth* ordains. And the *eneidfaeth* is infallible.

In his great speech to the court at Caernarfon following the burning of the Bombing School in Llŷn in 1936, Mr. Saunders Lewis could appeal to a law higher than English statutory law.[1] He could do so because he accepted the Catholic point of view that man's laws are not absolute. Emyr Llewelyn also urges the young people of Wales to 'obey laws higher than English law—our people's traditions and values' (p. 98). Yet these are not, in fact, 'higher' law because English law is the product of the English National Spirit. The whole point is that there are no 'higher' or 'lower' laws, only the product of our *eneidfaeth* and the product of their *eneidfaeth*. And he closes his argument with an appeal to follow something he calls '*Cyfraith Newydd Hywel*' (Hywel's New Law) in order to create 'a new social structure which will be an expression of the will of the Welsh people, and an expression of our age-old spirit, of our own internal laws' (p. 99). Goodness knows what that means!

The truth is that rhetoric cannot hide the ugly tinge of the totalitarianism which lies at the root of these ideas. What all this means is that the work of explaining the meaning of our age-old tradition in the context of the legal demands of our daily lives will fall into the hands of those who have responsible access to the admittedly incomprehensible mysteries of the *eneidfaeth*. The raising of the Welsh tradition above the demands of justice means repeating the same atrocity as that perpetrated in Hitler's Germany. As was stated in *Deutches Kulturrecht*, a volume published in Hamburg in 1936, the power of the State arises from 'the will of the people', and the discovery of this will is not a matter of counting votes in an election. It is to be found where the basic and half-conscious aspirations are formulated—in the 'national soul'. And who can interpret those aspirations? Who but the *Fuehrer*? 'The law which legalises the activities and policies of the Leader of the National Socialists emanates from the national soul'. When Alfred Rosenberg addressed the

German Law Academy at Weimar, he explained this concept quite simply: 'Justice is what is just in the opinion of the Aryan people; and injustice is what is rejected by them'. Emyr Llewelyn uses the same kind of reasoning to justify *Adfer* describing itself as 'the Protecting Government of the Republic of *Y Fro Gymraeg*'. It is the same *eneidfaeth* which authorises members of the *Adfer* to claim priority over others and to make themselves, at the same time, the only prophets of justice. In a word, we stand in the middle of the path leading us to 'the Principle of the Leader'. As was stated by one of the ministries of the German Culture Department in 1936, concerning the young men being imbued with 'national spirit': they, and they alone, like the *Fuehrer* today, will know in future what is right and what is wrong; they will know what the aim is, and how to achieve it'.

No more need be said to prove that we are here face to face with one of the most serious threats to legal fairness, to personal freedom and to democracy.

This has all arisen because Emyr Llewelyn's doctrine is a blow aimed at the heart of the Christian religion. It is a doctrine guilty of the ultimate blasphemy. It has taken an attitude to this world, and in deifying, it has broken the first commandment—'you shall not make for yourself a graven image'. This philosophy has placed society—the nation—and its culture on the throne of God. Immense claims are made about the *eneidfaeth* it produces. Its very name is blasphemous. Since when has man's genius been food for the soul? It's worth noting the properties the *eneidfaeth* is said to possess. It 'transforms our selfish urges into values', it is 'our people's only justification and objective'; it is 'the most valuable of all man's treasures' (p. 88); it gives 'rest to our souls'; it 'restores man's soul'; without it, 'man is lost in a mad vastness, a wanderer and a spiritual pilgrim' (p. 89); through it, 'man is safe from slavery and corruption' (p. 91). In line with the tendency to deify created objects, no consideration is give to the truth that a nation's spirit and culture are both tainted with the corruption of sin.

On the contrary, the *eneidfaeth* for Emyr Llewelyn carries the whole burden of salvation. It is in his scheme the redeeming force. Christ has been ejected from his position and is not even named in the last chapter. He has been swept aside so that man, now his own saviour, can occupy the middle of the stage. Every revelation necessary for our salvation comes from our nation's age-old tradition. Why need God reveal himself any more? Why need the Word become flesh?

And in the context of Emyr Llewelyn's book, there is one inexplicable mystery. What has this pitiful humanism to do with the age-old tradition of the Welsh nation? How has he come to such conclusions on the basis of the spiritual wealth given to us by St. David, Siôn Cent, Bishop Morgan, Morgan Llwyd, Williams of Pantycelyn and Gwilym Hiraethog?[2] Who exactly is Emyr Llewelyn trying to deceive with his claims of being able to solve the mysteries of the national spirit? This claptrap was produced by a handful of European philosophers, not by our age-old tradition. So, what is the use of talking loudly about limiting oneself to live one's whole life through the medium of the Welsh language and in the light of our national tradition? What about his beginning to revise his philosophy in the light of that particular Christian tradition?

I am, however, doing a slight disservice to Europe. It was because this doctrine was being forced down the throats of the German Christians that Karl Barth raised his powerful voice and men such as Martin Niemöller and Hans Lillje were imprisoned for refusing to bow to it. And that is why the German Confessional Church made its majestic statement at the Synod of Barmaen in May 1934:—

> 'Jesus Christ, as the Scripture testifies, is the only Word of God to whom we are to listen and whom we are to obey, and in Him shall we trust in life and in death. We condemn as falsehood the teaching that the Church should acknowledge as God's revelation, side by side with this unique Word, any other facts or forces . . .'

And what they had in mind, in particular, was the Nazi doctrine that the *Volksgeist*—the *eneidfaeth*—was the source of saving grace. And it is, at the same time, a blow against every attempt to dethrone God in Wales and replace Him with anything, however valuable or cherished. Our forefathers would have understood this perfectly because they were particularly jealous of the royal rights of the God who printed his covenant on our door posts and lintels over a period of fifteen hundred years.

Notes

1. This famous speech can be read in A. R. Jones and G. Thomas (eds.) *Presenting Saunders Lewis*, Cardiff: University of Wales Press 1973, pp. 115-26.
2. See *The Dictionary of Welsh biography*, London: the Honourable Society of Cymmrodorion, 1959.

Chapter Eleven

What is *Adfer*?*

Emyr Llewelyn

What is *Adfer*?[1] You could call *Adfer* a Limited Company which exists to buy houses in Welsh communities, but that would not answer the question. You could call *Adfer* a nationalist movement which tries to create a complete Welsh society in the west, but this does not completely answer the question either. Perhaps the best way to discover what *Adfer* really is would be to study the reason for establishing *Adfer* in the first place. The answer is in the purpose and aim of *Adfer*. What is the purpose of *Adfer*? The answer is quite simple—the purpose of *Adfer* is to ensure the continuation of our people. Lending money, preventing villages from becoming holiday villages, labouring together on working weekends, collecting money, buying land and businesses, are all done for this same purpose—ensuring the continuation of our people.

The *Adfer* idea is not a dilettante philosophy, *Adfer* is not an adventure, *Adfer* is not an experiment, *Adfer* is not a game, and *Adfer* workers are not people playing at revolution. *Adfer* is a necessity. The necessity to create a New Wales in the west, or face our extinction. And we are becoming extinct.

Ydd ym oll yn ddig	We are all angry
Yn bren heb un brig	A tree with no branches
Heb wreiddiau orig . . .	Soon without roots
Ein hetifeddiaeth ni a drowyd i estroniaid,	Our heritage has been given to foreigners,
A'n tai i ddieithriaid.	And our houses to strangers.[2]

* First published as one chapter of Emyr Llewelyn's (1976) *Adfer a'r Fro Gymraeg*, Pontypridd a Lerpwl, Cyhoeddiadau Modern Cymreig Cyf. 58-65, this was a speech delivered in August, 1973. The translation is by Mrs. Ann Davies; explanatory footnotes are by the editors.

We are being mutilated, dispersed, atomised. You cannot count a single county in the west as a Welsh county any more. Looking at a linguistic map of the west is like looking at a patchwork quilt. A patch of Welsh community here, then a patch lost to English, then another little patch of Welshness. Localities are cut off from one another, and within reasonably healthy localities the geographical distribution of the Welsh causes an atomising effect.

Our people are no longer a unit anywhere. We have no centre of gravity. We do not band together. By now, our oppressors do not have to fight the Welsh as a unit, but individual Welshmen and women. And it is so easy to deal with us one by one in the courts. They are not dealing with the whole body of a close knit society. It would be so difficult to conquer an entire village refusing to pay for a television licence, let alone a whole locality. Only when our people will be a social unit will we be able to bargain instead of beg, claim rather than protest.

Our legal freedom is on its way—there will be bilingualism in every public sphere before long—but this is not real freedom. We will still be without our real freedom—social freedom. We will still be powerless minorities in our villages and localities. The superficial status will come tomorrow—but where is your status, your social freedom? What do I mean by social freedom? Social freedom is being able to walk out of your house and be able to speak Welsh naturally to all you see in your village and locality. Most of the Welsh people in this Eisteddfod are not able to speak Welsh to the milkman or the shopkeeper in their own district. This is more of an oppression, more of an encumbrance to the Welsh language than the 'Welsh Not' ever was. Many clamour for civil rights for Welsh people these days, without realising that civil rights are something for individuals, and that the only real freedom for a language and people is social freedom.

Yes, look around you, to see your real freedom increasingly shrivelled every day. Don't you feel the pain as you see it all go, a house, a farm, a village, at a time? Every time a home in *Y Fro Gymraeg*[3] goes to a foreigner we die;

every time a young Welshman leaves *Y Fro Gymraeg* we die.

Can we now call this plundered country Wales? Is this Wales? No, this is not Wales. Haven't you heard? Wales has died. Our country, Wales, has ceased to be. Only the empty, meaningless name remains, without the substance of society and locality. Only the remains are left. The scattered remains of people. You who are middle-aged and elderly have seen the selling of bygone Wales. Yes, she was sold yesterday before your very eyes. The Wales of Dewi[4], the Wales of Glyndŵr, the Wales of our fathers, and the Wales of my childhood too, has 'SOLD' printed in capital letters over most of it, just as have the villages of my childhood, Llangrannog and Rhydlewis and hundreds of similar localities. And 'FOR SALE' has been written all over the little that remains unsold. Don't you believe me? There is no Wales anymore. She's gone. Sold. Sold. Sold. She's been sold.

And if you want her back, you will have to buy her back. You will have to pay with money, and with sweat and sacrifice to buy back every inch and part of her. But money alone cannot buy her back. You can't buy Wales back like buying a house—with everything ready-made—a carpet on the floor, a clean concrete path right up to the front door, central heating at the press of a button. No, you will have to create her anew, create her from the dust and the mud, from the foundations.

We want money for *Adfer* of course. But not just money. You cannot buy Wales back as she was with money. If you had thousands upon thousands and millions upon millions you could only buy back the land where a community of our people once dwelt, the land where Wales once was. You will have to recreate Wales from scratch—there is no other way. Gambling on the chance of an election or of a parliament of bourgeois socialism, which is so popular amongst nationalists, is not going to create a New Wales for you. On the other hand, dramatic action without doing the basic hard work will not create a New Wales either. I've done my share of dramatic actions, and I would be the last to deny their worth, otherwise I would be denying the value of the best years of my life—of course we need them. But it is foolish to trust protests alone. You are just as empty-handed the day after the protest as you were before, and the situation remains just as hopeless and stagnant.

There is no easy dramatic way of solving a problem that has taken centuries to create. Five hundred years of plunder on our land and people will not disappear overnight. There is no easy way out. There is only one answer—hard work, work, work, work. With no television cameras, with no attention from the press, with no reward apart from the reward of creation. We must not deceive ourselves that success should be measured according to the proportion of headlines in the English papers—rather according to the proportion of respect in the hearts of the Welsh people. Neither does progress come from speeches and rallies and verbal debates in the press, on radio and television, but from working in the dust and the mud until you feel the stone under your hand turning into a house for a Welshman in *Y Fro Gymraeg*. Until you can put your hand on the rough masonry of the house and say—here is progress, here is power, here is something permanent that will be here to be handed over to my children's children when the summer caravans will have rusted to nothing and the holiday chalets will have rotted—for ever.

I have tested many different methods of action, and I can honestly say that I reached this method of action the hard way, after pushing in vain along every other way until I came to the power in *Adfer*. I have felt so often in the last ten years—in the words of Llywarch Hen—'like a fieldmouse scratching at a crag'. And eventually learnt the lesson that there is no power for us other than the social power in *Y Fro Gymraeg*. Social power alone can solve our problem as a people—and Adfer is the key to that power.

The Welsh communities of the west are the starting point of any revolution to create a social or political power for the Welsh people. The scattered remains of our people must have an organic centre and central point. It is only by creating a centre for our people that we can make all the scattered and incoherent parts of our people aware of belonging to a united people. Not only a geographical centre, but a spiritual centre. Creating a centre in the west would not only give us a home and a society in which to lead a full life in our own language, but it would also be a means of the spiritual rebirth of our people. A new vision and hope would emerge, a cultural re-awakening would emerge, based on the ideals that guided our people throughout the ages.

So what if we have a centre? You say, won't most of our people still be scattered? Yes that's true. But the scattered ones will no longer be incoherent parts, because the centre in the west will be the heart and brains of it all: and it will all be a complete circle feeling the gravity of the centre keeping it together. When the heart beats once again, blood will flow to the scattered limbs and put new life into them.

How do we go about it? One of the most important things about *Adfer*—if not the most important of all—is that it is going to release the creative energy of the Welsh people. Our enemies have pushed us into using unproductive ways of action—but *Adfer* will release the creative vigour and energy of our people. Our people have never had the opportunity to show their creative ability, it has been restrained and confused, but once *Adfer* releases it we will have such a flood of creativity as to shock the world.

Our battle will be amongst *Y werin bobl*[5] and they are the decisive element in the success or failure of our battle. It is futile to try to create propaganda outside Wales—one cannot raise the battle to an international level without a strong foothold in *Y Fro Gymraeg*. This is the only true nationalism; the only true socialism is to work alongside the ordinary people, our people. We have chosen as a symbol of an *Adferwr*[6] a worker with a scythe in his hand. We have chosen this because the ordinary Welshman can identify with it. The academics and those who engage in empty talk will have to get some dirt under their fingernails and some sweat on their foreheads if they are to identify with this new symbol of the new Wales. After all, my battle is not in order to create more young bourgeois to inhabit suburbia, but in order to raise a generation of young people who are heroic and cultured, true to the people and civilised.

In the west, awaiting your leadership, is our unassuming peasantry—thoroughly lost, and voices from all sides deafening and confusing them. Materialistic English voices shout at them from all sides. They are confused, not knowing who they are or what to think. Everything surrounding an ordinary Welshman tells him that English, not Welsh, should prevail, tells him to forget his language and his people, and adopt foreign ones. He is lost, and turns to you, saying 'Show me the way, show me by your example, and I shall try to follow you'. And you must say to him 'Forget all the voices, I shall show you who you are and how you should be. I shall be here beside you, my sacrifice on your behalf shall be proof of my love and comradeship. This is the way, my brother, come, walk with me'.

> You must go to the people.
> You must live amongst them.
> You must learn from them.
> You must love them and serve them.
> You must start with what they know.
> You must build on what they know.[7]

Colonisation. That is the key to it all. You must return from exile in the non-Welsh-speaking areas, there is no vigour, no energy, no vision, no power there—nothing will emerge from there. We must entice the remainder of our people from the non-Welsh-speaking areas, and entice also those men and women who have lost the language but still feel its attraction—they must be enticed back to settle in *Y Fro Gymraeg.* The only way to build a country without fighting is through settlement. We must start from what little the ordinary people have in *Y Fro Gymraeg* —by adapting and developing the remains of the culture they have, and by entwining the brittle threads of the few strings which keep them Welsh into a strong knot that cannot be untied.

But *Adfer* is a dream, a fancy, a foolish dream, I hear you say. Yes, *Adfer* is a dream, a myth, and the New Wales is a myth. But, *Adfer* is our people's age-long dream, our people's age-long dream for a full, unfettered life. No-one can destroy the *Adfer* dream. No-one. Neither the strategy of enemies, nor time, nor violence, nor oppression. No-one can destroy the *Adfer* dream because it is an expression of our people's deepest aspirations, and expression of our people's yearning for speaking with their own voice, and expression of our people's thirst for justice. Only when the last of our people will have died will the *Adfer* dream die.

What kind of dream is the one we are battling to achieve? A dream about land and a dream about people. But not only land and not only people. Our battle is for the undefinable and invaluable wealth which existed in our people's community and was drowned in Tryweryn, in the reason why the mothers of Bryncroes wept outside the locked gates of their children's school. Our battle is for the most valuable of all things created by mankind in its age-long joint effort—namely the warmth and intimacy and comradeship that exist in a living community. Our battle is against those who wish to destroy people's emotional ties with their community and locality. The purpose of *Adfer* is to be a voice and utterance for those people who are fighting to keep a hold on that which gives a meaning to life for them. Preventing the breaking of the silver cord which the ages created between our people and their localities, the silver cord which makes us people.

But *Adfer* is not only a dream. It is a fact. The New Wales was a fact from the moment *Adfer* was established, from the moment the first house was bought, from the moment we had our first working weekend. *Adfer* is not a fantasy, our houses are real houses, the stones in their walls are real stones, the dirt on our hands is real dirt, the sweat on our foreheads is real sweat. Go, go to Doldre to see the sweat and labour of two year's work becoming fact. Go there to see the foundation stone of the New Wales.

What is *Adfer*? A cry.

'Thus Israel cried so strongly because their death was before their own eyes'.

Yes, a cry, *Adfer* is the last passionate cry of our people.

What is *Adfer*? It is what is left of the Welsh people's desire to continue.

What is *Adfer*? *Adfer* is the revolution. Revolution is an idea which has organisation. No company or companies can ever move our people geographically and root them anew in the west. Neither can any movement congregate our scattered people and return them to their localities—but an idea can. An idea is strong enough to do these things. Organisation is essential to act on the idea—the organisation has been created in the *Adfer* Company and the *Adfer* Movement. Realising the idea could take hundreds of years but the idea exists, and the foundation of the organisation exists and the revolution is inevitable.

Impossible, you say. When people say 'impossible' I think of Weizman telling the story about his friend Arthur Ruppin. Weizman was staying in the old ruined city of Jaffa when his friend called on him to take him for a walk over the sands outside the city. When they had both walked out a fair distance, and were surrounded by sand without a blade of grass or a stone anywhere—his friend turned to Weizman and said 'We are going to build a city here'. And there in the middle of the sand the marvellous city of Tel Aviv was built.

There were once three high courts in Wales, Aberffraw, Dinefwr and Mathrafal. The homes of the Princes of Wales and centres of our culture, but what remains of this splendour? Nothing. Go to Aberffraw, there is nothing there but a mound of earth, and as for Mathrafal—no-one even remembers its location. But we are going to build new towns and villages. I may not live to see this, but I say quite confidently that there will be new villages and towns built in our country again, called Aberffraw, Dinefwr and Mathrafal—there will yet again be a home and succour for our language and culture, where yet again will exist the splendour and glory that was.

I wish *Adfer* on you, as a curse and a nightmare to worry you in your exile from *Y Fro Gymraeg* in your luxurious lounges; but also as a blessing and a dream to sustain you in the hour of hardship and despair, a dream to sustain you in your cells.

We shall never surrender this land. It was our land, and shall be ours for ever and ever.

Notes

1. The *Adfer* group developed both as a registered business and as a movement to regenerate *Y Fro Gymraeg* (the Welsh-speaking area) through economic and practical means. Whilst its most prominent activists came from *Cymdeithas yr Iaith Gymraeg* (The Welsh Language society) they were to develop *Adfer's* perspectives with quite different emphases to those of the former organization.
2. This reference to the lamentations of Jeremiah, 5.2, is the first of several either to biblical sources or to Israel as example.
3. Lit. 'The Welsh-speaking area'. *Y Fro Gymraeg* refers to areas of west Wales where the language is still strong. See Chapter 2 for a discussion of models appropriate to this area.
4. Saint David.
5. A literal translation of this term could be 'the peasantry'; preferable alternatives could be 'the workers' or 'ordinary people'. Both the latter terms are used—from this point onward—to act as translation of this term. See Chapter 5 of this volume for a detailed discussion of the use of the term.
6. '*Adfer* member' or '*Adfer* worker'.
7. This series of exhortations bears close comparison with some of Mao Tse tung, particularly those contained in 'Talks at the Yenan Forum on literature and art' (1942) *Selected works of Mao Tse tung, Volume III*, Peking 1965, 69-98. At several points in other of his writings and speeches it is clear that Emyr Llewelyn has consciously or unconsciously used some of Mao's ideas and precepts.

Chapter Twelve

Language Planning and Minority Group Rights*

Colin H. Williams

In recent years, the discussion concerning the potential of language status planning in Wales, has focused too narrowly in my view, on the specific question of language maintenance, treating language promotion as a self evident right. This chapter seeks to examine the relationship between language planning and group rights and argues that a comprehensive elaboration of majority and minority language group rights is an essential prerequisite for any lasting and successful language planning programme. Some doubts as to the efficacy and direction of language planning *per se* are raised, for I am not as confident as others that the planning aspect is either the most appropriate or pressing means whereby Welsh may be more firmly rooted in contemporary life. However, given that language planning is firmly entrenched in many bi-cultural and multicultural societies (Eastman, 1982; Edwards, 1984), it is likely that the initial concern over its relevance will now give way to a major debate as to how to institute the principles of language planning within the everyday practice of local and national government service provision.

The debate has drawn on the experience of other states with a history of language planning, most notably Canada and Finland (Williams, C. H. 1978). It has related language erosion to other indicators of social and regional change (Williams, S. W. 1979) and has drawn attention to the danger and fallacy of interpreting language decline as an apolitical and purely 'cultural' phenomenon (Williams, G. 1979). The present paper reflects on the fundamental

* First published in *Cambria*, 9, 1982, 61-74, and specially revised by the author for this volume.

question of which rights and obligations language planning is meant to fulfil; this author believes that language rights in Wales are—in the main—only very generally defined,[1] and that the debate has currently lost sight of this basic aspect. As argued below this may prove, in the long term, to be a distinct advantage. In the short term, the absence of a codified system of language rights may hinder the development of language planning.

The decline in the Welsh-speaking population and the territorial shrinkage of Welsh-speaking regions has occupied the attention of language activists, politicians and social scientists for some considerable time. The number of linguistic domains within which the language is capable of being used continues to expand, as does its technical vocabulary. Yet, as Chapter 1 shows, the actual territory within which it is dominant, and can be used as a matter of course, is becoming more fragmented in the face of the challenge of the ubiquitous language of Wales' powerful neighbour. Concern over loss of territory is equated with a diminution of ethno-linguistic vitality and the promoters of Welsh are increasingly troubled as to which role the language will perform in the future. Encouraging signs in the language revival are reflected in the growth of the Welsh-medium schools sector, the development of Welsh language broadcasting and the increased use of Welsh in public administration and central government agencies in Wales. The significant feature of these developments is that they serve to institutionalize Welsh within the para-public state sector (Williams, C. H. 1984a).

In part the growth of a comprehensive Welsh public sector reflects the political pressures at the local and national levels described elsewhere in this volume. But it also reflects the growth in the sixties of a new class, a technical and administrative intelligentsia. This expanding professional class had a strong investment in Wales. After establishing the legitimacy of Welsh equivalents to U.K. ministries the decentralist trend had, as a logical outcome, the further establishment of Welsh-medium employment opportunities within Welsh-based ministries. Bound as they were by language loyalty, and a desire to reside in Wales, an element within the new intelligentsia saw limited opportunities in the English dominated bureaucracies of central government or of private corporate practice. They thus pushed for an expanded range of Welsh-medium public services, to be staffed by fully qualified bilingual civil servants. However, whilst the domestic growth rate of civil servants in Wales has been remarkable, little of this growth has been specifically engendered by the formal expansion of Welsh-medium services. Thus parallel with the development of the Welsh Office after November 1964 there has been a growth in the staffing levels and responsibilities of the Wales-based offices of other U.K. ministries, as in the Departments of Employment, Environment, Health and Social Security, Industry and Trade.[2] Notably it is in the Department of Education that Welsh has been promoted most as a language of government, administration and public interchange. Given the value system of this new bureaucratic, modernizing elite, it is perhaps not surprising that language planning has come to be regarded as a potentially sound instrument for the maintenance of a Welsh-speaking Wales. Although the impetus for language planning has come from a very small number of academics, journalists and language supporters, its inherently rational, purposeful and manipulable assumptions appeal to the bureaucracy of the local state.

The development of the Welsh-medium education sector is a prime example of language corpus planning, and reflects the increased awareness amongst the bureaucratic elite that the fortunes of the language can be markedly influenced by government policy. Attention has recently switched from corpus planning to status planning and the increased scope of local authority initiative in influencing the linguistic character of the socio-economic environment (Cooke, 1978). Such language planning is a logical outgrowth of the post-war developments in social and regional planning (Rees, G. and Rees,

T. L. 1980) where language functions are not treated *sui generis*, but as part of a larger social complex. However, such considerations are at an early stage of development. Each of the incremental reforms described above has done little to illumine the nature of language planning in its broadest sense in Wales. This unfulfilled potential stems from a failure to specify in a clear and consistent manner just what constitutes the language rights of the Welsh-speaking minority. In the long run it may be that this ambiguity is beneficial, in that it allows sympathetic local authorities a great deal of flexibility in the administration of Welsh-medium services. In the short term such ambiguity fuels language conflict. The thrust of recent developments within such sectors as education, local planning and public administration more generally, has been directed at a more self-conscious definition of the *needs* of Welsh-speakers. Thus linguistic considerations have, for the first time, influenced such activities as the development of structure plans, the granting or refusal of industrial and tourist development applications in predominantly Welsh-speaking areas, and the declaration by certain councils (e.g. Gwynedd County Council, Arfon, Dwyfor, and Glyndŵr District Councils) that henceforth language considerations will have equal weighting with the more traditional environmental and technical issues. Yet despite declaring the language a planning factor, the operation of this, especially at an appeal, has yet to be tested, so that much remains to be done to translate recommendations into normal working practice.[3]

These, and other non-public developments, speak of a greater recognition that Welsh both needs, and is amenable to, being planned i.e. that the language should be treated as any other socio-economic variable, such as housing and health. Of course, the key difference is that language has a more encompassing influence on the nature of services provided by government. Consequently the prospects for conflict are greater when a linguistic minority seek to change the resultant character of such services by demanding bilingual or unilingual reforms. Central to this process of linguistic change is the appeal to law, and the ensuing problems in determining the legitimacy of counter-claims in bi-cultural situations. The next section illustrates the primarily incremental development of the legal recognition of Welsh language rights.

Legal provisions and the ancillary concept of language

Historically, as Walters (1978) has detailed, the basis of legal provision in Wales is the Tudor system of English law and administration consolidated in the reign of Henry VIII. The Act of Union 1536 imposed English law on Wales to the exclusion of its rivals, and the statute of 1542 applied the English county system of local administration to Wales. The Act of Union, while acknowledging that

> 'the people of (Wales) have and do daily use a speech nothing like, nor consonant to the natural mother tongue used within this realm (of England)',

went on to provide that the language of the courts should thence forward be English and that

> 'from henceforth no person or persons that use the Welsh speech of language shall have or enjoy any manner or office or fees within the realm of England, Wales or other of the King's dominions . . . unless he or they use English'.

However, Welsh continued to be used after 1536 in legal and administrative matters, since the vast majority of the population were monoglot Welsh speakers. As British state integration continued apace the legal provisions enforcing the dominance of English became more binding. State education and formal administration completed the political incorporation of the population into state-wide structures and agencies, destroying many intermediate institutions, or making them arms of the state (Williams, G. 1981). In building a British nation out of a common territory, the established elite inevitably strengthened the state and its control over outlying areas through the process of bureaucratic centralization and standardization based on a common culture administered uniformly over a given territory. The legal recognition of a minority language, such as Welsh, in this state-building process, would have run counter to the political philosophy of the ruling parties. Indeed the most manifest expression of this centralist and uniform ideology was the 1870 Education Act. This involved the deliberate introduction of compulsory elementary education *exclusively in English*, a policy resulting from the conviction of commissioners appointed to inquire into the state of education in Wales that 'Welsh backwardness' was attributable to their ignorance of English. The results of this policy have been detailed elsewhere (Williams, C. H. 1980; Durkacz, 1983; Jones, 1984). So far as legal recognition of Welsh was concerned little was enacted until the passing of the Welsh Courts Act of 1942. This was the direct outcome of a petition, support for which was gathered over a period of twenty years by *Undeb y Cymdeithasau Cymraeg* (The Union of Welsh Societies). The provisions of the 1536 Act of Union forbidding the use of Welsh in court proceedings were replaced[4] by s 1 of the Welsh Courts Act 1942 which delcared that 'the Welsh language may be used in any court in Wales by any party or witness who considers by reason of his natural language of communication being Welsh'.[5] The 1942 Act also provided for the administration of oaths in Welsh and for the employment of interpreters, but s 3 (2) reiterated the Tudor principle that 'all proceedings of courts in Wales shall continue to be kept in the English language'. The Act marked a small advance for language supporters, made all the more remarkable in that it was passed during wartime (Walters, 1978).

Increased political and cultural pressure after the Second World War led the Conservative government in 1963 to establish a 'Committee on the Legal Status of the Welsh Language', chaired by Sir David Hughes Parry. The Committee reported in 1965 and in 1967 the Welsh Language Act was passed. The Report contained 31 recommendations, but the policy of both Report and Act may be said to make statutory 'the Principles of Equal Validity'.[6] By s 1, Welsh may be used by any person in any court proceeding in Wales and Monmouthshire.[7] Although the Act and subsequent local interpretations, have assisted in introducing Welsh into hitherto unilingual domains e.g. the supply of bilingual statutory forms and the judicial proceedings of Welsh courts, it has not kept pace with the growth of administrative law and the vast field of subordinate legislation. The regulations, roles, orders, by-laws, ordinances and proclamations which affect the rights and obligations of citizens are scarcely influenced by the existing statutes designed to promote the 'equal validity' concept of a bilingual community. Such ancillary and incidental legislation must be revised and expanded to cope with any proposed territorial division into language zones (Betts, 1976; Williams, C. H. 1978). The task of regulating the linguistic aspects of certain legislative measures is a complex political problem. A check list of the range of ancillary legislation necessary before language planners could operate effectively in Wales will suggest the comprehensive nature of the reforms required: provisions for interpreters, mixed-language juries, public notices by government inspectorates and tribunals, the use of language in local authority proceedings, municipal by-laws and notices, language qualification for local government employment, or even municipal office, official forms and returns as well as interpretive provisions in statutes. Sufficient examples have been cited to demonstrate that such language provisions are purely incidental of the exercise of jurisdiction (Sheppard, 1971).

And yet to approach language as a mere ancillary of jurisdiction is fruitless and misleading in bi-cultural situations where language is often asserted to be *the* prerequisite of minority group survival. Rather than language being ancillary to other ends, these ends are often deemed to be ancillary to the conservation of language, defined as the supreme social good.

Alternative directions for change: 1. Gradualism

Recognizing that language will continue to be a political issue in the forseeable future, the question of what changes language planning reforms will herald is deeply intertwined with the question of who governs Wales. The most realistic prospect is that of an extension of the ad hoc and incremental approach to language policy which has characterized Wales to date. This would then allow specific developments, without committing government to a wholescale involvement in elaborating the obligations of language legislation for each level in the administrative hierarchy. Such gradualism is in keeping with the British style of administration. However, all democratic countries in the twentieth century have experienced a shift from the laissez-faire to the positive state. The accompanying growth in the range and complexity of government activities has brought with it the need to grant increasing powers of discretion to the executive side of government. In the past the courts were the bulwark of individuals' rights and redress for the arbitrary or unjustified decisions of government were possible. Today, many argue that the ordinary courts have lost their flexibility and are no longer an effective instrument for remedying the wrongs of modern administrative action. Further, opponents of a gradualist approach to language legislation in Wales argue that the lack of a formally instituted set of language rights hinders the full realization of 'equal validity' granted under the Welsh Language Act. Their opposition is based upon two fears. First, that the slowness of a gradualist approach to language maintenance will militate against the effective revival of Welsh. Second, the singular emphasis on individual rights reflects the state's structural discrimination against minority language speakers. The tension between individual rights and group rights is critical in this situation and worthy of greater attention as it represents a second direction for change.

2. *Individual versus group rights*

The extension of the individual rights tradition in a bicultural community, as advocated by the gradualist approach, has tended to obscure the key issue of group conflict, namely the ability of the minority to preserve and, if possible, develop its own group characteristics in the face of state inspired assimilation. At first sight, therefore, it would seem foolhardy to attempt a solution to minority group grievances by legislating the right of an individual to use his/her language in specific domains, for that is not the issue. The issue in cases of conflict between groups of contrasting cultures, is the relative economic and social positions of the two linguistic communities, and the insistence by minorities of using their language as a medium of government and administration (Williams, C. H. 1980).

Glazer (1977) has shown that attempts to institute group rights, in such spheres as government, the civil service, university admission and business, have already been introduced in Canada, Belgium, Finland, India and Malaysia. Such attempts have been deliberately aimed at ensuring minority group representation in key areas of political and economic life. Yet in the United Kingdom, the attempt to reserve places by a quota system for minority representation is strongly resisted as a subversion of individual rights. The establishment of an officially unilingual Welsh-speaking region would provide a classic example of the tension generated between individual rights and group rights. If, for example, Welsh fluency was required for employment in the Civil Service of a proposed unilingual region (*Y Fro Gymraeg*), are we depriving the majority of non-Welsh-speakers their traditional rights? Defenders of an unilingual region would argue that as there exist ample opportunities for English-speaking civil servants to be employed elsewhere within the United Kingdom, such a region would be a 'special case' and deserving of special preference for Welsh-speakers. Opponents would argue, as they did in the American South in relation to Black rights, that this might lead to less qualified applicants gaining admission in preference to non-Welsh-speakers, and would insist on being considered on merit, in accordance with their individual rights.

There are two notions of justice in opposition here. One which says justice is the apportioning of rewards to groups on the basis of proportionality, the other which suggests that justices should only consider the established rights of individuals, regardless of national origin, language, religion or any other cultural marker (Glazer, 1977). In our individualistic society the majority would favour merit as a guiding principle of selection. How then would language planning be able to force compliance in the field of language rights, and which solution to this dilemma would prove most effective in fulfilling planning aims and reducing inter-group tension? Are there any guiding principles which suggest which path to follow: whether to reduce discrimination by establishing quotas and preferential places to minority group members, or alternatively to focus on the right of individuals without regard for their cultural origin?

Glazer (1977) has suggested that it is the model of society the state upholds which determines this choice. If the state adopts a diffusion perspective of ethnic change, viewing group identities as malleable and group membership as a purely private affair, it will conceive of group rights as a barrier to minority assimilation and a basis for maintaining permanent divisions within the state. However, if the state conceives of its constituent cultural groups as forming part of an established, ethnically plural society, as does Canada, then it must legislate for what the rights of each group shall be. At present, we are capable of choosing between both approaches, depending upon one's interpretation of British state ideology. If we choose the group-rights approach in Wales, we admit that the needs of both speech communities are so great that they cannot be met on the basis of individual rights. We also institute the legal separation of one culture from another, which in turn will lead to a strengthening of group distinctiveness and group boundaries.

The problem in Wales is whether effective language planning can be introduced prior to a full elaboration of which language rights are to be guaranteed. Critics suggest that language plans that involve differential treatment of British citizens within varying language zones would perpetuate and accentuate existing divisions, which in themselves are a source of conflict. Alcock (1977) has argued that it is the *exact opposite* that is true.

> 'The point about divided societies—in South Tyrol, Cyprus, Canada, Switzerland, Belgium, Lebanon, *is that they wish to remain divided*. Each group draws its strength, its group consciousness, the basis for the exercise of its power, from the fact that it *is* different, *and that it wishes to remain different*. Those who see divisions as a source of conflict overlook that conflict arises because of threats to the factors which make for division—threats to separate identity or coexistence of the group, whether these threats be active (such as legislation or violence) or passive (such as non-recognition or cold-shouldering of the group or benign neglect by the majority in face of economic, social or technological change or pressure).'

Language activists thus press for the creation of new rights which will allow them to maintain their cultural group distinctiveness. Such rights, when allowed, are often retroactive in their application. But new language laws are bound to create conflict between those groups and areas for whom the law creates a new right, and others whom it also appears to deprive of long established patterns of behaviour, and expected, but now unfulfilled, rights. Thus, for example, the right of the Welsh-speaking majority in Gwynedd and Dyfed to promote Welsh clashes with the right of the Anglophone minority there to use their mother-tongue, a feature especially evident in recent education changes. We have here a second conflict over rights, between two similar claims, both of which represent acquired rights and hence entitled to be respected. However, the respecting of legitimate, acquired rights provides little basis for settling the question of priority which must face language planners if they are to be effective in redressing the grievances of conflicting petitioners in such circumstances.

The greatest difficulty facing language legislators, and planners as interpreters of such legislation, is the question of priority, not that of balance. As a rule, where the same acquired right, that of using one's preferred language, is claimed by two or more groups, then the right of the numerically stronger group would take preference.[8] This would seem to argue for a territorial solution to language rights. Where Welsh-speakers form a geographical majority their language should be used as a matter of course, with the personality principle ensuring the rights of the Anglophone minority within the Welsh language zone. However, arguments derived from acquired rights are weak elements in the modern state, especially for minorities, due to the legislative and constitutional sovereignty of the people and their representatives in the central legislature. Such arguments acquire strength only in relation to the degree to which the established political institutions are willing to recognize them. We should not be surprised, then, to discover that the most ardent advocates of Welsh language rights are also advocates of Welsh independence, for they have already concluded that the desired rights can be maintained only where the polity is willing to enforce them. There may be a Welsh language problem, but there is not yet a unilingual Welsh administrative region. It may be that for the majority the limits of the achievement reflect accurately the limits of the aspiration. From current experience it seems unlikely that any Welsh region will become functionally unilingual, as the territoriality principle diminishes in its general utility. What, then, are the chief merits and drawbacks of a territorial perspective on the question of how best to provide governmental services to a linguistically heterogeneous clientele?

3. *A territorial approach*

It is rare for a government to opt for a purely territorial solution to its language problem. Many have attempted to follow a middle way between the territoriality and personality principles by classifying their territory according to a flexible system of both unilingual and bilingual districts (Williams, C. H. 1981b). As more Welsh local authorities become bilingual or predominantly Welsh in their internal deliberations, and as the development of

Welsh-medium education and commerce in these areas continues apace, it is possible that some system of official language districts will be enacted in the future.[9] Initially this would seem to argue for a formal organization of territory which would categorize the whole local authority unit according to a language criterion (Betts, 1977). However, the Canadian experience has demonstrated that formal organization of territory is not always the most apposite way of guaranteeing language rights (Cartwright, 1981; Cartwright and Williams, 1982). An alternative, functional approach, argues for less universal, formal, designation of territory, and for a closer adherence to spatial patterns of language usage. This approach argues that actual patterns of inter-cultural interaction are more important for realizing government service provision, than the absolute numbers and spatial distribution of a minority-language population alone. In other words, need, not distribution, governs the allocation of government service. As Welsh-speakers are scattered throughout the nation a functional organization of territory should lead to a greater degree of linguistic harmony than would a system predicated on formal principles of territorial organization. District categorization could be determined by a standardized language intensity index and a multi-variate socio-cultural framework derived from the details of 'local needs' couched from survey work. This would allow a more responsible designation than would the existing univariate census-based attempts at language zoning (Betts, 1977; Williams, C. H. 1978). The primary task is an elaboration of language needs, coupled with intensive fieldwork to assess whether or not the bilingual district is the most appropriate instrument of language policy in this case.

Advantage of adopting bilingual districts in Wales

1. In principle, it could serve as an attempt to depoliticize the language issue in the long term, though in the short term we must accept the likelihood of intense opposition.

2. It would legitimize and institutionalize Welsh within a wider range of local and central government services provided in any bilingual district.
3. Automatic adjustment after each decennial census to reflect changes in the linguistic proportions of the population would provide an element of flexibility to accommodate 'local needs', as is attempted in Finland.
4. Bilingual districts could provide the institutional basis for other agencies concerned with the socio-economic structure of primarily Welsh-speaking regions, along the lines suggested by the experience of the *Údarás na Gaeltachta* in Ireland.

Disadvantages of adopting bilingual districts

1. The original concept of bilingual districts was developed to solve a specific practical problem, namely, at what threshold of concentration should language minorities receive national and local services in their own languages? There is a danger, that, in attempting to make bilingual districts the primary instrument of language planning, we shall overburden the system and discredit the concept (Cartwright and Williams, 1982). The geolinguistic imbalance between the Welsh and non-Welsh speakers in Wales is a widely recognized problem, but it is questionable whether the solution can be advanced significantly through establishing—or not establishing—bilingual districts, and in proposing different solutions for Welsh and English minorities the opportunities for depoliticization may be lost.
2. The limited scale of a settled Welsh-speaking population might detract from any attempt at territorial subdivisions through language zoning. Limitations of finance, plus a lack of experienced personnel, coupled with the complexity of the problem, suggest a greater concentration of bilingual civil servants at the Welsh Office, rather than an expansion of local bureaucracy at the point of consumer contact.
3. It is possible to argue that bilingual districts were feasible in 1951, or even as late as 1961, but with the

territorial shrinkage of the Welsh-speaking regions the personality principle is by 1981 the most apt criterion for language planning.

4. It is possible to argue that the existing legislation and planning procedures allow sufficient consideration of language requirements under the ambit of social and environmental planning without need for recourse to further, and perhaps irrelevant, reforms.
5. The fragmented nature of Welsh-speaking communities must predispose one to adopt a pragmatic service-orientated approach, aimed at a piecemeal development of Welsh-medium services through local authority agencies, from the ground up rather than as part of an enforced national plan.
6. The adoption of any system of bilingual districts would be unrealistic, given that no major party, has as yet, adopted a policy of linguistic zoning in Wales.
7. It could increase, rather than decrease, language conflict and be interpreted as 'reverse apartheid'.
8. No comprehensive set of linguistic legislation for minority group rights exist to date. Any attempt to establish language planning zones, whether unilingual or bilingual, would politicize the planner and could increasingly transform his/her role from that of servant and interpreter to that of policy director and arbitrator.
9. Whilst formal territorial demarcation appears feasible, the current functional pattern of service provision would minimise the efficacy of a comprehensive territorial solution. For example, in North Wales, several of the principal services are directed from regional headquarters in England *viz* MANWEB in Chester, British Telecom in Chester and Shrewsbury, British Rail in Manchester. Bilingual service provision would only be possible were these regional service functions to be relocated within Wales, and even that would not necessarily guarantee an increase in Welsh-medium services.[10]

Discussion

Any proposal to establish formal language districts in Wales is fraught with difficulties, especially in the absence of a precise elaboration of which language rights and services such districts would fulfil. The recent upsurge of interest in language planning as an instrument of socio-economic change may be welcomed because it promises to set language problems within a wider socio-political and developmental frame. But there are dangers also in imputing to language planning a real ability to change an adverse climate for language reproduction. Language planning deserves critical scrutiny, along the lines suggested by G. Williams (1979, 1981) and C. H. Williams (1981, 1984a, 1984b), particularly in relation to the ideological base and political implications of its liberal, consensus epistemology. Such scrutiny, however, should not deter us from accepting that in very particular situations, formal language planning can have a marked effect on language reproduction. It is in the field of Welsh-medium education that such language planning has had its greatest impact, not only in sociolinguistic terms, but also in terms of the language's areal spread and in producing a relatively youthful Welsh-speaking population in the densely settled districts of the south-east and north-east (Aitchison, Carter and Williams, 1985). Conceivably we may be witnessing a radical alternative base for language reproduction in Wales, where the school operates as the single most important socialisation agency in the process of language acquisition. If this is accepted, severe problems may be engendered for the wider society once the constraints of a formal bilingual education no longer sustain a viable and well-integrated bilingual population. Adulthood may pose quite different problems of language choice from childhood, and clearly we need more detailed research on patterns of language use in these industrialised regions. Should an alternative base be supported in these regions, clearly questions relating to the value messages imparted by the medium of Welsh will be raised. Disquiet has already been expressed as to both linguistic and social class differences within the Welsh-speaking population, a trend which future developments may very well exasperate and intensify into a real conflict of interests between constituent interest groups within society.

In terms of the territorial aspects of such language struggle, both methodological and interpretative aspects need detailed investigation before answers to, as yet, unresolved questions are provided. I conclude with some key geographic questions pertinent to language planning. Should language zones be delimited primarily in terms of formal administrative criteria or in terms of functional-efficiency criteria? What are the minimum thresholds of population of either main language group that can sustain the formal establishment of a language district? How important are the criteria of spatial contiguity and territorial compactness in this form of regionalization procedure? To what extent would, or should, language priorities be independent of other planning programmes?

Until comprehensive evidence to answer such questions is provided it is unlikely that we shall deviate from the incremental, piecemeal approach to implementing basic language rights in Wales. Ultimately the emphasis on searching for a territorial solution may be misguided and the loose principle of personality that operates today may be sufficient. If so, it is possible that the short term will see increased pressure on government and the local state to specify in more detail the nature of language rights in Wales, whilst the long term will see far more profound internal conflicts concerning the very essence of both the definition and survival of the Welsh.

Acknowledgements

The research for this chapter was supported by a British Academy award. I am grateful to the editors and publishers for their permission to reproduce portions of the original papers which first appeared as 'Language planning and minority group Rights' in *Cambria* 1982, volume 9, 61-74 and 'The territorial dimension in language planning', in *Language problems and language planning*, 1981, volume 5, no. 1, 57-73. The Uni versity of Texas Press. I also acknowledge the critical comments made by Clive James, Gwynedd County Council.

Notes

1 Details elaborating the nature of language planning may be found in Williams, C. H. (1978; 1981b) Wood, R. (1979), Eastman (1982) and in the journal Language Problems and Language Planning.

2 In the ten years since 1969 the number of non-industrial civil servants has risen from 18,500 to more than 31,000 which is well above the U.K. growth pattern (Balsom, D. and Burch, M. 1980).

3 I am grateful to Clive James for this comment.

4 Some prior legislation facilitated the use of Welsh in public affairs e.g. the Local Government Act 1888 led some of the new county councils it created to keep their records in Welsh. Although Walters (1978) claims this clause may have been repealed by the Statute Law Revision Act, 1887, and s 1 of the 1942 Act states that where doubt exists this clause is to be treated as repealed.

5 However, in R v Merthyr Tydfil Justices, Exparte Jenkins (1961. 1. A11 ER636) the Divisional Court construed this provision to mean that a Welsh-speaker could not insist on giving evidence in Welsh, on the grounds that 'his native language' was as much English as Welsh (Walters, 1978).

6 This principle did not commend itself to all Welsh language supporters, many of whom would have preferred the third option i.e. the principle of bilingualism whereby all legal and administrative business should be carried out in both languages side by side (Walters, 1978).

7 Following the reorganization of Local Government in Wales, Monmouthshire was declared to be part of Wales.

8 For comparative material see Bourhis (1984) and the series Discussion Paper in Geolinguistics.

9 The county of Gwynedd has a population of about 225,000—about two-thirds of whom are Welsh speaking. In 1974 the County Council adopted a series of bilingual policies, one of which, through use of a simultaneous translation service, ensured bilingualism in all its committees and sub-committees. Dwyfor has adopted a more thorough-going language policy. Welsh is the official language of all meetings, internal documents, letters to rate payers and dealings with national and local government. The only exceptions are for those who address the district council in English.

10 I owe this observation to discussions with Clive James.

References

Aitchinson, J. W. Carter, H. and Williams, C. H. (1985) 'The Welsh language at the 1981 Census'. *Area*, 17, 1, 11-17.

Alcock, A.E. (1977) 'A new look at the protection of minorities and the principle of equality of human rights'. *Community development journal*, 12, 2, 85-95.

Ambrose, J. E., Williams, C. H. (1981). 'On the spatial definition of minority'. In E. Haugen et al (eds.) *Minority languages*. Edinburgh, Edinburgh University Press.

Balsom, D., Burch, M. (1980). *A political and electoral handbook for Wales*. Llandysul, Gomer Press.

Betts, C. (1977) *Culture in crisis*. Wirral, The Ffynnon Press.

Bourish, R. Y. (ed.) (1984) *Conflict and language planning in Quebec*. Clevedon, Multilingual Matters.

Cartwright, D. (1981) 'Language policy and the political organization of territory: A Canadian dilemma'. *Canadian Geographer*, XXV, 3, 205-16.

Cartwright, D., Williams, C. H. (1982) 'The bilingual district as an instrument of Canadian language policy'. *Transactions, Institute of British Geographers*, 7, 4, 474-93.

Cooke, P. (1978) 'Some problems and contradictions for Welsh language planning', *Cambria*, 5, 2, 167-72.

Durkacz, V. E. (1983) *The decline of the Celtic languages*. Edinburgh, John Donald Publishers.

Eastman, C. M. (1983) *Language planning*. San Francisco, Chandler and Sharp.

Edwards, J. (ed.) (1984) *Linguistic minorities: problems and policies*. London, Academic Press.

Glazer, N. (1977) 'Individual rights against group rights'. In E. Kamenka (ed.) *Human Rights*. London, E. Arnold.

Jones, G. E. (1984) *Modern Wales*. Cambridge, Cambridge University Press.

Rees, G., Rees, T. L. (ed.) (1980). *Poverty and social inequality in Wales*. London, Croom Helm.

Sheppard, C. A. (1971) *The law of languages in Canada*. Ottawa, Queen's Printers.

Walters, D. B. (1978) 'The legal recognition and protection of pluralism', *Acta Juridica*, 305-26.

Williams, C. H. (1977a) 'Non-violence and the development of the Welsh Language Society'. *Welsh History Review*, 8, 4, 426-55.

Williams, C. H. (1977b) '*Cynllunio ar gyfer yr iaith yng Nghymru*. Part 1', *Barn*, 179, 392-93. 'Part 2', *Barn*, 180, 2-5.

Williams, C. H. (1978) 'Some spatial considerations in Welsh language planning'. *Cambria*, 5, 2, 173-181.

Williams, C. H. (1980) 'Language contact and language change in Wales: A study in historical geolinguistics'. *Welsh History Review*, 10, 2, 207-38.

Williams, C. H. (1981a) 'On culture space'. *Études Celtiques*, XVIII, 273-96.

Williams, C. H. (1981b) 'The territorial dimension in language planning: an elevation of its potential in contemporary Wales'. *Language problems and language planning*, 5, 1, 57-73;

Williams, C. H. (1981c) 'Official-language districts: a gesture of faith in the future of Canada'. *Ethnic racial studies*, 4, 3, 334-47.

Williams, C. H. (ed.) (1982) *National separatism*. Cardiff, The University of Wales Press.

Williams, C. H. (1984a) 'Ideology and the interpretation of minority cultures'. *Political geography quarterly* 3, 2, 105-25.

Williams, C. H. (1984b) 'When Nationalists challenge: When Nationalists rule'. *Environment and planning*, C. 3, 27-48.

Williams, G. (1979) 'Sociological bases of a language planning programme in Wales'. *Cambria*, 6, 1, 70-76.

Williams, G. (1981) Review of E. Allardt 'Implications of the ethnic revival in modern industrial society', *Journal of multilingual and multicultural development*, 1, 4, 363-70.

Williams, S. W. (1979) 'Language erosion: a spatial perspective'. *Cambria*, 6, 1, 54-69.

Williams, S. W. (1981) 'The urban hierarchy, diffusion and the Welsh language: a preliminary analysis 1901-71'. *Cambria*, 8, 1, 35-50.

Wood, R. (ed.) (1979) 'National language planning and treatment', *Word: Journal of the International Linguistic Association*, 1-2, 1-186.

Chapter Thirteen

Wales: A Separate Administrative Unit*

David Foulkes, J. Barry Jones, R. A. Wilford

In strictly legal terms Wales, since the Tudors, has not existed but has been part of the legislative hybrid 'England and Wales'. Wales never acquired those autonomous institutions of statehood which Scotland enjoyed—an established church and separate legal, banking and educational systems—and retained despite the Act of Union of 1707. And yet the sense of Wales as a separate administrative and, periodically, a political entity has never been entirely extinguished.

Until the sixteenth century Wales was little more than a geographic expression, a westward facing promontory of the British Isles within which an anarchy of petty princedoms was perpetually at war, an inherently unstable situation exacerbated by the proximity of the Marcher-Lordships along the Anglo-Welsh border. At the commencement of the fifteenth century the initial success of Owain Glyndŵr suggested that an effective central authority might be imposed upon Wales. The shadowy structure of a nation state began to emerge but the Glyndŵr regime lasted only a decade, hardly enough time for national institutions to be established. The sense of a separate Welsh entity was further obfuscated during this pre-Tudor period by the ambivalence in the Welsh attitude towards England which was coloured not simply by a desire for separation but for the restoration of the historic unity of Southern Britain. It was an attitude which Henry

* First published as Chapter 1 in Foulkes, D., Jones, J. B. and Wilford, R.A. (eds.) *The Welsh veto: the Wales Act 1978 and the Referendum*. Cardiff, University of Wales Press, 1983, as their subject matter is extensively dealt with elsewhere in this volume, the tables present in the original are not reproduced here. As a result minor editorial changes have been made.

Tudor was to exploit prior to the Battle of Bosworth and which was recognised by contemporary observers, notably the Venetian Ambassador who reported to his government that 'the Welsh may now be said to have recovered their former independence for the most wise and fortunate Henry VII is a Welshman'.[1]

Despite the high expectations of his countrymen, Henry VII did little for Wales, preoccupied as he was with the larger and more pressing concerns of establishing the Tudor Dynasty. However, in deference to Welsh sensibilities he named his first son, Arthur, Prince of Wales and in 1501 carried into effect a scheme first mooted in Edward IV's reign to establish a Council of Wales and the Marches. Arthur's untimely death frustrated the experiment whereby the Prince of Wales served as the Council's Chairman and the Council declined in significance until, in 1534, Rowland Lee was appointed and charged with the task of restoring law and order. An initial series of punitive measures was followed in 1536 by an Act of Union which ordained that Wales should be entirely incorporated within the realm of England, with all Welshmen given the same privileges, rights and laws as Englishmen. It was nothing less than a constitutional settlement in which the chaotic Marches completely disappeared, either incorporated into existing Welsh or English counties or merged to form the five new counties created by the Act. But fundamentally the Act reflected 'Henry VIII's ambition to fuse the English and Welsh people and bind them with indissoluble links of common aspirations'.[2] Although the Act of Union is highly significant in as much as it brought the whole of Wales within the realm of England and under the authority of Parliament, it was but the last stage in a process of assimilation that had been taking place for over two centuries and it took a further six years for the administrative machinery necessary for full incorporation with England to be set up. This was accomplished by the Act of Union of 1542: 'Broadly therefore it may be said that the Act of 1536 enunciates the general principle governing the Union and that of 1542 the details. Together they form the constitution under which Wales was henceforth to be governed'.[3] Under the Union the counties and boroughs henceforth sent representatives to Parliament. Welshmen were granted equality with Englishmen before the law: the severe disabilities previously applied to them were abolished. The English system of land tenure was introduced and *gavelkind*, where it still obtained in Wales was, over a period, displaced. The English system of local government was applied to Wales. The country was divided into twelve counties, grouped into four areas each with three counties. Sheriffs, coroners and other officers were appointed, and eight Justices of the Peace for each county: 'Local Administration was now placed in the hands of men drawn from local families and the energies of these families were now directed to the prevention of disorder rather than its perpetration as hitherto'.[4]

However, the system of government differed in some respects from that of England. Wales was given its own system of courts, the Courts of Great Session, largely independent of the courts at Westminster: in effect the system which had operated in North Wales for two and a half centuries was extended to the whole country. In these courts English law was administered—and in English, for the Act of Union required all official business to be in that tongue (out of a concern for administrative simplicity). Wales also had a separate organisation for revenue purposes, each group of three counties serving also as a fiscal unit with its own exchequer and system of audit. Finally, the Council of Wales and the Marches, formerly a prerogative court, was continued by the Act of Union as a permanent administrative body responsible to the Privy Council. 'Wales thus became a special administrative area'.[5] But the integrity of these Welsh institutions was not maintained. During the Civil War the Council fell into abeyance and, although it was revived in 1660, its authority was much restricted and the Glorious Revolution of 1688 finally brought it to an end. The other distinctive Welsh administrative institution, the Courts of Great Session, was significantly weakened by the

Council's demise and in 1830, after a century of rivalry with the Westminster Courts, the Great Sessions were abolished in the face of the unanimous opposition of Welsh MPs and a considerable body of Welsh public opinion. With their abolition, the last vestiges of an identifiably Welsh system of government, erected by Henry VIII for the Welsh people, disappeared.

Consequently the emergence of Welsh political nationalism during the latter half of the nineteenth century occurred when Wales was devoid of distinctive legal and administrative institutions and disregarded as a separate political entity. Henry Richard speaking in the wake of the 1868 political evictions in Wales chided the House of Commons 'that no question relating to Wales had occupied the attention of Parliament in the memory of man'.[6] However, this situation was to change dramatically. The General Election of 1868 following the extension of the franchise in the previous year, marked the beginning of 50 years of 'Welsh political nationalism as a major force in British public life', in which the distinctive needs of Wales were brought 'into the general context of British politics after the obscurity and isolation of centuries'.[7]

The first administrative admission of Wales as a separate entity in the modern period was the Welsh Intermediate Education Act of 1889 which virtually created the modern system of Welsh secondary education. In 1896 an Inspectorate and Examining Body, the Central Welsh Board (CWB) was set up to administer the Act. However, there was by no means unanimous support in Wales for the Act. The Conservative *Western Mail* censured the government, claiming that the Act would enable 'bigoted and uneducated councillors to remove clerical masters from [church] schools. The paper went on to assert that the councillors 'want to cripple the influence of the church and pave the way for Welsh Home Rule'.[8] Thus, even at this early stage, the restructuring of Welsh administration could not be separated from political considerations, a tendency which became increasingly apparent during the course of the referendum debate. Subsequent to the 1889 Act there were regular demands for a Welsh National Council for Education but they fell on deaf ears until 1907 when the Liberal Government introduced a bill proposing a Council for Wales composed of representatives from Welsh local authorities which would regulate education policy throughout Wales. It generated a considerable volume of opposition which was largely concerned with the difficulty of ensuring fair representation on the national body for the rest of Wales as against the heavily populated South—another issue which is not infrequently raised today. The Bill was passed by the Commons but rejected by the Lords and by way of a consolation prize the Welsh Department of the Board of Education was set up in 1907; it was none the less a significant development creating the first regionally oriented department within a central government ministry. But too much should not be read into this; the Permanent Secretary had his office not in Cardiff but in London and the attempt to obtain a similar reform in the Ministry of Agriculture was rejected. However, the founding of the University of Wales in 1883 and the creation of the National Library and the National Museum in 1907 are further testimony to the growth of Welsh institutions.

The decade of 1910-20 represents a period during which a coherent and consistent policy of administrative devolution to Wales can be identified and when Wales came to be regarded as a 'special administrative area' for subsequent legislation. The passage of the National Insurance Act in 1911 followed by the establishment of the Welsh Health Insurance Commission in 1913 and the foundation of the Welsh Board of Health in 1919 all reflect this devolutionary trend. The same year also saw the creation of the Welsh Department of the Ministry of Agriculture responsible for a wide range of functions in Wales. Another issue to the forefront of political life in Wales during the first two decades of the twentieth century was the demand for the Disestablishment of the Church in Wales or, as it was seen, of the Church of England in Wales. As with any other issue affecting Wales, the Welsh interest in Parliament had to persuade a major British political party to its view—at this time this could of course only be the Liberal Party. Disestablishment was eventually provided for by the Welsh Church Disestablishment Act 1914, but did not take place until 1920. The impetus generated by these initiatives was not maintained during the inter-war years largely because of the decline of Liberalism and preoccupation of all politicians with the Depression. However, Wales still made demands for special administrative treatment. In 1927 the Central Welsh Board, the Welsh Federation of LEAs and the University of Wales jointly called for a National Council for Education in Wales. The request was repeated in 1931 and 1935 but it was not associated with a significant political force and, despite the administrative attractions of the scheme, nothing was done.

The Second World War with the consequent dispersal of government departments and the appointment of Regional Commissioners (including one for Wales) renewed the process of administrative devolution. In 1940 the Welsh Board of Health acquired responsibility for a whole range of local government services in Wales. Two years later a Welsh Reconstruction Advisory Council was set up and recommended a 'new decentralised administrative pattern' to solve the post-war problems in Wales. In the immediate post-war years much was done in this direction; Wales was recognised as one of the Treasury 'standard regions' and a regular Conference of the Heads of Government Departments in Wales (of which there were 15 in 1945) was held which produced annual reports on government economic policies. Thus 'in the absence of a Department for Wales the Government evolved the necessary machinery to fill the gap, so that when the Welsh Office was created it did not have to work in a vacuum'.[9] Wales was created as an administrative unit by the National Health Service Act 1946 (the Welsh Regional Hospital Board) and the Gas Act 1948 (the Wales Gas Board—not at all convenient administratively); but not by the Electricity Act 1947 (South Wales Electricity Board and Merseyside & North Wales Electricity Board). On the education side some rationalisation took place with the setting up in 1948 of the Welsh Joint Education Committee which took over from the C.W.B. and also acquired additional powers of recommending educational proposals to Welsh local authorities. In the same year an advisory Council for Wales and Monmouthshire was also established; a nominated body, whose function was to meet (in private) for the exchange of views and information, and to ensure that the Government was adequately informed on the impact of government action on the general life of the country. Thus by the end of the 1940s there was extensive administrative machinery in Wales but it was the result of a series of *ad hoc* decisions and the arrangements, which lacked both political direction and supervision, fell short of the demands voiced fifty years previously.

The desire to invest the Welsh identity with a political as well as an administrative dimension had been explicit in the aspirations of the *Cymru Fydd* (Young Wales) Movement in the closing decade of the nineteenth century. It was linked with the Home Rule campaign but whereas in Ireland it blazed dangerously, in Wales it flickered only uncertainly. A National Institutions (Wales) Bill was introduced to Parliament in 1891 which proposed—in addition to a Welsh Education Department and a National Council for Wales—a Secretary for Wales. The Bill failed to arouse either the interest or the approval of Parliament and similar legislative initiatives by private members were equally unsuccessful in 1908, 1921 and again in 1955. In the 1930s the Welsh Parliamentary Party, consisting overwhelmingly of Labour and Liberal MPs, launched a series of initiatives to persuade successive governments to establish a Welsh Office and to give Wales a voice in the Cabinet; in effect to adopt the system that had applied to Scotland since the middle of the nineteenth century. But the requests were rejected, first by Chamberlain in 1938 and then by Churchill in 1943, on the grounds of cost, administrative disruption and the belief that Wales would not receive any practical advantage from the co-ordination of activities in a single department. Furthermore,

Chamberlain, expressing an opinion that was to find echoes in the referendum debate, claimed that the analogy of Scotland could not be advanced because whereas Scotland had a different system of law and administration, Wales's close incorporation with England precluded the need for a separate minister. After the war, when Labour had the political power, the hostility of Morrison and Bevan prevented the creation of a separate Welsh Office. Bevans's concern—which also found expression in the referendum campaign—was that such a devolution of authority 'would divorce Welsh political activity from the mainstream of British politics'.[10]

Despite the Labour party's close association with Wales it was a Conservative government which created in 1951 the office of Minister for Welsh Affairs, but it was a curious arrangement as the post, which existed until 1964, was always held in conjunction with another office—until 1957 by the Home Secretary, and from then until 1964 by the Minister of Housing and Local Government. In 1951 the Welsh Office of that Ministry had been created and in 1957 a Minister of State for Welsh Affairs was created as a junior officer in that Ministry. The Permanent Secretary of the Welsh Department of Education whose office had until then been in London was also given an office in Cardiff; and the office of the civil servant in charge of the Welsh Department of the Ministry of Agriculture was upgraded.

In 1957 the Council of Wales produced a memorandum which set out the case for a Secretary of State for Wales and a Welsh Office. The government remained unconvinced (its response included the appointment of the Minister of State referred to), but the report must have added weight to those in the Labour Party who had been arguing the case for some time. An undertaking to appoint a Secretary of State was given by the Labour Party in its manifesto for the 1959 general election and reaffirmed in the 1964 manifesto. Despite the long campaign and the undoubted sincerity of several leading Labour politicians, notably James Griffiths, at the time deputy leader of the

Labour Party, the manner in which the Welsh Office was established and the functions of the new Welsh Secretary were announced, illustrates a lack of clear administrative thinking and suggests that the exercise was a political expedient to placate aggrieved Welsh interests. In the debate on the Queen's Speech on 3rd November 1964 Mr. Grimond, the leader of the Liberal Party, commenting on the appointment of Mr. James Griffiths to the new Office of Secretary of State, admitted himself perplexed as to the powers the new minister was to receive. Mr. Griffiths was unable to enlighten him. It was the 19th November before the Prime Minsiter felt able to define the responsibilities of the Secretary of State for Wales. They were somewhat vague; the Secretary of State was to take over 'virtually all executive responsibilites of the Ministry of Housing and Local Government in Wales; to take over responsibility for the Welsh Roads Division of the Ministry of Transport and to co-operate with the First Secretary of the DEA in respect of regional economic planning in Wales'.[11] A former minister at the Welsh Office suggests a reason for the vague and tardy definition:

> Whitehall had made little or no preparation for the coming of the Welsh Office. The 'Charter' Secretary of State for Wales and his two ministers were immediately appointed, only to find themselves without functions to perform. Despite the fact that Labour's 1964 manifesto clearly envisaged executive responsibility for the Secretary of State covering housing, local government, health, education and agriculture, moves were afoot in Whitehall to confine his role to that of a watch-dog, a general oversight function over all government activities as they affect Wales. There were to be no executive functions. The Secretary of State's first major task was to demand and extract from Whitehall some real and effective powers.[12]

Initially the executive functions of the Secretary of State were those which had been administered by the Welsh Office of the Ministry of Housing and Local Government, mainly town and country planning, housing, water, sewage and other local government matters, together with economic planning and the responsibilities for roads in Wales formerly exercised by the Minister of Transport. The Secretary of State was also authorised to exercise 'over-sight within Wales of the execution of national policy by the Ministry of Agriculture. Fisheries and Food, the Department of Education and Science, the Ministry of Health, the Ministry of Transport, the Board of Trade and the Ministry of Labour'.[13] However, it would appear that the powers were extracted from Whitehall in a random fashion. If the Welsh Secretary was to play a significant part in the formulation of regional plans, why were the functions of the Board of Trade and Ministries of Power and Transport not taken over? Another curiosity of the establishment of the Welsh Office concerned the exclusion of education from the Secretary of State's responsibilities. This perplexed many people including Lord Crowther. Some years later, as the first Chairman of the Commission on the Constitution (on his death he was succeeded by Lord Kilbrandon), he enquired of the Permanent Under-Secretary at the Welsh Office:

> May I ask if there is any reason why it [education] was not transferred? One would suppose it is the oldest specific Welsh Department and it is a field in which there have been differences in policy and practice between Wales and England for longer than most. One would suppose it would be the very first function to be transferred. Is there some special reason why it was not?[14]

No complete or convincing answer stating the administrative reason for the exclusion was forthcoming. The lack of any clear administrative principle in the allocation of responsibilities to the Welsh Office is even more vividly illustrated in the case of the Secretary of State's 'over-sight' powers. Mr. James Griffiths interviewed in November 1968 had a very clear view of these powers:

> The Secretary of State is the master of the Welsh situation: [he] has oversight of other departments in Wales and gives instructions to the regional controllers of all seventeen government departments in Wales.[15]

Other observers have reached different conclusions which cast serious doubts on the 'oversight' power of the Welsh Secretary, inferring the possibility of a conflict of loyalties. Professor Cross, examining the new Office, reported that 'Welsh controllers do not necessarily inform the Welsh Office of every possible future development of departmental policy in Wales if the knowledge might prove embarassing to their own department'.[16] The delay and the confusion surrounding the announcement of the Welsh Office's functions and the divergence of views regarding the 'oversight' role of the Welsh Secretary raise serious doubts as to the administrative principles behind the establishment of the Office which are reinforced by Crossman's opinion that it was 'a completely artificial new office for Jim Griffiths—all the result of a silly election pledge'.[17]

With the passage of years the Welsh Office has acquired additional functions the effect of which has been to make the office a more viable administrative department. In later stages the Welsh Office took over direct responsibility for the health service, forestry and agriculture, ancient monuments, tourism, child care and primary and secondary education in Wales and for financing the National Museum and National Library of Wales. In 1975 the Welsh Office acquired significant economic powers arising from Section 7 of the Industry Act with reference to the role and activities of the Welsh Development Agency. Taken together these functions have enabled the Welsh Office to present itself as a custodian of Welsh interests and as an administrative expression of the Welsh identity.

The Welsh dimension has also been taken account of in Parliament. Under the House of Commons (Redistribution of Seats) Act 1949 Wales is guaranteed a minimum of 35 seats and presently has 36 although on the basis of her population should only have 31 seats. Since 1964 and the establishment of the Welsh Office, government action in Wales has been subjected to the same parliamentary scrutiny as all government departments. With regard to parliamentary questions Welsh Office questions are taken first every five weeks. In addition it has become the practice in each parliamentary session to have a 'Welsh Day' which usually consists of broad-ranging debate covering the whole area of government activity in Wales. The Welsh Grand Committee, for which Welsh parliamentarians of all political persuasions had campaigned since 1886, was established on a sessional basis in 1960 and became a permanent standing committee in 1969. It consists of all 36 Welsh constituency MPs together with not more than 5 others. The committee meets about three times a session and has power only to 'consider such specified matters relating exclusively to Wales as may be referred to them' by agreement through the 'usual channels' and to 'report only that they have considered the said matter'. Votes are not taken: nor does it consider estimates or Bills. Furthermore its recommendations, if any are made, have no force. Thus it is no more than a forum for debate serving to air Welsh grievances and debate Welsh issues; in short, a 'talking shop' exhibiting all the vices and virtues of that type of institution.[18]

The Acts relating exclusively to Wales are very few in numbers. The Sunday Closing (Wales) Act 1881, referring to the closing of public houses, was the first Act to apply to Wales a legislative principle that did not apply to England. Even at that time it did escape notice that the principle of treating Wales as a national unit could be extended to matters other than liquor licencing. (The present statutory provisions are found in the Licensing Act 1964, as amended by the Local Government Act 1972, which give a local option exercised by referendum organised on a district council basis). One notable and exceptional piece of legislation relating to Wales alone was the Welsh Church Disestablishment Act (1914). Since the war, such particularistic legislation includes provision for the use of the Welsh language on election forms (Elections (Welsh Forms) Act 1964) and its use in official documents and the administration of justice (Welsh Language Act 1967). There has additionally been a series of Acts which enable Welsh local authorities to support financially various

Welsh cultural institutions. However, such legislation remains extremely rare and for the overwhelming majority of cases England and Wales are treated as a single unit.

Although reform of local government in England and Wales was accomplished by the same Act of Parliament (Local Government Act 1972), the consultative procedures leading to the legislation were quite different for Wales. In fact, the structure of local government in Wales was under separate consideration from that in England from the end of the Second World War. Under the Local Government Act 1958, separate Commissions were created for England and Wales to make recommendations on the boundaries of counties and county boroughs. The Welsh Commission's draft proposals for, *inter alia*, a reduction to five counties met with hostility, and revised proposals, which were not more favoured, were rejected by the Government. In 1965 the first Secretary of State for Wales, James Griffiths, set up an Interdepartmental Working Party of senior official of relevant departments to look at the problem again. The Working Party consulted informally a number of people experienced in local government in Wales as a result of which three broad lines of thought were noted:

(a) that the then existing structure should be retained but with fewer and stronger authorities;
(b) that the structure should be replaced by a single tier of all-purpose authorities;
(c) that some kind of regional or sub-regional authority should be formed.

Those who favoured a single tier system based on 16 authorities also, it seems, took the view that some functions could be exercised more effectively on all-Wales level and favoured an elected all-Wales council.

Thus from the mid-sixties proposals for reform of local government in Wales were entangled with proposals for devolution, a fact of some significance during the course of the referendum campaign. The government having considered the report of its Working Party opted for a two-tier system consisting of five counties, three county boroughs and 36 districts. The single tier proposal was rejected and with it proposals for a new all-Wales body.[19] However, the government acknowledged the need to improve the then existing machinery in Wales for advisory and promotional work. In 1965, a Welsh Economic Council had displaced the advisory Council for Wales and Monmouthshire. The Government now proposed, and in 1968 proceeded to the creation of, a more prestigious Welsh Council to provide a forum for the inter-change of information, to assist in the formulation of plans and to advise the Secretary of State on major land use matters, etc. In March 1970, following the report of the Redcliffe-Maud Commission on Local Government in England, another White Paper[20] produced by the Welsh Office proposed three unitary authorities for the area of the then counties of Glamorgan and Monmouthshire. The incoming Conservative Government of 1970 thought that it was wrong to treat that area differently from the rest of Wales, and proposed a two-tier system for the whole of Wales, with 7 (later increased to 8) county councils and 36 district councils. It was on this basis that the Welsh clauses, together with the Bill itself, were approved by parliament in the form of the Local Government Act of 1972. Subsequently, the Local Government Act 1974 created a Commission for Local Administration in Wales (the local government ombudsman) separate from that in England.

The treatment of the reform of local government in Wales reveals the extent to which Government in the late 1960s and early 1970s was increasingly identifying Wales as a separate administrative unit. The Welsh Arts Council, a regional committee of the Arts Council of Great Britain since 1945, was established as a financially autonomous body in 1967. In 1968 the Countryside Commission appointed a Committee for Wales (after consultations with the Secretary of State) to which it delegated all its functions in Wales. The following year, 1969, the Development of Tourism Act created a Wales Tourist Board to promote the industry in the Principality, and in 1972 a Sports Council for Wales was created by Charter.

The Health Service in Wales, as a result of the 1973 reorganisation,[21] also differs from that in England in that in Wales there are no Regional Health Authorities, only Area Health Authorities which are responsible for certain functions additional to those vested in English AHAs. Furthermore there is in Wales a special health authority created by the Secretary of State, to provide various services on an all-Wales basis for the NHS in Wales, including design and construction of major capital works and computers. The Welsh Development Agency was set up in 1975 to promote Wales as a location of industrial development, to promote industrial efficiency and safeguard employment. The Community Land Act of 1975 enabled public authorities (in England and Scotland, local authorities) to acquire land for development. However, in Wales, an all-Wales body—the Land Authority for Wales—was established to exercise these functions. Significantly the Minister expressed the hope that the Authority was 'an interim measure in the context of future devolution'.[22]

It would not be appropriate to attempt to provide here an account of the significance of the Welsh language in Wales politics and in the devolution discussions.[23] But it should be noted that the Welsh language has increasingly become recognised as a medium for the administration of government and justice in Wales. The linguistic restrictions imposed by the Act of 1536 were to some extent repealed by the Welsh Courts Act 1942. The Elections (Welsh Forms) Act 1964 authorised the use, in connection with elections in Wales, of translations of statutory forms into Welsh. The Committee on the Legal Status of the Welsh Language (Cmnd. 2785) recommended in 1964 that there should be a 'clear, positive, legislative declaration of general application, to the effect that any act, writing or thing done in Welsh in Wales or Monmouthshire should have the like legal force as if it had been done in English'. It was followed by the Welsh Language Act 1967 which authorised the use of Welsh in any legal proceedings in Wales by anyone who desires to use it, and provided for Welsh versions of statutory forms.

As has already been indicated, the lack of distinctive Welsh institutions from the sixteenth to the twentieth century functioned to erode social cohesion. During that period it was only the language that could claim to give meaning to a separate Welsh identity and this, in part, explains the pressure during this century to accord it full legal and administrative status. Consequently, the loss of language, which for many represents a sense of dispossession, is rendered all the more acute in Wales in comparison with, for example, Scotland which has a comprehensive range of national institutions. This loss is empirically verifiable. In 1901, 50 per cent of the population of 2 million claimed to be Welsh speaking; by 1971 the proportion had shrunk to under 21 per cent of the population of 2.7 m. The language is now largely concentrated in North and West Wales, areas which support the Welsh Nationalist Party, Plaid Cymru. It is these areas that have experienced a not inconsiderable amount of rural depopulation between 1911 and 1971. These figures suggest that the prospects for the language appear bleak. Welsh speakers become an aging population as the traditional influx of retired English-born into these areas proceeds.

Industrialisation was a key factor in fostering migration not only from rural areas of Wales into its developing urban areas, but also from England into Wales. The scale of this movement into the Welsh industrial enclaves is not even remotely approached in the equivalent areas of Scotland and Northern Ireland. The high points of this movement coincided with the boom in the coal industry but it has continued and increased despite the decline of coal during the 1960s; the proportion of English-born residents in Wales at the time of the 1971 Census was 15 per cent. But all the traditional industries of Wales, slate quarrying and agriculture, as well as coal mining, have undergone substantial decline since 1921 in terms of job losses. The consistent decline in manpower in these industries has had a consequent weakening effect upon traditional industrial communities. The other traditional industry, iron and steel making, has also experienced marked job-losses particularly during the 1970s with the total closures at Ebbw Vale and East Moors, Cardiff, a trend continued after the referendum by the ending of steel making at Shotton and cutbacks at Llanwern and Port Talbot. Thus, the economy of Wales has undergone substantial change during this century. An index of this change is also provided by the growth of the tertiary or service sector in Wales which in 1975 accounted for more than half (52.7%) of the labour force.[24] The advent of the white collar workers, and the consequent *embourgeoisment* of Wales has been in part assisted by successive governments who have sought to relocate administrative departments in Wales and develop Cardiff as the administrative capital thereby fostering a further wave of English-born migrants into the Principality and cementing the bonds of integration and assimilation between the two nations. Cumulatively, these demographic shifts and socio-economic changes—with their inevitable deleterious effects upon Welsh language and culture—have served to complicate and render less certain a consensual perception of Wales as a separate and distinct entity.

Finally, discussion of institutions reflecting Wales as a separate entity is incomplete without reference to the non-governmental institutions that have been set up since the Second World War.[25] The major political parties now have recognisable Welsh identities. The Liberals set up North and South Wales Liberal Federations in 1886 and 1887 respecitively and formally created the Welsh Liberal Party in 1897. The Labour Party created the South Wales Regional Council of Labour in 1937; ten years later it was merged with its North Wales counterpart to create the Welsh Regional Council of Labour which in 1975 was retitled 'Labour Party—Wales'. The Conservative Party has also had a 'Welsh area' within its organisational structure since 1930 and has held 'Welsh Annual Conferences since 1972. In fact, all three parties, no doubt stimulated by the existence of Plaid Cymru, have assumed an increasingly Welsh profile. The creation of the Wales TUC in 1973, matched by the first annual conference of the Wales CBI in 1978, gave added weight to a general momentum creating a framework of Welsh institutions. However, the *ad hoc* institution building in Wales, whilst performing the manifest function of recognising the need for a distinctively Welsh administrative framework, also has promoted the assimilation of the Principality into the British body politic, part of the process of acculturation—popularly termed 'Anglicization'. The process, whether intended or unintended, has acted to integrate the periphery into the dominant British political culture. We later discuss the effects of acculturation upon the referendum vote, but here it is pertinent to note that the unspoken, but underlying, question in the referendum was whether the Welsh identity achieved in the developed administrative and political institutions should be crowned by a national Assembly or whether the continuing socio-economic and political integration of Wales with England had vitiated the assumed residual aspiration for a Welsh identity, thereby rendering the whole exercise of the referendum redundant.

Notes

1 Quoted in D. Williams, *A history of modern Wales*, 1950, p. 20.
2 I. Jones, *Modern Welsh history*, 1934, p. 22.
3 W. Rees, *The Union of England and Wales*, 1967, p. 49.
4 D. Williams, *op. cit.*, p. 44.
5 Rees, *op. cit.*, p. 49.
6 K. O. Morgan, *Wales in British politics: 1868-1922*, 3rd edn., 1980, p. 2.
7 *ibid.*, p. 297.
8 Quoted by Carter in *Welsh studies in public law*, 1965, p. 48.
9 *ibid.*, p. 53.
10 Quoted in J. Griffiths, *Pages from memory*, 1969, p. 161.
11 H of C Debate Vol. 702 col. 623, 19 November 1964.
12 E. Rowlands, 'The politics of regional administration: The establishment of the Welsh Office', *Public Administration*, Vol. 50, 1972, p. 333.
13 See Welsh Office written evidence to the Commission on the Constitution (para. 33-37) vol. 1, pp. 91-111.
14 Minutes of Evidence I: Wales, *Commission on the Constitution*, 1970, p. 12.
15 Quoted by P. Byrne, J. McCarthy, M. Tudor and J. W. Jones, 'The Welsh Office', unpublished research paper, UWIST, 1970, p. 7.
16 J. A. Cross, 'The regional decentralisation of British government departments', *Public Administration*, Vol. 48, 1970, p. 439.
17 R. Crossman, *Diaries of a cabinet minister*, Vol. I, 1975, p. 117.
18 For a fuller discussion see Borthwick, Research Paper No. 5, *Commission on the Constitution*, 1973.
19 Local Government in Wales, Cmnd. 3340, 1967.
20 Local Government in Wales, Cmnd. 4310, 1970.
21 National Health Service Reorganization Act 1973.
22 Standing Committee G. Col. 933: 12 June 1975.
23 For a discussion of this issue see, M. Stephens (ed.), *The Welsh language today*, 1973.
24 *Digest of Welsh statistics No. 26*, 1980.
25 A full description of the development of Welsh institutions is given in A. Butt-Philip, *The Welsh question*, 1975, Chs. 9-10.

Chapter Fourteen

Organizations, Political Movements and their Backgrounds*

Ian Hume

This work focuses on Welsh political movements and other organizations which have political effect in the 1980s. Rather than cataloguing these in comprehensive manner,[1] the concern is to link them to the rapidly changing political dynamics of Wales since the early 1960s.

One substantial body of social scientists have contended that in the context of a larger system, the minorities at its periphery will become—as that society becomes industrially and commercially more developed—less unique in their culture (and in economic, social and political structures). The centre, they contend, will act as a powerful standardizing device propagating administrative, educational, commercial, cultural and other norms which gradually overcome the distinctiveness of the minorities by a process of diffusion, resulting in progressive acculturation.[2] If this contention is correct in the context of the British Isles we should expect to see fewer and weaker political manifestations of Welsh identity—both in terms of organizations and their actions—as time goes on. However, elsewhere in this volume[3] we have the work of observers writing from a different critical standpoint. In the context of the 1960s and early 1970s they observe if anything an increase in manifestations of political distinctiveness of the Welsh nation.

The 1970s and 1980s have seen writers who examined the political movements and political actions of the years leading up to the 1979 Devolution Referendum, the various

* Specially written for this volume.

elections of that year, and the General Election of 1983. Whilst doubting the absolute validity of the ideas of the first-mentioned grouping, in this sequence of events they have perceived a considerable acceleration in the process of diffusion of 'English' values, ideas, techniques and institutions in Wales.[4]

During the period 1979-1983 there were substantial moves away from the electoral near-hegemony achieved by the Labour Party in the 1960s, and by 1983 Labour retained only the seats of the industrial north-east and south-east and that of Carmarthen; Conservatives represented the more 'anglicised' shire counties, much of the northern seaside belt, and several of the south-eastern suburban and residential area seats; the Liberals and Plaid Cymru in general held the more Welsh speaking rural and peripheral areas. The emergence of this pattern[5] has led various media commentators to question whether the 'Welsh radical tradition'[6] in politics still exists, and to ask if the political structure and culture in Wales has now become no more than a reflection of patterns to be found elsewhere in the United Kingdom. If one also refers to the undoubted historical function of firstly the Liberal Party and later the Labour Party in integrating Welsh people into the British parliamentary and administrative system,[7] then a picture of decline of political characteristics that are significantly influenced by distinctively Welsh features can be built up. Further, it may be posited that the growing concern of the post-1945 Conservative Party to structure itself to the Welsh situation has similarly contributed to, rather than detracted from, a process of acculturation to British norms and values. And during the last months of the Labour administration of 1974-9 even the most distinctively Welsh of all parties, Plaid Cymru, for tactical legislative reasons, worked alongside that government. This it could be argued, further aided the assimilative and acculturative processes.

There is reason too, to see the debate around the question of the 1979 Devolution proposals as a political watershed, and the electorate's firm rejection of the scheme as a sign that Wales was rapidly losing its political distinctiveness, this being subsequently confirmed by the elections of that year and of 1983. However, these kinds of analysis depend in large part on the use of aggregated electoral data, which can hide complexities and contradictions beneath.

It is well known that the aggregation of individual votes conceals the reasons why individuals make the choices they do; in the Welsh context several parliamentary constituencies have now seen contests where any one of the four main parties has had a good chance of success, and where tactical voting probably played a considerable part. With all four parties now normally contesting each parliamentary seat, voting behaviour in Wales is a more complex phenomenon than it is in England—even more so when one considers the factor of preferential vote for a particular candidate.[8] It is reasonable to suppose that, for example, a significant percentage of people not normally voting for Plaid Cymru do so in Meirionydd because of the charisma of Dafydd Elis Thomas. In Ceredigion and Pembroke North it could be reasonably argued that the 'natural' Plaid Cymru vote is reduced because of the cultural-nationalist appeal of the Liberal Geraint Howells. Tactical voting too undoubtedly influenced the defeat of the Conservative Delwyn Williams in the Montgomery constituency in 1983. These are examples, and indeed, they may be debatable, but further evidence as to the importance of the factor of candidate in electoral contests comes from the fact that the County Councils and district councils of Gwynedd, Clwyd, Dyfed and Powys return large numbers of independent candidates.[9] There is also evidence from industrial and urban areas of the operation of these factors.[10]

Again the aggregate of votes in the 1979 Devolution Referendum conceals a variety of responses differentiated by region, language, and other factors. Surveying readers' letters in the weekly press at this time[11] one could see potential voters in, for example Gwynedd, declaring their intention to vote 'No' for an identical cluster of reasons that led other writers in Glamorgan to register a 'Yes' response. When one begins to look at voting data in relation to such factors a much more complex impression of a pluralism within parties, within Wales and its regions, begins to emerge. From this perspective one may even venture so far as to question whether the importance of the 1979 Devolution issue lies only in its rejection by the voters. Perhaps social scientists should now put more emphasis on an analysis of the social, economic and cultural factors which made such a debate essential. Voting behaviour itself is not the sum total of politics, and is indeed only one indicator of political beliefs and activities and of underlying social interests.

Parties in the 1960s and 1970s—Labour hegemony and breakdown

The steady rise in electoral support for the Labour Party in Wales between 1945 and 1966 and its subsequent decline should not be mistaken for the totality of political relations in post-war Wales; no party system, let alone one party, can encompass all significant politics. The question of a party's organization and ideology is, though, highly relevant to the maintenance and development of its level of support based on this totality of politics.

Winning increased electoral support challenges a party to develop its ideology and practice; if it takes up this challenge too weakly it endangers not only its hold on the newly-won votes but also the stability of its old core of support. Wherever people from different social and economic backgrounds and from different geographical areas are won over their interests must be considered. Whenever greater victories are won, levels of enthusiasm, expectations and desired involvement are all likely to increase. Just as the Liberal Party was latterly unable to accommodate—either ideologically or organizationally—the growing real demands for class-based social action from its supporters, so the Labour Party was unable to cope in comprehensive manner with either the rise of national sentiment or of the widening of its own bases of support in the 1960s and 1970s. From winning 25 out of 36 parliamentary seats in the 1945 General Election, Labour went on to its peak in 1966 when it captured 32 of these seats. This period above all was one when it was considered the 'Party of Wales'. Yet during this time there were many contradictions contained within the aggregate of its voting support, and within the aggregate of its MPs, candidates and officers.

Labour support then came virtually from all regions of Wales and from a wide variety of social classes.[12] There were also new structural features in the leadership composition, particularly with regard to MPs and candidates. The victories of the period 1959-66 had progressively given Labour hegemony in the Welsh speaking agricultural heartland areas of the north and west, and had resulted in the election by 1966 of 11 Welsh-speaking Labour representatives in Wales; but in industrial south Wales, the Labour Party's strongest area, there was an increasing trend during the period from 1964 onwards toward supplanting retiring MPs from working class backgrounds with candidates from middle class backgrounds or occupations. This increased the numbers of those within the hierarchy who emphasized the international character of Labour's task, seen by them as one to unite with the working classes of other nations, progressing forward together against the forces of capitalism; in this respect they differed from many of those representing Welsh speaking areas, for the 'internationalist' view of factors of national uniqueness was that they should be regarded as secondary to the class factor. The distinct cultural characteristics (particularly that of the Welsh language) of the regions—apart from the industrial south—were rarely considered, and if regarded at all by this group were seen as potential obstacles to the primary unity of class. Increasingly Labour thus both seemed to be minimising the philosophical importance of a powerful section of the radical rural tradition whose support it had only just won, and, through its choice of new non-working class candidates, moving further away from an emphasis on its roots in the structures of Welsh industrial society.

Whilst the argument that international factors were more important than national ones became increasingly predominant by the late 1960s, it was only occasionally presented with full class rhetoric, the implication rather being that Wales remained predominantly a one-class, *gwerin*-like,[13] nation of unproblematic composition. The pluralities, inequalities and polarities within Wales and between Wales and Britain were again seen as relatively unimportant in the face of this assumed unity.

For some there may have been an instrumental basis for this viewpoint, for to adopt a view of Labour as a coalition of interests, ideas and areas would have been a threat to old established power bases. Indeed the major part of the industrial south Wales 'establishment' of councillors, and several of the MPs of the area, probably would have been alarmed by any hint that there might be such a plurality of interests. Thus at the very time it should have been developing its social and political philosophy, the party instead centred upon drawn-out considerations as to whether Wales should have a Secretary of State with a cabinet seat as of right. The discussion of this particular administrative scheme took the attention and energies of party members until 1959, when Labour's manifesto at last ensured Labour's commitment to a Welsh Office.[14] During the 1964-70 period of Labour government, Cledwyn Hughes as Secretary of State for Wales (1966-68) was influential in developing more ambitious plans,[15] but his successor (1968-70) George Thomas was unenthusiastic about virtually any form of political devolution.[16] By 1969, in its evidence to the Royal Commission on the Constitution, the Welsh Labour Party foreshadowed its stance of the 1970s and showed a strong emphasis on local government perspectives and a particular hostility toward any federal features.

Attitudes toward devolution within the party therefore moved throughout this period progressively further toward a planning and administrative perspective, confirming that the power of the 'contributionists'[17] in the Labour Party was increasing. Insofar as it subscribed to the latter perspective, Labour, as the Liberals before it, had a mission to deliver Wales as a loyal and united block, contributing to United Kingdom solidarity against the Conservatives. Therefore, it is not surprising that during the 1964-70 period of Labour government, which saw a continuation of the increase in expressions of radical and national sentiment both within and outside the parties in Wales, the Labour Party did not seem organizationally and philosophically adaptable enough to incorporate these new elements.[18] Party membership was actually falling and fewer young people were joining; it had also gone far from the days when political education played a prominent part in branch and regional activities. With the Wilson government's enthusiasm for national planning, an economic rather than political perspective was placed well to the fore; thus one of its first acts was to establish a Welsh economic council to advise Westminster on Welsh matters. In the 1970s the Party continued to discuss various schemes for further devolution and the possibility of an elected assembly for Wales, but it was here that the contradictions between the MPs of industrial south Wales and those for the rural areas became most apparent. United Kingdom government perspectives increasingly required a series of standardized administrative structures for the regions and it is from this economic *planning* imperative rather than from the social and political factors that much of the impetus for the devolution debate within the Labour Party in Wales then came.

Because of the Party's internal contradictions the various schemes since 1959 involved considerable compromise, and it therefore moved progressively further from the wider political situation. With the planning emphasis went an implied reliance on sound and representative local government institutions, thus the various revelations and allegations of corruption in south Wales councils at this time was a decided embarrassment. Therefore in many ways the Party was unprepared for the strong decentralist challenge mounted by Plaid Cymru, which was to affect Labour's vote at all levels;[19] since 1945 Labour had been conditioned to seeing the Conservative Party as the main enemy—and that on the United Kingdom as much as the Wales level. This was a further indication of the growing strength of the centralist perspective within its ranks. Thus during the 1960s and 1970s the Welsh Labour Party may have sowed the seeds of its subsequent electoral decline. The upsurge in Labour representation since 1945 had occurred for a variety of reasons, and beneath the seeming unity of aggregated votes lay a complex political sociology. Labour's electoral support was a product of plural interests; it was progressively to be broken down by assaults from the other parties, initially by Plaid Cymru, latterly by others.[20]

The schizophrenic attitude of the Party during the 1978-9 Devolution Referendum campaign—indicative of its then existing cleavages—was further destructive of its unity. A prominent group of six Labour MPs[21] spearheaded a tenacious 'Vote No' campaign; although they acted against agreed party policy, no disciplinary action was ever taken against them. Encouragement given by this group within the heart of the Labour Party certainly influenced formerly loyal Labour voters to desert the official policy. Having once done so on March 1st 1979, it is quite possible that some of them felt equally able to do so in the subsequent General Election.

Other arguments apart, the scheme for an Assembly that was finally put to the public test, was undoubtedly unexciting and lacking in detail. As the product of so many compromises within and outside Wales it never reflected the vitality and plurality of Wales and its cultures that had been manifested in increasingly vigorous form since 1945. The devolution issue had been progressively removed from the area of significant social and political discussion and latterly was more associated with questions of bureaucracy and administration. At the very time when Margaret Thatcher was vigorously promoting a new and popular anti-bureaucratic line in the Conservative parliamentary opposition, the official Labour referendum campaigners in Wales were supporting a scheme which could only be seen as adding to bureaucracy.[22]

Whilst Plaid Cymru was to join with the official Labour group in supporting the 1979 Referendum proposals, it did so with caution and with some reservation, for it had gained electoral support in the 1960s and 1970s by offering a decentralist and less bureaucratic alternative in politics—a perspective hardly associated by the public with the 1979 proposals.

Several kinds of explanation of the upsurge in the support for Plaid Cymru during the late 1960s were used by the London based media, yet rarely did they refer to continuing social, economic and cultural factors; rather they tended to label the events as temporary or illogical by the use of such phrases as 'the protest vote', 'the Celtic fringe', and by associating this support with the activities of the Free Wales Army and *Cymdeithas yr Iaith Gymraeg* (The Welsh Language Society).[23] Yet within Wales all the major political parties were to revise their policy and organization during this period in order to take account of the upsurge in expressions of national feeling, thereby recognising the sound basis for these sentiments that lay in the history of Wales as a political nation.

Politicians and academics were influenced subsequently and considerably by the work of Michael Hechter[24] who applied the colonial analogy to the nations at the periphery of Britain. Wales, as periphery, was seen as historically subordinate economically to Britain's 'core', producing labour and raw materials in return for finished products and consumer goods. This economic under-development of Wales, sustained by a colonial-type relationship directed from London, he maintained, was bound to produce successive reactions, social and political, in Wales. Therefore, those of the 1960s were a logical and predictable response to a continuing situation rather than simply a momentary and arbitrary aberration. Hechter's influence on academic analysis is well covered elsewhere in this volume,[25] however, we should note here the considerable effect that both he and another major commentator, Tom

Nairn,[26] had on political thinking. Nairn placed Wales in a comparative framework with Scotland and Ireland—just as did Hechter—and emphasized the logic in the willingness of the nationalities at the periphery of Britain to put forward a radical alternative to centralised government during a time of British national decline. However, he also extended the comparison to other minority nations within larger European states. In doing this he distinguished those which were or had been relatively highly developed economically and had produced a relatively articulate middle class able to sustain demands for semi-independent, semi-autonomous, cultural and administrative institutions, and those which were largely peasant societies depleted of their population and natural resources in the early period of industrialisation, leaving a fragmented economy, infrastructure and culture. Indeed, in the description of the first of these types of development a number of academics and politicians recognised the role of the middle class in Wales which had led the construction around the turn of the century of the cultural monuments[27] of the University Colleges, the National Library and National Museum; at the same time it had built up pressure for creation of a range of other semi-independent educational and administrative institutions, culminating in the establishment of the Welsh Office in 1964. Similarly, the placing of Wales by both Nairn and Hechter in the latter category of historical dependency and relative deprivation emphasized the political vitality of the 1960s and early 1970s as a product of an historical relationship paralleled elsewhere and not as a simply isolated phenomenon. From these perspectives, the chances of Welsh political activity developing into a reinforcement of political nationalism were high.

Previously associated with the more conservative social and cultural aspects of nationalism, Plaid Cymru had been reorganizing its social and political philosophy.[28] By the mid-1950s it had begun tentatively to acknowledge that support from the populous industrial (and largely English-speaking) areas was essential if it were to make political capital. To create a widespread perception of a relatively-deprived Wales required a new economic and social perspective, with a wider appreciation of the various cultures of Wales. Whilst this shift in ideological emphasis slowly was evolving to encompass more of those unhappy with centralised British government, unemployment and industrial decline in Wales, and Labour's administrative rather than socio-political solutions, there was the development of something akin to a *cadre*[29] policy. A considerable increase in active membership in south-east Wales in the early 1960s laid the basis for the dramatic by-election near wins in Rhondda West (1967) and Caerphilly (1968) and subsequent impressive gains in local government elections in Merthyr, Rhymney, and other areas. Following on from the triumph of Gwynfor Evans in the October 1966 by-election in Carmarthen these results indicated that Plaid Cymru now had an electoral appeal in many different areas of Wales. Yet, just as the Labour Party at the height of its period of electoral success lagged behind in the creation of an organizational and ideological framework which reflected the plural bases of its support, so too in some respects did Plaid Cymru. In terms of active membership and voters, by the late 1960s it had support from industrial workers, farmers, tertiary-sector employees, intellectuals, conservative cultural nationalists and socialists, small business people and trade unionists, language activists and those relatively indifferent to its fate.[30]

Whilst in the late 1960s the Party commissioned a series of reports on economic and constitutional matters which paved the way for debates about what an autonomous Wales could take, there were to be problems regarding party policy and organization. These had been foreshadowed by the development in 1962—at the same time as the new infusion of membership from south-east Wales—of *Cymdeithas yr Iaith Gymraeg* (The Welsh Language Society). Although this body was quite separate from and independent of Plaid Cymru there was a large degree of intermembership. The feeling that Plaid Cymru should engage in direct, even illegal, action to secure the future of Wales has been present ever since its foundation, and over the years several of its prominent members had featured in such campaigns. However, Plaid Cymru did not show any sign of organizing such activities even, for example, during the 1959 drowning by Liverpool Corporation of the Tryweryn Valley. The more active approach of *Cymdeithas yr Iaith Gymraeg* in support of Welsh language and culture appealed in particular to the younger generation of Plaid Cymru members, especially those from the various colleges of the University of Wales, and with the late 1960s being the golden years of student protest throughout the world it was to become progressively more militant. At the same time the experience immediately following the passage of the Welsh Language Act in 1967—designed to ensure equal validity of both Welsh and English in the courts and in administrative matters—was that the authorities were relatively unenthusiastic in implementing its provisions; this ensured a response from *Cymdeithas yr Iaith Gymraeg*, and in early 1969 for example, it launched a campaign to obliterate monolingual English roadsigns. Whilst important areas of public opinion in Wales, notably the churches, were favourable to this campaign, overall public reaction was hostile. And within Plaid Cymru was a strong body of opinion wishing to dissociate itself from what it saw as illegal or dubious activities which could detract from electoral support. It therefore, distanced itself as a body from such activities, whilst being sympathetic and analytic about the underlying factors behind the protests. Thus from the later 1960s, as *Cymdeithas yr Iaith Gymraeg* became more militant, numbers of its membership chose to put more of their energies into the activities of this pressure group than into the party, Plaid Cymru.

Despite its widening of membership there was to remain in Plaid Cymru a strong emphasis on the socially conservative aspects of cultural and linguistic nationalism. From the standpoint of most of the new members and supporters from south-east Wales the activities of *Cymdeithas yr Iaith Gymraeg* and the emphasis in the party on cultural nationalism were both of far less importance than the pressing economical and social problems of the major industrial areas of Wales. They were also probably concerned about the revelations and allegations of corruption in local government—which had contributed to many of them moving from Labour to Plaid Cymru—and were therefore anxious to see the party define in detail a new way forward for political democracy, including work-place democracy. Yet its economic plan of 1970 concentrated on a relatively generalised description of economic and social development,[31] about which it was hard for the active member to become enthusiastic in everyday discussions in the factory or the street. Also missing from policy considerations during these two decades, despite the efforts of the late 1950s, was a sustained attempt to develop an awareness, a consciousness, of the various distinctive cultural aspects of Wales which were expressed through the medium of the English language. There remained for the public a continuing association between Plaid Cymru and a Welsh-language based culture—a culture to which most would never have means of access.

Thus, whilst Plaid Cymru achieved successes as far as the mid-1970s[32]—both in electoral terms, and in terms of influence on the policies of other parties—the organizational tasks of blending together disparate elements, of creating an electoral strategy where it had hardly existed before, and of developing a series of detailed economic and cultural policies could be but partly successful, simply because of their enormity. As Labour found, the retention of new electoral support depended on the rapid development of ideas and organisation as well as a willingness to accommodate potentially conflicting interests. Paradoxically Plaid Cymru's electoral victories and subsequent concentration on an electoral strategy, latterly involving co-operation with the 1974-9 Labour government in order to obtain legislation beneficial to Wales, bound it more closely and intimately to Westminster, an association which may have led some of its supporters to doubt whether after all it was so radically different from other parties.

Once again there were factors internal to party policy and organization which contributed toward electoral decline; to keep mobilization and enthusiasm levels high after the first phase of Plaid Cymru's success would require considerable ideological and organizational development. Yet whilst language activism had been firmly moved away into *Cymdeithas yr Iaith Gymraeg's* area of activity there remained in the party the heritage of conservative cultural nationalism; this both acted as a brake on the development of a 'multi-cultural' approach and, paradoxically, as a continuing imagined association in the minds of some outside the party with 'extremist' language protest.

Like Plaid Cymru, the Liberal Party's association with Wales has long been perceived as linked with its support of traditional culture and, in particular, religious non-conformity. Its post-1945 electoral support firmly anchored it in the rural areas of west and north Wales, yet by 1966 the Liberals were to hold only the Montgomeryshire seat. A long period of co-operation between them and the Conservative Party ended around this time; it had undoubtedly contributed to a loss of support, as it permitted Plaid Cymru to appear as an alternative for disillusioned radicals in Welsh-speaking areas of rural Wales. Associated since the last century with devolutionary moves, the Liberal approach to this issue during the 1950s was neither as firm nor as united as before, its presence in the Parliament for Wales campaign[33] of that era being overshadowed by the small but active group of Labour MPs. The regeneration of national feeling in the 1960s led them though to re-emphasize their Welsh identity; in 1966 a separate Welsh Liberal Party was set up to take part in a federal Britain-wide structure; in 1967 Emlyn Hooson put forward in parliament an unsuccessful Government of Wales bill, and a new emphasis was put on membership and candidate selection.

Despite its virtual parliamentary extinction in 1966, by 1985 it came to hold three mid-Wales seats, indicating that whilst it had failed immediately to profit from the new political situation of the 1960s, the radically inclined Welsh electorate had not completely deserted the original 'Party of Wales'.[34]

Whilst the Conservative Party remained staunchly unionist in policy and practice, it had developed 'devolutionist' features by its emphasis since the 1960s—through a series of reports—on seeing Wales as a specific planning unit. Similarly since 1972 it had held an Annual Welsh Conference. In power it had placed emphasis on the development of the Welsh cultural tradition by financial support through the Welsh Office of, for example, *Urdd Gobaith Cymru* (the Welsh League of Youth), the National Eisteddfod[35] and Welsh medium education. In addition it had stated concern to recruit parliamentary candidates with Welsh or Welsh-speaking backgrounds in order to rectify an imbalance in the Party existing in the 1950s and early 1960s.[36] Whilst these factors may have been secondary to the overall political appeal of Mrs. Thatcher in the General Elections of 1979 and 1983 they have obviously helped to increase the attractiveness of the Party for both rural and urban voters in Wales. These new features imply a persisting, even developing, importance for Welsh administrative bodies during times of Conservative government.[37] In order to develop its vote in Wales the Conservative Party must continue to support and develop cultural and administrative institutions which bolster Welsh identity.

However, the loss of the Montgomery seat in 1983, and the Brecon and Radnor seat in 1985—both to the Liberal/SDP Alliance—may give some indication of the permanence of Conservative appeal in Wales. High voting figures for the Conservatives are a new feature in post-war Wales; despite the efforts to make the party appear less unionist and more responsive to the Welsh cultural context, the party by mid-1985 had gained relatively few new members and activists, and its bases of support showed signs of movement back to the pre-1979 profile of the northern holiday coast plus the 'anglicized' areas of the south.

To review, the highlight of the 1960s and early 1970s appeared to be the remarkable rise of Plaid Cymru, and its concomitant acceptance of a parliamenary strategy. Yet could it be that Plaid Cymru was largely the beneficiary of discontent and disappointment within other parties at a time of national *cultural* resurgence? As outlined, they too shared the problems of the other parties in organizing and maintaining political support. Whatever the reality, the development of a 'Wales first' perspective and its political articulation and elevation to electoral prominence by Plaid Cymru's successes, marked a turning point in Welsh politics; all the major parties during this period reviewed their electoral and organizational strategies and made new and binding commitments to Welsh perspectives. The growth in political vitality in Wales was a real phenomenon; yet it was articulated in many ways other than through political nationalism of the 1960s and 1970s and other than through the electoral system. The ability of a Westminster-orientated system adequately to represent the needs of Wales should not be overestimated.

Institutions and interest groups—their influence in the 1960s and 1970s

Since the latter part of the nineteenth century Wales has developed institutions that in a real and symbolic way identify it as a nation.[38] The University Colleges, the National Library at Aberystwyth, the National Museum, and the revival of the National Eisteddfod are products of that period. Bridging differences of region, class and status in their construction and their activities, they offered to Welsh people not only tangible cultural benefits but also physical and ideological location points where they could recreate themselves as a visible nation. These structures, whilst in several ways contributing to Wales' integration with Britain, certainly demonstrated the existence of a new type of national cultural consciousness. Their continuing presence in the twentieth century was a positive and continuing example for those who wished to create distinctively Welsh institutions, societies, trade unions and the like.

Recent foundations such as *Undeb Amaethwyr Cymru* the Farmers' Union of Wales (1955), *Undeb Cenedlaethol Athrawon Cymru* the National Association of Teachers of Wales (1940), *Merched Y Wawr* Daughters of the Dawn (a break-away from the Women's Institute in 1967) are all examples of organizations which grew up in order to represent the separate and distinct characteristics of Wales. These and similar movements enjoyed considerable growth during the 1960s and 1970s, a further indicator that the changes in electoral preference of that period had a firm social and historical foundation, rather than a location in illogical 'protest'.

Although many of these groupings appear from their titles to be orientated exclusively to Welsh-speaking Wales it should not be assumed that they have no special appeal or basis outside that community. For example, whilst *Undeb Cenedlaethol Athrawon Cymru* conducts most of its business through the medium of Welsh it does have non-Welsh speaking members, and because of its Wales-wide local structures which reach to all Welsh counties the Farmers' Union of Wales is a body where both languages are used with equal validity. Even in organizations dedicated to the maintenance of the Welsh language such as *Urdd Gobaith Cymru* (the Welsh League of Youth) and *Mudiad Ysgolion Meithrin* (Nursery Schools Movement) there is often a solid dependence (for example in south-east Wales) on monolingual English-speaking parents and supporters. Here there is obviously no question or differences of language or region being divisive forces as regards organization or policy.

Turning to a different area, it may be argued that because it purports only to represent unionized working people and consists largely of unions affiliated to the Labour Party, the Wales TUC[39] is therefore by nature a homogeneous body. However, within that aggregate of unions and members are contained many of the diverse and potentially contradictory aspects of Wales—differences of language, culture, and region which in other contexts have proven incompatible. Indeed, of all the interest groups the Wales TUC provides the classic example of an organization which has faced these traditional differences of Wales, and has created an economic and political unity from diversity. In the 1970s the work of the Wales TUC ensured as much as did that of any political party that Wales should be considered as an economic planning unit in its own right. It may not be that the creation of the Wales TUC owed consciously to the antecedent institutionalised culture movement, but the process of its creation paralleled the experience and example. In many respects it demonstrated how a Welsh assembly could have operated, as it acted as an area for discussion and policy making on key Welsh issues, and brought together working people of various political opinions and from the different sub-regions of Wales in one representative forum. Owing to the split in Labour's ranks at the time of the Devolution Referendum it further acted as a powerful alternative locus of organization for the vote 'Yes' campaign. During the 1980 steel strike and the 1984/85 miners' strike it was again to demonstrate its ability to organize support and publicity on a Wales-wide basis.

This large group of various social, educational and cultural organizations specifically founded to service Welsh national characteristics showed few significant signs of weakening of influence or suffering a decline in membership in the period through to the 1980s—offering a further indication that the apparent electoral rejections of Welsh dimensions in 1979 and 1983 are but one part of a complex socio-political whole. The existence of pressure groups and interest groups orientated toward specific social, economic or cultural features of Wales—whether middle class or working class in composition, or whether they bridge these divisions—indicates the continuing political vitality in Wales, and the continuing influence of its cultures on its politics.

The 1980s: continuity and change

Despite the changes in voting pattern since 1979 and the obvious and persistent 'anglicising' or 'acculturation' forces at work—the dominance of east-west rather than north-south communications, the predominant position of the London-based newspapers, radio and television services—there are still remarkable and continuing Welsh characteristics in the arenas of politics. These characteristics owe their existence not only to tradition but to its reinterpretation and development.

The growth of the Welsh Office as an administrative expression of Welsh identity with wide-ranging economic powers and direct responsibility for areas such as health, primary and secondary education and agriculture has given further impetus to pressure groups and other interested bodies to organize on a Wales basis and develop distinct Welsh perspectives.[40] Similarly a growing emphasis of EEC regional policy on the peripheral areas has given increased importance to bodies organized to promote the concerns of Wales. Whilst clearly bringing them more closely into a network of centralised relationships—focussing on policy made in London and Brussels—there is an undoubted enhancement of visible Welsh identity and greater opportunity thereby for its promotion in other areas of life. The pressure and interest groups outlined in the previous section continue to develop, and thereby enhance a sense of Welsh identity. Added to this factor, the Welsh Language Act of 1967 has encouraged visible and audible bilingualism in public and semi-public bodies.[41]

Advertising slogans on the ubiquitous Telecom vans urge us, in both languages, to greater use of the network; British Rail's sign system at stations is progressively being made bilingual; road signs offer information and direction in Welsh and English. The practice has also spread into wider commercial areas; bilingual cheque books are readily available; Tesco stores guide their customers by bilingual signs; a Wales-based airline makes bilingual flight announcements and boasts aircraft with their registration marks *G-YMRU* and *G-WLAD*.[42] From the seemingly inconsequential to the manifestly profound, these examples add up to a continual and public reminder that Wales has national characteristics.

In electoral politics all the major parties have an enhanced Welsh profile and orientation both in organization and policy. And with each one of them—especially since the late 1960s—attempting to capitalize on this, is it unreasonable that Welsh voters should become more discriminating in their choices? The plurality of cultures and interests in Wales may have been more effectively represented by Labour than by the single party as exists in some socialist states, but there are inevitable and obvious problems for representative and democratic politics in either situation. The rejection of single party dominance of Welsh politics by no means implies a loss of distinctive cultural features, but rather a realignment based upon them.

Thus the July 1985 Liberal victory under the Alliance banner in the Brecon and Radnor parliamentary constituency offers contradictory as well as confirmatory evidence for the acculturation hypothesis. Whilst local issues predominated in the campaign, Welsh *national* issues were not well to the fore, thus giving apparent weight to the opinion that the electorate behaved—albeit in sophisticated manner—in a way that voters in England would. However, there is now a solid belt of Liberal territory from the Ceredigion and Pembroke North constituency on Cardigan Bay in the west, through to the Montgomery and Brecon and Radnor constituencies, which form a substantial part of the eastern boundary of Wales. And to the north of this are Plaid Cymru's Caernarfon and Meirionydd-Nant Conwy seats forming a similar block. Voters in these and neighbouring constituencies could come to perceive this as the basis of a potentially powerful unity, both real and symbolic, uniting the Welsh speakers of the west with the English speakers of the east of the area.[43] It is too much to say that a new and conscious territorial alignment is already in existence, but the possibility of electoral support for the two parties in these areas acting as an accelerator to their existing support in constituencies such as Ynys Môn, Conwy, Clwyd South-West, Carmarthen, and Pembrokeshire, is by no means inconceivable.[44] In 1979 it was possible to travel from north to south Wales from Anglesey to Gwent through Conservative Party territory; perhaps following the next General Election the same journey from north to south will be possible through Plaid Cymru and Liberal/SDP territory. This scenario would see Labour remaining in power only in industrial south Wales and industrial north-east Wales, the Conservatives retaining but a few northern coastal and south Wales residential area seats. It would not necessarily involve the possibility of any kind of prior or subsequent alliance between Liberals/SDP and Plaid Cymru. Rather it would refer to the possibility of Welsh rural consciousness, whether English or Welsh language based, manifesting itself more visibly in opposition to centralist parties than during the past six years—during which time, by the criterion of aggregate voting in parliamentary elections, it was declining. The suggestion of such a result to the next General Election is highly speculative, but if it were to occur a distinctively new Welsh political profile could be established for some decades.

This is an area of speculation which involves several assumptions, one of which is that language need not be a divisive factor in Welsh electoral politics. Since the 1960s even Plaid Cymru was anxious that it not be over-associated with language factors in the eyes of the electorate. There are, though, contradictions, *Cymdeithas yr Iaith Gymraeg* freed of constraints of association with Plaid Cymru became more militant in support of language issues, arousing strong *pro* and *anti* feelings in the process. The logic of preserving and developing the language involves, though, more than cultural factors and *Cymdeithas yr Iaith Gymraeg* has progressively researched social and economic issues, and on that basis has pressed the various county councils toward use of linguistic considerations in planning. Because of this broadening of scope and emphasis its members have not only been prominent in other Welsh language orientated ventures such as *Cymdeithas Tai Gwynedd* (Gwynedd Housing Association), *Cymdeithas Tai Clwyd* (Clwyd Housing Association) and *Antur Teifi* (Teifi Venture—a co-operative development enterprise), but also in other organizations with socio-political objectives which span the linguistic communities. Thus its members have often been involved in the activities of CND Wales,[45] various ecological groups, and miners' support groups (during the 1984/5 strike). The membership of *Cymdeithas yr Iaith Gymraeg*, whilst overwhelmingly Welsh speaking, shares the characteristics of CND Wales in that it cuts across a variety of regional, status and class loyalties. The involvement of some CND and *Cymdeithas yr Iaith Gymraeg* members in a common complex of social and economic issues surrounding their individual aims—despite the variety of their members' backgrounds—is evidence of a continuing co-operation across sub-regional and linguistic boundaries in Wales. A further instance of this was the action under the auspices of the Wales TUC in support of the 1980 steel strike and the 1984/5 miners' strike. Especially significant was the Wales-wide organization of support groups for the miners;[46] the structure of these support groups, again bridged the traditional divides mentioned above and, in particular, brought women forward as political activists in traditional male territory. Notable too, is the fact that the impetus for the Greenham Common encampment came from Welsh women—an example not only of the move of women into the male-dominated arena of political activism, but of Wales taking a political initiative into England.[47] The development of debate on wider issues within groupings like CND, *Cymdeithas yr Iaith Gymraeg* and the Wales TUC, may well have been influenced by the failure to obtain a Welsh Assembly. Just as other Wales-wide bodies in the old institutionalized culture movement acted as forums for the debate of Welsh issues as a result of lack of provision elsewhere in the political structure, so now do these groupings. Further, insofar as the political parties are unable to adapt to the actions and sentiments encompassed by these groups, so the latter will grow in significance as *foci* of action at the expense of parties.[48]

The major party-political attempts to capitalise on these areas of activity have come from the Labour Party and Plaid Cymru respectively. The Labour Party, particularly through its traditional appeal to the working class of industrial Wales, may have had large numbers of active members in those groupings not based on the Welsh language factor and will undoubtedly benefit from the experience gained in these areas. Plaid Cymru with its mixed feelings over the parliamentary road and its geographical imbalance caused by the loss of a considerable number of votes in the south-east Wales industrial areas in the past ten years, has recently placed more strategic emphasis on identifying with all types of these groupings. In October 1981 it amended its constitution to declare one of its principal aims as the establishment of a Welsh decentralised socialist state. Since that time, it has been debating the way in which to fulfil this new socialist objective; it has been a stormy process and rival groupings on the left and right of the Party have often been clashed. However, the unity of the Party appears to have been held—despite some resignations—and both the National Left grouping and others less sure of the role of socialist ideology have all seen the organizational future as one which should link together the kind of experiences mentioned above. So far success has been patchy, and if Plaid Cymru is to challenge the Labour Party in this area it will have to re-emphasize the type of *cadre* policy that led to the gain of committed active political workers in the industrial south-east some twenty years ago. In the 1980s Plaid Cymru has been able to develop and sustain campaigns on several issues of widespread interest in Wales. Prominent amongst these were efforts to publicise the fact that despite providing so much water for England, the price of water to consumers in Wales is often considerably in excess of that over the border; its place in the campaign to secure from the Conservative government the fourth television channel that had been promised for Wales again brought Plaid Cymru into the headlines of the British press and gained it some measure of political *kudos* in Wales itself.[49]

Whilst the major parties and pressure groups attempt to co-ordinate action which is within the frameworks of present government structures and legality, the 1980s saw a continuation of direct action taken by groups outside those areas. There were a series of minor explosions at sites symbolic of British control of Wales, including one outside an army recruiting office in Pontypridd, and the first in a series of burnings of holiday cottages in rural and Welsh speaking areas occurred in December 1979.[50] Operating within the constraints of legality, but far from the perspectives of other groups, dissatisfied by the efforts of the Labour and Communist Parties and Plaid Cymru to achieve substantial devolution or self government for Wales, and horrified by the effects on unemployment of the anti-inflationary policies of the 1979 Conservative government was the Welsh Socialist Republican Movement (January 1980). Its organization was virtually destroyed by a combination of internal contradictions and the close attention paid to its members by the police during their efforts to trace those responsible for the burnings and explosions.[51] A further movement which spurns contact with the conventional parties is *Adfer*.[52] Founded in the late 1970s by those feeling that the efforts of *Cymdeithas yr Iaith Gymraeg* and Plaid Cymru were not strong enough to ensure the survival of the Welsh speaking cores of Wales in Gwynedd and Dyfed, *Adfer* placed its emphasis on the achievement of areas of monolingualism, where Welsh language and culture could develop without what they saw as the destructive intrusions of Anglo-American cultural influences. Bilingualism to *Adfer* was anathema, and as a policy considered corrosive of traditional Welsh areas. More controversial than its insistence on the creation of Welsh heartlands in the west, where it would be made hard for any language other than Welsh to be used, was the virtual denial of Welsh nationality to those not speaking Welsh and their disdain for those who do speak Welsh but chose to live outside the heartlands. *Adfer* aimed to be active in the areas of housing and co-operative ventures, and whilst achievements in these areas have been limited, the group has maintained its membership and political presence.

The very fact that these differing movements have continued to exist outside or in opposition to the formal political structure, or in limited contact with it, indicates that there are distinct tensions continuing to be generated by factors explicit to Wales and unlikely to be satisfied by the presently-constituted formal political structures and processes.

Conclusion

Both within and outside its formal structures Wales retains, revises and develops its national and political identity. There obviously have been strong challenges to these distinctive features from the larger and centralised British system and the influence of its attendant norms. Yet not all influence from outside is destructive of distinctly Welsh features. For centuries Wales has assimilated and put to its own use ideas from outside. Perhaps it is no coincidence that the late 1960s and early 1970s—years of considerable political change in Wales—were times when much of the rest of the world was experiencing radical political activity, from the Cultural Revolution in China to the worker-student challenge to the French state and the vigorous anti-Vietnam war demonstrations in the United States. Without doubt these events affected the perspectives of political activists in Wales. Similarly, albeit sometimes less dramatically, continuing progress of other minority nationalities within larger states—particularly those of western Europe—towards various forms of self-assertion has not escaped attention in Wales.

Whilst Wales, like the rest of Britain, listened to and indeed adapted to the ideas of radical Thatcherism from

1979 onward, the process has neither been uncritical nor uneventful. What will be reconstructed from this continual process of re-evaluation is hardly likely to be another 'Party of Wales' of hegemonic nature; instead Wales may now be moving towards a more sophisticated politics where the role of interest groups takes on increasing significance for the conventional political parties, wedded as the latter are to the requirements of the Westminster model.

One of the more helpful signs for those convinced of the existence of Wales as a nation, but uncertain as to how it may be defined and articulated through political action, has been the recent publication of works which look at the questions of Welsh nationality and political identity as answerable by reference not simply to historical and political 'facts' but rather to how people interpret them in relation to their present and future positions. Just as the works of Hechter[53] and Nairn substantially have affected political and economic thinking in Wales, so too will the diverse ideas of those such as Emyr Humphreys, Raymond Williams, and Gwyn A. Williams.[54] These are works which overcome the traditional use of opposed categories such as Welsh speaker and English speaker, northerner and southerner, industrial worker and farmer. Their richness and complexity will take some time before being absorbed into the thinking of those active in politics but without doubt will be of considerable influence on the revision of political ideas with regard to the question of nationality.

Whilst this contribution has concentrated on a description of only selected features of the background to Welsh organizations and groupings of political effect, it has done so with a purpose: for it contends that there has been since 1979 an underestimation of the distinctive features of Welsh social and political life.[55] For some academics and media commentators the loss of Labour Party hegemony and a decline in electoral support of Plaid Cymru indicated an irreversible breakdown of ethnic, class, or *gwerin* solidarity. There is no longer a 'Party of Wales' but this does not mean that a distinctive Welsh politics has ceased to exist. Wales rejected the 1979 Devolution proposals; in 1896 it rejected the Home Rule ideas of *Cymru Fydd*. In both these instances a blow was dealt to certain political ambitions, but in neither case did it mean that the social and political uniquenesses of Wales, which had necessitated the widespread debate of these issues, had in turn declined.

The 1980s have brought with them considerable possibilities for the development of sentiment that recognizes Wales as a political unit.[56] In times of austerity mere regions can take on a political identity of considerable magnitude. Wales has a history of relative deprivation; in the severe years since 1979 many individual events have become connected with reinterpretations of that history, giving an opportunity for development of the pluralistically-based all-Wales identity of the kind that was needed for a 'Yes' vote in the Referendum. Indeed the considerations that the 'Yes' campaigners wished to present may be capable of better articulation and reception after the rejection of 1979. In February of that year Saunders Lewis wrote to the *Western Mail* newspaper as follows:

> Sir, we are asked to tell the Government on St. David's Day whether we want a Welsh Assembly or not. The implied question is: 'Are you a nation or not?' May I point out the probable consequence of a 'No' majority? There will follow a general election. There may be a change of government. The first task of a new Westminster Parliament will be to reduce and master inflation.
>
> In Wales there are coal mines that work at a loss; there are steelworks what are judged superfluous, there are still valleys convenient for submersion. And there will be no Welsh defence. (*Western Mail*, 26.2.1979)

This letter was prophetic in nature; yet the fact that the Referendum rejection left Wales less well defended was, paradoxically, part of the means of creating a new response.

Notes

1 A comprehensive listing will be found in Butt Philip, A. (1975) *The Welsh question: nationalism in Welsh politics, 1945-70*, Cardiff, University of Wales Press, 1975; this can be up-dated by reference to Morgan, K. O. (1981) *Rebirth of a nation: Wales 1880-1980, The history of Wales, vol. VI*, The Claredon Press, Oxford and the University of Wales Press, Cardiff, chs. 12 & 13.

2 These approaches are reviewed in: Hechter, M. (1975) *Internal Colonialism: the Celtic fringe in British national development 1536-1966*, London, Routledge and Kegan Paul. In the Welsh context 'acculturation' is popularly known as 'Anglicization'.

3 Chapter 8, Nairn, T. (1976) 'Culture and politics in Wales'; Chapter 9, Hechter, M. (1975) 'Towards a theory of ethnic change'.

4 Jones, J. B. and Wilford, R. A. (1983) 'Implications: two salient issues', in Foulkes, D., Jones, J. B. and Wilford, R. A. *The Welsh veto: the Wales Act 1978 and the referendum*, Cardiff, University of Wales Press, and Balsom, D. (1985) 'The three-Wales model' in Osmond, J. (ed.) *The national question again: Welsh political identity in the 1980s*, Llandysul, Gomer Press, both offer observations on recent trends in the 'acculturation' process.

5 Described in Balsom, D. (1985), *op cit.*

6 For a short but stimulating academic discussion of the 'radical tradition' in Welsh politics see Chapter 6 of: Morgan, P. and Thomas, D. (1984) *Wales: the shaping of a nation*, Newton Abbot and London, David and Charles. In particular this addresses the question of 'how the Welsh remained faithful to Labour for so long without experiencing the revival of Conservatism occurring elsewhere in Britain in the 1950s, and without Liberal revivals . . .' (p. 148).

7 Morgan, K. O. (1981) *op. cit.* and Osmond, J. (1977) *Creative conflict: the politics of Welsh devolution*, Llandysul, Gomer Press, and London, Routledge and Kegan Paul, review this experience.

8 To re-emphasize: the point here is not that these features are unique to Wales, but that its political system exhibits them for reasons that owe some measure to the cultural distinctiveness of Wales as well as for reasons common to the United Kingdom system as a whole.

9 This gives rise to a distinctive style of decision-making in these county and district councils; in Gwynedd in particular there is an emphasis on achievement of consensus, details of policy and practice being worked out in committees and sub-committees, the full council having previously agreed general policy, normally without divisive voting. A case study by this author of the development of decision making in relation to the policy of bilingualism in secondary education in Gwynedd will be found in Block II of D208 *Decision making in Britain* (1983) the Open University Press, Milton Keynes.

10 For example the victory of S. O. Davies as Independent Labour Candidate for Merthyr Tudful in the 1970 parliamentary election, achieving 52 per cent of the poll as against the 29 per cent of the official Labour candidate.

11 Hume, I. (1981) 'The Welsh experience' in Bochel, J., Denver, D. and Macartney, A. *The Referendum experience, Scotland 1979*, Aberdeen, Aberdeen University Press.

12 Labour then held all parliamentary seats apart from Barry (where the Conservatives held control by a mere 2.6 per cent over Labour) Denbigh, West Flintshire, and Montgomery.
13 See Morgan, P. (1967 and 1985) 'The *gwerin* of Wales: myth and reality' (Chapter 5 of this volume) for a discussion of this term and its usage.
14 The problems of achievement of this commitment, and the related divisions within Labour ranks on the question of the place of nationality in socialist politics are covered by Morgan, K. O. *op. cit.* Ch. 13, Osmond, J. *op. cit.* Ch. 3, and Butt Philip, A. *op. cit.* (1975) (particularly Ch. 11).
15 It is instructive that Cledwyn Hughes took up the recommendations of the Hughes-Parry report with vigour, resulting in the 1967 Welsh Language Act, which was designed to ensure equal validity for both languages in legal and administrative areas.
16 For evidence of this see George Thomas's autobiography (1985) *Mr. Speaker*, London, Century Publishing, 124 and 127-8.
17 For discussion of the origin of the term and its effect see: Thomas, Ned (1985) 'Images of Wales' in Osmond, J. (1985) *op. cit.*; also his still-stimulating volume (1971) *The Welsh extremist*, Talybont, Y Lolfa, especially Chapter 2.
18 However toward the end of this period several study groups were set up to examine broadcasting, bilingualism, rural depopulation and traditional industry decline (Osmond, 1977, *op. cit.*).
19 The victory of Gwynfor Evans in 1966 Carmarthen by-election was followed by impressive votes for Plaid Cymru in the constituencies of Rhondda West (1967—40 per cent of the poll), Caerphilly (1968—40 per cent of the poll); by October 1974 it held the former Labour seats of Caernarfon, Carmarthen, and Merioneth, and in a 1972 by-election polled 37 per cent in Merthyr Tudful. By 1976 it had gained control of Merthyr Tudful council, and had become the largest party in the Rhymney Valley.
20 The intervention of Plaid Cymru began the process of breakdown in the hegemony of Labour; this has had an effect on traditional voting loyalties to this day, and it is not unreasonable to hypothesize that this indigenous factor may even have influenced the swing to the Conservatives in the parliamentary elections of 1979 and 1983.
21 Its members were: Leo Abse, Donald Anderson, Ifor Davies, Fred Evans, Ioan Evans, and Neil Kinnock (notably they were all representatives of south-east Wales constituencies).
22 For a full discussion of the referendum issues and campaign, particularly the role of the parties, see Foulkes, Jones and Wilford (1983) *op. cit.* A shorter summary is Hume, I. (1981) *op. cit.*
23 For the background to these explanations see Graham Day (1979 and 1985) and Glyn Williams (1977 and 1985), Chapters 6 and 7 respectively of this volume.
24 Hechter, M. (1975) *Internal colonialism*, *op. cit.* Chapter 9 of this volume is an extract from that work.
25 See Chapters 6 and 7.
26 Nairn, T. (1976) *op. cit.*
27 These are products of a broad-based movement, which is often identified collectively by the title 'Institutionalized culture movement'.
28 For a description of Plaid Cymru's strategy and tactics in this period see: Davis, J. (1985) 'Plaid Cymru in transition' in Osmond, J. (ed.). 1985 *op. cit.*

29 The term 'cadre' refers to a disciplined and motivated activist, who is part of an integrated administrative or party structure. It is more often used in the context of socialist or communist parties, but no such ideological connotations are implied by its usage here.

30 See Chapter 7 of Butt Philip, A. (1975) *op. cit.* for a detailed profile of Plaid Cymru voters and supporters in this period. Whilst it should be noted that the most likely supporter of Plaid Cymru in the late 1960s was 'a Welsh-speaking non-Anglican Welshman, aged between 21 and 35, living in north or west Wales' (150) it is also pertinent that by 1969 four in every ten members came from Glamorgan and Monmouthshire (172). Further, 'throughout the 1960s the rank and file of the *Blaid* was becoming more youthful and drawn more from the manual-worker section . . than previously' (169).

31 The move towards economic planning was understandable in terms of the party's previous neglect; yet it also could be interpreted as following the United Kingdom planning agenda set by the 1964 Wilson government.

32 Plaid Cymru's gains in the 1976 and 1977 district and county elections were followed by losses in 1979. An explanation of this apparent decline (and a full listing of recent electoral results) occurs in Balsom, D. and Burch, M. (1980) *A political and electoral handbook for Wales*, Farnborough, Gomer Publishing. Jones, Beti (1977) *Etholiadau seneddol yng Nghymru 1900-1975, Parliamentary eletions in Wales 1900-1975*, Talybont, Y Lolfa, also provides useful basic information.

33 The 'Parliament for Wales' campaign, presided over by Lady Megan Lloyd George, involved Liberal, Labour and Plaid Cymru members. The five major supporters from the parliamentary Labour Party (with the exception of S. O. Davies of Merthyr Tudful) represented rural constituencies; for these activities they were under constant threat of discipline by the party.

34 Roberts, D. 'The strange death of Liberal Wales' in Osmond (1985), *op. cit.* examines the realignment of the party during this period, and in particular the crucial role of the SDP-Liberal alliance.

35 In 1959 the parliamentary bill was passed, allowing local councils to contribute to the National Eisteddfod from rating income.

36 Keith Best, the English-born member for Ynys Môn, and Chris Butler, the 1985 by-election candidate in Brecon and Radnor, have both made efforts to learn Welsh.

37 The influential Hughes-Parry report that led to the 1967 Welsh Language Act was commissioned by Sir Keith Joseph whilst Minister for Housing and Local Government and Welsh Affairs.

38 Morgan, P. and Thomas, D. (1984) *op. cit.* 213-229.

39 Constituted in its present form in 1973.

40 See: Osmond, J. (1985) 'The dynamic of institutions' in Osmond, J. (ed.) *op. cit.*; Foulkes, D., Jones, J. B. and Wilford, R. A. (1983) 'Wales: a separate administrative unit'—Chapter 13 of this volume.

41 The role of *Cymdeithas yr Iaith Gymraeg* in persuading (by various means) these and other commercial and cultural bodies to implement the spirit of the Hughes-Parry report and the resultant act has been crucial.

42 In English these are 'Wales' and 'Country' respectively; the use of *Gwlad* in relation to Wales also has connotations of national spirit and pride.

43 There is though a strong tendency in some quarters to identify as distinctively Welsh only those features which are articulated through the medium of the Welsh language or by reference to linguistic considerations. See for example some of the chapters in Osmond, J. (ed.) (1985) op. cit.

44 The creation of the Liberal/SDP alliance obviously injects a new dynamism and significance from outside Wales; yet the electoral traditions of Wales owe much to the Liberal Party's experience within that country. How far Wales and its regions will adapt to, or adopt, the United Kingdom-wide features of the Alliance is referred to in two articles in *Cambria: a Welsh geographical review*, vol. 10, 2, 1983: Carter, H. Some geographical observations on the 1983 general election in Wales and its implications for the country's future political pattern' 74-88, and Prentice, R. C. 'The rise of the 'Alliance' parties in the 1983 general election in Wales: continuity or discontinuity in voting correlations?', 89-111. In Osmond (ed.) 1985 *op. cit.*, Denis Balsom's Chapter 1 'The three-Wales model' offers further information and, incidentally, a pessimistic conclusion regarding the future of Welsh identity 'not anchored by the Welsh language'. Of relevance is the different and detailed analysis of Wales as culture region, with specific discussion of a variety of spatial models of core and periphery seen in Chapter 2 of this volume—Pryce, W. T. R. (1978) 'Wales as a culture region: patterns of change 1750-1971'.

45 CND Wales has developed its own distinct identity, based both on current and past experience in Wales. Long-established pacifist, ILP, and internationalist tendencies have linked with such new factors as an upsurge of activity in CND by women in Wales and a widespread and growing level of commitment by county and district councils to an anti nuclear weapons stance.

46 An interview of Kim Howells, touching on the distinctive features of the miners' strike in Wales, brings out the socio-cultural aspects of what initially may appear to have been a purely economic confrontation in *Planet: the Welsh internationalist*, 51, 1985.

47 Williams, Gwyn A. (1985) *When was Wales? A history of the Welsh*, Harmondsworth, Penguin Books' 298-9, notes the key role in CND of women in particular and of the south-east Wales valleys in general.

48 It is also noticeable that young people form a substantial part of membership of these groups, whilst all political parties currently are having difficulty in the area of youth recruitment.

49 Whatever factors are considered, the separation of the languages—with Welsh language programmes now broadcast only on *Sianel Pedwar Cymru (S4C)*—turned out to be a relatively popular solution.

50 The development and activities of the 1960s para-military movements, *Mudiad Amddiffyn Cymru* (Wales Defence Movement) and the Free Wales Army, are documented in Clews, R. (1980) *To dream of freedom*, Talybont, Y Lolfa.

51 Osmond, J. (1984) *Police conspiracy?* Talybont, Y Lolfa, and Griffiths, R. (1985) 'Resolving contradictions between class and nation' in Osmond, J. (1985) *op. cit.*

52 See Chapter 11 of this volume.

53 Hechter's monumental work, using Weberian categories of status rather than Marxist categories of class in the analysis of Wales' social structure may well have over-estimated the uniformity, the integrated nature, of Welsh political response to English dominance and control of the UK economy; in turn this may have reinforced the notion that Wales' distinctive political features *required* predominant representation by one radical party.

54 Humphreys, E. (1985) *The Taliesin tradition*, London, Black Raven Press; Williams, G. A. (1985) *op. cit.*; Williams, R. (1985) 'Wales and England' in Osmond, J. (ed.) (1985) *op. cit.*

55 Whilst political nationalism has had relatively few successes in electoral politics, these latter have played a key role in the reshaping of Welsh politics. Their significance cannot be dismissed as simply temporary and relative. Underlying those electoral expressions of political nationalism is a diversity of opinion and sentiment that owes much to the distinctive cultures of Wales—whether they be of class, language, region or occupation. A related point is that a decline in the fortunes of political nationalism in electoral terms does not necessarily indicate the decline of the distinctive cultures and structures which gave rise to it; the expression associated with them—perhaps because of a lack of an adequate forum for them in presently constituted electoral politics—often moves to other non-electoral areas of politics or to primarily cultural areas, which in turn take on political significance.

56 Clearly the activities of some of the groupings outlined, for example *Adfer*, are not directed towards the recognition of Wales as a valid political unit constituted by its plural interests. However the majority, whatever their sectional interest, do subscribe to and reinforce this image of Wales as a single distinctive unit.

Chapter Fifteen

The Mass Media in Wales: Some Preliminary Explorations*

Ian Hume

This chapter centres on the role of the Welsh mass media of the 1980s in presenting to their audiences images of Wales and the world. Because of observed differences, it concentrates upon a broad comparison of news presentation in the media in the English language and the Welsh language respectively. It does not seek, other than peripherally, to outline the influence of the London-based press or broadcast media.[1]

The title of this chapter indicates its primary aim. It seeks to stimulate thought, encourage debate, and provide impetus for further research in the area. A definitive history of the mass media in Wales has yet to be written. The accounts that do exist often disagree both over questions of emphasis and of fact. Thus for the social scientist seeking to examine the pattern of 1980s there must be caution in relying on any particular historical source. Whilst the series of tables at the end of the chapter mainly consist of original data, obtained from primary research undertaken by the author during 1979-85, a caution should still be made. Owing to inherent difficulties of standardisation and measurement, and to the relatively short period of survey time represented by each table, these data should not in themselves be subject to over interpretation. This therefore is a chapter which explores selected aspects of the mass media of Wales in the 1980s, rather than a comprehensive history. It does not seek for example to examine patterns of ownership, control, or finance. Rather, through its comparison of the media in the English language and the media in the Welsh lang-

* Specially written for this volume.

uage, it directs the reader to consider the significance of their similarities and differences in relation to the interplay of factors from within the Welsh context and the British context respectively. It builds in conscious manner on several preceding chapters. The reviews of Day (Chapter 6) and Williams (Chapter 7) indicate a whole range of perspectives and evidence considered to be of importance by social scientists working on Wales; more particularly the concepts and ideas suggested by Nairn (Chapter 8) and Hechter (Chapter 9)—which relate to larger economic and social processes—could form a useful exploratory framework of reference for the data in this Chapter. Similarly, Pryce (Chapter 2) and Bowen (Chapter 3) use spatial models and related perspectives which could cast light on distinctive features of the contemporary mass media.

A lively tradition of communication has long been apparent in Wales, and although continually influenced by the practices and values of English journalism, it is not until comparatively recently that this influence has become almost overwhelming. Whilst not all the Welsh media are operating on the basis of the norms and methods of journalistic procedure developed in England, it is now but a small part which is distinctively different. At the time of writing the three-year experiment of *Sianel Pedwar Cymru*/Channel Four Wales (*S4C*) is due for review. Whilst appraisal must take place, the question of *S4C*—and particularly its output in the Welsh language—has dominated public discussion of the mass media almost to the exclusion of other areas and aspects. Carrying, as it does, programmes in English and in Welsh *S4C* may be seen as representative of the interface, and the interaction, between Wales and England. Why then confine the debate to the suitability of its Welsh-language output to its Welsh-language audience? Indeed, why should we not debate in detail the whole pattern of newspaper, radio and television provision in Wales? Such a comprehensive review is both desirable and necessary.

Local and national newspapers of Wales

A prime means of mass communication in Wales of the second half of the nineteenth century was the weekly press. Its growth during this period was considerable; by 1880 there were twenty national and local weekly newspapers in Welsh, and by 1883, forty in English. K. O. Morgan refers to the period from the 1880s as 'a golden age' for the radical journalist, with its immense array of local newspapers and periodicals'.[2] D. Tecwyn Lloyd sees the years 1850-1910 as a 'heyday-period'.[3] The development of journalism in Wales, they maintain, was part of a larger upsurge in the production of pamphlets, journals and books in both languages, but more notably in Welsh. By the closing decades of the nineteenth century a new class of professional writers was to be found in key towns such as Caernarfon, Denbigh, Aberdare and Merthyr Tudful, providing an enhanced status for these places as regional centres for political as well as commercial activities. Naturally, the intensity of political debate was heightened by the franchise reforms of 1867 and 1884 and in particular by the rise of the Liberal Party in Wales. Indeed, K. O. Morgan maintains that 'Liberalism permeated Welsh life at every point during this period'.[4] This was a time when Wales began to find new and structural means of asserting its identity, a period when far greater numbers of Welshmen, if not women, were able to participate in a new framework of politics. Just as politics became more 'popular', so the Welsh press itself became more involved in the discussion of political issues. The ethos of Wales at this time, one of radical non-conformity, was both mirrored in and developed by the press. And just as nonconformity and its political associate of Liberalism had developed a tradition of informed and constructive debate so too, it seems, did the press. According to Morgan the extent to which it did so varied according to area,[5] for whilst the Liberals were certainly concerned with social equality and civil libertarianism, their world was also a 'highly local one'.[6] In this local context these wider values were 'modified always by the ethic of middle-class chapel respectability'.[7] Editors from Liberal backgrounds (the majority) were thus varied in their concerns and emphasis. Was this perhaps a reflection on the nature of the Liberal coalition itself? In this connection Morgan draws as an example the contrast between the style and coverage of the English-language *South Wales Daily News* (Cardiff) and *Y Genedl Gymreig* (Caernarfon)—both of which were supporters of Liberalism. The *Daily News*, he maintains, gave little prominence to Welsh cultural or educational affairs, concerning itself more with the pre-occupations of the 'bourgeois elite, Conservative as well as Liberal, who dominated the civil life of Cardiff at its greatest period of expansion'.[8] *Y Genedl Gymreig* he describes as having a considerably wider outlook. This distinction in style, he writes, 'speaks volumes on the cultural and social gulfs that existed within the Welsh Liberal Coalition'.[9]

D. Tecwyn Lloyd similarly notes 'that the majority opinion in most of these papers was Liberal and radical'.[10] However, in comparison with Morgan he tends to see the press, particularly that in the Welsh language, as a relatively uniform body whose newspapers 'became true platforms for the discussion of most of the social, political and religious issues of their time not only as these affected Wales but as they appeared in Europe and the world.'[11] He further sees the press as creating 'a new vocabulary of political and educational controversy in Welsh that is felt to be vibrantly alive today'.[12] Lloyd tends to see the weeklies in the Welsh language as developing a radically independent assessment of world affairs and a distinctive approach toward journalism that was in several respects different to that of the British press. However, just how far the Welsh language press was independent of British sources and influence, and how far they were uniformly successful in creating a new vocabulary of debate is open to some question.[13] Yet whatever its other characteristics, its close relationship with the concerns of Liberalism gave the Welsh press the opportunity to develop reporting and discussion of issues then seen as being of national importance in Wales.

However, in the twentieth century improved communications and delivery systems opened up even the innermost areas of Wales to the popular London dailies, and to an increasing number of new English-language *weeklies*.[14] The former brought the political vocabulary of greater Britain; the latter, almost without exception, were highly localised in their reporting and rarely developed coverage of all-Wales issues. Few editors from the English language press of Wales have achieved in the twentieth century a distinctively high reputation. 'Campaigning' seldom occurs; national events are rarely treated; editorials—if they exist at all—are either homily-like and moralistic, or idiosyncratic. Staff are kept to a minimum and advertising to a maximum; this results in a low proportion of news to total column inches.[15] The use of local correspondents, often paid on a wordage basis, is common. This discourages professionalism in style, and encourages low level verbosity.[16] Even in strongly Welsh-speaking areas these papers rarely have had other than a token amount of Welsh in their columns,[17] and events which are conducted totally in Welsh are more likely to be reported in English.[18] Through a combination of localised perspectives, low quality reporting, and failure fully to reflect Welsh culture, these papers have possibly contributed to a process of anglicisation, and at best have reflected only superficial kinds of local or regional identity.

As data presented at the end of this chapter evidences, in aggregate the English language weeklies have insignificant coverage of international, British, or Welsh national issues.[19] The 1978/9 Devolution Referendum campaign was surely a period when editors of local papers could have shown their mettle. Yet, most of the papers did little more than report local campaign meetings and publish readers' letters;[20] virtually none provided the kind of background information necessary for a reasoned interpretation of this news and opinion. For example one of the rare articles on the issue in the *Pontypridd Observer* was written by a person who had changed from an intention to vote 'Yes' to an intention to vote 'No' and therefore naturally emphasised the latter perspective. The neighbouring *Merthyr Express* contained a neutral pre-Referendum editorial which referred to the 'quality of the letters' it had received on the issue; while these had been the usual cross-section, they hardly added up to an overall debate. This paper, like most of its rivals, did little to provide its readers with a balanced assessment of these letters and reports; indeed, in an article published in the issue of 1st February 1979 purporting to provide background information, it maintained 'if you vote 'No' it doesn't necessarily mean that you disagree with devolution—simply that the present plan for an assembly is a born loser and that Welsh people deserve a better way of running their affairs'. However, this was sophistication itself compared with the pre-Referendum leading article in the (weekend) *Wrexham Leader* which ended by offering 'two fingers' to the proposals!

In contrast the editors of the Welsh language national weeklies *Y Cymro* and *Y Faner* have continued to report matters of Welsh significance. Whilst *Y Faner* is a paper offering serious comment on social, cultural and political issues as they affect Wales and with little in the way of current news reportage, *Y Cymro* is a paper popular in style which covers news from all localities of Wales (although mainly from the north) and national issues, as well as containing a broad mixture of features—from religion and gardening to sport and pop music. Both newspapers appear to operate on the assumption that their readership shares and subscribes in conscious manner to a sense of national identity.

In contrast the English language newspapers of Wales tend to see the country as a series of counter cultures and competing sub-regions,[21] thus militating against the presentation of issues in national form. Whilst the circulation of the Welsh language national papers is tiny,[22] they often have a much wider influence. Many of Wales's most influential figures contribute to the columns of

Y Faner and in particular it often acts as an area of refinement of issues, aspects of which subsequently feature in discussions in other arenas from parliament to broadcasting. However, neither of these papers can give adequate immediate coverage to events outside Wales. *Y Faner* relies almost exclusively on contributed articles, *Y Cymro* has but a tiny staff. Thus foreign news in particular finds little place in the Welsh language press.[23]

The English language dailies had their origins in the latter part of the nineteenth century. Neither morning paper, the *Western Mail* (Cardiff) and the *Liverpool Daily Post* (Welsh edition), with their restricted circulations outside the south and north respectively,[24] can be considered as truly national. The four evening papers have their circulations in Cardiff, Swansea, Newport and Wrexham and their hinterlands respectively. Whatever differences exist in their history, these morning and evening dailies—apart from the *Western Mail*—have rarely sought to develop a systematic reporting of issues of Welsh national significance. As Figure 23 shows, the evening newspapers concentrate almost exclusively on news which originates in, or has an immediate effect on, their own circulation areas; news from outside these areas is often presented directly in the form in which it was obtained from agencies. Where reporting of Welsh issues exists it is often tinged with a vocabulary of polarisation: whilst terms such as 'industrial' and 'rural Wales', 'Welsh' and 'English', 'north' and 'south', 'core' and 'periphery', are sometimes useful simplifying devices, behind them there exists a much more complex and multi-faceted reality. The relative lack of political sophistication, and associated inability to explain or develop Wales-wide issues is again exemplified by the treatment of the 1978-9 Devolution Referendum debate, where fairness and systematic reporting was often subordinated to erratic coverage and idiosyncratic editorial or lead article opinion.[25] In contrast, during the devolution debate *Y Faner* and *Y Cymro* were to offer a good level of information by means of news coverage, contributed articles or features, including comparisons with the situation in Scotland, and other European countries which had experienced devolution of powers to their national regions. Whilst further research would be required before one could accurately substantiate the contention that among the weekly and daily press of Wales it is only its Welsh language component that attempts systematically to sustain a relatively high standard of political debate on major national and international issues, certainly there are sufficient observable differences to warrant serious investigation. However a hypothesis that the whole of the Welsh-language press was of this character would have to consider the phenomenon of the *papurau bro*,[26] which rarely consider other than highly localised issues.

In summary we can say that there is little in the English-language press—particularly the weeklies—which offers any support to the idea that Wales is a distinct nation; through emphasis and re-emphasis of local news, local priorities and issues, tendencies toward competitive and localised identity are accelerated. And whatever criteria are used for evaluation, the Welsh language press would appear to be a shadow of its former self. If the latter part of the nineteenth century really was a 'golden age' for Welsh journalism, how is it that its traditions and practices seem virtually to have vanished? Perhaps one should even question the use of the term 'golden age', for it may have the effect of over-emphasizing the extent to which the press was consciously 'Welsh' in its perspective and presentation. Much of the emphasis of Liberalism in Wales was on the achievement of reforms within the United Kingdom political structure; the Welsh press was undoubtedly influenced by the priorities and perspectives of this aspect of the relationship. Thus, as emphasised at the outset of this chapter, one should certainly look for comparisons with the larger social and political processes of change at work in Wales of the late nineteenth and twentieth centuries.

Broadcast media

It was well into the history of broadcasting before Wales—after considerable pressures—achieved any kind of service appropriate to its needs as a nation. In 1937 a Welsh Home Service of BBC radio was established. Broadcasting mainly in English, with around five hours a week in Welsh, its pattern was not to change much until the mid-1960s by which time there was an output of around 25 hours each week. Of the early years of this service it has been said that there was 'an undue emphasis on the more sombre and traditional aspects of Welsh culture, with chapel services at length and seemingly interminable hymn singing'.[27] Although by the 1960s television had become widespread in Wales, combined local services of both BBC and ITV equalled little more than 24 hours of broadcasting per week, with an almost equal split between the two languages. By the mid-1970s there had been little significant change, although slowly and steadily the output of radio had been increasing.

Given such provision there could not be a comprehensive service for Wales in either language; however, from this low level there was to be significant development. In 1977 the combined radio service was split into channels broadcasting in the English and Welsh languages respectively; by 1984 *Radio Wales* was broadcasting approximately 72 hours per week in English and *Radio Cymru* around 80 hours per week in Welsh. In late 1982 there emerged a new pattern whereby English and Welsh television programmes were separated. *S4C* became the fourth television channel in Wales, and from that date carried all the Welsh language output. *BBC Wales* and *Harlech Television* (HTV) carried the English language services—as they did before the change.

The current service pattern with regard to radio is that *Radio Wales* is on the air each weekday from 6.25am to 6.00pm; the pattern for *Radio Cymru* is similar, apart from a close-down between 2.00pm and 5.00pm. The latter's service in the evening dovetails neatly with *S4C*, which normally broadcasts in Welsh from 6.30pm to

8.00pm and again from 9.00pm to 10.00pm. There is a resumption of both radio services most evenings for around one hour at about 10.30pm.[28] Thus, apart from the mid-afternoon there is a continuity of radio or television programmes in the Welsh language from early morning to late night. This is not true of the English-language broadcasts of Wales, with little other than the early evening news on BBC and HTV constituting the 'national' television service. *BBC Wales* and *HTV* together offer a total of 16 hours per week of local programmes in English. News programmes apart, these are often during 'unsocial hours'. Given the small and scattered nature of this output compared to *S4C*'s use of Welsh in peak hours, these two contributions, whether taken individually or together, can hardly be described as a comprehensive national service. As Figure 28 shows,[29] over half of the material presented is news or news headlines, leaving very little time for other areas of interest.

In the nature of the service they offer both *Radio Wales* and *Radio Cymru* may be categorised as being rather like a combination of *Radio Two* and *Radio Four*, with a strong element in both of magazine style programmes that alternate news with popular music and interviews, and chat shows and 'phone-ins. However, for those contributing to *Radio Cymru*—and also to *S4C*—whether as programme presenters, interviewers or interviewed, there is a particular sense of being *Cymry*—sharing a common ethnicity and above all a distinctive language. Particularly in the news programmes of *S4C* and *Radio Cymru* there is no doubt that Wales is presented as a distinct nation, and not simply as a region of the United Kingdom; the very use of Welsh terms such as *Cymry* and *Gwlad* indicates a sense of nationality which can never be conveyed by the use of the equivalent terms 'the Welsh' and 'the country' in services in the English language. The former services may also have contributed to an enhancement of national identity amongst Welsh speakers by offering to them a chance of hearing the varying accents and dialects of their own country. Rather than an exclusive emphasis on a form of 'standard Welsh' the broadcasting authorities have indeed allowed presenters to use their own local forms of speech. This assists the process of comprehension of the various regional forms of Welsh speech.[30]

Similarly, whilst both radio services feature programmes on popular culture in Wales there are a number of aspects which are not immediately understandable to the audience for English programmes, for example from *cynghanedd* and *cyd-adrodd*[31] through to a thriving area of Welsh rock and pop music.[32] Concepts and ideas such as these receive little attention from *Radio Wales*, as a considerable amount of explanation is required to convey them in intelligible form.

Whilst *Radio Wales* and *Radio Cymru* give broadly similar amounts of time to the coverage of news and current affairs *Radio Wales* shares with English language television services in Wales the tendency to adopt the 'adversarial' approach. This is particularly noticeable in the presentation of issues of all-Wales significance, especially those involving the relative status of the two languages. Related current affairs programmes often adopt the structure of staged 'contests', involving little chance of the two sides engaging in analysis or exploration. Indeed, if controversy is not forthcoming the programme presenter will frequently encourage dissent and bipolarity in order to obtain a 'lively' programme. Thus the real or imagined polarisations often receive the most attention, rather than the cultural and regional pluralisms of Wales.

With regard to the coverage of international issues, radio and television services broadcasting in the Welsh language are markedly superior in three respects. Firstly, as Figure 25 shows, the combined total coverage of international news is greater than that on the English language services. Whilst *Radio Wales* and *Radio Cymru* (Figure 27) devote 15 per cent and 17 per cent respectively of their early morning news bulletins to international issues, neither *BBC Wales* or *HTV* (Figure 25) offer any international news coverage comparable with *S4C*'s 12 per cent. Secondly, this international coverage by services in the Welsh language is often linked to events or opinions in Wales. Thirdly, ever since the introduction of *S4C*, *Y Byd ar Bedwar* ('The World on Four') has been a regular programme that examines world events from Welsh perspectives. In addition, there are also programmes and series with similar emphasis such as *Newid Byd* ('Changing World'), *Bobol Bach* ('Minority Peoples'). A glance at the television programme journals will show that the English language radio and television services have scarcely any coverage of this latter nature. Thus, with regard to world events, the Welsh language audience has the better level and standard of provision.

One further area worthy of note is that of broadcasts for the younger generation. Whilst *S4C* broadcasts almost an hour of children's programmes each week-day, there are virtually no special programmes for the English-speaking children of Wales. As Alwyn D. Rees remarked in 1975 'They are treated as if they are already anglicised.'[33]

Patterns of news broadcasting in Wales are illustrated in Figures 25 and 27 below. These tables show details of various early evening television news services before and after the change in service pattern in late 1982, and of the main morning news bulletins for *Radio Wales* and *Radio Cymru*. For comparative purposes Figure 26 also gives information concerning news broadcasts of the BBC Midlands' Region. With regard to television,[34] it is noticeale that before the advent of *S4C* there was virtually no news coverage of international issues. This is still so in the case of the two programmes in the English language but for *S4C* it now forms about 12 per cent of its total coverage. Whatever the language of the service, news originating in other parts of the United Kingdom, or presented as of United Kingdom significance, formerly received much the same coverage. It now occupies a considerably greater part of television services in Welsh (and a significant part of the headlines).

News from the various localities of Wales receives much the same amount of coverage today on the English language television services as before 1982, whilst on *S4C* it has been reduced considerably. However, *Newyddion Saith*'s predecessor *Heddiw* had a much more extended magazine type of format, and local issues and personalities were frequently dealt with in short features; *S4C* now has a number of current affairs, history and popular culture programmes which take on this function. Both services in the English language now appear to give more time to issues of Welsh national significance. Is this perhaps in part owing to an increasing tendency to take issues out of their purely local context and to report them as being of Welsh national significance? More detailed research is needed to clarify the nature of this apparent development—but should this be so it is a small but heartening sign that a more Wales-orientated approach may be building up among production teams.

As figure 25 shows, before the 1982 change in television broadcasting there was a remarkable statistical similarity in the English-language and Welsh medium news services of *HTV*. Indeed, there was also an almost identical presentation style; often the sequence and subject of headlines and reports was virtually identical, location items being shot twice with the same presenter successively making the report first in Welsh, then in English, or the other way around. Studio items were frequently translated quite literally from the original English or Welsh or *vice versa*. However, despite sharing production and studio facilities it is noticeable that the pattern of programmes produced by *Heddiw* and *Wales Today* (BBC) was different (see Figure 25). By the time of its demise *Heddiw* had developed a firm identity and a distinctive approach to the news. The sequence of items was often quite different to that of *Wales Today*, as was the time devoted to particular topics. *Heddiw* did not accept the conventions of British broadcasting uncritically. Rather it often blended them with historically developed Welsh perspectives. This can be illustrated by its reporting and analysis of the build up to and the progress of the south Atlantic war. For example, in the early stages its reports were underlayed with references to historical connections with Wales particularly with regard to the Welsh *Gwladfa.*[35] In the latter part of the campaign increasingly *Heddiw* was to rely on the categories of analysis received from London based reportage, but nevertheless it maintained a distinctive perspective. None of the other Welsh based television news services reflected this style or these concerns to such a remarkable degree.

Heddiw's successor *Newyddion Saith* (both are produced by the BBC) has attempted to develop a Welsh outlook in key areas of United Kingdom and international significance. It maintains a regular parliamentary correspondent located in Westminster, and has access to Eurovision and satellite links. However, it still shares studio and other production facilities and must rely on BBC London-based sources for the majority of its film and reportage from outside Wales. Technical factors put pressure on the Welsh editors to reproduce reports virtually in original form. As received, the verbal and visual elements of such reports are already edited together in order to form a coherent story. Thus it is hard to do other than simply to transmit the visual element of the original and to provide a translation of its soundtrack. To do otherwise could destroy continuity. So, with considerations of urgency and immediacy continually at work, new perspectives are harder to introduce. Thus, during the 1984-5 miners' strike there was the use of categories received from the UK media such as 'picket line violence', 'split communities', 'the working miner',—together with a similar concentration at one stage on the portrayal of the issues as revolving around the personalities and utterances of MacGregor and Scargill. However, there was also use of differing styles of analysis based on categories such as 'defence of communities' in Wales-originated reports. The same pattern could also be observed in the reporting of the English language services, but with a rather greater emphasis—it would seem—on the former UK categories and constructions.

In summary, it would appear that the pattern of television news broadcasting both before and after the 1982 changes is one which appears to be differentiated in style and presentation according to language used. Whilst further research is still required, it would appear from Figure 25 that in terms of proportion the television news services in the Welsh language were providing considerably more coverage of UK and international events than its English language counterparts. Whilst, as Figure 27 indicates, the situation for the two radio services is broadly comparable, this still adds up to an imbalance. Whilst further work is certainly needed to confirm this point, the broadcast media in the Welsh language appear to have a relatively clear identity, linked to a perception of Wales as a spatially defined political, social and cultural entity. This must, though, be qualified by reference to the increasing use of conventions of English journalism in the presentation of British and foreign news. Despite this, it appears that the non Welsh-speaking population are provided with a news and current affairs coverage which is much less conscious of Welsh perspectives, whether in relation to Wales or its place in the world.

Conclusion

Whilst parallel and different structures (differentiated by language) often exist in Welsh cultural, social and political life, we find in reality that people often move between various linguistic domains quite freely, and locate their identity in a plurality of ways. Thus there are other than linguistic bases in the composition of Welsh identity. However the effect of the English language mass media in Wales—particularly the press—seems to be one which does not advance the idea that the country is in reality a nation based as much on its similarities as its differences.

Future research could usefully examine the extent—and significance—of vocabularies of polarization used in the Welsh media, particularly with regard to the use of concepts emphasizing linguistic division. The data presented in this chapter clearly need to be supplemented before firm conclusions may be drawn in relation to this aspect. However, in relation to international issues less qualification is necessary. The small amount of foreign coverage by the English language media (Figures 23, 25, 27 and 28) gives little opportunity for English-speaking Welsh people to develop an image of Wales as a distinct territory in a multi-cultural Europe—something which the Welsh language media (Figures 23, 25 and 27) appear to do better at least in terms of proportion of news coverage. Neither the evening nor the weekly newspapers in English carry any serious and sustained reference to the role of Wales in the world (Figure 23) and certainly do not offer other than occasional or peripheral glances at the Celtic heritage. The English language broadcast media of Wales have but few explanatory items which place Wales in a larger European or global context; English language television in particular has pitifully few hours to do so (Figure 28).

Overall the English language media in Wales seem heavily to rely on localisation of issues (Figures 23, 25 and 27); whilst this feature is also present in the Welsh language media (Figures 23, 25 and 27), the impact there is lessened by the presence of international coverage, and possibly by the sense of national identity referred to and enhanced by the use of the Welsh language. Nevertheless, even the former factor must be qualified by the extent to which *Newyddion Saith* has to rely on non-Wales originated material for its foreign reports.

Whilst it is natural that small circulation weekly papers (including the *papurau bro*) should cover local issues and personalities almost to the exclusion of other topics, it has been argued that these media could make a much greater contribution to an understanding of Wales and the world.[36] A basic problem relating to this and other areas is that whilst many excellent journalists are at work, their total number is very small. The virtual monopoly of a small group in news and current affairs presentation in all media has a predictable effect on style, presentation, and content of articles and programmes. In addition, the radio and television services in Welsh in particular use only a small number of expert contacts in these areas—this serves to exacerbate the previously-mentioned tendencies. And however much broadcasters and writers seek to formulate and develop distinctive vocabularies and other features of presentation that reflect the uniquenesses of Wales, these are constantly seen against a background of comparison with other British media—with a dominant bases of the comparison being criteria of professionalism developed outside Wales.

In a comparative view of the media in Britain Jeremy Tunstall concludes that 'The Welsh media are much less Welsh than the Scottish media are Scottish.'[37] He adds that Wales in some respects is the opposite of Scotland, with an extremely Anglicised press in English, but with 'a uniquely rich set of regional offerings'[38] in radio and television. Whilst agreeing with the former contention it must be pointed out that in the broadcast media the richness appears mainly to be confined to the Welsh language sector. Both *Radio Cymru* and *S4C* are relatively sure of their identity, and when considered together offer a firmly-based national service to Wales. However, neither in terms of structure or content of broadcasting can the combined English language services of *Radio Wales, HTV* and *BBC* be so considered. The comparison of news coverage in the English and Welsh sectors of the media as a whole is evidence that the English language media in Wales urgently requires the provision of a background understanding that could be developed by a system including a television channel dedicated to the needs and characteristics of English-speaking Welsh people. At the moment the broadcast media in English, like the English press in Wales, present a picture of their territory through vocabularies and procedures of compilation and presentation which are very little different to those put forward by their media colleagues based in Birmingham, Bristol, or Manchester.

References

1 A good general introduction to the media in Britain as a whole is Tunstall, J. (1983), '*The media in Britain*', London, Constable. For an outline history of the modern Press in Wales see the treatment by Lloyd, D. Tecwyn (1979), 'The Welsh language in journalism' in Stephens, M. (ed), *The Welsh language today*, Llandysul, Gomer Press, and his 1980 *BBC Cymru* Annual Lecture, *Gysfenu i'r wasg gynt*—Lloyd, D. Tecwyn (1980) Llundain (London), *Y Gorfforaeth Ddarlledu Brydeinig* (BBC).

There are notable insights into the role of all the modern mass media in Wales in Morgan, K.O. (1981), *Rebirth of a nation: Wales 1880-1980, the history of Wales, vol. VI*, The Clarendon Press, Oxford, and the University of Wales Press, Cardiff; in Williams, G. A. (1985) *When was Wales? A history of the Welsh*, Black Raven Press, London, and Penguin Books, Harmondsworth; in Humphreys, E. (1983) *The Taliesin Tradition: a quest for Welsh identity*, London, Black Raven Press, and from Butt Philip, A. (1975) *The Welsh question—nationalism in Welsh politics 1945-1970*, Cardiff, University of Wales Press.

An interesting chapter by St. Leger, F. Y. (1979) 'The mass media and minority cultures', in Alcock, A. E., Taylor, B. K. and Welton, J. M. *The future of cultural minorities*, Basingstoke and London, MacMillan, explores the range of policies available to governments concerned with encouragement of diversity in multicultural societies.

2 Morgan, K. O., 49.

3 Lloyd, D. Tecwyn (1979), 155.

4 Morgan, K. O., 49-51;

5 *Ibid.*

6 *Ibid.*

7 *Ibid.*

8 *Ibid.*

9 *Ibid.*

10 Lloyd, D. T. (1979), 156.

11 *Ibid.*

12 *Ibid.*

13 For example, work shortly to be published by Dr. Cyril Parry of the University College of North Wales, Bangor, will offer evidence which could cast doubt on a number of key contentions of D. Tecwyn Lloyd. I am grateful to Dr. Parry for advance notice of some of his findings.

14 Richards, P. and John, L. (1981) 'Who owns the local rag?' in *Arcade: Wales fortnightly* 21, find 46 English language weeklies currently published. This figure excludes a number of other weeklies which are very similar to their 'parent' paper.

15 See Figure 22. The features mentioned in this paragraph and notes in the appropriate Figures are, of course, also found in the weekly press in England.

16 Lloyd D. Tecwyn (1979) 161-2 gives examples.

17 See Figure 22.

18 Several years of reading the English-language weeklies confirms this; for example, meetings of bodies such as *Merched y Wawr* (a breakaway movement from the Women's Institute), *Mudiad Ysgolion Meithrin* (Welsh Nursery Schools Movement) and proceedings of local eisteddfodau are normally reported in English, and rarely in Welsh.

19 See Figure 23.

20 Hume, I. (1981) 'The Welsh Experience', in Bochel, J., Denver, D. and Macartney, A. *The referendum experience: Scotland 1979*, Aberdeen, University Press, 153-168, provides this evidence and the examples that follow.

21 This is particularly apparent by the way in which they often present the interests of north and south, Welsh speaker and non-Welsh speaker as inevitably conflicting. Again see Hume, I. (1981), also Osmond, J. (1983) 'The Referendum and the English language press' in Foulkes, D., Jones, J. B. and Wilford, R. A. (eds.), *The Welsh veto: the Wales Act 1978 and the referendum*, Cardiff, University of Wales Press, 153-164.

22 See Figure 24.

23 See Figure 23.

24 Osmond, J., 153, evidences this.

25 Osmond, J., 157-164, and Hume, I. *passim.*

26 Lit. 'area papers'. Circulation of these (normally monthly) papers averages about 1,400 per title. Dating from the early 1970's they are published in the Welsh language, largely by voluntary efforts, and concentrate almost exclusively on local, if not parochial matters. Several short articles by Norman Williams in *Y Casglwr* (The collector) have documented their progress; also Lloyd, D. Tecwyn (1980), *Y Casglwr*, Mawrth 1983, shows 49 *papur bro* in Wales, with a combined circulation of nearly 70,000. If one assumes a readership of three times that sale, then an astonishing proportion (around 52 per cent) of those declaring themselves literate in Welsh at the 1981 census are reached by these papers (Source: Office of Population Censuses and Surveys: *Census 1981—The Welsh language in Wales.* London, H.M.S.O., 1983, 3). Although these papers are largely confined to the Welsh-speaking areas of the north and west, there is a thriving *papur bro* in Cardiff, and several others are published by Welsh communities outside Wales.

The size and nature of circulation areas can be instanced by the following:
Cwlwm—Carmarthen area, circulation 1,800, est. 1978.
Y Bedol—Rhuthun area, circulation 2,150, est. 1977.
Nene—Rhosllanerchrugog, circulation 1,000, est. 1978.
Y Dinesydd—Cardiff, circulation 4,500, est. 1973.

27 Morgan, K. O., 251, reports this opinion.

28 This pattern varies slightly throughout the year.

29 Data refers to *HTV Wales* service.

30 *c.f.* the situation in Brittany, where Breton speakers have virtually no provision for hearing their language in the broadcast media—this does not help a situation where many from one Breton speaking area already have difficulty in understanding those from another.

31 'Rhyming' and 'recitation in unison' respectively.

32 Parenthetically it would be instructive to compare the lyrics of modern English and Welsh language pop music in Wales; even a superficial acquaintance leaves one with the clear impression that references to nation and other aspects of national identity plays a significant part in Welsh language lyrics, but only an insignificant part in those written in English.

33 Rees, Alwyn D. (1975) 'The Welsh language in broadcasting' in Stephens, M. (1979) op. cit.

34 See Figure 25.

35 *Gwladfa*—perhaps best translated as 'colony', it refers to the nineteenth and twentieth century Welsh settlements in Patagonia. A tragic irony of the South Atlantic War of 1982 is that men of Welsh origin and cultural background may have fought each other—descendants of the original Welsh settlers are known to have been in the Argentinian forces which opposed the British forces, the latter partly comprised of units from Wales.
36 In an article published in *Y Faner*, (5 Awst, 1983) Dafydd Elis Thomas sees the *papurau bro* as encouraging localization—even parochialization—of identity, portraying each area as a collection of inner personalities. He concludes that their outlook is often one rooted in a sentimental view of the past and a conservative one of the present and implies that this should not be so.
37 Tunstall, J. *op. cit.* 228.
38 *Ibid.*

Figure 22: Newspapers of Wales, contents analysis (column inches)

	Column inches		
	English Language		Welsh Language
	Weeklies	Dailies	*Y Cymro*
	per cent	*per cent*	*per cent*
Editorials and other leading articles	4	4	3
News	21	22	44
Sport	7	8	5
Readers' letters	1	1	1
Non-news features	6	4	6
Photographs	4	4	5
Welsh language items	1	*	*
Advertising	56	57	36
	100	100	100

Notes

Data obtained from a representative selection of 25 weekly newspapers; also the *Western Mail, Daily Post, Wrexham Leader, South Wales Echo*. These papers, and *Y Cymro* were surveyed for the months of January 1979 and November 1984.

* *Y Cymro*, apart from a large part of its advertising material, uses exclusively the Welsh language. The dailies use an insignificant proportion of that language.

Figure 23: Categories of new coverage in daily and weekly newspapers and in *Y Cymro* (as a percentage of total news coverage*)

	Evening	Western Mail	Liverpool Daily Post	*Y Cymro*	English language weeklies
	per cent	*per cent*	*per cent*	*per cent*	*per cent*
Local	90	26	23	30	88
Wales national	4	24	9	54	6
UK excluding Wales	5	35	59	8	5
International	1	15	9	8	1
	100	100	100	100	100

Note:
* Survey period as in Table 22 above; sport and non-news features are excluded; the *South Wales Echo* and *Wrexham Leader* are the evening newspapers surveyed; the *Rhondda Leader, Carmarthen Journal, Brecon and Radnor Express, Llandudno Advertiser,* and *Caernarfon and Denbigh Herald* are the English language weeklies.

Figure 24: Welsh newspaper circulations in the 1980s

Western Mail (Cardiff, morning)	94,000
Daily Post (Welsh Edition: Liverpool, morning)	50,000
Wrexham Leader (Mon-Fri., Evening)	35,000
South Wales Echo (Cardiff, Evening)	120,000
Llanelli Star (Weekly)	18,000
North Wales Weekly News (Weekly)	27,000
Y Cymro (Weekly)	8,000
Y Faner (Weekly)	1,800

Figures, which relate to representative years in the early 1980s, are rounded to the nearest 1,000, and are from various sources including *Willings Guide to the Press;* Foulkes, D., Jones, J. B. Wilford, R. A. (1983) *op. cit.*; and *Arcade* 21 (1981) *op. cit.*

Figure 25: News broadcasting in Wales: early evening television news services, 1981/2 and 1984/5. Type of issue as percentage of headlines and as percentage of total programme duration.

1981/2	Welsh language services *Heddiw* (BBC)		*Y Dydd* (HTV)		English language services *Wales Today* (BBC)		*Report Wales* (HTV)	
	Headlines	Total	Headlines	Total	Headlines	Total	Headlines	Total
Wales, localities	52	46	61	58	54	55	58	58
Wales, national	38	42	33	35	41	38	36	34
UK excluding Wales	8	8	5	6	4	5	5	6
International	2	4	1	1	1	2	1	2
	100	100	100	100	100	100	100	100

1984/5	*Newyddion Saith* (S4C)		(BBC)		(HTV)	
	Headlines	Total	Headlines	Total	Headlines	Total
Wales, localities	23	26	38	50	42	55
Wales, national	34	42	52	45	47	40
UK excluding Wales	38	20	10	5	11	5
International	5	12	*	*	*	*
	100	100	100	100	100	100

Notes:
Survey period: Monday-Friday evenings for the months of November 1981, September and December 1982, and April and May 1984, September 1985; sport is excluded from the analysis (no significant differences observed).

* Insignificant coverage

Figure 26: Early evening television news services of BBC Midlands' region.

	per cent
Midlands, localities	62
Midlands, regional	35
UK news, excluding Midlands	3
International	*
	100

Notes:

Survey period: month of June 1984; sport is excluded from the analysis.

* Insignificant coverage.

Figure 27: News broadcasting in Wales, early morning main news bulletins, 1985. Type of issue as percentage of headlines and as percentage of bulletin duration.*

	Radio Cymru		*Radio Wales*	
	Headlines	Total	Headlines	Total
Wales, localities	8	20	14	25
Wales, national	25	39	40	37
UK excluding Wales	40	24	31	23
International	27	17	15	15
	100	100	100	100

* Survey period, 1st July 1985-5th July, 1985, 30th September 1985-4th October, 1985; sport is excluded from the analysis (no significant differences observed).

Figure 28: HTV Wales: Hours of service in English*

Category	*Hours*
News	187
Current Affairs	25
Headlines	36
Farming	10
Adult Education	3
Schools	7
Childrens	NIL
Light Entertainment	35
Drama	NIL
Documentary	30
Sport	12
Religion	9
Weather	6
Total transmission of locally originated programmes	360

* Source: communication from HTV, dated 16.8.85.
Data are for 1984.

INDEX

A
Abbot of Aberconwy, 76
Aberdare, 5
Aberdaron, 105, 106
Abergavenny, 46
Abergwili, 45
Aberhafesb, 40
Aberporth, 111-14, 124-29
Aberystwyth, 6, 54, 76, 94, 104, 154, 174, 176
 school, 178, 179
Abraham, William (Mabon), 146
absolute numbers (Welsh speakers), 13
acculturation, 58, 167, 292-93
activity rates, 166
Acts of Union, 1536 and 1542, 75, 274
Adfeilion by Alwyn D. Rees, 103
Adfer, xxiv, 210, 234-43, 315-16
administration, 273-90
Aeron—R., 67
Afon Menai (Menai Straits), 7
age structures (Welsh population), 24
agents of anglicisation, 53
Agrarian Revolution, 142
Agricultural, community in south-west Wales by D. Jenkins, 124-29
agricultural labour, 100, 126, 127-28
Agricultural Labourer—Royal Commission on the, 92
Agricultural Show—Royal Welsh, 98
agriculture, 80, 125-26, 185
Aitchison, Dr. J. W., 7, 11, 13, 18
Alcock, A. E., 263
Alliance, SDP-Liberal, 311, 312
Alun—R., 66
America—North, 34
Amman Valley, 9
Andaman Islands, 95
Anglesey (Ynys Môn), 7, 12, 13, 14, 16, 17, 27, 30, 52, 54, 55, 59, 67, 74, 79, 82
Anglican Church, 53
 services (language), 36 *et. seq.*
Anglican clergy, 36, 43, 135
Anglicans, 141, 143
anglicising agent, 53
Anglo-Americanisation, 121
Anglo-Norman, 78, 80, 82, 83
Anglo-Saxons, 68, 171
Anglo-Welsh, 159
anthropologists—social, 179
anthropology, 129, 177
 historical, 125
 social, 121
anti-English feeling, 123
anti-urban, 156
Archbishop of Wales, 76
Arenig Mts., 66, 72
Arensberg, C. M., 94, 96, 116, 154
Arfon, 7, 16, 67
Arfon District Council, 256
arable cultivation, 68
Atlantic features, 68
attitudes to Welsh, 24

B
bagpipe playing, 110
Bala, 40, 82
Balkans, 154
Balsom, D., 293, 312
Banbury, 107
Bangor, 6, 76
Baptists, 82
Baptist Union, 76
Barn, xix, 104, 160
Barnes, Prof. J. A., 115, 116
Barnet, 107
Barth, Frederik, 223, 225
Barth, Karl, 242
Basque Country, 202, 206,
Battle of Chester, 68
B.B.C. Wales, 332-38
Bedwas, Gwent, 41
Beddgelert, 7
benefit clubs, 145
Bersham, Clwyd, 83
Berwyn Mts., 72, 108
Bethel, nr. Caernarfon, 140
Betts, Clive, 259, 265
Betws, (Newport, Gwent), 41
Betws Cedewain, Powys, 40
Betws Diserth, Powys, 46

bilingual districts, 265-70
    road signs, 160
    schools, 17
    zones, 43-45, 47, 51-52, 56
    Welshmen, 28, 29
bilingualism, 45, 47, 245
bishops, 36
Bishop of St. David's, 45
Blaenau Morgannwg, 71
Blue Books, 1847, 143, 144, 145
Blygain Fawr, Y, 99
'bobol bach', 335
'bois y pop' ('the pop boys'), 111
bond villages, 69
bonedd, 140
Border, The, 75
borderline, 27
Borderland, 16, 17, 23, 24, 27, 39, 48, 56, 75
borough towns, 44
Bosherston, Dyfed, 50
Bosworth, 75
Boughrood, Powys, 44, 50
boundary changes, 4
    ethnic, 168
Bowen, Prof. E. G., 35, 52, 56, 57, 325
Bradney, Sir J., 46
Brady, Prof. A., 236
branch establishments/plants, 165, 187
Brecon, 26, 41, 78, 80, 81, 82
Brecon and Radnor Express, 344
Brecon and Radnor Parliamentary Constituency, 306, 311
Brecon Beacons, 66
Brecknock, 16
Brecknockshire—*see also* Breconshire, 16, 41, 44, 50, 51, 52, 59, 80
Breconshire—*see also* Brecknockshire, 12, 14, 30, 72, 139
Britain, 68, 75, 153, 164, 167, 171, 180, 183
British, 178
    economy, 183
    Isles, 97
    Legion, 116
    society, 168
British Sociological Association, 176
Brittany, xvi, 201, 334
broadcast media, 331-40
Bro Morgannwg, 67, 71
broadcasting, 86, 331-40
Bryngwyn, Rads., 50
Brynmawr (Brec/Mon), 139
buchedd A/B, 111-14, 122, 124, 125
Builth Wells, 50
burgher mobility, 188
Butt-Philip, A., 160, 292, 297, 302, 324
Byd ar Bedwar, Y, 334-35

C
Cadair Idris, 66, 72
Cadoxton (Neath), Glam., 42
Cadwaladr, 75
Caerffili (Caerphilly), Glam., 52
Caerleon, Gwent, 44
Caernarfon, 6, 26, 27, 42, 79, 140
Caernarfon and Denbigh Herald, 344
Caernarfon Parliamentary Constituency, 311
Caernarfonshire, 12, 14, 30, 31, 52, 54, 59, 67, 105, 164
Caerphilly, *see* Caerffili
Caerphilly Parliamentary Constituency, 302
Calvinism, 82
Calvinistic Methodists, 76
Cambrian Mts., 9
Campaign for Nuclear Disarmament (CND), 313
Canberra, Aust., 75
Canterbury, 74, 76
Capel Curig, 7
capital, 187
Cardiff, 7, 11, 17, 18, 23, 42, 44, 49, 76, 77
Cardigan, 79
Cardigan Bay, 58
Cardiganshire, 12, 14, 27, 30, 42, 52, 53, 55, 59, 72, 107, 108, 111, 125
Carmarthen, 6, 26, 72, 82
Carmarthen Bay, 83
Carmarthen Journal, 344
Carmarthenshire, 12, 13, 14, 27, 30, 31, 45, 59, 72, 80, 82
Carter, Prof. H., 7, 11, 13, 18, 52, 57, 312
Carter, I., 92
cartographic techniques, 47
Cartref Bychan, Carms., 80
Cartref Mawr, Carms., 79-80
Cascob, Powys, 50
Castell Caereinion, Powys, 44

castle—Norman, 138
towns, 42
castles, 80
Catalonia, 202, 205, 206
catechism, 41
Cefnllys, Powys, 50
Celtic, 134
Church, 69
folklore, 94
languages, 67, 78, 94
studies, 104
Celts, 167, 171
Cemais Comawndwr (Kemeys Commander), Gwent, 46
census, 1801, 35
1891, 35
1981, 2
religious, 1851, 143
reports, 26
Central Advisory Council for Education in Wales, 32, 33
central Wales *see also* Mid Wales, 6, 15, 31, 49, 66, 78
centrifugal forces, 70
centripetal forces, 70
Ceredigion, 16
Ceredigion and Pembroke North Parliamentary Constituency, 294, 311
chancery towns, 27
change—ethnic, 217-31
Channel Four—Wales (S4C) (Television), 315, 325, 332-38
chapel(s), 106, 108, 109, 110, 113, 117, 121, 122, 123, 124, 143, 144, 145, 154, 189
deacons, 112
dominated society, 121, 123
goers, 111
'Chapel Romanticism', 138
charity school, 36
cheap labour, 187
Chester, 78
Battle of, 68
Chirk, Clwyd, 83
Christian values, 113
Christianity, 138
church, 117, 118
Church—Anglican, 53
Celtic, 69
Established, 53
in Wales, 277
Circulating Schools (Griffith Jones), 138
class, 155, 156, 157, 159, 162, 168, 169, 179, 180, 189, 190, 217-31, 296
class differences, 114
divisions, 111, 116
land owning, 102
lower, 135
middle, 134, 141, 145, 146
structure, 92
working, 135, 146
Cleddau Ddu—R., 67
Cleddau Wen—R., 67
Clergy—Anglican, 36, 43, 135
Clews, Roy, 315
cluster analysis, 19-20, 22
Clwyd, 73
County Council, 294
Clwydian Range, 72
Clwyd—R., 66
Vale of, 6, 15, 67
Clyro, Rads., 50
coal, 164, 165, 185
Coalbrookdale, Shrops., 83
coalfield—Glamorgan, 49, 52
north Wales, 83
south Wales, 83, 84, 93, 164
coalfields—Welsh, 83
coal mines, 84
owners, 85
Cogan, Glam., 44
Colony—Internal, 3, 166-70
Colwyn Bay, 6
Commission on the Constitution, 282
common folk, 134, 135
community, -ies, 4, 19, 21, 23, 43, 56, 91, 158, 179
definitions, 91
urban, 102
rural, 91-133
studies, 91-133, 154, 160, 173, 178, 180
village, 118
Communities in Britain by R. Frankenberg, 102
Comte, Auguste, 235
conflict, 115, 117, 118, 119, 122, 159
Conservative Party, 289, 293, 298-99, 306-7
'contributionism', 297
Conwy—R., 6, 7, 42, 66, 73, 74
Vale of, 53

co-operation—in farming, 127-28
mutual, 123
Cornwall, 68
corporations—multi-national, 183
Corsica, 201
Corwen, 40
cottagers, 126, 127-28
Council for Wales and the Marches, 75
Council for the Welsh Language, 1978, 17
Countryside—Life in a Welsh, by Alwyn D. Rees, 94-104
County Clare, Irel., 94, 95
county schools, 140
courts (of law), 257-59
counter urbanisation, 16
Cowbridge, Glam., 42, 44
crafts, 69
craftsman,-men, 69, 108
Cross, Prof. J., 283
Crwys—*see* Williams, Crwys,
cultivation—arable, 68
cultural changes, 141
differentiation, 171
division of labour, 167, 168, 169, 170, 181, 187
factors, 170-71
geography, 35, 154
idiom, 116
invasion, 51
nationalists, 135, 156
pluralism, 53, 60
relativism, 180
Revolution, 316
values, 33
culture, 1, 6, 31-63, 67-68, 69, 70, 85, 86, 87, 97, 102, 115, 141, 142, 144, 145, 146, 155, 157, 167, 170, 178, 180
area, 60
definitions, 31-63
material, 97, 105
non-material, 105
religious, 142
rural, 102, 154
surrogate, 33
culture symbols, 58
transition, 43
urban, 157
village, 102
culture region, 26-63, 325
Mormon, 56
cultures, 77
culturalist explanation, 187-88
Cumbria, 68
Custom and conflict in Africa by Max Gluckman, 115
Cwyn yn erbyn gorthrymder by T. Roberts, 135
cyd-adrodd, 334
Cydweli, Dyfed, 44
Cyfraith Newydd Hywel, 240
cymdeithasfa, 76
Cymdeithas yr Iaith Gymraeg (see, also, Welsh Language Society), 17, 160, 300, 302-305, 312-13
Cymmrodorion—Honourable Society of, 26
Cymro, 70
Cymro, Y, 329-30
Cymru ddi-Gymraeg, 56
Cymru Fydd by O. M. Edwards, 137, 144, 146, 279
Cymru Gymraeg (see, also, Welsh Wales), 56, 57, 159
Cymry, 68
cynghanedd, 334
Czechs, 136

D

daily newspapers in Wales, 86, 324-40
Darby, Abraham, 83
Darwin, Charles, 65
Davis, J., 301
Davies, Elwyn, 104
Davies, S. O. (MP), 294
Day, Graham, 114, 300, 325
deacons—chapel, 112
debating society, 113
Dee—R., 67, 72
Deeside, Clwyd, 159
definitions of community, 91
Deheubarth, 71-72
de-industrialisation, 173
demographic trends, 29
Denbigh, 6, 26, 79
Denbighshire, 12, 13, 14, 30, 39, 59, 67-68, 83, 114
Deorham, Gloucs., 68
dependence theory, 161, 163, 166

deprivation—relative, 169, 183
Derfel, R. J., 136, 144
determinism—economic, 167
development—economic, 172
regional, 170, 172
social, 172
uneven, 183, 184
devolution, 153, 273-90, 293-95, 318
Devolution Referendum, xix
differentiation—cultural, 171
regional, 171
diffusion, 217-21, 292
diffusionist model, 167
Dinas, Pembs., 55
Dinefwr, 6
Diocese of St. Asaph, 36, 37
dis-establishment of the Church, 76, 277, 278
dispersed settlements, 97, 102
Dissenters, 53, 141, 143
Dissent—Older, 142
division of labour—cultural, 167, 168, 169, 170, 181, 187, 225, 227
Dolgellau, 75
Dowlais, 83
drovers, 108
Dwyfach—R., 67
Dwyfor, 7, 16
Dwyfor District Council, 256
Dwyfor—R., 67
Dyfed, 6, 9, 14, 52, 58
County Council, 294
Dyfi—R., 8, 9, 67, 72
Dyfrdwy—R., 66
Dysynni—R., 67

E
English academics, 185
Crown, 72
intelligentsia, 122
language, 146
markets, 164
middle class, 145
monoglots, 43, 48
Service in Wales Act, 1863, 36
speakers, 117, 121, 122
speaking territories, 45-47, 49-51
villages, 98
zone, 49-51
English villages of the 13th century by G. C. Homans, 94
Englishmen, 144
Englishry, -ies, 27, 45, 78, 122,
Eryri, 66
Er mwyn Cymru by O. M. Edwards, 139
E.S.R.C., 185
Established Church, 53, 80
ethnic, ethnicity, 34, 180
boundaries, 130, 159, 168, 177, 181, 182, 190
change, 217-31
identity, 217-31
nationalism, 180
European Economic Community (EEC), 310
Evans, Prof. E. Estyn, 97
George Ewart, 129
Gwynfor, 302
evening papers in Wales, 86, 324-40
Ebwy—R., 67
Economic and Social Studies Research Council, 177
economic determinism, 167
development, 172
investment, 184
structure, 153
economism, 172
economy, 288-89, 298
British, 183
education, 112, 146, 189, 276
Welsh medium, 254, 255, 265, 306
Education Act, 1870, 258
Education—Central Advisory Council for, in Wales, 32, 33
Edwards, O. M., 135, 136, 137, 139, 140, 146
Eglwysilan, Glam., 52
eisteddfod, -au, 69, 144
local, 113
Eisteddfod—National, 98, 136, 209, 306-307
elections—local, 108
electronics industry, 185
elites, 159
emigration, 164
Emmett, I., 96, 120-24
employment, 185
eneidfaeth, 234-43
England, xvi, 45, 70, 83, 84, 99, 102, 103, 107, 124, 142, 169, 170, 176, 178, 182

south east, 165
Midland, 165
English, 3, 10, 29, 33, 37, 38, 39, 40, 41, 42, 44, 45-47, 49-51, 53, 54, 55, 75, 77, 80, 82, 107, 122, 123, 124, 142, 145, 154, 159, 169, 185

F
factories—branch, 165
false consciousness, 179, 180
family farming, 100-101
organisation, 130
solidarity, 99
Faner, Y, 329-30
farm building type, 97
servants, 100, 127
size, 126
farmers, 127-28
Farmers' Union of Wales, 308
farming, 125-26, 165
co-operation, 127-28
family, 100-101
interdependence, 126-27
Febvre, Lucien, 66, 87
female employment, 185
feminist movement, 180
Fitton, Martin, 114
Fitzhanon, 71, 78
Flint, 6, 79
Flintshire, 12, 13, 14, 30, 53, 59, 83
folk dancing, 110
folk-life studies, 129
folk lore, 94
football, 119
Ford, Prof. C. Daryll, 94, 176
foreign, foreigners, 78, 82
forest, 68
Foulkes, D., 293, 329
Fourth TV Channel, Wales (S4C) 17
Frank, A. G., 161, 169, 218
Frankenberg, R., 102, 114-20, 124, 176
free markets, 168
French regional geographers, 35
social science, 180
Friesland, 202
Fro Gymraeg, Y, 56, 59, 155, 234-70
functionalism—structural, 188, 191
future for Welsh, 11, 58-59
Fyrnwy—R., 66

G
Galicia, 201
Gaul, 68
Geertz, Clifford, 223
Gellner, Ernest, 223, 225
gender, 188, 190
Genedl Gymreig, Y, 327
Geneva, 142
gentry, 40, 46, 54, 55, 113, 125, 141, 156
geographers—French regional, 35
Geographical introduction to history, A, by Lucien Febvre, 66
geographical location, 60
mobility, 170
geography, xiv, 105, 174, 177
cultural, 35, 154
human, 129
social, 107
of Wales, 64-87
Giraldus Cambrensis, 99
Gladstone, 136
Glamorgan, 71, 78, 83, 141
coalfield, 49, 52
Mid, 5, 16, 23
West, 6, 9, 23
Vale of, 16, 43, 71, 93
Glamorganshire, 12, 13, 14, 27, 29, 41, 42, 44, 49, 50, 59, 80
Glan-llyn, Merions. 108-11
Glaslyn—R., 67
Glazer, N, 261-62
Gloucester, 78
Gloucestershire, 68
Gluckman, Prof. Max, 115, 118, 176
Glyn Ceiriog, Denbs., 114, 124
Glyn Dŵr, 74-75, 76
Glyndŵr District Council, 256
Glywysing, 71
Goebbels, J., 237
gossip, 118, 123, 124, 129
government—local, 26
Gower, 27, 43, 45, 51, 72, 78, 82
Peninsula, 67
Graig-parc, Swansea, 136
grammar schools, 80
Great Ormes Head, 53
Greeks, 64
Greenham Common, 313
Griffiths, James, 280-82, 285

groups—ethnic, 34
social, 33
growth pole, 184
Gruffydd, Rhys ap, 72
Gruffydd, Prof. W. J., 135, 139, 140
Guest, John, 83
Guilsfield, Montg., 49
Gwaun—R., 9, 67
Gwendraeth Fach, 67
Fawr, 67
Gwent, 16, 23, 43, 46, 50, 78
gwerin, 134-5, 156, 297, 317
Gwerin Cymru by Crwys Williams, 137
gwerinos, 134, 135
gwerin-bobl, 135
Gwilym Hiraethog, 136
Gwlad Morgan, 71
Gwladfa, 336
Gwynedd, 58, 72, 74, 186, 187
County Council, 256, 294
Gymraeg, Cymru (*see also* Welsh Wales), 56, 57

H
Hardie, Keir, 84
Harlech Dome, 66, 72
Harlech Television, 332-38
harvest labour, 93
health service, 287
Heartland, (see also *Cymru Gymraeg* and Welsh Wales), 7, 16, 21, 23, 41, 51, 56
heavy industries, 185
Hebrides, 110, 111
Hechter, Prof. Michael, 161, 166, 169, 170, 172, 177, 180, 181-2, 199, 200, 204, 300, 317
Heddiw, 335-38
Henry VII, King, 75
Hereford, 78
Herefordshire, 82
Herodotus, 64
Heylyn, Peter, 64
hierarchy—social, 113, 121
Hillery, G., 91
hill forts, 68, 69
Hiraethog lowlands, 66
moorlands, 72
historians, xv, 171, 172
Welsh, 136, 172
Histoire de France by Jules Michelet 64
historical anthropology, 125
Historical geography of the Holy Land by Sir George A. Smith, 65
historical records, 98
history, xiv, 64-87, 102, 157, 163, 184
oral, 129
political, 273-90
Welsh, 35
Hobsbawm, Eric, 201
holiday resorts, 51
Holyhead, 6, 7
Homans, G. C., 94
homes—second, 16
Honourable Society of Cymmrodorion, 26
hosiery trade, 108
house types, 97
Hughes, Cledwyn (Lord), 297
Hughes, Prof. T. Jones, 105, 106-107,
Hughes Parry, Sir David, 258
human geography, 129
Humboldt, Alexander von, 65
Humphreys, Emyr, 317
Hywel Dda, 240

I
iaith, 69
ideology, 182
Ieuan Gwynedd (Evan Jones), 136
illegitimacy, 99, 121, 123
improvement societies, 145
income levels, 166
increase in population, 84
independent Wales, 75
Independents, 80, 82, 143
industrial, 146
areas, 10, 29, 157, 165
development, 141
location, 184
towns, 107
Wales, 107, 146, 153, 177
Industrial Revolution, 51, 59, 77, 83, 84, 142
industrialisation, 26, 31, 35, 38, 44, 45, 47, 92, 103, 141, 164, 169, 173
industrialized environments, 10
industry, 154
electronics, 185
heavy, 185

metallurgical, 38
mining, 38
inequalities—regional 183
in-migrants, in-migration, 16, 93, 124, 164, 189
Inner Wales, 35, 51, 52, 53, 55, 56, 58-59, 77, 78, 80, 82, 83, 85, 86, 155
innovation—technological, 129
integration—national, 168
intelligentsia—English, 122
interdependence—farming, 126-27
interest groups, 307-18
internal colony, 3, 166-70, 172, 177
colonialism, 217-31
Internal colonialism by M. Hechter, 166-70, 172, 199, 300, 325
interpellation, 180, 190, 191
institutionalized culture movement, 277, 301, 307
investment—economic, 184
Iolo Morganwg, 142
Ireland, 72, 84, 107, 164, 185
Irish, 47, 84, 116, 146
famine, 84
life, 70
studies, 95
Irish Countryman, The, by C. M. Arensberg, 94, 116
iron, 164
Iron Age B, 68
settlers, 67, 68
iron industry, 84
masters, 85
Isle of Anglesey *see* Anglesey

J
Jenkins, Dafydd, 92, 111-14, 122, 124-29, 176
Jeremiah—Lamentations of, 244
Jesus College, Oxford, 93
Jones, Sir D. Brynmor, 93, 139
Jones, Edward (folklorist), 142
Prof. Emrys, 33, 107-108, 176
Evan (Ieuan Gwynedd), 136
Griffith, 138
Prof. Ieuan G., 145
J. B., 293, 329
Prof. J. Morris, 135, 137
Rev. Michael D. (Bala), 136
William (Llangadfan), 141-42

K
Kemeys Commander *see* Cemais Comawndwr, 46
Kent, 107
Kidwelly *see* Cydweli
Kimball, S. T., 94, 154
King Henry VII, 75
King Offa, 68
kinship, 112
Kluckhohn, C., 31
Kohr, Leopold, 197-98
Kroeber, A. L., 31

L
labour—agricultural, 100, 126, 127-28
cheap, 187
cultural division of, 167, 168, 169, 170
harvest, 93
unskilled, 108, 126
Labour Party, 289, 292-315
Land in Wales—Royal Commission 1894-96, 93
Land of Morgan, 71
land—owning class, 102
gentry, 113
land tenure, 93
Landsker—Pembrokeshire, 14, 43, 49
language, xvi, 33, 36, 69, 102, 104, 124, 130, 137, 141, 143, 144, 154, 158, 159, 160, 177, 188, 189
areas, 1961-81, 1-25, 33
change 1961-81, 1-25
divide, 40, 57
front, 58
indicator of culture, 1, 31-63
planning, 253-70
policies, 58-59
sociology of, 189
stadials, 47
statistics (mapping of), 2-5
zones, c1750, 38
zones, 1900, 48
Language Society—Welsh (see also *Cymdeithas yr Iaith Gymraeg*), 17, 160, 300, 302-5, 312-13
languages—Anglican church services, 36 et. seq.,
Celtic, 78
law—Medieval Welsh, 99, 101
lead—mines, 164

Leckwith (Lecwith), Glam., 44
Lee, Rowland, 75
Leipzig, 65
Le Pays de Galles by E. G. Bowen, 35
Leri—R., 67
Lewis, Oscar, 179
Lewis Saunders, 206, 209, 213, 240, 318
Liberal Party, 305-306, 311-12, 326-29, 331
'Lib-Labbism', 146
Life in a Welsh countryside by Alwyn D. Rees, 94-104, 128
life styles—rural, 16
urban, 16
linguistic division, 338
minority, 171
pluralism, 53
literacy levels—Welsh, 3, 9, 10, 11, 21, 24
literary tradition, 154
Liverpool Daily Post, 330
'Llan', 96, 107, 120, 122
Llanaelhaearn, Caerns., 7
Llanbedr-y-cennin, Caerns.,53
Llanblethian, Glam., 44
Llanbryn-mair, Montg., 80
Llandaf, 76
Llandeilo, Carms., 45
Llandough, Glam., 44
Llandrindod Wells, 46, 50
Llandudno, 6, 53
Llandudno Advertiser, 344
Llandybie, Carms., 45
Llandygai, Caerns., 54
Llandysilio, Angl., 54
Llandysilio-yn-Iâl, Denb., 54
Llanelli, 5, 6
Llanelli Star, 344
Llanerfyl, Mont., 55
Llanfaches, Angl., 80
Llanfair Caereinion, Montg., 36-38, 44
Llanfair Pwllgwyngyll, Angl., 54
Llanfrothen, Mers., 120, 122, 124
Llanfihangel-yng-Ngwynfa, Montg., 95-103, 105, 108, 125
Llanfyllin, Montg. 43, 80-81
Llangors, Brecs., 51
Llangattock *see* Llangatwg
Llangatwg Dyffryn Wysg (Llangattock nigh Usk), 51
Llangeitho, Cards., 82
Llangollen—Vale of, 54
Llangorwen, Cards., 54
Llangwyllog, Angl., 7
Llangynog, Montg., 40
Llanllwchhaearn, Montg., 40
Llanofer, Mon., 46
Llanover *see* Llanofer
Llanrhaeadr-ym-Mochnant, Montg., 39
Llanrhidian (Gower), Glam., 51
Llansamlet, (Swansea), Glam., 54
Llantrisant, Glam., 42
Llanuwchllyn, Merions., 9, 109, 140
Llanvetherine *see* Llanwytherin
Llanwytherin, Mon., 46
Llanycil, Merions., 40
Llanywern, Brecs., 52
Lliedi—R., 67
Lloyd, D. Tecwyn, 326-29
Llwchwr—R., 67
Llwydiarth, Angl., 54
Llwynrhudol, 135
Llŷn, 52, 67, 105, 106
Llywarch Hen, 70, 247
Llywel, Brecs., 41
Llywelyn, Emyr, 234-43
Llywelyn Fawr, 74, 78, 82
Llywelyn-Williams, Prof. A., 138
local government, 26
Local Government Act, 285, 286
local radio stations, 86
location—industrial, 184
lock out—Penrhyn, 140
London, 70, 75, 76, 108, 164
London School of Economics, 120
London Welshmen, 108
Loughor, (*see also Llwchwr*) Glam., 44
Lord Powis, 40
Lord Rhys, 72
lower classes, 135
Ludlow, 75
Luogh, Co. Clare (Ireland), 95
Lyell (geologist), 65

M
Mabon (William Abraham), 146
Machynlleth, 75
'macro-idea', 33
male employment, 185
Manafon, Montg., 51

Manchester, 115
Mandelbaum, D. G., 1
manorial system, 80
manual workers, 112
Mao Tsetung, 249
mapping techniques, 47
maps of language statistics, 2-5
marginal areas, 165
marginalisation, 184, 191
market forces, 162, 165, 168
  town, 107
markets—English, 164
marriage customs, 99
Marxist, Marxism, xxiv, 179, 181, 182
mass communications, 86
material culture, 97, 105
  resources, 69
Mawddach Estuary, 72
Mayo, P. E., 157, 198
media, 189
  mass, 17, 189, 324-40
  Scottish, 340
Media in Britain, The, by J. Tunstall, 340
medieval Wales, 101
Meinig, D. W., 34, 35, 56
Meirionydd, 8, 9, 27, 52
Meirionydd Nant Conwy Parliamentary Constituency, 294, 311
Menai Straits (Afon Menai), 7
Merchant Navy, 113
Merched Y Wawr, 124, 174, 308, 328
Mercia, 68
Merioneth, 67, 75
Merionethshire, 12, 14, 27, 30, 52, 120
metallurgical industries, 38
methodology, 94
Methodism, Methodists, 37, 82, 110, 141, 142,
Methodist Revival, 82, 113, 139
  Calvinistic, 76
  Wesleyan, 106
  'metropolis', 162
metropolitan society, 24
Merthyr Express, 329
Merthyr Tudful (Tydfil), 5, 43, 84, 85
Michelet, Jules, 64
middle classes, 135, 141, 145
Midlands—English, 165
Microcosmos by Peter Heylyn, 64
Mid Glamorgan, 5, 16, 23
  Wales, 158, 164
Middle Ages, 64
migration, 16, 49, 83, 93, 124, 164, 166, 170, 186, 187
migration—in, 189
Miner, Horace, 94
miners, 85
Miners' Strike 1984-5, 313-15, 337
mines—lead, 164
mining industries, 38
  valleys, 157
minority—linguistic, 171
mobility, 188
  burgher, 188
model-culture region, 34, 43, 56-58
  diffusionist, 167
modernisation, 181
Mold, 11, 17, 23
Môn Mam Cymru (Anglesey), 74
Monmouth, 76, 80, 83
Monmouthshire, 12, 14, 27, 29, 30, 41, 44, 45, 50, 59, 80, 139
monoglot—Welsh, 2, 27, 28, 29, 42, 52, 56, 61
  English, 43, 48
Montgomery Parliamentary Constituency, 294, 306, 311
Montgomeryshire, 12, 14, 30, 36, 40, 41, 43, 49, 51, 55, 59, 79, 80
Morgan—Land of (Gwlad), 71
Morgan, Dr. Kenneth O, 146, 292, 293, 297, 326-29
Morgan, Dr. Prys, 114, 297
Morgannwg, 78
Morgan's Land, 71
Mormon culture region, 56
motor car, 85
motorways, 86
Mudiad Ysgolion Meithrin (see also, nursery schools movement), 308
multi-national companies, 183
music, 334
  halls, 146
mutual co-operation, 123
Mynydd Hiraethog, 8

N

Nairn, T., 159, 163, 300-301, 317, 325
nation, 69, 74, 136, 190
  state, xvi
National Eisteddfod, 76-77, 98, 136, 209, 306-307

national feeling, 70, 76
identity, 74
institutions, 74, 98
integration, 168
National Library of Wales, 98
Museum of Wales, 98
national regions, xxiv
nationalism, 159, 195-215, 182, 188, 189
cultural, 135
parties, 153
political, 136
Scottish, 195-215
nationalist(s), 158, 161
resurgence, 157
voters, 189
nationality, 145
natural defences, 72
resources, 164
Neath, 14, 42, 44
Nedd—R., 67, 71
Nefern—R., 67
Newid Byd, 335
Newby, H., 92
Newport, Mon., 41, 43
newspapers, 324-40
Newtown, 40, 81
Newyddion Saith, 335-38
Nicholas, Dr. Thomas, 145
nonconformist(s), 51, 136, 138, 143, 146
bodies, 76
community, 109
values, 113
'nonconformist populism', 145
'nonconformist radicalism', 136
nonconformity, 98, 136, 144, 146, 154
non-material culture, 69, 105
Normans, The, 71-72, 74, 78, 137
Norman, Anglo-, 78, 80, 82, 83
Castle, 138
Conquest, 70
manorial system, 80
manors, 73
North America, 34
north Wales, 6, 15, 17, 45, 96, 120, 122
coalfield, 83
North Wales, parish, A, by I. Emmett, 120-24
North Wales Weekly News, 344
north-east Wales, 17, 18, 24, 26, 29, 38, 43, 48
north-west Wales, 122
nuclear settlements, 69
numbers—absolute (Welsh speakers), 13
relative (Welsh speakers), 6-7
nursery schools movement, 308

O
Occitania, 201
occupation (social structure), 112
occupational structure, 185
Offa, King, 68, 71
Offa's Dyke, 69, 70
Ogwr—R., 67
Open University, xv
oral history, 129
organisation—social, 183
tribal, 99
Osmond, J., 198, 293, 297, 310, 315
Oswestry, 45, 81
Outer Wales, 35, 51, 56, 58-59
out migration, 166
outsiders, 116, 124, 129
Outer Wales, 78, 80, 82, 83, 85
Owen, Hugh, 145
Owen, Trefor M., 108-11, 176
Oxford—Jesus College, 93

P
Palestine, 65
Pantycelyn, 82
papurau bro, 331, 339
Parry, Dr. Cyril, 327
pastoral tradition, 68, 70
patriotism, 144
pattern, xvi-xviii
Pays de Galles, Le, by E. G. Bowen, 35
peasant societies, 116
peasantry, 136, 141, 142
Pembroke Landsker, 14, 43, 49
Pembrokeshire, 12, 14, 16, 23, 27, 30, 42, 43, 45, 49, 50, 55, 56, 59, 72, 78, 80, 82, 83
Penarth, Glam., 44, 49
Pendeulwyn, Glam., 54
Pennal, Merions., 75
Penrhyn lock-out, The, 140
'Pentrediwaith', 96, 114, 117
peripheral region(s), 161, 162, 167
Peris—R., 66
Peterston, Glam., 42
physical geography, 66, 67, 70-71, 77

Plaid Cymru, 208, 288-89, 293-94, 301-16
Planet, 198
planning, 177
pluralism—cultural, 53, 60
linguistic, 53
pluralistic society, 34
poaching—salmon, 121, 122-23
'pobl y capel' ('chapel people'), 111
'pobl y dafarn' ('pub people'), 111
Point of Ayr, 83
point symbols, 47
polarization—vocabularies of, 338
policies—language, 58-59
policy—regional, 165
political consciousness, 121
political life, 146
nationalism, 136
upheavals, 135
structure, 163
politics, 102, 115, 119, 130, 159, 160, 188, 190, 195-215, 273-90, 292-318,
Scottish, 195-215, 301
Pontypool, Mon., 44
Pontypridd Observer, 328-29
Pool (Welshpool), Montg., 45
Poor Law Unions, 92-93
pop music, 334
population—born outside Wales, 186
changes 1901-71, 29, 59
Possibilist School, 66, 87
post industrial, 31
potatoes, 127, 128
Powis, Lord, 40
Powys, 71
County Council, 294
Vale of, 67, 71
pre-industrial, 26, 41, 48, 136
Prentice, R. C., 312
pre-Roman, 71
Preseli District, 16
pressure groups, 307-18
prestige—Welsh ladder of, 121
primary production, 185
primitive societies, 98
Princeps Wallia, 74
principal components analysis, 19
process(es), xvi-xviii, 115, 118, 146
restructuring, 187
social, 115
production—primary, 185
Protestant Reformation, 80
Pryce, Dr. W. T. R., 325
psychology, 177
public houses—Sunday opening, 119
Pumlumon, 66, 75
Puritan churches, 81
Puritanism, 80, 145
Puritans, 83
Pwllheli, 6, 7

Q

Quakers, 82
Quarter Bach, Dyfed, 9
questionnaires, 94, 120

R

Radcliffe-Brown, A. R., 98
radicalism, 146
nonconformist, 136
radio 77, 85, 324-40
Radio Cymru/Wales, 332-38
Radnor, 79
Radnorshire, 12, 14, 27, 29, 30, 41, 44, 45, 50, 59, 80, 82
railway building, 55
train, 108
railways, 84, 85
Ratzel, Friedrick, 65
Ravenstein, E. G., 27
Rebecca Riots, 55
Red Dragon, 75
Redfield, Robert, 179
reductionalism, 182
Rees, Alwyn D., 94-104, 116, 118, 119, 124, 125, 129, 154, 157, 176, 178, 179, 335
Rees, Brinley, 104
Rees, David (Llanelli), 136, 145
Ress, Dr. Thomas (Swansea), 145
William (Gwilym Hiraethog), 136
Referendum-Devolution, 284, 294-95, 299, 318, 328-31, 344
Sunday Closing, 284
region(s), 184
Mormon culture, 56
peripheral, 161, 162, 167
satellite, 162
regional development, 170, 172
differentiation, 171
disparities, 161
geographers, French, 35

inequalities, 183
policy, 165
imbalance, 167
relative deprivation, 169, 183
numbers (Welsh speakers), 6-7
religion, 102-103, 125, 130, 141, 241
religious affiliations, 33
census, 1851, 143, 144
culture, 142
meeting, 109
revivals, 69, 82, 138, 154
society (*seiat*), 113
upheavals, 135
Renaissance, 64
research-scientific, 166
residents born outside Wales, 187
residential segregation, 168
resort towns, 46, 51
restructuring—social, 188
process, 187
Rheidol—R., 67
Richard, Henry (MP), 136, 145
Rhiwabon, Denb., 6
Rhondda, 5, 49, 67
Rhondda Leader, 344
Rhondda West Parliamentary Constituency, 302
Rhosllanerchrugog, Clwyd, 6
Rhuthun, 43
Rhymni—R., 67
Rhys, Sir John, 93, 139
Riddell, D., 159
rights—minority, 253-70
Ritter, Karl, 65
Roath (Cardiff), 44, 49
Roberts, Thomas, 135
S. (Llanbryn-mair), 136
Roman, 71
Rome, 80
Royal Commission on the Agricultural Labourer, 1893, 92
on Land in Wales, 1894-96, 93
Royal Welsh Agricultural Show, 98
Ruabon *see* Rhiwabon,
Rug Chapel, Corwen, 40
rural, 142, 146, 180
areas, 153, 156
communities, 91-133
life (style), 16, 129
ruling class, 159
culture, 101, 103, 154
peasantry, 136
societies, 103, 156
Wales, 19
Ruthin *see* Rhuthin
Rynamona (County Clare), 95

S
St. Asaph, 76
Diocese, 36, 37
St. Davids, 75, 76
Bishop of, 45
St. Harmon, Rads., 41
St. Hilary, Glam., 50
St. Lythan's, Glam., 42
salmon poaching, 121, 122-23
Sasiwn, 76
satellite—region, 162
Saxon, 68, 137
Saxon—Anglo, 68
Savigny, Friedrich Karl von, 238
scandal, 118
scattered habitat, 69, 97, 102
School—Aberystwyth, 178, 179
school—charity, 36
schools—bilingual, 17
county, 140
Sunday, 138, 139
Welsh medium, 17
Schools—Circulating, 138
scientific research, 166
Scotland, 70, 84, 164, 185
Scots., 146
Scottish National Party, 195-215
nationalism, 195-215
second homes, 16, 124, 130, 158
Seebohm, Fredric, 94
segregation—residential, 168
spatial 34
Seiat (religious society), 113
Seiont—R., 66
settlement(s) patterns, 97, 102
urban, 107
Severn (Hafren, A.)—R., 40, 45, 66, 71, 78, 164
sex typing, 188
sheet steel, 164
Shrewsbury, 76, 78, 164
Shropshire, 83
Sianel Pedwar Cymru (S4C) see also, Channel Four, Wales, 17, 315, 325, 332-38
singing festivals, 69
Sirhowy—R., 67

slate, 164
small holder, 126, 128
Smith, Sir George A., 65, 77
Snowdonia, 7, 73, 120
social activity, 117
    administration 177
    anthropology, 121, 179
    change, 124
    class divisions, 156, 157, 168
    conditions, 129
    development, 172
    geography 107
    groups, 33
    hierarchy, 113, 121
    interaction, 111
    organisation, 96, 183
    processes, 115, 118, 129
    restructuring, 188
    science, French, 180
    sciences, xv
    scientific theory, 129
    structure, 34, 116, 125, 129, 184
    study, 94
    system, 101, 111
    upheavals, 135
Social Science Research Council, 177
society—British, 168
    chapel dominated, 121, 123
    metropolitan, 24
society pluralistic, 34
    rural, 156
    transactional, 24
    urban, 157
sociologists, 158, 171, 173
socio-cultural differentiation, 180
socio-economic groups, 186
sociolinguistics, 189
sociology, xiv, 129, 156, 176
    of development, 160, 172
    of language, 189
    of plantation, 122
    of Wales, 153-92, 173
    of Wales Research Group, xxii, 177
Somerset, 93
South Atlantic War, 336-37
south-east Wales, 16, 24, 41, 47, 49
south Wales, 6, 9, 26, 29, 44, 139
    coalfield, 83, 84, 93, 164
South Wales Daily News, 327
South Wales Echo, 330, 344
south west Wales, 49, 50, 128
spa resort towns, 46
sparsely inhabited areas, 130
spatial relationships, 105
    segregation, 34
    variations, 172
speakers—Welsh, 186
speech—Celtic, 67
spiralism, 170, 189
Sports Council for Wales, 286
squirearchy, 135
Stacey, Prof. M., 91
stadials—language, 47
state welfare, 189
statistical information, 94
    techniques, 19
statistics—language, 2
status, 168-69, 217-31
steel, 165, 185
stocking industry, 109
story telling, 110
structure—occupational, 185
    social, 184
structural functionalism, 178, 188, 191
structure plans, 256
suburbia, 108
Sunday Closing Act, 1881, 284
Sunday opening (public houses), 119
    school teachers, 112
    schools, 138, 139
surrogates (culture), 33
Sussex, 46
Swansea, 51, 54, 76, 82, 136
    University College of, 82
    Valley, 14
symbiosis, 127
symbiotic relationships, 45
symbols—culture, 58

T
Taf—R., 67
Taliesin, 70
Tanat—R., 66
Tawe—R., 67
teachers—Sunday school, 112
technological innovation, 129
Teifi—R., 67, 72
    Vale of, 72
Teifiside, Dyfed, 49
television, 17, 77, 85, 324-40
Tepozlan, 179
Tewdrig—Meurig ap, 71

theatres, 146
theories—social scientific, 129
Thomas, Dafydd Elis (MP), 294
Thomas, D. Lleufer, 92
Thomas, George, 297
Thomas, Ned, 198, 297
Thucydidas, 64
Tikopia, 95
tinplate, 164
Tithe Survey, 1842, 95
Toriad y dydd by J. Morris Jones, 137
tourism, 55
town—market, 107
towns, 156
borough, 44
castle, 42
chancery, 27
industrial, 107
resorts, 46, 51
tradition—village, 98
Traeth Mawr, 73
Trallong (Llywel), Brecs., 41
'transactional society', 24
'Treason of the Blue Books, 1846-47', 143, 144
Tredunnock *see* Tredynog
Tredynog, 44
Trefecca, Brecs., 82
Trelawnyd (New Market), Flints., 43, 53
Tremeirchion, Flints., 54
Tregaron, 105, 107-108
Trevethin (Pontypool), Mon., 44
tribal heritage, 102
organisation, 99
tribesmen, 69
Trobriand Islands, 95
Troed-yr-aur, Cards., 53, 125, 126
truck shops, 85
trunk roads, 85
Tryweryn, Merions., 303
Tudors, 75
Tunstall, Jeremy, 340
Turner, Victor, 120
Tynged yr Iaith by Saunders Lewis, 206
Tywi—R., 6, 67, 72

U
underdevelopment, 26
unemployment, 164-65, 166
uneven development, 183, 184
Ulster, 202
Undeb Amaethwyr Cymru (Farmers' Union of Wales), 308
Undeb Cenedlaethol Athrawon Cymru (National Union of Teachers of Wales), 308
Undeb y Cymdeithasau Gymraeg, 258
Union—Baptist, 76
of the Independents, 76
Unitarians, 82
universities, 75
University, College of Wales, Aberystwyth, 94, 104, 174
College of Swansea, 82
Court, 76
London School of Economics, 120
National, 144
Open, The, xv
of Wales, 74-75, 76, 98, 129, 138, 144, 176, 209, 277, 301, 303
unskilled workers/labourers, 84, 108
urban 107, 154, 157
anti, 156
communities, 102
culture, 157
life styles, 16
settlements, 107
urbanism, 103
urbanisation, 16, 26, 45, 92, 166
Urdd Gobaith Cymru (Welsh League of Youth), 174, 306, 308
Usk—R., 41, 66-67, 71, 78, 80
Uzmaston, Pembs., 51

V
Vale of Clwyd, 6, 15, 67
Conwy, 53
Glamorgan, 16, 43, 54, 71, 93
Llangollen, 54
Powys, 67, 71
Teifi, 72
Tywi, 6
valleys—Glamorgan, 93
values—Christian, 113
cultural, 33
nonconformist, 113
Venetian Ambassador, 75
Vietnam War, 316
village-centred culture, 102
community, 118
Village on the Border by R. Frankenberg, 114, 118

village tradition, 98
Visitation Returns, 36, 45
Volksgeist, 234-43

W
Wales—Archbishop of, 76
C.B.I. 290
central (*see also*, Mid Wales), 6, 15, 31, 49, 66, 78
Central Advisory Council for Education in, 32, 33
industrial, 107, 146, 153, 177
Inner, 35, 77, 78, 80, 82, 83, 85, 86
Medieval, 101
Mid, 77, 158, 164
National Library of, 98, 209, 283, 301
National Museum of, 98, 277, 283, 301
north, 6, 15, 17, 45, 74, 85, 96, 120, 122, 155
north-east, 17, 18, 24, 26, 29, 38, 43, 48
north-west, 122
Outer, 35, 78, 79, 80, 82, 83, 85
population, 1901, 1971, 59
population, born ouside of, 186, 187
rural, 19, 107
sociology of, 153-92
south, 4, 6, 9, 26, 29, 44, 139, 155, 158-59,
south, coalfield, 164
south-east, 16, 24, 41, 47, 49, 77
Wales: the shaping of a nation by P. Morgan and D. Thomas, 293, 307
Wales—south-west, 49, 50, 128
Tourist Board, 286
T.U.C. 289, 309-15
University of, 74-75, 76, 98, 129, 138, 176
Welsh', 7, 16, 41, 52
west, 6
Wallas, 68
Warner, Lloyd, 154
Wars of the Roses, The, 74
water, 164
Weber, Max, 224
Weberian concepts, xxiv, 181
welfare state, 189
Welsh—surrogate of culture, 33
Welsh and English in the schools of Wales, The place of (Report 1953), 32
Welsh archbishopric, 74
Welsh in education and life, (Report 1927), 32
Welsh bilinguals, 28, 29
change statistics, 22, 28, 29, 30
coalfields, 83
core areas, 52-56
culture region, 26-63
customs, 78
Development Agency, 187, 283, 287
feudal state, 74
future for the language, 11, 58-59
Grand Committee, 284
Heartland, 79
historians, 136, 172
history, 35
Intermediate Education Act, 1889, 276
Joint Education Committee, 279
language, attitudes, towards, 24
language, 1901-1971, 27-31
Language Act, 1967, 17, 258, 260, 284, 303, 310
Language Council 1978, 17
Language Society (*see also*, *Cymdeithas yr Iaith Gymraeg*), 124, 160, 300, 302-305, 312-13
language writers, 135
laws, 99, 101
League of Youth (*see also*, *Urdd Gobaith Cymru*), 174, 306, 308
literacy levels, 3, 9, 10, 11, 21, 24
medium schools, 17
monoglots, 2, 27, 28, 29, 42, 52, 56, 61
Office, 160, 255, 280-83, 297, 301
Parliament, 74-75
Welsh people, The, by D. Brynmor Jones, 93
Welsh prestige ladder, 121
readers and writers of, 2-3, 9, 10, 15
Welsh Republican Socialist Movement, 315
Welsh rural communities, edited by E. Davies, 104, 108, 114

Welsh speakers, 79, 117, 186, 253-70
  1870s, 27
  1901, 1981, 12, 59
  1981, 1, 5, 8
  absolute numbers, 13, 59
  age structures, 24
  increases 1971-81, 17, 18
  relative numbers, 6-7, 30
Welsh-speaking population, 253-70
Welsh state, 70, 72, 74
Welsh veto, The by D. Foulkes et al, 293-329
'Welsh Wales' (*see also, Cymru Gymraeg*), 7, 16, 41, 52, 82, 155, 159
'Welsh ways of life', 142, 154, 158, 178, 179
Welsh zone, 38-45
Welshness, xiii, 52, 53, 121, 123, 144, 170
Welshpool, Powys (*see also*, Pool), 45, 49
Welshry, -ies, 78, 122
werin, 134
Wesleyan Methodists, 106
West Glamorgan, 6, 9, 23
west Wales, 6
Western Mail, 276, 318, 330
Widston, Mon., 50
Wilford, R.A., 293, 329
Wilkinson, John, 83
Williams, D. T., 57
Williams, Prof., Caerwyn, 139
Williams, Crwys, 135-39
Williams, Prof. Glanmor, xx
Williams, Dr. Glyn, 300, 325
Williams, Prof. Gwyn A., 136, 145, 146, 317
Williams, Prof. Raymond, 317
Williams—Elis, Sir Clough, 122
Wilson Government, 298-99
Winchester, 70
Wnion—R., 67
women, 116
  in politics, 313-15
Woodcock, George, 199
working classes, 135, 146
Wrexham, 6, 11, 80, 81, 85
Wrexham Leader, 329, 343
Wye—R., 66-67, 78
Wyre—R., 67

Y
Ynys Môn (*see also*, Anglesey), 7, 12, 13, 14, 16, 17, 27, 30, 52, 54, 55, 59
Youth—Welsh league of (*see also*, Urdd Gobaith Cymru), 174
ysgol feithrin, 18
Ystradfellte, Brecs., 41
Ystwyth—R., 67

Z
Zelinsky, Prof. Wilbur, 32